# ACHIEVING

# SERVICE

# EXCELLENCE

*Strategies*

*for*

*Healthcare*

# ACHIEVING SERVICE EXCELLENCE

*Strategies*

*for*

*Healthcare*

Myron D. Fottler

Robert C. Ford

Cherrill P. Heaton

Health Administration Press
ACHE Management Series

Your board, staff, or clients may also benefit from this book's insight. For more information on quantity discounts, contact the Health Administration Press Marketing Manager at (312) 424-9470.

**Library of Congress Cataloging-in-Publication Data**

Fottler, Myron D.
    Achieving service excellence : strategies for healthcare / Myron D. Fottler, Robert C. Ford, Cherrill Heaton.
      p. cm.
    Includes bibliographical references.
    ISBN 1-56793-190-1 (alk. paper)
    1. Medical care—Customer service.   2. Patient satisfaction.   3. Customer relations.   I. Ford, Robert C. (Robert Clayton), 1945–   II. Heaton, Cherrill P. III. Title.

R727 .F684 2002
362.1'068—dc21

2002068569

The paper used in this publication meets the minimum requirements of American National Standard for Information Sciences—Permanence of Paper for Printed Library Materials, ANSI Z39.48-1984. ⊗™

Project manager: Jane Williams; Book/Cover designer: Matt Avery; Acquisition manager: Marcy McKay

Health Administration Press
A division of the Foundation of the
   American College of Healthcare Executives
1 North Franklin Street, Suite 1700
Chicago, IL 60606-3491
(312) 424-2800

# Contents

v

# Foreword

*Quint Studer, founder, The Studer Group*

THE NEED TO have a sense of purpose, the opportunity to do worth-while work, and the desire to make a difference are reasons people enter healthcare and stay in healthcare. Direct caregivers and those who support them feel a great sense of accomplishment in seeing a patient get better; in knowing that a family appreciates that they preserved the dignity of a dying loved one; and in hearing people in the community make positive comments about their hospital, medical center, or clinic. Each healthcare worker also feels sadness when a patient, family member, or physician is not satisfied with the care and service provided. Although it is difficult if not impossible for patients to measure clinical outcomes, it is not hard for them to measure other aspects of their experience. All patients and family members can measure the courtesy they are shown, length of wait times, speed of admission, response to call lights, management of pain, quality of food, cleanliness, and home care instructions they receive.

Over the past 15 or so years, something happened in healthcare. Formerly dependent on a group of individuals taking care of others, the essence of healthcare somehow lost out to the pressure of the bottom line. On a daily basis, healthcare leaders are bombarded with reimbursement cuts, labor shortages, patient safety issues, medical staff challenges, and a multitude of other crises. Boards of directors can go for months without discussing patients at their meetings. Patients, physicians, and employees today wonder what happened to healthcare's core function of providing care.

In the beginning of the movie "It's A Wonderful Life," two characters in heaven are talking. One says to the other, "You have to go down to earth and help George Bailey." The other replies, "Why, is he in trouble?" The first responds, "Even worse. He is discouraged." As I travel around the country working with healthcare organizations, leaders, and staff, I find the word "discouraged" appropriate to describe how many patients, physicians, and healthcare employees feel about the state of healthcare service today.

What happened? Did the advent of DRGs, Medicare, managed care, increased pharmaceutical costs, labor shortages, etc., change healthcare? Although all of these issues have had an impact, I feel that the number one culprit is the failure of healthcare's leaders. In 1998, the American Hospital Association published responses from a survey it conducted on over 3,700 healthcare executives. The survey asked, "What are you doing to move your organization ahead?" Patient satisfaction, employee satisfaction, and clinical outcomes did not make the top 10 responses given. Maybe many healthcare executives did not add those three responses because they thought it was just common sense to focus on patients, employees, and physicians. Maybe so, but I have found that common sense is often very uncommon. I know it was for me. As a healthcare leader I was guilty of moving away from patient and staff interaction. Managed care negotiations, building programs, mergers, consolidations, cash collection, and debt financing all crowded out time with patients and staff. Even so, I could always rationalize my behavior.

In 1993, I became senior vice president and chief operating officer of an inner-city hospital in Chicago called Holy Cross Hospital. Much to my dismay, I was put in charge of patient satisfaction. After some false starts, I finally surrendered. I did not know what to do, so I sought help. I visited non-healthcare companies with great reputations in service. The most important thing I did was ask the staff what we should do. The next key thing I did was I listened. I started my journey back to why I got into healthcare. At first I was worried that all this satisfaction stuff would take away from our bottom line, but I soon realized that focusing on patient satisfaction led me to employee and physician satisfaction. For us to have great patient satisfaction, employee and physician issues needed to be addressed first.

As each month went by, I learned more. As employee satisfaction increased, employee turnover decreased. A more stable workforce decreased length of stay, increased patient satisfaction, and increased physician satisfaction. These outcomes led to increased volume and leverage with managed care companies. Most surprising of all my discoveries was that not focusing on the bottom line increased the bottom line; in fact, this increase was the most dramatic I had ever seen.

From January 1993 to June 1996, a group of employees at Holy Cross taught me so much. Our team effort led to Holy Cross winning numerous awards, including the 1994 AHA Great Comeback Award. In June 1996, I took the lessons I learned at Holy Cross, and from other hospitals, to Baptist Hospital, Inc., in Pensacola, Florida. There, I found that the same approach of focusing on satisfaction rather than on the bottom line worked again. As more hospitals benchmarked Baptist and as I spoke at hospitals around the country, I began to gain an even greater understanding of the "must haves" in healthcare. These pillars, principles, and practices I learned again produced results for my organization: Baptist placed in the top 1 percent of organizations for providing patient satisfaction and it placed first in employee satisfaction and quality. Baptist also received the *USA Today* quality cup in 2000. To show that these service principles stick if "hardwired" to the organization's culture, Baptist was named as one of the top 10 places to work by *Fortune* magazine in 2002. While at Baptist, I developed a seminar to give me an opportunity to share with others what I had learned. This seminar led me to establish my own coaching organization, allowing me to make an even greater difference now that I can share my experiences full time.

What have I learned and continue to learn? Although it is important for each organization to have its own style, it is imperative that organizations identify the causes of their success and study them. Organizations must improve their patient, staff, and physician satisfaction, but more importantly they must return to their core values—their purpose for existing, their ability to do worthwhile work, and their calling to make a difference.

This book is deceptive because although it is easy and fun to read, it is also a comprehensive text on customer satisfaction theories and applications. It is filled with relevant examples and illustrations. I appreciate the Lessons Learned section that organizes critical points in each chapter and serves as reminders of the patient-focused concepts that each chapter contains. These practices can help healthcare executives improve their organizational results, especially in today's highly competitive healthcare environment. Both patients and employees know, by word of mouth and by reading the large amount of information available, who is doing a good job and who is not.

I hope you enjoy this book. Knowing Myron Fottler, Robert Ford, and Cherrill Heaton personally, I know they have worked very hard to provide each reader with "take-aways" that can make a difference. Although the authors have won awards for their writing from the American Academy of Medical Administrators, their biggest reward is making a difference. To the authors, thank you. As George Bailey ultimately learned in "It's A Wonderful Life" through the guidance of his angel, Clarence, you should never underestimate the difference you can make.

# Preface

THIS BOOK, *Achieving Service Excellence: Strategies for Healthcare,* is an attempt to organize and present the best available practices and information related to providing patients with a superb total healthcare experience. It is designed for executives and managers who want to implement a customer-focused service strategy in any healthcare organization that wants to compete successfully in today's customer-driven market. The book joins the findings of the most significant research on services, healthcare services in particular, with specific examples of the best practices of leading healthcare and other service organizations.

A proven principle of providing excellent service anchors each chapter of this book; a list of these principles is provided on page XXIV. Leading healthcare organizations have found these principles to be important, workable, and useful. They represent the key points to remember when putting the book's concepts into practice and can guide healthcare organizations and their managers as they seek to reach the levels of excellence achieved by benchmark organizations. We conclude each chapter with "Lessons Learned," a summary of the most important management recommendations of that chapter.

The book is divided into three parts, each of which is devoted to examining one of healthcare management's three major components—strategy, staff, and systems. Each *s* is important, but no one is more important than the others. *Strategy* is the plan a healthcare organization must have to be effective. *Staff* represents the personnel who deliver the high-quality healthcare experience that distinguishes the excellent healthcare organization from the merely good. An effective array of *systems* needs to be in place to support staff as they deliver superior clinical and nonclinical service. The healthcare organization's strategy, staff, and systems are interrelated; have one focus—the patient; and exist to fulfill one overriding purpose: to provide a positive, even superb, total healthcare experience.

Part I (The Healthcare Service Strategy) comprises chapters (1 through 5) that explain the effect on healthcare of the "new consumerism" and discuss the differences between products and services; the meaning of guestology; the planning process to assess and meet customer expectations; the three parts of the healthcare experience; and the definitions of quality, value, and cost in a customer service context. In addition, Part I chapters discuss quantitative and qualitative forecasting tools; demographic trends; and the link between the organization's healthcare service strategy and its vision, purpose, and mission. Many real-world examples are used in each chapter to illustrate the principles and best practices.

Part II (The Healthcare Service Staff) chapters (6 through 9) discuss how to recruit and hire "persons who love to serve" and how to train, motivate, and empower them to provide outstanding customer service. Chapter 9 is devoted to how the healthcare organization can, when the conditions are right, encourage and help patients and their families to coproduce—that is, to participate in—their own healthcare experiences.

Part III (The Healthcare Service Systems) chapters (10 through 15) address ways of glueing the different parts of the healthcare experience together by communicating information to the right person at the right time. Because no organization's service provider-system combinations can match demand perfectly, Part III offers techniques for managing the inevitable wait times for healthcare service. Because organizations want to provide perfect experiences, this part discusses ways to avoid service failures and problems. Because no healthcare systems have yet been designed that can provide a perfect healthcare experience every time, we also discuss how to fix service failures when they occur.

So that organizations and service providers can know how they are doing, Chapter 14 presents some ways of measuring service quality and customer satisfaction. Part III explains how the organization's people, units, and their efforts are tied together to provide remarkable customer service that delights patients and their families. This blending of parts and people is accomplished with outstanding organizational leadership.

The healthcare experience in many organizations is too often less than excellent, driving dissatisfied patients to defect to competing healthcare providers. Healthcare providers and managers are increasingly aware that if they want patients to keep coming back to their HMO, clinic, or dental practice, they must learn to provide outstanding service and positive clinical outcomes. Healthcare consumers know the problems with healthcare, so they are constantly looking for answers to Who does it right and how? This book aims to help any healthcare organization or manager who wants to provide better service to patients.

Myron D. Fottler, Ph.D.;
Robert C. Ford, Ph.D.;
and Cherrill P. Heaton, Ph.D.
April 2002

# Acknowledgments

WE WOULD LIKE to thank many people for reading our manuscript and offering suggestions for revision. Their insightful comments added great value to our project.

Myron Fottler would like to thank his wife, Carol, for her patience during the approximately eighteen-month period of manuscript preparation. He also thanks several students in the health services administration master's program at the University of Central Florida who made contributions to this book, including Amanda Stewart, Linda Skrosky, Sergio Correa, Danielle Louth, Lisa Pitram, and Reid Oetjen. Amanda Stewart's assistance was crucial in the preparation of the final manuscript. He would also like to thank Dr. Aaron Liberman, chair of the department of health professions, for his support of this project.

Robert Ford wishes to thank his wife, Barbara, for her patient support throughout this project. Her tolerant understanding of and helpful willingness to do all that had to be done to produce a book like this are gratefully acknowledged. He also wishes to acknowledge and thank his "guestology" mentor Bruce Laval, retired senior vice president of planning and operations of The Walt Disney Company, for his willingness to share his incredible knowledge on managing outstanding guest service organizations.

Cherrill Heaton would like to thank his wife Marieta for her help and support during the writing of the book. He also thanks Dr. Allen Tilley for his support and encouragement.

The authors would like to thank Audrey Kaufman, assistant director of Health Administration Press, for her encouragement, support, and patience. We would also like to thank Jane Williams, editor at

Health Administration Press, for her editorial assistance in shortening and focusing the manuscript. Finally, we would like to thank Quint Studer for inspiring us to see the need for and value of taking what we know about excellent customer service and making it relevant and useful to the healthcare industry.

# The Principles of Achieving Service Excellence

1. Identify and manage all aspects of the healthcare experience
2. Meet or exceed the quality and value that customers expect
3. Identify and focus on the key drivers of customer satisfaction
4. Provide the healthcare setting that customers expect
5. Define and build a culture committed to providing superb service for all parts of the healthcare experience
6. Find and hire clinically competent people who love to serve
7. Train your employees, then train them some more
8. Motivate, empower, and reward your employees for achieving customer service goals
9. Empower patients and their families to help meet their own healthcare needs
10. Keep the patient, family, and employees informed
11. Provide a seamless healthcare experience
12. Manage all parts of the customer's wait
13. Eliminate all sources of disappointments positively and quickly
14. Measure the important things, then pursue the superb healthcare experience relentlessly
15. Lead others to achieve a superb healthcare experience

# PART ONE

## The Healthcare Service Strategy

*Chapter 1*

# Healthcare and the New Consumerism

Healthcare Principle: *Identify and manage all aspects of the healthcare experience*

Whatever your discipline, become a student of excellence in all things. Take every opportunity to observe people who manifest the qualities of mastery. These models of excellence will inspire you and guide you toward the fulfillment of your highest potential.

—*Micheal Gelb and Tony Buzan*

IN THIS CHAPTER, we address the rise of the new aggressive, informed healthcare customer; the healthcare market trends driven by the patient-customer; and the ways benchmark service organizations, and some cutting-edge healthcare organizations, are responding to this market reality. We also enumerate the three fundamental concepts—focus on the customer, treat the customer like a guest, and manage the total healthcare experience—that serve as the basis of the 15 principles of achieving service excellence (see page xxiv). Both the traditional healthcare term patient and the broader term customer are used throughout the book. These terms are not interchangeable, as all patients are customers but not all customers are patients. A more specific definition is as follows: *Patients* are people who receive either clinical services from healthcare providers or processing services from third-party payers. *Customer* is a broader term that includes everyone to whom the healthcare organization seeks to provide service. The *primary customers* are the patients. The *secondary customers* include physicians, family members, visitors, third-party payers, vendors, and staff.

3

## THE RISE OF THE NEW CUSTOMER

The healthcare industry is made up of organizations that provide health and health-related services to patients and organizations that pay for and regulate the provision of health services. This varied industry includes HMOs, PPOs, other third-party payers, government agencies, outpatient clinics, medical practices, nursing homes, and of course hospitals. Because we think the principles and practices presented in this book have wide application, we are going to use this more expanded concept of the industry. Historically, these organizations have concentrated on meeting the expectations of their key stakeholders—medical staffs and third-party payers.[1] Because most physicians are affiliated with more than one hospital, they have the power to decide where their patients receive healthcare services. Healthcare organizations therefore go to great lengths to make their medical staffs and unaffiliated community physicians happy. Because third-party payers, rather than patients themselves, often pay the bills, healthcare organizations also spend considerable effort in satisfying these key stakeholders. To retain the approval of third-party payers, healthcare managers focus on increasing market share, restructuring, decreasing costs, and expanding revenues; to keep their medical staffs satisfied, they provide sophisticated technology and in-house amenities.

Even though patients are also considered as key stakeholders, and hence need to be satisfied, healthcare managers have typically focused on meeting their *clinical* needs rather than their needs as healthcare *customers*. Only recently have healthcare managers begun to expand their focus to meeting the needs, wants and expectations of their customers, not only for positive clinical outcomes but also for positive total healthcare experiences.[2] Even the term patient implies passiveness of the person who "patiently" waits for service from the healthcare providers. These healthcare providers often provide services but offer minimal consultation or explanation in environments or under conditions that cater to the needs of providers but not the patients.

Such treatments have led to increasingly unhappy and vocal patients. Voluntary Hospitals of America commissioned a survey that reported that public trust in healthcare institutions has markedly declined, with health plans losing more ground than physicians or hospitals, from 1993 to 1998.[3] The decline in trust was especially pronounced among consumers age 40 to 59; those with higher income and education levels; and those who had recently changed, added, or selected a physician or hospital. Customers gave hospitals only a 67-percent satisfaction rating: compared with 31 other industries, hospitals ranked 27th. This ranking placed them just above the Internal Revenue Service and only 10 percentage points below the tobacco industry. Moreover, a separate survey by the National Coalition on Health Care revealed that 80 percent of those surveyed felt that hospitals have cut corners to save money, and 77 percent believed those cuts have endangered patients.[4] These results are not particularly surprising because services paid for primarily by private insurers and government are not as likely to fulfill consumer preferences for convenience and personal control as those paid directly by the consumers.

In the summer of 1998, the National Partnership for Women and Families undertook a research project to examine women's mindsets regarding health and healthcare in the United States.[5] DYG, Inc., a national social and market research company, conducted six focus groups for the project. Results indicated that focus group members believed the following are flaws of the U.S. healthcare system:

1. It promotes an emphasis on money rather than care
2. The greed of insurance companies and providers represents a real threat to quality
3. Costs to consumers are high and rising
4. Average people are treated poorly by uncommunicative and arrogant healthcare providers and insurers
5. Access is often constrained or denied, even for those with employer-provided insurance coverage.

Most focus group members said the healthcare process *increased* their stress levels by being very time insensitive, inefficient, and needlessly complex.[6] For example, women felt strongly that requiring a referral from a primary care physician to see a gynecologist is unnecessary, offensive, shows a lack of respect, and wastes their time. In response to such conditions, women have become activists for and increasingly vocal about healthcare issues that concern them.[7] The public now values self-reliance in all areas of life, including healthcare. In keeping with that self-reliance, the women in the focus groups reported many instances in which they had personally confronted the system or an individual provider, plan, or employee regarding their healthcare. The women in these focus groups reflected one critical aspect of the trend toward consumers being in charge: the demand to be treated with respect.

The unique characteristics of the healthcare industry (i.e., third-party payments, physician decision roles, regulatory structure, and so forth) have led it to pay less attention to its customers than other types of service organizations. Various environmental changes now require the industry to be more responsive to customer needs, wants and expectations for healthcare convenience, comfort, information and for having personal control of their healthcare experience. Although good relationships with physicians and third-party payers continue to be crucial, good relationships with patients are becoming increasingly important in determining organizational success or failure. Healthcare executives, therefore, must find ways to respond to these new customer expectations.

Today's healthcare consumers have more knowledge about and access to information on the value and quality of healthcare alternatives. They use the Internet to evaluate protocols and providers and, consequently, are more involved in the decisions about how their dollars are spent.[8] In addition, increasingly vocal consumer groups have encouraged healthcare customers to change their attitudes, transforming them from patient "patients" to active participants.[9] Author Regina Herzlinger describes the new healthcare customers as well-informed, overworked, and overburdened with child and eldercare responsibilities whose demands for convenience and control have caused many American businesses to greatly enhance their quality and control their costs.[10]

### The Patient-Customer

The increasingly involved patient-customer and the newly evolved hypercompetitive market are forcing healthcare institutions to reconsider the old principle of catering to doctors and third-party payers and to focus on meeting the patient's desire for a satisfying total healthcare experience, not just a positive clinical outcome. When the patient has choices, being a good healthcare provider at a reasonable price is no longer enough. Now, the healthcare organization must also persuade the customer that its service is most responsive to *all* of the customer's needs and meets customer expectations for a total healthcare experience. This new paradigm means that providers must spend much more time and energy providing and marketing services to their customers.

How the customer determines the value and quality of the total healthcare experience is based on more than the success or failure of the medical procedure or clinical service. The customer's holistic perception of the total experience begins before admission and ends after discharge and bill payment. To sustain the relationship with the customer, the healthcare organization must continually remind the customer, through advertisement and other communications, that it is a high-quality provider to which the customer should seek to return if the need arises.

## MARKET TRENDS

Gaining a competitive advantage in today's healthcare environment is increasingly difficult, so examining today's trends is important. A healthcare organization will sustain such an advantage only so long as the service it delivers has attributes that correspond to the key "buying criteria" of a substantial number of customers in the targeted market. Sustained competitive advantage is the direct result of an enduring "value differential"—a difference in clinical quality, service quality, and/or price—between the services of an organization and those of competitors in the minds of its customers. Benchmark healthcare organizations know that the quality and value of the service experience they provide are largely, if not entirely, determined in the mind of the customer.

One way to achieve a competitive advantage is to develop organizational capabilities, which are difficult for other organizations to duplicate in the short run or, even better, in the long run.[11] Such capabilities are the organization's ability to deploy tangible resources, intangible resources, and competencies to produce desired services. Implementing appropriate principles and practices that have been proven effective by the best guest-service and other service organizations offers an additional and powerful capability.

### Trend 1: Knowing Customer Expectations

Table 1.1 lists eight major customers of healthcare organizations, their customer type (whether they are primary or secondary and external or internal), and their service expectations (all eight customers have the same expectations for service excellence). As Table 1.1 shows, the patient is the primary customer and most customers are secondary or external; the Table also indicates that the service expectations of these eight customers overlap. The term secondary does not indicate that a particular customer is unimportant. For example, staff physicians (internal stakeholders) and affiliated community physicians (external stakeholders) are both extremely important. However, we believe healthcare systems should be built around the needs and service expectations of patients.

Excellent customer service requires understanding the expectations and key drivers of all these customers because knowing these can help the organization design its strategy, staff, and systems to meet customer needs and expectations.

Because patient families, vendors, visitors, staff members, and third-party payers are all customers of healthcare organizations, we should consider their needs and expectations carefully. However, the patient is the principal customer and the ultimate reason that the healthcare organization exists. Although the concepts in this book are helpful in dealing with all customers, our primary purpose is to focus on providing an outstanding healthcare experience to the primary customer.

### Trend 2: Involving Customers in Quality Initiatives

Previous efforts to improve the quality of healthcare have focused on the provider's orientation and needs rather than the needs of the patient. For example, in 1991 the Joint Commission on Accreditation of Healthcare Organizations adopted "continuous quality improvement" (CQI) as one criterion for accreditation. The Joint Commission proposed that healthcare leaders set expectations, develop plans, and implement procedures to assess and improve the governance, management, clinical services, and support services of their organizations. The focus of these proposals was on organizational structures and processes.[12] Although continually improving quality seems like a worthy goal, the results of CQI have been mixed at best.[13] Further, the proposals have been aimed at improving caregiving not from the viewpoint of patients but of providers. The recommended process does not require consumer input or benchmarking against the best practices of service organizations outside of healthcare.

The Joint Commission also collects data for its Indicator Measurement System (IMSystem)—a repository of clinical quality and financial outcome indicators.[14] However, participation in the IMSystem is voluntary, and most healthcare organizations do not choose to participate. The cost of generating the requested information is high, and

**Table 1.1: Customers of Healthcare Organizations, by Type and Service Expectations**

| Customer | Customer Type | Service Expectations (beyond clinical excellence) |
| --- | --- | --- |
| 1. Patients | External/Primary | Personalized care, prompt attention, professionalism, communication, respect, privacy, and clear information |
| 2. Patient families | External/Secondary | Professionalism, communication, respect, privacy, and clear information |
| 3. Visitors | External/Secondary | Professionalism, respect, and clear information |
| 4. Third-party payers | External/Secondary | Prompt attention, professionalism, privacy, and clear information |
| 5. Vendors | External/Secondary | Prompt attention, professionalism, and clear communication |
| 6. Clergy | Internal or External/Secondary | Professionalism, communication, privacy, and clear information |
| 7. Physicians | Internal or External/Secondary | Respect, conflict resolution, teamwork, communication, privacy, and clear information |
| 8. Staff | Internal/Secondary | Professionalism, conflict resolution, communication, respect, privacy, teamwork, and clear information |

many organizations do not have information systems that are capable of generating it. From the customer's point of view, the indicators collected may not necessarily be desirable or useful in assessing the quality of the healthcare experience. So far, individual patients have had minimal input into these reporting initiatives.[15]

An effort to enhance quality while seeking to give consumers some information that can help them make better decisions about health plans and providers is embodied in the "report card" movement. The National Committee for Quality Assurance (NCQA) developed a performance measurement system that compares different health plans using the Health Plan Employer Data and Information Set (HEDIS).[16] Developed by a coalition of large employers, the intent of HEDIS is to create a database that the participants can use to compare the performance of their health plans against other plans according to a consistently measured and reported set of criteria (e.g., percent of enrollees receiving mammograms, immunizations, and so forth).[17] The data collected by the Joint Commission and NCQA are unaudited and rarely reflect the customer's point of view. For example, *Consumer Reports* notes that HEDIS data on health plans are uncorrelated with its own surveys of patient satisfaction.[18] Some dimensions of the customer experience generally ignored in providers' measures of quality include patient comfort, convenience, satisfaction, and service quality. The equivalent of customer satisfaction surveys, like the Zagat Survey of restaurants and the J.D. Power surveys of automobile quality, has yet to appear in healthcare.[19]

Customers now have access to more information through provider report cards, the Internet, and other means. Why should such information access create competition among providers and make them more responsive to consumers than they have been in the past? One author suggests that the major environmental forces leading to the increase in competition and greater provider responsiveness to consumers include excess capacity, the consumer movement, deregulation of the healthcare industry, and increased managed care.[20] Whatever the reason, it has resulted in greater interest in redesigning healthcare organizations to make them more customer focused. One example is the decision by United Healthcare (an HMO) to give physicians final authority over patient care. This is in response to United Healthcare's customers' wish to have their own doctors make more decisions with patient input and collaboration, instead of having the doctors rely on the organization's administrators and policies.

## Trend 3: Allowing Customers to Make Choices

After long relying on managed care and capitated health plans to defend them against rising employee healthcare benefit costs, some U.S. employers are making a fundamental change in their healthcare cost-management strategies: turning healthcare decisions over to their employees through defined-contribution plans.[21] This idea is driven by a confluence of interacting forces including:

- the backlash against managed care;
- the popularity of 401(k) plans, which permit employees to make their own investment decisions;
- the use of Web-based information to help consumers make more informed healthcare decisions;
- the resurgence of high healthcare costs, despite the efforts of managed care organizations; and
- a growing feeling that the nation's healthcare market will not work well until patients themselves hold the purse strings.[22]

The new trend to let employees handle their own healthcare benefits just as they do their retirement money adds momentum to the growing customer involvement in healthcare decisions. Many employers have created web sites to help employees make health benefit decisions and sign up for plans. Entrepreneurs are responding to this trend by offering Web-based services that greatly reduce the need for employers to manage this information. These entrepreneurs are more creative than the employers themselves in providing customers with new tools to navigate the healthcare system and to make decisions.[23]

Corporations are also self-insuring in increasing numbers. This means that healthcare services are increasingly paid for by corporations instead of by insurance companies. One significant advantage of self-insurance is that it allows greater flexibility in the health plans offered to employees. Furthermore, when the employer manages the plans, the employee usually has a significantly greater voice in how these plans work and what they provide. Employees or their union representatives only need to persuade the employer to change healthcare providers or plans.

## Trend 4: Publicizing Performance Ratings

Information on how U.S. healthcare organizations and providers are performing is easily accessible. National magazines like *U.S. News and World Report* publish lists of "best hospitals," while local television and newspaper outlets rate the best doctors. Local magazines in cities like Boston and Philadelphia provide annual lists of the best regional physicians and hospitals.[24] Some states publish physician malpractice statistics, while others like Florida provide nursing home performance indicators on the Internet. The Massachusetts Department of Public Health offers ratings of the state's skilled nursing facilities on its web site, which is updated every six months. The department measures seven patient-satisfaction factors, and the results are publicized in newspapers and on television.[25] The publication of the ratings of healthcare organizations and providers only emphasizes to healthcare providers the importance of treating the patient as a customer.

Data generated by the Health Care Advisory Board suggest that healthcare executives are beginning to respond to the trends discussed above. Interviews with 321 health industry executives in 1998 found that overall they "agree" (i.e., a response average greater than 4.0 on a 5-point scale) with each of the following statements:

1. Individual consumers' new predominance in the healthcare marketplace is increasingly influencing policy, strategy, operations, and investment decisions of healthcare organizations within all segments of the industry.
2. Healthcare organizations will provide education and readily available data to encourage and empower consumers to be direct purchasers of care.
3. Healthcare organizations will develop new products, offer more choices, and provide service enhancements to respond directly to consumer preferences.
4. Healthcare organizations will increasingly invest in feedback mechanisms to ensure that they are in touch with consumer needs and are meeting customer expectations.[26]

Another study of healthcare executives noted that the increasing competition among healthcare providers has given more power to consumers.[27] Here are two predictions from that study[28]:

The marketplace is going to be more consumer- and customer-driven. Price and value are going to be tied together, and the consumer is going to have a lot more say about it.

Pressure from patients should help to remind healthcare providers to recreate and resurrect the fact that we're about caring for people and helping them in their own development toward wellness.

To compete in this new customer-driven environment, healthcare managers must understand and use the successful practices of benchmark organizations in their own and in related service industries. The times are changing, and healthcare organizations must change with them to survive and prosper.

## LESSONS FROM BENCHMARK ORGANIZATIONS

The modern economy is dominated by service organizations, which already represent 75 percent to 80 percent of the U.S. economy but are still expected to grow. Author Roland Rust points out that even businesses that deal primarily in physical goods "now view themselves primarily as services, with the offered good being an important part of the service (rather than the service being an augmentation of the physical good)."[29] These businesses have adopted such traditional services terms as customer satisfaction, customer retention, and customer relationships.

Throughout this book, we use lessons learned from benchmark healthcare and service organizations to show how contemporary healthcare organizations can use their strategy, staff, and systems to provide each patient with a seamless healthcare experience, paying close attention to its three components—the product, the setting, and the delivery. Provision of each component will at least meet the patient's expectations, but satisfaction in all ideally will make the patient say, or at least think, "They did their best for me. What a superb healthcare experience!"

From the neighborhood clinic to the national HMO and from the small community hospital to the huge academic medical center, the principles of managing the total healthcare experience are the same. As explained in the book and as illustrated in the practices of the benchmark organizations, these principles of customer service also stress the nonclinical aspects of the healthcare experience in a way that is not often addressed in today's academic programs and seminars on healthcare management.

Although a trip on a Southwest Airlines plane or a visit to a Disney theme park is quite different from an overnight stay at or a visit to a healthcare facility, many service excellence principles and practices used in those industries are transferable to healthcare. This book shows that the most successful healthcare organizations treat their customers like guests and offer them not just successful clinical outcomes but positive, superior total experiences.

Most organizations that treat customers like guests and provide memorable experiences do not come from the healthcare industry but elsewhere—often from the hospitality industry, from which many of our examples come. For example, many writers on service excellence consider The Walt Disney Company to be the best at treating customers like guests. An "experience economy" is emerging. Disney was the first to think in terms of providing experiences rather than goods and services, and no one does it better. So Disney makes a worthwhile model for any organization, including those in healthcare, that aims to provide an outstanding customer experience.

The dissatisfaction of many healthcare customers with their providers suggests that the industry has much to learn from the benchmark organizations in hospitality and other service fields. There is plenty of room for making improvements, and these improvements will carry over to the bottom line, which is especially noteworthy when many U.S. hospitals are operating at a loss.

## The Challenges of Healthcare Management

Traditional bureaucratic structures and manufacturing management principles get turned on their heads in the healthcare sector. Designing, organizing, and controlling the work process and motivating a workforce are done differently when the product is tangible and the production process takes place in a big factory. Totally different challenges arise when the product is intangible: Healthcare is intangible, and the components that comprise the healthcare experience may not even physically exist. Designing and producing such an experience is quite different from designing and producing tangible goods when the customer is consuming the product as it is being produced. These "production" problems in the healthcare industry are matched or exceeded by the challenge of managing employees who must be carefully trained to provide a service whose quality and value are defined not by internal quality control experts or external evaluators but by each patient. Moreover, employees have to be taught to provide this service not behind closed doors but while customers are watching and asking questions. Patients and their families may even participate in producing the healthcare experience!

Manufacturing managers sometimes moan about how hard it is to teach their employees to perform the necessary manufacturing steps accurately. They should talk to their colleagues in the healthcare industry who not only have to teach their employees how to "manufacture" the product but also how to do so with the patient and family watching and sometimes participating. Healthcare managers know that the principles taught in smokestack management courses in traditional business schools do not seem too relevant in the healthcare industry.

The unique reimbursement systems with which healthcare organizations must cope also set apart the healthcare industry. In manufacturing and other service industries, the customer pays the producer or service provider directly. In contrast, most healthcare organizations receive the bulk of their revenue through multiple third-party payers like HMOs, PPOs, Medicare, and Medicaid. These third-party payers impose rules, regulations, guidelines, clinical protocols, and incentives on service providers that constrain the services (as well as where and how the services are delivered) that organizations can provide to particular patients. Failure to be responsive to these pressures may result in a denial of reimbursement for the services provided. Although becoming more customer focused is obviously important from a strategic and competitive perspective, this goal must be achieved within political and economic constraints that are less relevant in other industries.

Only recently have healthcare researchers and management scholars begun to consider the management of the total healthcare experience as part of the healthcare manager's responsibility. Therefore, much of what is known in this area is still based on anecdotal information and case study examples, which makes perfect sense. In the early stages of inquiry into any field of business, the logical approach is to find the best organizations and study them to discover the principles that drive what they do. A review of the service-management literature quickly reveals several benchmark organizations; these include Southwest Airlines, Marriott, Ritz-Carlton, Nordstrom's, USAA Insurance Company, and The Walt Disney Company.

Some healthcare organizations, such as Shouldice Hospital, Selnick Healthcare Services, and Baptist Hospital (in Pensacola, Florida), have learned the importance of understanding what their customers expect from all parts of their service experience, and they manage their businesses around satisfying those expectations. Because they have studied their customers long and hard, they know what their customers want, what they are willing to pay for it, and how to give it to them. Outstanding healthcare organizations meet customer expectations, of course, then they exceed them in a thousand ways. As a result, customers, clients, patrons, and patients return to the great organizations—whether in manufacturing or in service industries.

## THREE FUNDAMENTAL CONCEPTS

Three fundamental concepts, based on the practices of successful healthcare organizations, underlie the fifteen principles of achieving service excellence. They are (1) focus on the customer, (2) treat the customer like a guest, and (3) manage the total healthcare experience.

### Focus on the Customer

Everything the organization does should focus on the customer, most usually on the patient. Too many healthcare managers think first about *their* reimbursement procedures, *their* clinical requirements, and *their* physician needs. They are used to starting the process with themselves, their third-party payers, or their physicians when they design their product, create the setting or environment in which the patient interacts with the organization, and set up the system for delivering the healthcare services that their patients receive. They manage from the inside out. The first fundamental concept, however, requires managing from the outside in: start the process with the customers. Study them endlessly to find out what they need, want, value, and expect and what they actually do. Then focus everyone in the organization on doing a better job of meeting and exceeding customer expectations in a way that allows the organization to achieve its financial goals.

Another way of viewing customer focus is to "think retail." This means following the retail model of taking the perspective of the customer (i.e., the end user) and developing service features and attributes that will prompt the customer to buy from your organization.[30] Retailers employ three basic strategies to maximize satisfaction and create loyalty:

1. Enhance the customer experience
2. Capture a greater share of the consumer's spending for related needs
3. Create new sources of revenue by discovering unmet or unacknowledged needs

Independent doctors who do not accept health insurance at all exemplify this trend toward a consumer focus. These doctors accept a limited number of patients, provide quick appointments, and take an above-average amount of time with each patient. Independent doctors are popping up fastest in affluent cities and suburbs,[31] given that most of the patients earn middle- to higher-level incomes and therefore can afford better service. These doctors lobby Congress to create more financial incentives for employers to offer workers medical savings accounts, which let people put aside pretax earnings for healthcare expenses. They believe if more people held cash, they would vote for independent doctors.

Healthcare organizations with a customer focus have the best opportunity to achieve patient satisfaction and improve their competitive position. The successful organizations of the future will be managed by leadership teams that are committed to customer service and able to instill a service philosophy in their entire staffs.[32] The most successful organizations and leaders will focus on their core competencies and set and sustain standards that enable them to satisfy the needs of their customers at all times in all service locations. They know that each interaction with a customer or potential customer represents a "moment of truth" that needs to be endowed with caring and courtesy. When multiple organizations consolidate into regional systems, the service excellence philosophy must be consistent among the leaders at each facility so that the customer service focus prevails across the entire system.[33] The culture must also be embraced by the system's outsourcing partners so that all services are performed at the same high level throughout the system. The process is ongoing, beginning with employee selection and training and continuing through measuring results and rewarding employees for customer service accomplishments.

### Treat the Customer Like a Guest

Because patients are the organization's primary customers, this second fundamental concept is doubly important for dealing with them. Implementing this concept goes beyond a simple change in terminology —replacing the term patient for guest; it requires a change of attitude. In fact, many outstanding service companies are proud that they now use the term guest instead of customer. They have learned the importance of constantly reminding their employees to think of their customers as guests. Disney even coined the term *guestology* to refer to the scientific study of guest behavior to learn more about meeting, and exceeding, the expectations of their guests. Even though we will generally use the traditional terms patient and customer, healthcare organizations need to think of these people as guests and treat them like guests. Staff should also be trained to think of the people in front of them as their guests, whom they are hosting on behalf of the organization.

Looking at a customer as a guest changes the way the healthcare organization and its employees perform their responsibilities. For example, if a patient-customer comes to the healthcare organization seeking and expecting a healthcare service, the only obligation of the healthcare organization and its staff is to provide the appropriate, effective clinical service or treatment. As a result, the patient may be satisfied with the healthcare provider. But with the guest mindset, the organization and its staff can go further: They can provide a positive total healthcare experience in addition to a satisfactory clinical outcome. As a result, the patient will think "What a superb experience!" Creating such an experience, instead of only providing clinical services, exceeds the expectations of most patients, and that encourages them to return and even refer others to the facility. Excellent healthcare organizations know that repeat business and referrals are the key to long-term profitability.

Apply the concept to your own experiences as a customer. Don't you feel like going back to the business if they exceeded your expectation rather than treated you merely as a component in a commercial transaction? Your patients-customers are the same way. Customers are increasingly aware of who treats them right and who does not, they know more about what service does and does not have value for them, and they expect more from the organizations they deal with.

### Manage the Total Healthcare Experience
The patient's main concern is for a positive clinical outcome, but the process by which that outcome is achieved is also important but often

neglected to the detriment of both the customer and the healthcare organization's long-term viability. The physical and psychological environments, interpersonal relations, communication processes, and efficient and responsive delivery system all contribute to the total healthcare experience, and these components must all be managed.

A characteristic of the contemporary economy is that for many consumers, receiving well-rendered clinical services may no longer be enough.[34] The patient's total healthcare experience is the sum total of the components of the experiences that the patient has on a given occasion or set of occasions. In Chapter 2, we outline the components of the total healthcare experience, which consists of three parts: service product, service setting, and service delivery system. We also show how benchmark healthcare and hospitality organizations use their strategy, staff, and systems to provide each patient (viewed as a guest) with a seamless three-part experience.

## CONCLUSION

Although focusing on the customer, treating customers like guests, and managing the total healthcare experience seem simple enough, they are actually huge managerial challenges that the innovators in healthcare services spend considerable time and energy resolving. Despite the challenges they pose, they must be followed: The healthcare organizations that use these principles are taking business away from those organizations that still do not understand their value. The best organizations keep raising the bar, making it increasingly difficult for the rest to compete.

## LESSONS LEARNED

1. Identify the expectations and needs of the emerging new healthcare customer.
2. Develop a plan to overcome and reverse negative customer perceptions of healthcare organizations in general and your healthcare organization in particular.
3. Use the Internet to provide links between your web site and other information that would be useful to your customers.
4. Determine what the best healthcare and other service organizations do to serve their customers and then emulate those techniques that make sense in your environment. In other words, benchmark against the best in customer service.

5. "Think retail" to develop service features and attributes that will prompt the customer to buy healthcare services from your organization.
6. Manage the total healthcare experience.

## NOTES

1. Blair, J. D., and M. D. Fottler. 1990. *Challenges in Health Care Management: Strategic Perspectives for Managing Key Stakeholders.* San Francisco: Jossey-Bass; M. D. Fottler, J. D. Blair, C. L. Whitehead, and M. J. Laus. 1989. "Who Matters to Hospitals and Why? Assessing Key Stakeholders." *Hospital & Health Services Administration* 34 (4): 525–46.

2. Ford, R. C., S. A. Bach, and M. D. Fottler. 1997. "Methods of Measuring Patient Satisfaction in Health Care Organizations." *Health Care Management Review* 22 (2): 74–89; M. D. Fottler, R. C. Ford, V. Roberts, and E. Ford. 2000. "Creating a Healing Environment: The Importance of the Service Setting on the New Customer Oriented Healthcare System." *Journal of Healthcare Management* 45 (2): 91–106; B. J. Pine and J. H. Gilmore. 1998. "Welcome to the Experience Economy." *Harvard Business Review* 78 (4): 97–105.

3. "Consumer Attitudes." *Alliance* (May–June 1998): 11.

4. National Coalition on Health Care. "How Americans Perceive the Health Care System." [Online article]. http://www.nchc.org/perceive.html.

5. National Partnership for Women and Families. 1998. "A Study of Women's Attitudes Toward Health and Healthcare." [Online article]. http://www.nationalpartnership.org/healthcare/org.htm.

6. *Ibid.*

7. *Ibid.*

8. Green, H., and C. Himmelstein. 1998. "A Cyber Revolt in Health Care." *Business Week* (October 19): 154–156; "Consumers Use Web to Fight Back." 2001. *Orlando Sentinel* (May 23): E1.

9. Herzlinger, R. 1997. *Market Driven Health Care: Who Wins in the Transformation of America's Largest Service Industry.* Reading, M A: Addison-Wesley.

10. *Ibid.*, pp. 3–4.

11. Stalk, G., P. Evans, and L. Shulman. 1992. "Competing on Capabilities: The 'New' Rules of Corporate Strategy." *Harvard Business Review* 70 (2): 57–69; D. Ulrich and D. Lake. 1991. "Organizational Capability: Creating Competitive Advantage." *Academy of Management Executive* 5 (1): 77–85.

12. Joint Commission on Accreditation of Healthcare Organizations. 1991. *Quality Improvement Standards.* Oakbrook Terrace, IL: JCAHO.

13. Bigelow, B., and M. Arndt. 1995. "Total Quality Management: Field of Dreams?" *Health Care Management Review* 20 (4): 15–25.

14. Joint Commission on Accreditation of Healthcare Organizations. 1991. *Quality Improvement Standards.* Oakbrook Terrace, IL: JCAHO.

15. Hibbard, J.D., and J. J. Jewett. 1996. "What Types of Quality Information Do Consumers Want in a Health Care Report Card?" *Medical Care Research and Review* 53 (1): 28–47.

16. Epstein, A. 1995. "Performance Reports on Quality: Prototypes, Problems, and Prospects." *Journal of the American Medical Association* 333 (1): 57–61.

17. Slovensky, D. J., M.D. Fottler, and H. W. Houser. 1998. "Developing an Outcome Report for Hospitals: A Case Study and Implementation Guidelines." *Journal of Healthcare Management* 43 (1): 15–34.

18. "How Good is Your Health Plan?" 1996. *Consumer Reports* 61 (8): 34–35.

19. Herzlinger, R. 1997. *Market Driven Health Care: Who Wins in the Transformation of America's Largest Service Industry.* Reading, MA: Addison-Wesley.

20. Arnold, A. 1991. "The Big Bang Theory of Competition in Health Care." *Business Forum* 15 (4): 6–9.

21. Cohn, L., and P. L. Moore. 2000. "Managed Care Takes to the Sickbed." *Business Week* (May 15): 44.

22. Weber, D. 1997. "The Empowered Consumer." *Healthcare Forum Journal* (September/October): 28.

23. Winslow, R., and C. Gentry. 2000. "Medical Vouchers: Health Care Trend—Give Workers Money, Let Them Buy a Plan." *Wall Street Journal* (February 8): A1, A12.

24. Clark, R. H. 1999. "Marketing Health Services." In *Health Care Administration: Planning, Implementing and Managing Organized Delivery Systems,* edited by L. P. Wolper, pp. 161–82. Gaithersburg, MD: Aspen Publishers.

25. Frye, L. 1998. "Patient Services Shows How Massachusetts Hospitals Stack Up." *The Boston Globe* (November 13): A1.

26. Health Care Advisory Board. 1999. *Hardwiring for Service Excellence: Breakthrough Improvements in Patient Satisfaction,* p. 7. Washington, DC: Health Care Advisory Board.

27. Wan, T. H. 2000. "Evolving Health Services Administration Education: Keeping Pace with Change." *Journal of Health Administration Education* 18 (1): 11–29.

28. *Ibid.*, p. 21.

29. Rust, R. 1998. "What Is the Domain of Service Research?" *Journal of Service Research* 1 (2): 107.

30. Goldman, E. F., and K. V. Corrigan. 1998. "Thinking Retail in Health Care: New Approaches for Business Growth." *Alliance* (May/June): 9–11.

31. Lau, G. 2000. "MD Defiance: Doctors Stay Away from HMOs in Quest for Better Patient Care." *Investors Business Daily* (July 5): A10–A11.

32. Girard-DiCarlo, C. B. 1999. "The Importance of Leadership." *Healthcare Executive* 14 (6): 48.

33. *Ibid.*

34. Pine, B. J., and J. H. Gilmore. 1998. "Welcome to the Experience Economy." *Harvard Business Review* 78 (4): 97–105.

*Chapter 2*

# The Customer As Guest

Healthcare Principle: *Meet or exceed the quality and value that customers expect*

Hail guest! We ask not what thou art: If friend, we greet thee, hand and heart; if stranger, such no longer be. . . .

—*Arthur Guiterman*

SERVING PATIENTS AND making products are such different activities that they require different management principles and concepts. Catching a defective tire or a paint blemish at the final inspection stage is one thing; it is quite another to listen to irate patients or family members tell you in no uncertain terms that your hospital, clinic, group practice, or HMO has failed to deliver the service experience they expected. In the first instance, the quality inspector—one of many middlemen between the maker of the product and the final customer—can send the defect back so that the customer never sees the faulty product. In the second situation, no one may be able to fix an unsatisfactory experience or satisfy the dissatisfied customer.

The challenge for healthcare organizations is ensuring that their employees always offer the high level of service that the customer wants and expects—every time, perfectly. Even more challenging is the simple reality that service quality and service value are defined not only by administrators, third-party payers, and governmental oversight agencies but also by the patient-customer. Although *Consumer Reports* has from time to time evaluated HMOs, in the final analysis the decision about the quality and value of a healthcare experience is made anew by each individual patient in every transaction with a specific unit of a healthcare

23

organization on a particular date with a certain service staff. On a particular day, a particular patient could deem the nursing home to be of poor quality, the doctor inept, or the hospital a major disappointment. One unfortunate incident can negatively influence the opinion of the patient, and anyone the patient talks to, about the quality of service provided by that particular organization across its entire service area.

In this chapter, we explore the concept of *guestology* and discuss the nature of service and service products. We also examine the components of the total healthcare experience that patients evaluate: the service product, the service setting, and the service delivery system. We also discuss the relationship between quality, value, and cost.

## WHAT IS GUESTOLOGY?

Guestology is a term coined by Bruce Laval, retired senior vice president of planning and operations of The Walt Disney Company, that has application for any organization that deals with customers. It is the scientific study of their customers' demographic characteristics, needs, wants, expectations, and actual behavior relative to the experience the organization seeks to provide. Guestology turns traditional management thinking on its head because instead of focusing on organizational design, managerial hierarchy, and production systems to maximize organizational efficiency, it forces the organization to look systematically at the healthcare experience from the customer's or patient's point of view. The goal is to create and sustain an organization that can effectively respond to the customers' needs and actual behavior while still meeting its objectives.

For a healthcare organization, guestology involves studying the patients' needs and expectations as well as observing their behavior while in the healthcare organization. The findings of such study are then turned into the organizational practices that provide outstanding healthcare experiences, aligning the organization's strategy, staff, and systems to meet or exceed the patient-customer's (or guest's) expectations regarding the three aspects of the healthcare experience: the service product, service setting (also called service environment), and service delivery. These aspects are carefully woven together to give patients, as well as other healthcare customers, what they want and expect plus a little bit more. As a result, "It all starts with the customer" becomes more than an inspirational slogan; it becomes the truth that everybody accepts and lives up to.

What does it mean to treat a patient as a guest? Basically, healthcare organizations need to address "functional quality characteristics"—attributes of quality that are important to customers and relatively easy for them to evaluate. Among the most important functional quality characteristics are:

- Responsiveness: willingness to help and provide services.
- Assurance: knowledge and courtesy of staff.
- Empathy: caring and individualized attention.
- Tangibles: availability of equipment and appearance of physical environment.
- Reliability: ability to perform the promised service dependably and accurately.[1]

Author David Stamatis identifies the key customer service attributes: comforting, observant, mindful, friendly, obliging, responsible, and tactful.[2] Healthcare organizations need to ask how well they are meeting their patients-customers' expectations in all of these areas and what could be improved.

## External Customers' Expectations

Most patients have the same general expectations when they go to a healthcare organization for service. Surveys and interviews are not required to determine that most patients expect a positive clinical result, cleanliness, courtesy, responsiveness, reliability, and so on. Patients complain when they do not get what they expect or when they encounter situations that they do not expect, so one way to understand patients' expectations is to examine their complaints. Examining what customers do not want can provide insight into what they do want. Service expert Len Berry has listed the ten most common customer complaints in his book *Discovering the Soul of Service*. A common thread that runs through these complaints is that customers feel disrespected. Berry's list helps us identify some critical patient expectations:

1. *Complaint:* lying, dishonesty, unfairness
   *Patient Expectation:* to be told the truth and treated fairly
2. *Complaint:* harsh, disrespectful treatment by employees
   *Patient Expectation:* to be treated with respect

3. *Complaint:* carelessness, mistakes, broken promises
   *Patient Expectation:* to receive careful, reliable healthcare and the promised clinical outcome
4. *Complaint:* employees without the desire or authority to solve problems
   *Patient Expectation:* to receive prompt solutions to clinical and nonclinical problems
5. *Complaint:* waiting in line because some service lanes or counters are closed
   *Patient Expectation:* to wait as short a time as possible
6. *Complaint:* impersonal service
   *Patient Expectation:* to receive personal attention and genuine interest from healthcare employees
7. *Complaint:* inadequate communication after problems arise
   *Patient Expectation:* to be kept informed of problem-solving efforts after reporting or encountering problems or service failures
8. *Complaint:* employees unwilling to make extra effort or who seem annoyed by requests for assistance
   *Patient Expectation:* to receive assistance rendered willingly by healthcare employees
9. *Complaint:* employees who do not know what is happening
   *Patient Expectation:* to receive accurate answers to common questions from informed healthcare employees
10. *Complaint:* employees who put their own interests first, conduct personal business, or chat with each other while the customers wait
   *Patient Expectation:* to have their interests come first[3]

Being aware of common patient concerns and expectations should be part of any healthcare organization's knowledge base. As we shall see later, benchmark organizations dig deeper to discover the more specific patient expectations, which allows them to personalize each patient's experience as much as possible. Some organizations actually record patients' expectations, along with their clinical record, to ensure that they are met on the patient's next visit.

Many healthcare organizations try to provide their patients with accurate information ahead of time so they come to the experience with realistic expectations, which the organization can meet or exceed. Hospitality and other guest-services organizations know the importance of creating guest expectations and living up to them. People who frequent Wendy's have very well-defined expectations, so they notice quickly when the food is not up to par, the restrooms are dirty, or something else is different from what they expected. In contrast, the expectations of patients are more ambiguous because they usually have infrequent interactions with the healthcare provider.

What determines patients' expectations in the first place? Among the crucial influences are the individual patient's needs, values, previous experiences, information, intentions, attributes, moods/emotions, perceived consequences of outcomes, social/demographic background, social norms, group pressures, and perceptions of equity.[4] First-time patients may have general expectations; for example, most first-time patients of a major hospital expect clean rooms, knowledgeable and helpful staff, and a positive clinical outcome. Repeat patients may have more specific expectations based on past experiences. A guestologist seeks to understand and plan for these expectations before customers— whether patients, clients, or family vacationers—ever enter the service setting, so that everything is ready for each customer to have a successful experience. For example, at Disney World the road from the Magic Kingdom's Main Street square to Tomorrowland is wider than the road to Frontierland because studies have shown that more people choose to go to Tomorrowland. This is guestology in practice, and every organization can benefit from similar study of customer behaviors and expectations.

To preserve its reputation and customer base, the healthcare organization must meet or exceed the needs, wants, and expectations of its customers. If it cannot or does not, it must either change its strategy and create different customer expectations or change its service product and/or service delivery system so that it can meet customer expectations. The alternative to not changing is perishing. These days, happy and unhappy patients are no longer restricted to talking with friends and neighbors over the backyard fence or on the phone; they are also equipped with the Internet, which can spread their message to the whole world. Web sites dedicated to bashing organizations that customers perceive to have treated them badly are easily found. Therefore, if enough people perceive that your organization has provided them a terrible experience, your reputation will be severely affected.

The excellent organizations spend extra time and money to ensure that the experience of each patient—whether first time or repeater— not only matches but exceeds that patient's expectations. This is an especially big challenge when one considers the high expectations some patients have about some organizations—say, the Mayo Clinic. First-time customers have received a doctor's referral, have read articles about the superior healthcare provided at Mayo, and have heard the Mayo Clinic name for years; they know of the clinic's outstanding reputation. Repeat patients arrive with high expectations based on prior experiences. If the organization cannot meet expectations, it should not say that it can or promise more than it can deliver.

During difficult times in the airlines industry, no-frills Southwest Airlines has continued to do well. One reason for this is that they deliver superb service, but a more important reason is that they were honest about what they could provide. Ed Perkins, retired editor of *Consumer Reports' Travel Letter,* said: "They give people what they say they will give them. You go in there with realistic expectations. They do not say, 'Come fly our luxurious airplanes.'"5 Healthcare organizations that want to compete can learn from Southwest's practice. They must assess patient expectations, assess their own competencies, decide which patient expectations they can reasonably meet, communicate them widely, and try to meet or exceed them wholeheartedly. Communication of realistic expectations is the responsibility of all healthcare managers who come into contact with customers.

Meeting or exceeding the expectations of present and past customers is extremely important because recruiting new customers is five times more costly than retaining an existing customer base.6 Other service industries have already discovered this truth and are building customer loyalty, satisfaction, and product quality through a customer-oriented approach. The healthcare industry in general is just beginning to adopt this customer-service orientation. In many cases, customer service is an area in healthcare that is given lip service but not the resources for selecting, training, and rewarding employees who possess or can develop customer-service skills.7

### Internal Customers' Expectations

Internal customers include persons and units within the organization that depend on and serve each other. The principles for providing an outstanding service experience for external patients or clients also apply to these internal customers. For example, when the x-ray laboratory serves its internal customers—the physicians requesting the x-rays— it must understand and fulfill the physicians' expectations, just as the organization seeks to meet and exceed the expectations of all its customers. If the x-ray department does not meet the expectations of its internal customers, then the healthcare experience provided to external customers falls short of their expectations.

This logic can easily and rightfully be extended to the individual-employee level. The organization must meet or exceed the expectations of employees about how they will be treated. Benchmark healthcare organizations know that employees deserve the same care and consideration that the organization encourages employees to extend to patients. Extending guest-like treatment to employees is so important to organizational success that much of Chapter 8, on employee motivation and empowerment, is devoted to it.

The competition for customer loyalty and dollars is intense and will grow more so in the future. Therefore, those organizations hoping to survive and prosper in this competitive environment need to master and practice the principles of guestology. If they do not provide the total experience that their customers expect, someone else will.

## THE NATURE OF SERVICE

We have frequently spoken of service—a word with numerous meanings. A common way to think of service is as the *intangible* part of a transaction relationship between a provider organization and its customer, client, or patient.[8] Another way to think of service is strictly from the customer's point of view, rather than the organization's.

### Relationship Between Provider and Customer

Table 2.1 displays four different types of relationships between service provider and customer, with examples of each type noted inside the respective boxes. Different service situations call for different strategies in systems, staff, and settings by the service provider. If the provider is not going to be present in the encounter (upper-left cell of the Table), the service system must be foolproof for all types of customers who will use it. Automatic teller machines in South Florida, for example, ask customers whether they want to read the instructions on the screen in English or Spanish. Some ATMs have phones for people who cannot figure out the instructions. On the other hand, if the provider is present, then the organization must focus on the customer's interactions with that provider as a major means for adding value to the experience. A vision care center or clinic, for example, relies extensively on its employees to deliver the value in the healthcare experience; the owner of vending machines does not.

Many services are delivered with customers present at some stages. At car dealerships, for example, most car repairs take place out of the customer's sight, but the customer still meets the service provider at two points—the customer service desk at the beginning and the payment window at the end. Each type of customer contact may call for a different managerial strategy, environment, and delivery system.

Obviously, healthcare services are typically delivered within the lower-left cell (see Table 2.1) with both the provider and patient present. The healthcare exceptions would include such service providers as laboratory technicians, insurance claims processors, and plant maintenance personnel. These roles are similar to "back-of-the-house" personnel in the hospitality industry (e.g., cooks, administrative and accounting staffs). However, some of the most exciting advances in healthcare are seen in situations described in the upper-left cell, where the patient may be present and the provider is far away, but they are able to communicate over the Internet.

## The Implications of Service Intangibility

Services and manufactured products have different characteristics. *Manufactured* products tend to be tangible—produced, shipped, and purchased now for consumption later; they require minimal, if any, interaction between the manufacturer and the consumer. *Services* tend to be intangible—purchased (if not always paid for) first, then simultaneously produced and consumed later; they are accompanied by considerable provider-customer interaction.[9]

Services are partly or wholly intangible. If the service rendered includes a tangible item (eyeglasses, a prosthetic device, a prescription drug), then the total healthcare experience is the sum of the product-service mix, the environment within which it is delivered, and the service product's delivery. Because part or all of the service product is intangible, many implications exist. First, intangibility makes *assessing the product's quality or value accurately or objectively* (or inventorying or repairing it) *impossible,* although correcting service failures will be discussed later. Because the customer decides whether or not the quality is acceptable or value is present, the only way to measure either quality or value is through subjective assessment techniques, the most basic of which is to ask the customer. A second implication is that *every health-*

**Table 2.1: Interaction Relationships Between Customer/Guest/Patient and Service Provider**

|  | Customer Present | Customer Not Present |
|---|---|---|
| Service Provider Not Present | electric/gas utilities, ATM, vending machines | answering services, TV security services |
| Service Provider Present | healthcare, hospitality, other professional services | lawn service, watch repair |

*care experience is unique.* Even though City Hospital looks the same to everyone, for example, the overall experience at the hospital will be different for each patient. The less tangible the service provided, the more likely that each patient will define the experience differently.

A third implication is that *healthcare organizations cannot keep an inventory of healthcare experiences.* The stockpile of 10:00 a.m. appointments at the clinic is gone after the time passes. Tonight's unused hospital beds cannot be held over until tomorrow night, nor can today's operating room capacity be used tonight. The lack of inventory has important results for healthcare organizations. At the level of healthcare organization design, capacity is the crucial issue. At the managerial level, because capacity is limited and healthcare experiences take place over periods of time, capacity must be carefully managed to meet demand. If demand exceeds capacity, then someone has to wait or go to another facility or provider. If capacity exceeds demand, then the healthcare organization's human and physical resources sit idle.

A fourth implication is *intangibility makes the services difficult to comprehend fully before they are delivered and experienced.* Organizations wanting patients to consider or favor their services rather than those of competitors' must make tangible the intangible through including photographs in advertising pieces, posting on the Internet a view of the organization's interior or the "after" of a successful facelift, promoting positive word of mouth by former patients, publicizing data on patient satisfaction or accreditation information, displaying diplomas on the office wall, endorsements by famous people, and so forth. Such efforts to give tangible evidence of service quality help the employees comprehend the expected healthcare experience as well. Tangibles help them form a mental image of what the service should be like and what its quality level should be and help them better understand how they should perform their jobs.

Yet another implication is that *services are consumed at the moment or during the period of production or delivery*. Even if the patient takes home the product of the service—the eyeglasses, the prosthesis, or the prescription drug—the service as a whole and from the customer's perspective was consumed as it was being delivered and as a result could not be taken home; in other words, the patient can take the eyeglasses home but not the service. Therefore, the organizational systems must be carefully designed to ensure that the service is reliably produced so that each patient has a high-quality experience that is nearly equal to that experienced by every other patient as well as equal to the experience that the same patient had in previous visits.

The healthcare organization must think through the service delivery process by working from the patient backward. Working backward to meet customer desires and expectations is a major difference between benchmark healthcare organizations and the typical bureaucratic functional organization, which is often designed for the convenience and efficiency of organizational members. Instead of concentrating on managerial control systems to ensure consistency and employee predictability, benchmark healthcare organizations concentrate on employee empowerment. They know that no manager can watch every patient-employee interaction and that the healthcare experience cannot be inventoried until the boss checks it for errors, as would be true of a new book, tractor, or suit. Therefore, the frontline service provider who cares about the service, the organization, and the patient must be trusted to deliver the healthcare experience as well as that person can. Instead of following the traditional model of reviewing performance after the fact, healthcare managers must guide their employees from the beginning, teaching them new skills and helping them understand how and why consistent delivery of a high-quality healthcare experience is critical to patient satisfaction and organizational success; all this empowers the employees to provide excellent service. Instead of managing information and authority from the top down, the patient-focused organization must manage these from the bottom up.

The last implication is that *intangible services usually require interaction between the service provider and the customer, client, or patient*. This interaction can be as short as the brief encounter between the customer and the order taker at McDonald's or as long as the lifetime relationship between the patient and the family physician. These interactions can be face to face; over the phone; or by mail, Internet, or fax.

## THE NATURE OF SERVICE PRODUCTS

Most service transactions include tangible materials or equipment as well as intangible services. At the dentist's office, the service may include a product, tooth filling for example, that can be seen and touched; similarly, at the hospital, the healthcare visit may include a room and the doctor may use a stethoscope, tongue depressor, and a thermometer to check the patient's health. Both settings also provide intangible parts of the transaction that the patient or customer cannot take home. This bundle or combination of tangible product and intangible service comprises the service product or service package.

The term service product is also sometimes used to describe completely intangible services because these services may be *the* product that the organization offers for sale. Although these overlapping meanings can be confusing, the way the term is used in context should make clear what we are talking about. One necessary distinction is that the service product does not refer specifically to the tangible items that may accompany the transaction, though it can include them—that is, if you go to a clinic for a flu shot, the actual shot is not the service product; it is just a tangible part of one service product (i.e., the treatment for flu) that the clinic delivers. The intangibles may include the friendliness and responsiveness of staff, promptness in providing the service, and an efficient system for providing the shot.

Both the healthcare organization and the customer define the service product, and the definitions may not be the same. The organization may think the service product is the successful heart transplant, but the patient may perceive it to be the successful heart transplant performed in clean surroundings by informed and cheerful providers and capped off by outstanding follow-up care. Patients may remember the cleanliness of the surroundings, the positive attitude of the staff, and the bedside manner of the surgeon as well as the clinical aspects of their hospital stay. Because everything is defined and assessed by the patient, the healthcare organization should define its service product not only in terms of its own interests but in terms of what patients need, want, and expect; these needs, wants, and expectations go far beyond clinical outcomes. Charles Revson, head of Revlon, Inc., long ago drew this important distinction between what his organization makes and what the clientele buys: "In the factory we make cosmetics, in the store we sell hope."[10]

A characteristic of the contemporary economy that a few leading organizations were among the first to understand is that, for many consumers, receiving well-made goods or well-rendered services may no longer be sufficient. More and more, today's consumers want their goods and services packaged as part of a positive, memorable experience. Of course, today's hospitals are still expected to provide high-quality clinical services at a fair price, doctors to prescribe appropriate treatments, and HMOs to pay the bills in a timely fashion. But the most successful healthcare organizations, and an ever-increasing number of organizations in many other fields, are providing more—carefully designed experiences for the customers that unfold over a period of time. Authors B. Joseph Pine and James H. Gilmore maintain that just as we moved from an industrial to a service economy, we are now in transition to an experience economy.[11] If that is so, thinking in terms of providing customer or client experiences will become important for many organizations in varied industries; in the healthcare industry, such thinking is rapidly becoming essential to a successful competitive strategy.

Patients are not statistical entities, vague concepts, or abstractions to the well-managed healthcare organization. The organization understands that individuals comprise the heterogeneous mass of people they serve or want to serve, each of whom has a different bundle of needs, wants, and expectations. Some patients arrive at the facility happy and excited about whatever is going to happen to them, while others arrive unhappy, frustrated, fearful, or even angry. The healthcare organization must strive to satisfy each of these varied patients by managing their healthcare experience. The first step in accomplishing this task is to understand the patient, to whatever extent possible. Ideally, this understanding would include not only the traditional clinical assessment and demographics but also the psychographic breakdown of how patients feel; what their attitudes, beliefs, and values are; and what kind of experience they need, want, and expect the healthcare organization to deliver.

Meeting the expectations of a customer who arrives needing but not really wanting the service and angry at the service provider is difficult. Most dental patients coming in for a root canal will neither enter nor leave the dentist's office filled with joy. Many patients arrive so apprehensive and concerned about a clinical problem that providing them with a positive, totally satisfying healthcare experience is extraordinarily challenging, and if the clinical outcome turns out to be negative, the challenge intensifies. The healthcare literature shows that even if the clinical outcome is negative, attending well to the other aspects of the healthcare experience can reduce negative consequences such as lawsuits and poor patient-satisfaction evaluations.

Figure 2.1 shows that as the probability of a good clinical outcome decreases, the more important clinical aspects of the healthcare experience become to the patient. Patients who know that their chances of survival are slim unless their clinical treatment is provided with great skill are not going to be much impressed by guestology while life and death hang in the balance. Conversely, the more likely a positive outcome, the more important the nonclinical aspects of the experience become to the patient. Because most patients go to the healthcare provider expecting and in fact experiencing a favorable outcome, the nonclinical aspects are usually quite important. Even if the outcome is negative, its effects can be offset to an extent by a positive total healthcare experience (if the outcome is not too negative). Understanding and appreciating that patients and their needs, wants, and expectations are so varied should motivate the patient-focused organization to design each healthcare experience from each patient's point of view, offering a personalized, tailor-made experience insofar as possible.

## THE HEALTHCARE EXPERIENCE

The healthcare experience is the sum total of the experience, including the service product, service setting, and systems for delivery, provided to the patient on a given occasion or set of occasions. As mentioned earlier, no two healthcare experiences are exactly alike because each patient is unique and has unique needs. That uniqueness is what provides the primary challenge to healthcare service providers; although they cannot meet the expectations of every patient, they must at least try. On the other hand, patients do respond to some experiences in similar if not identical ways. These categories of responses can be sampled, studied, and modeled to produce extremely accurate predictive models of what patients will do and how they will behave. Probabilistic statistics are a major tool for healthcare managers in identifying how their organizations can best respond to the needs, wants, and expec-

**Figure 2.1 Relationship Between Probable Clinical Outcome and the Importance of Service Quality**

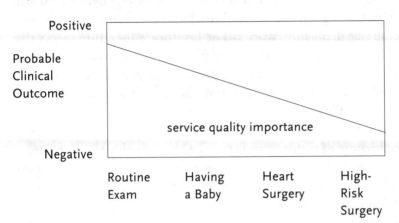

tations of their targeted patient markets. Benchmark healthcare organizations spend considerable time, effort, and money studying their patients to ensure that each part of the total healthcare experience adds something positive. They also expend significant resources attending to the inevitable mistakes as best they can.

Author Wendy Leebov has stated the relationship between great service and meeting customer needs as follows:

> The definition of great service in healthcare depends on customer requirements. Patients have certain requirements of hospitals, employees have other requirements, and physicians expect different things. Good customer service involves identifying the requirements of all the different groups of customers and lining up the environment, people, and systems to deliver them.[12]

The three components of the healthcare experience—the service product, service environment or setting, and service delivery systems—are described more fully below.

## The Service Product

The service product is why the customer, client, or patient comes to the organization. An organization's reason for being is often embodied in the name of the business—for example, Orlando Regional Medical Center, Orthopedic Associates, Eckerd Pharmacy, Jones Chiropractic Clinic, Millhopper Family Dentistry, Shouldice Hospital, and VisionCare. Most service products have both tangible and intangible elements and can range from mostly product with little service to mostly service with little if any product. In most healthcare service encounters, the service product more often than not is entirely or almost entirely intangible (i.e., the expertise of the service providers). Patients go to healthcare providers primarily for the intangible service part of the service product. They go for the inserting of the artificial hip and the expertise that results in successful hip replacement, not for the hip itself. Thus, the new hip is the tangible component of the service product, and the service provider expertise constitutes the intangible component.

## The Service Setting

The terms servicescape and healthscape—the landscape within which service is experienced—have been used to describe the physical aspects of the setting that contribute to the patient's overall physical "feel" of the experience. A healthcare organization that pays careful attention to the details of the physical setting adds value to the healthcare experience and can promote healing. A careful layout for waiting lines, spotless surroundings, neat and clean employee clothing, pleasant background music, comfortable chairs in waiting areas, appropriate lighting, and signs that let patients know where to go next can all communicate to customers that the organization understands their needs and has made every effort to meet their expectations.

## The Service Delivery System

The service delivery system includes the human components (like the orderly who brings dinner or the surgeon and clinical staff who perform the operation), the physical production processes (like the kitchen facilities in the hospital or the operating theater's sophisticated technology), and the organizational and information systems. Unlike a factory's assembly line system, which is generally closed to customers, many parts of healthcare delivery systems are visible to patients. Although the output produced on an assembly line can be touched, physically owned, and looked at, the many services produced and delivered in healthcare are experienced.

Although all aspects of the healthcare service delivery system are important, the people interacting with customers or patients are by far the most important component and the most challenging to manage. The attending physicians, orderlies, shift nurses, billing clerks, admission staff and their attitude, friendliness, genuine concern, and helpfulness largely determine both the value and the quality of the experience for the patient and other customers. At the moment or across the series of moments when the service is delivered and experienced, that one person or that single service provider is the service provider's department, the entire organization, and perhaps in effect the entire healthcare industry to the patient. The feeling that the patient takes away from the healthcare experience is largely derived from what happens during the encounters or interactions between the patient and the various employees; the less tangible the service product, the more important the service providers become in defining the quality and value of the healthcare experience. No wonder the benchmark service organizations spend endless hours and countless dollars finding, training, and supporting their frontline employees. If these staff members do not do it right, the patient and everyone the patient ever tells about the experience may be permanently lost to the organization.

## Moment of Truth

Although many service situations or interactions between organization and customer are now automated, the automatic teller machine being a familiar example, the term service encounter is usually reserved for the actual person-to-person interaction or series of interactions between the customer and the person delivering the service.[13] The encounter is a period of time in which the interaction occurs. The length of a typical service encounter will vary from one healthcare provider or healthcare experience to another. Having a chest x-ray taken is a brief service encounter, while the interaction between patient and clerk at a billing office is usually somewhat longer. A stay in a hospital may involve dozens of service encounters.

Service encounters or interactions, and especially certain critical moments within them, are obviously of crucial importance to the patient's evaluation of service quality; they can make or break the total healthcare experience. Jan Carlzon, former president of Scandinavian Airline Services (SAS), refers to the key moments during such interactions and to some brief encounters or interactions, as moments of truth.[14] (When Carlzon took over SAS, he was confronted with tough labor unions, disheartened management, a stagnant market, and an obsolete corporate strategy. He knew that SAS's only chance of survival was to transform it into a customer-focused organization. Carlzon used all available communication tools to make this cultural change and sent every employee, from shop workers to top management, to a two-day customer service training.[15] Today, the entire organization is focused on service, from the executive suite to the check-in terminal.)

The distinguishing characteristic of most healthcare experiences is how the people providing the service did it. Even if the nursing home, surgery team, or HMO is excellent overall, a rude or careless service person can wreck the healthcare experience in a moment. If that happens, all of the organization's other efforts and expenditures are largely wasted. Little wonder that the benchmark healthcare organizations spend serious time and money to manage those moments. For example, Carlzon managed his entire airline to provide good service at the moment of truth—"the first fifteen golden seconds" in which the mammoth airline is represented to one customer by one service provider—because the success of the entire organization depends on that first fifteen seconds. In a healthcare organization, the first fifteen seconds are important but may not be a make or break moment. The original definition of moment of truth was Carlzon's, but other writers have expanded this definition to include any significant or memorable interaction between service provider and customer or, if no service provider is present, between organization and customer. In addition, some writers have expanded this notion to include interactions with objects such as an ATM or a hospital room. If the customer's first impression with the object is negative (that is, if the organization has slipped up and forgotten to clean the room, for example), a crucial moment has not been properly managed.

The success or failure of the healthcare experience may depend on how a single moment of truth involving the healthcare employee and the patient or relative is handled. Management's responsibility is to ensure that each moment of truth has been prepared for (managed) as well as humanly possible to yield a satisfying, even a superb, experience for the patient. To this end, some hospitals have created diagrams highlighting all points of contact between external customers and internal hospital staff.[16] Especially at the initial point of contact, surely a critical moment, the organization wants customers to receive the information, care, and direction they need. For example, one hospital establishes its first point of contact by placing a red-jacketed guest relations representative in each parking vestibule; this employee's responsibility is to greet customers and direct them to their destination.[17] This service prevents customers from becoming confused or frustrated as they try to find their way through the maze of hospital hallways.

In 1995, Baptist Hospital in Pensacola, Florida, ranked close to the bottom in national surveys of patient satisfaction, and their patient census was declining. Today, the hospital is among the top 2 percent in customer service surveys, and its market share has jumped by 4 percent.[18] It generated $4.5 million in additional revenue in 1999 while reducing costs by $3.5 million. These gains were achieved by establishing ten employee teams that focused on the numerous moments of truth in the healthcare experience and made hundreds of seemingly small improvements. These improvements have added up and have paid off in big ways. Baptist Hospital, which provides an excellent example of how a healthcare organization can go "from bottom to benchmark," will be discussed in more detail in future chapters. The moment-of-truth concept is very important, as each patient may have only a few moments of truth during a healthcare experience or in a lifetime relationship with a healthcare provider, but each healthcare provider is responsible for many make-or-break moments of truth every day.

Another term sometimes seen in the service industry literature is critical incident. Author Mary Jo Bitner and colleagues cite 12 types of critical incidents (both favorable and unfavorable) that can occur during the service encounter.[19] These critical incidents are factors within the customer experience that may be classified as dissatisfiers, neutral, or satisfiers. For example, a customer survey might let the organization know the satisfiers or the moments of truth that are critical to customer satisfaction. The survey might also reveal the dissatisfiers, which the organization can rectify by tracing their root causes. One study of convention hotel attendees identified guest arrival, coffee break, lunch, and the conference room as critical incidents or factors. Once the hotel knew the critical incidents identified by convention guests, it concentrated on making those incidents smooth and seamless.[20] Examples of possible critical incidents in healthcare might be patient complaints about the wait for an appointment, special requests or preferences, patient failure to comply, verbal abuse by a patient, and patients breaking organization policies.

## QUALITY, COST, AND VALUE

In the service industry, the terms quality, cost, and value have specialized meanings to fit the guest-focused orientation of the benchmark organizations. The same is true in healthcare. Two equations (discussed later in this section) can help make these meanings clear and show why we say that quality and value are determined not in any absolute sense but by the customer.[21] Because service is intangible and patient expectations are variable, no objective determination of quality level (and therefore of value) can be made. In some areas of business, a quality inspector might be able to define and determine the quality of a product before a customer ever sees it. In the healthcare field, that is not possible. Physicians and other experts can determine what they think are the best methods or protocols for achieving positive clinical outcomes. They can assess the effectiveness or quality of the delivered healthcare from the organization's or clinical perspectives. However, in the current hypercompetitive healthcare environment, the healthcare customer's assessment of quality and value has become crucially important in determining the success of healthcare organizations. The organization may think it has designed high-quality services, environment, and delivery systems, but if the patient is dissatisfied with any of these elements, the organization has failed to meet the patient's expectations and hence has not provided a healthcare experience of acceptable quality and value.

To meet or exceed the expectations of all different types of customers with their different medical needs, wants, experiences, and moods is a fundamental and exciting challenge for healthcare organizations. If the healthcare manager does not believe that the patient is always right (at least in the patient's mind), then the manager had better find a new career. Even when patients are wrong according to any reasonable standard, the healthcare manager must find ways to let them be wrong with dignity so that their self-esteem and satisfaction with the healthcare experience and the organization continue to be high.

### Quality

The quality of the total healthcare experience or of any part of it is defined as the difference between the quality that the customer expects and the quality that the customer gets. If the two are the same, then quality in this special sense is average or normal: you got what you expected and you are satisfied. If you got more than you expected, quality was positive; if less than you expected, quality was negative. Let us say that you have some routine medical tests done at an academic medical center and some other tests done at a neighborhood health clinic. If the academic medical center did not live up to your (high) quality expectations and the neighborhood clinic exceeded your (somewhat lower) quality expectations, then you would likely conclude that the clinic experience was of higher quality.

The first equation—$Qe = Qed - Qee$—describes these relationships for the quality of the healthcare experience, $Qe$. It is equal to the quality of the experience as delivered, $Qed$, minus the quality expected, $Qee$. If the delivered quality and expected quality are about the same, quality is not zero as it would be if these were true mathematical equations, but it would be average or normal—the expectations have been met. If the quality of the healthcare experience is average or above average, the patient can be described as satisfied with the quality of the experience. If quality is below average, the patient is dissatisfied. Thus, customer satisfaction is determined by customer expectations.

As reflected on the right side of the equation, quality as perceived by the patient will be affected by changes in either patient expectations or organizational performance. If $Qe$ is high enough, the patient had an exceptional, memorable, or superb healthcare experience. The quality of any aspect of the healthcare experience could be described in the same way.

Quality is independent of cost or value. Quality can be high and cost can also be high; quality can be high and cost low, and so forth. Also, the customer may be satisfied with the quality of the experience but dissatisfied with the value received, or vice versa.

## Cost

The cost to a patient selecting your eyecare center rather than someone else's is of course the incremental costs of the eye exam and glasses over what a third party reimburses to you. In addition, experienced eyecare facility managers appreciate that the patient has also incurred other less-quantifiable costs, including the so-called opportunity costs of not going to a different facility, of foregoing experiences or opportunities other than having an eye examination at that time, of the patient's time, and of any risks associated with entrusting a precious set of eyes to your center. The patient's time may not be worth an exact dollar figure per minute or hour, but it is certainly worth something to the patient, so time expenditures (time spent getting to your eyecare center, waiting for the examination or for glasses to be ground) are also costly. Finally, the patient at your center runs some risks, slim but real and potentially costly, like the risk that your center cannot meet expectations or the risk that your service staff will do some damage to the patient's vision.

All of these tangible and intangible, financial and nonfinancial costs comprise the "all costs" denominator of the value equation's right side. They make up the total burden to the patient who chooses a given healthcare experience.

**Value**

The value of the healthcare experience is equal to the quality of the experience (Qe) as "calculated" in the first equation divided by the costs of all kinds to the patient of obtaining the experience:

$$Ve = Qe/all \ costs.$$

If the quality and cost of the experience are about the same, the value of the experience to the patient would be normal or about average; the patient would be satisfied by this fair value but not greatly impressed. Low quality and low cost, and high quality and high cost, satisfy the patient about the same because they are a good match for the patient's expectations. Most people do not expect low quality to come at high cost or high quality to come at low cost. Organizations try to "add value" to the healthcare experience by providing additional features and amenities for patients without increasing the cost to them.

An important concept in service organizations is the cost of quality. Interestingly enough, it is often used to serve as a reminder not of how much it costs the organization to provide service quality at a high level but of how little it costs compared to the cost of not providing quality. If the organization thinks about the costs of fixing errors or compensating patients for errors, low employee morale, patients who never return, or negative word of mouth that can result from poor service, the cost of quality is low indeed and the cost of not providing quality is enormous. That is why the benchmark organizations expend whatever resources are necessary to accomplish two complementary goals: exceed expectations and prevent errors. Because preventing and recovering from errors are so important, we devote Chapter 13 to these topics.

## CONCLUSION

Although guestology is obviously helpful in organizing knowledge about the management of hospitality businesses like hotels and restaurants, which have traditionally spoken of their clientele as guests, it can also be applied to healthcare organizations or for that matter to any organization that serves people in some way. Even manufacturing firms have guests or people that they should treat like guests: their own employees, their customers, and their strategic partners.

Why bother to consider the guest part of guestology seriously? Why should I think of my subordinate as a guest, the person walking into my healthcare facility as my guest, or the physician coming to practice at my hospital as a guest? Let us look at the service situation from the other side for a moment. What healthcare organizations would you personally choose, and what kind of healthcare facility would you yourself want to work for? Those that treat you like a special person or those that make you feel like you are interrupting their organizational procedures and policies?

The answers to all of these questions are obvious. The healthcare organizations and facilities you prefer are the ones that take the time to figure out what you seek in the healthcare experience, offer it to you, and then make clear in all they say and do their sincere appreciation that you sought it out from them. If they understand you and give you what you seek in that experience, you will like them, ascribe high value to the healthcare experience they provide, return again when you need that service, and tell your friends and neighbors what a terrific place that healthcare organization is.

Of course we recognize that the clinical part of the healthcare experience, about which our book has little to say, is of primary importance. If serious medical errors occur or if the outcome of the clinical treatment is negative, patients may not care whether or not they were treated like guests or whether they were the focus of genuine staff attention and caring. When matters of life and death are involved, the nonclinical side is clearly secondary. What makes this book important is that the nonclinical aspects of healthcare are becoming increasingly the competitive margin that can determine organizational success or failure in an increasingly competitive environment. Take hospitals as an example. Most healthcare services are relatively similar—one appendectomy is not all that different from another appendectomy. Factors other than the skills of the clinical staff are the basis on which hospitals can favorably differentiate themselves.

## LESSONS LEARNED

1. Treat each patient like a guest.
2. Your patient defines the value and the quality of your service, so find out what your patient wants.
3. Ask, ask, ask your patients what they want and expect.
4. Provide memorable experiences that exceed patient expectations when possible.
5. Manage all three parts of the healthcare experience—the service product, the service environment, and the service delivery system—and manage both the processes and the people.
6. The less tangible the healthcare experience, the more important to the patient's perception of quality and value are the frontline staff providing the service.
7. Underpromise and overdeliver.
8. The cost of providing quality is very low, compared to the potential cost of not providing quality.
9. Equation for managing the healthcare experience:
Service Product + Service Environment + Service Delivery System = Healthcare Experience

## NOTES

1. Mittal, B., and W. Lassar. 1998. "Why Do Customers Switch? The Dynamics of Satisfaction Versus Loyalty." *Journal of Services Marketing* 12 (1): 177–91; A. Parasuraman, V. A. Zeithaml, and L. L. Berry. 1988. "SERVQUAL: A Multiple-Item Scale for Measuring Consumer Perception of Service Quality." *Journal of Retailing* 64 (1): 38–40.

2. Stamatis, D. 1996. *Total Quality Service Principles, Practices, and Implementation.* Boca Raton, FL: St. Lucie Press.

3. Berry, L. L. 1999. *Discovering the Soul of Service,* p. 31. New York: The Free Press.

4. Thompson, A., G. H., and R. Sunol. 1995. "Expectations as Determinants of Patient Satisfaction: Concepts, Theory, and Evidence." *International Journal for Quality in Health Care* 7 (2): 127–41.

5. Marbella, J. 1999. "Airline Passenger Complaints Soar." *The (Florida) Times-Union* (January 3): F-2.

6. Mittal, B., and W. Lassar. 1998. "Why Do Customers Switch? The Dynamics of Satisfaction Versus Loyalty." *Journal of Services Marketing* 12 (1): 177–91.

7. Mayer, T., R. Cates, M. J. Mastorovich, and D. Royalty. 1998. "Emergency

Department Patient Satisfaction in Customer Service Training Improves Patient Satisfaction and Ratings of Physician and Nurse Skill." *Journal of Healthcare Management* 43 (5): 427–38.

8. For more on the intangibility of services, see C. A. Congram and M. L. Friedman. 1991. "The Quality-Leadership Connection in Service Businesses." In *The AMA Handbook of Marketing for the Service Industry*, edited by C. A. Congram and M. L. Friedman, pp. 3–19. Chicago: American Marketing Association.

9. Congram, C. A., and M. L. Friedman. 1991. "The Quality-Leadership Connection in Service Businesses." In *The AMA Handbook of Marketing for the Service Industry*, edited by C. A. Congram and M. L. Friedman, pp. 3–19. Chicago: American Marketing Association; C. H. Lovelock. 1981. "Why Marketing Management Needs to Be Different for Services." In *Marketing of Services*, edited by J. H. Donnelly and W. R. George, pp. 5–9. Chicago: American Marketing Association.

10. Levitt, T. 1972. "Production-Line Approach to Service." *Harvard Business Review* 50 (5): 50.

11. Pine, B. J., and J. H. Gilmore. 1998. "Welcome to the Experience Economy." *Harvard Business Review* 76 (4): 97–105; B. J. Pine and J. H. Gilmore. 1999. *The Experience Economy*. Cambridge, MA: Harvard Business School Press.

12. Leebov, W., and G. Scott. 1994. *The Customer Relations Strategy for Health Care*, p. 14. Chicago: AHA Press.

13. Lytle, R. S., P. W. Hom, and M. P. Mokwa. 1998. "SERV*OR: A Managerial Measure of Organizational Service-Orientation." *Journal of Retailing* 74 (4): 460.

14. Carlzon, J. 1987. *Moments of Truth*. New York: Ballinger.

15. *Ibid.*, pp. 26–27.

16. Stamatis, D. 1996. *Total Quality Service Principles, Practices, and Implementation*. Boca Raton, FL: St. Lucie Press.

17. Hiebler, R., T. Kelly, and C. Ketteman. 1998. *Best Practices for Building Your Business with Customer-Focused Solutions*. New York: Simon and Schuster.

18. Nathan, S. 2000. One Hospital Mends Customer Service. *USA Today* (May 5): 5B.

19. Bitner, M. J., B. H. Booms, and M. Stanfield Tetreault. 1990. "The Service Encounter: Diagnosing Favorable and Unfavorable Incidents." *Journal of Marketing* 54 (1): 71–84.

20. Danaher, P. J., and J. Mattson. 1994. "Cumulative Encounter Satisfaction in the Hotel Conference Process." *International Journal of Service Industry Management* 5 (4): 69–80.

21. Adapted from J. L. Heskett, W. E. Sasser, Jr., and C. W. L. Hart. 1990. *Service Breakthroughs: Changing the Rules of the Game,* p. 2. New York: The Free Press.

*Chapter 3*

# Meeting Customer Expectations Through Planning

Healthcare Principle: *Identify and focus on the key drivers of customer satisfaction*

Those who fail to plan, plan to fail. Leaders who are not planners are simply caretakers and gatekeepers.

—*Major General Perry Smith, U.S. Air Force*

GIVING CUSTOMERS WHAT they expect takes detailed planning, forecasting, and sound intuitive judgment. Managers of excellent healthcare organizations try to mix all three together into a strategy that allows them to give patients and other customers exactly what they need, want, and expect. Customers will return and will speak well of an organization only if their experiences meet if not exceed their expectations. The service strategy is the organization's plan for providing the healthcare experience that customers expect and even a little bit more.

Planning and strategy making are simple to talk about and difficult to do. In theory, all one has to do is to assess the environment within which the organization operates, assess the organization's capabilities, decide where the organization wants to go within that environment and in light of those capabilities, and then make a plan to get there. Unfortunately, the expectations of real patients change quickly, competitors eventually duplicate the organization's strategic advantage of the moment, governments pass new laws, and advances in technology require the organization to scrap expensive parts of its old healthcare delivery system and create new ones. In other words, people and their needs and expectations change, the competitive environment changes, and the healthcare organization changes. Finding ways to deliver what customers expect in light of the uncertainties created by such changes is a major challenge.

In this chapter we explore the healthcare planning process, internal and external environment assessments, the service strategy, and the action plans. We also provide methods of enhancing customer service strategies and examples from benchmark organizations.

## THE HEALTHCARE PLANNING PROCESS

Providing customers with an outstanding healthcare experience, both clinically and nonclinically, is how benchmark healthcare organizations become outstanding. Benchmark organizations try to imagine the kinds of experiences customers will find satisfying, then plan ways to deliver them. Examples of these innovative strategies abound. Maternity patients did not know how much staying in family suites (birthing and recovery rooms that allow family members to be part of the event) would help ease the intensity of childbirth until they actually experienced it. Similarly, bank customers did not know the convenience of debit cards (cards that deduct expenditures directly from the customer's bank account) until banks began to offer them. In the late nineteenth century, travelers did not realize that they were being inconvenienced by the unavailability of ready cash, or by having to carry too much cash, until American Express created the traveler's check. HMOs did not know they needed a 1-800 phone number with 24-hour instant response until the idea was introduced.

Benchmark organizations in all fields anticipate, and sometimes even create, the future needs of their target markets. The way to achieve these ends is through the strategic planning process. The process has two basic steps: (1) assessing external and internal environments and (2) figuring out what to do on the basis of that assessment. The external assessment of environmental opportunities and threats leads to the generation of strategic premises about the future environment. The internal assessment of organizational strengths and weaknesses leads to a redefinition or reaffirmation of organizational core competencies.

As shown in Figure 3.1, healthcare planning follows an ongoing cycle that begins at the big-picture level and ends at specific action plans including departmental or project budgets and individual yearly objectives. Typically, healthcare planning is done annually and begins with management's simultaneous consideration of three components: (1) the external environment and its opportunities and threats, (2) the internal organization and its strengths and weaknesses, and (3) the organizational vision and mission and their relationship to the other two components.

The environmental assessment, or the "long look around" for opportunities and threats, defines the strategic premises. These premises result from the managers' assessment of all long-term aspects of the external environment and their attempt to use them to predict what patients will expect and what the key drivers of patient satisfaction will be in the intermediate-term and longer-term future. Although patients do not always know the key drivers of their future satisfaction, the organization must still try to find out the kinds of experiences customers think will meet their expectations. The internal assessment, or the "searching look within" for strengths and weaknesses, defines the organization's core competencies and considers the organizational strong and weak points in terms of its ability to compete in the future.

The vision statement articulates what the organization hopes to look like and be like in the future. Rather than presenting specific principles, goals, and objectives, the statement creates a picture of that toward which the organization aspires and provides inspiration for the journey ahead. The vision statement is used to unite and inspire employees to achieve the common ideal and to help external stakeholders understand what the organization is all about. The mission statement articulates the organization's purpose—the reason it was founded and the reason it continues to exist. It defines the path to the vision, given the strategic premises and the organization's core competencies, and it guides the organization's overall service strategy which in turn drives the design of the healthcare service product, service environment, and service delivery system. Examples of vision and mission statements will be presented later in the chapter.

Table 3.1 outlines the steps that convert the planning process into customer-focused outcomes. Once the mission, vision, and values are articulated and the environmental scanning is completed, the organization can develop a service strategy (addressing the strategy, staffing, and system), put resources in place to implement the strategies, and implement the strategies. The healthcare planning process is never complete; it should begin again in some predefined time frame. The planning process should never stop because the world in which any healthcare organization operates never stops changing.

**Figure 3.1: The Healthcare Planning Process**

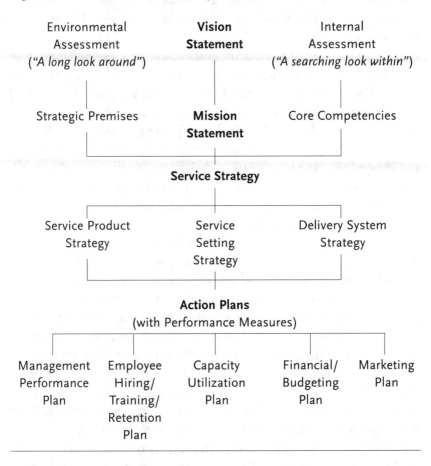

## The Necessity of Planning

The process illustrated in Figure 3.1 is an attempt to apply rationality to an irrational world and to predict an unpredictable future; it will therefore be accompanied by errors, wasted time, and frustration. Nevertheless, the planning process is worthwhile. Every healthcare organization needs a road map to unite and focus the efforts of the organization's members to prepare for the future that the organizational planners predict. Everyone makes decisions today that they must live with in the future, and most managers want to make those decisions as rationally as possible. Even though no one, including planners, knows what the future will bring, only by creating and implementing plans can we communicate to those both inside and outside the organiza-

**Table 3.1: Steps to Enhance Customer Service**

*1. Mission, Values, and Vision*
- Ensure that the organization's mission statement creates the framework for a customer service initiative
- Gain support of upper management for the concept of a customer focus

*2. Environmental Scan*
- Scan the external environment to identify opportunities and threats for satisfying present and future customer key drivers
- Scan the internal environment to identify all strengths and weaknesses to enhance core competencies of staff that are responsible for customer service

*3. Service Strategy*
- Study similar organizations that excel in customer service and benchmark against them
- Use a service audit to survey customers based on quality, value, service, and achievement
- Develop a strategy to reduce the gaps between desired and actual customer service expectations

*4. Action Plans*
- Use cross-functional teams to create tactical plans that focus all parts of the organization on customer service
- Use cross-functional teams to integrate all of the tactical plans
- Use various techniques, like brainstorming, to create customer service initiatives in each tactical area
- Carefully select one or two customer service priority areas for intense focus
- Empower employees to meet customer expectations
- Include customer outcome measures in assessment strategies

tion where we want to go, what criteria we should use to allocate our scarce resources, and which activities we should pursue or avoid.

## EXTERNAL ASSESSMENT

The healthcare planning process starts with a careful study of the opportunities and threats that the future holds for both the organization and its industry. The many available forecasting techniques range from the heavily quantitative or objective to the highly qualitative or subjective. The quantitative techniques include the powerful tools of statistical forecasting, design day, and yield management. The qualitative techniques, to be discussed later, include brainstorming, the Delphi technique, focus groups, scenario planning, and pure creative guesswork.

Most forecasting techniques are based on the idea that the future is somehow related to the past—that what has already happened has some predictable relationship to what will happen. For example, if a hospital's patient growth rate has been about 10 percent per year for 30 years, then forecasting that this growth rate will continue next year seems reasonable. Similarly, if records show that 20 percent of all patients scheduled to come into a clinic on a particular day are already on the premises by 10 a.m., then any day's total patient count can probably be reliably forecasted by 10:01 a.m. On a grander scale, if the growth rate of new residents coming to a metropolitan city has been 10 percent per year for the past decade, then predicting that this growth rate will continue for at least a few more years seems reasonable.

The problem with assuming that the past can be used to predict the future is that all too frequently the assumption does not hold true. In the early days of the telephone, the ratio of phones to operators was very small. If that ratio and population trends were used to predict the number of telephone operators needed today, many millions of people in the United States would have been predicted to now be working as telephone operators. Innovations can destroy statistical trends. Major improvements in technology and work productivity have greatly increased the ratio of telephones to operators, making the prediction in the example above highly unlikely. Any forecast based only on the past will be thrown off by unexpected technological or other dramatic change.

Over the years, some astute human beings have made some lifestyle-changing predictions. For example, when the automobile began to be commonly available, some people predicted that increasing numbers of motorists would need roadside hotels. Similarly, Walt Disney foresaw the impact of sound on movies, of television on entertainment, and of the interstate highway system on the theme-park industry. Moreover, during the 1970s several entrepreneurs correctly predicted that employers and government would be looking for ways to rein in healthcare costs. One result of this prediction was the establishment and growth of for-profit healthcare providers and managed care organizations.

Forecasting techniques are useful to capture the impact of current trends on future business. However, they are only one source of input into the creative process by which thoughtful healthcare managers develop strategic plans.

## Quantitative Forecasting Techniques

### Statistical Forecasting

Statistical techniques used for forecasting have several major types: econometric, regression, time series, and trend analysis. Each is based on the idea that definable and reliable relationships exist between what the organization wishes to forecast and some other variable or variables. Accurate forecasts of the future demand for various health services allow the organization to provide appropriate capacity to meet customer service expectations.

*Econometric* models are elaborate mathematical descriptions of multiple and complex relationships that are statistically assembled as systems of multiple regression equations.[1] An example is the impact of population growth, income changes, and changing demographics on projected demand for a particular health service. In *regression analysis,* variations in dependent variables are explained by variations in one or more independent variables. *Time series* and *trend analysis* are simply extrapolations of the past into the future. If we know how much our market has grown each year for the past ten years, a time series forecast will project that rate of growth into the future and allow us to project total demand, patient waits, occupancy rates, and so forth. Because change is constant, these numbers can be adjusted to account for recent changes in the economy.

### Design Day

A basic problem for many healthcare organizations is that future demand is uncertain and capacity is fixed. An important concept in capacity planning for service organizations is the *design day*—the day of the year chosen by management to determine the capacity of a facility. Whenever a new clinic, hospital, specialty practice, or other similar facility is created, management must determine how big to build it or how many people it should handle at one time. A hospital should not be designed to accommodate demand during a potential natural disaster or terrorist attack because its capacity will exceed demand during other periods. But if an inpatient hospital in South Florida is designed to meet the typical demand during the winter "snowbird" season, demand will exceed capacity the rest of the time. Hospitals also have been able to estimate expected utilization patterns for inpatient care or emergency room care based on past patterns. For example, inpatient care is usually down considerably during the Christmas holidays, while emergency department care is up on weekends. However, natural disasters or terrorist attacks can and do cause significant deviations from the expected use patterns.

A clinic considering expansion could use past and predicted patient volume figures to set the design day at the 50th percentile. Overall clinic demand (and demand for particular clinical departments) would then exceed capacity on about half the days, and about half the time capacity would exceed demand. But a customer-focused clinic does not want patients to experience excessive wait times for half the days of the year. The clinic designers must decide what percentile level they want to establish for their design day. The higher the percentile level chosen, the lower the number of days they will exceed their design-day wait-time standards. For example, if they choose a 75th percentile design day, the clinic will exceed wait-time standards on 90 days of the year; if they choose a 90th percentile design day, they will exceed their wait-time standards on only 36 days per year. But resources will remain idle more often than if a 75th percentile day is chosen.

The design-day percentile is a critical management decision. A higher percentile day means increasing capital and human resources investments to increase clinic capacity. A lower percentile day will cost less initially, but patient dissatisfaction will probably be higher; once the design-day capacity is exceeded, the quality of the experience will be diluted for some patients. This dissatisfaction will have a negative impact on repeat visitation, long-term revenue growth, and avoidance of litigation. Management must balance the tradeoff between investment costs and patient service very carefully. The design-day concept is one way to address the challenge of finding the best balance between carrying the costs of excess capacity and ensuring the quality and value of each patient's experience. Costs are associated with buildings, grounds, and people. Customers expect the service to be available to them when they need it; otherwise they are dissatisfied with the quality and value of their experience.

For any healthcare organization, the original design-day decision is based on forecasts, information derived from organizational past experience, and perhaps from knowledge of similar facilities. Once real information can be gathered through real experience with real patients, the design-day decision can be refined. Because most healthcare organizations would rather add capacity than tear down existing capacity or let it stand idle, the original design-day decision for a new or expanded facility should probably use conservative estimates.

### Yield Management

A capacity-management concept that has gained substantial favor in the hospitality industry and can have direct application to healthcare is *yield management*. Yield management is the management of the sale of units of capacity to maximize the profitability of that capacity. Successful yield management involves selling the right capacity to the right customer or patient at the most advantageous price to maximize both capacity utilization and revenue. This concept is based on the idea that patient demand patterns can be predicted to some extent. Those predictions can be used to allow the healthcare organization to charge different rates to different people (or groups) based on

1. the bargaining power of the group, based on its relative importance to the organization;
2. current demand by other customers; and
3. the capacity projected to be available at any given time.

For example, HMO patients might receive the lowest prices, and patients who are not part of a group might be charged more. Balancing capacity, demand, and price is the job of the computerized yield-management system.

Yield management is an important capacity-planning device for any organization that has capacity limitations and a perishable commodity. Because the organization's planners must have accurate and timely information about customer demand and available capacity, true yield management in the modern sense can hardly be accomplished without the computer.

### Qualitative Forecasting Techniques

Healthcare organizations can use forecasting tools to make more qualitative or subjective projections. Among them are brainstorming, the Delphi technique, focus groups, and scenario building or war gaming.

### Brainstorming

The old strategy of asking a group of people to ponder the future and what it may mean, based on what they already know, is called *brainstorming*. This pondering can be formal and structured, requiring participation from everyone, or informal and unstructured. As a forecasting tool, it assumes that everyone has some degree of creativity, that people will voluntarily contribute their best ideas in an open group discussion, that the sharing of those ideas will spark the generation of good new ideas, and that the sum total of those ideas will be a more accurate forecast than the forecast of any one person. Unfortunately, these assumptions do not always hold up, and participants encouraged or forced to brainstorm often view the time spent as wasted. However, many organizations have found that placing creative people in discussion sessions (like brainstorming) can provoke new ideas or ways of looking at things.

### The Delphi Technique

The Delphi technique is a more formal way of tapping the forecasting skills of experts. If a hospital wants to know what percent of overall surgical capacity will be filled at this time next year, the Delphi technique would be a good tool to use. This is how it works: A group of industry experts make individual estimates for next year, and the estimates are combined or averaged. If that average estimate is not sufficient for organizational purposes, the average may be shared with the experts, along with the individual estimates and the thinking that went into them. The experts are then asked to consider this new information and to make a second round of estimates.

Even though this process cannot guarantee an accurate forecast of such future unknowables, such as how many elderly people will need hip replacements, how many patients will seek laser eye surgery, or how many doctors will prescribe generic substitutes, combining expert estimates can yield the best composite estimate available.

### Focus Groups

Focus groups are asked to concentrate on an issue and to discuss their thoughts about it with a trained group-discussion leader. Although focus groups are perhaps most frequently used in assessing the quality of service already rendered, and are discussed in more detail in a later chapter, they can also be helpful in forecasting what people are apt to like and not like about a service experience. If an organization has an innovation in mind, it can form a focus group that is demographically and psychographically representative of its target market to see how the group reacts to the innovation. For example, groups of senior citizens living in trend-setting areas are frequently used to predict healthcare expectations of aging patients.

### Scenario Planning

Scenario building, or war gaming, has become a fairly popular subjective forecasting technique. With this technique, we assume a certain future situation or scenario, then try to assess its implications for our organization. For example, if a clinic specializes in diagnostics, a future scenario of concern might be the rapid development of online diagnostic services. If this scenario occurs, making quick and easy access to diagnosis possible for millions of people, we assess the scenario's impact on the present willingness of people to travel to fixed-site healthcare locations for diagnosis. Organizational leaders should prepare contingency plans that respond to such a scenario. Although scenario building stimulates the imaginations of organizational planners, managers must be careful not to be ruminating at the scenario stage while the competition is actually building facilities.

### Predicting Other External Factors

The healthcare organization must try to assess the uncertain future in terms of potential changes in the following factors: demographics; technology; social expectations; economic forces; competitors; other relevant groups (e.g., suppliers of resources, capital, and labor); and surprise factors. All these factors will have varying effects on the organization, and the organization will also have varying abilities in forecasting the factors fully. Some factors are both predictable and simple, such as demographics. For example, estimating the number of teenagers eligible to work in ten years is a straightforward calculation because these children have all been born already.

On the other hand, some other factors are simple but unpredictable. Using the demographics factor again, an estimation of skilled and trained employees who will be available in a certain geographical area in 20 years is a simple number to calculate. But the calculations rest on unpredictable information such as unknown changes in family formation, net migration into the area, and other factors.

As is true of simple future elements, complex future elements are either predictable or unpredictable. Once a certain number of people are in a geographical area, a relatively predictable percentage will come to any given healthcare facility on any given day. Calculating the number of people who will be in the area, however, is a complex process; it depends on growth rates, travel into and out of the area, and employment levels.

The complex and unpredictable outcomes are of course the hardest to forecast. An example would be changes in technology. If technology develops to the point that the experience of going to a major healthcare facility can be duplicated through virtual reality technology, then people would not have to expend time and trouble going to the healthcare facility for medical services. If this happens, the entire area surrounding a major facility will suffer a severe economic decline.

Some forecasts are easy because the elements comprising them (which are themselves forecasts) are predictable and the calculations simple, while others are difficult. Healthcare organizations must try to make the forecasts relevant to their futures, regardless of ease or difficulty, and include them in their strategic planning processes. Because things that can be counted are often more comfortable to deal with than those that cannot, managers are sometimes tempted to emphasize those factors that are quantitative and ignore those that cannot be easily measured. Unfortunately for those managers, in real life the important factors are usually those that we cannot put a number to in spite of how hard we try.

The healthcare organization draws conclusions about the future of its industry and market from its environmental assessment, then uses them to make the assumptions (called strategic premises) on which the service strategy is based. Premises are educated guesses. The organization may guess wrong, or even if it guesses right it may devise the wrong strategy. But not to guess at all means reacting day to day to whatever seems to be going on without a plan or a focus for organizational activities.

## INTERNAL ASSESSMENT

The internal assessment or audit is the searching look within. The healthcare organization cannot plan with any confidence until it admits its weaknesses and identifies its central strengths, frequently termed its core competencies.

## Core Competencies

The definition given by authors Hamel and Prahalad is helpful: An organization's *core competence* is the bundle of skills and technologies (often called, confusingly enough, competencies) that gives the organization an important difference in providing customer benefits and perceived value.[2] Here are examples: Chrysler's core competence is making cars, while HealthSouth Corporation's is physically rehabilitating people following surgery and/or after suffering injuries. The core competence of Baptist Hospital in Pensacola, Florida, is wider in scope: providing an outstanding healthcare experience. As shown in Figure 3.1, there are connections and relationships between an organization's vision statement, mission statement, strategic premises, core competencies, service strategy, service setting strategy, and action plans. The core competence, for example, ought to be embodied in the mission statement, and knowing its areas of competence will enable an organization to make a key strategic decision: What shall we *not* do?

The point is that every successful organization has developed a core competence—an ability to do something very well. As long as it sticks to activities appropriate to that core competence, it will probably continue to succeed. When it strays from its core competence, it may find itself pitting its weaknesses against the strengths of other organizations. For example, when some hospital systems in the 1990s diversified by buying physician practices or health insurers, their top management had moved beyond their core competency in providing inpatient care. As a result, most of these systems failed in their new ventures.

Successful managers must have two skills or qualities: management ability and expertise in a specific industry or functional area; these skills comprise their core competence. They know, just as successful organizations know, that they should focus on developing their management ability and industry expertise. A factory manager and a hospital manager may have many of the same managerial skills, but the successful factory manager may fail as a hospital manager because the core competence leading to success, for managers as well as for organizations, will be different in the two industries.

The internal assessment tells the healthcare organization where it stands now, what new strengths it must develop, and what weaknesses it must eliminate to build the core competence it will need to succeed in the future industry it foresees. If a surgery practice accurately perceives itself to have undeveloped potential in elective surgery and foresees the future of such surgery to be promising because aging baby boomers, many of whom have substantial discretionary income, will want and be able to afford various kinds of elective surgery, then that practice should probably focus on developing that surgical specialty.

### Internal Assets

An internal assessment includes an evaluation of all the organization's *internal assets*. Each organization has internal assets that help define its core competencies; these assets include the organization's reputation; human capital (employees); managerial capabilities; resources; and competitive advantages based on its technology, patents, brand names, copyrights, and customer loyalty. For example, internal assessment of its assets helped Baptist Hospital in Pensacola, Florida, earn the RIT/*USA Today* Quality Cup in 2000 as one of the best hospitals in the United States. Baptist Hospital developed programs and strategies that promote patient satisfaction, employee empowerment, and physical support,[3] all of which support its core competence in providing service excellence in hospital care. Much like Jan Carlzon's success with Scandinavian Airline Services (see Chapter 2), Baptist Hospital is an example of a "turnaround" organization rather than an organization with decades of service excellence like Marriott or Disney. Nevertheless, in a very short period of time (the turnaround process began in 1997), Baptist Hospital has become a benchmark healthcare organization in terms of service excellence.

### The Vision and Mission Statements

Most organizations spend a great deal of time trying to articulate their vision and mission statements, and the reason is clear: If you do not know what you want to do, you cannot decide how you will do it. Most companies write mission and vision statements, and other statements such as credos, beliefs, and values, but some know what they are doing and where they are heading without writing down the details. Vision and mission statements vary from the simple to the complex, and the simpler the better. Figure 3.2 is a listing of vision and mission statements of some healthcare organizations.

### Vision

The *vision statement* describes what the organization should look like in the future and what significant contributions it expects to make.

**Figure 3.2: Mission, Vision, and Values Statements of Various Healthcare Organizations**

*Valley Cardiac Surgery, California*
*Mission:* To provide quality and comprehensive cardiovascular services in a cost-effective manner to those we serve throughout California and beyond.

*St. Joseph Health Services, Rhode Island*
*Mission:* To preserve, restore, and enhance the health of individuals and families we serve within our communities guided by our core values of respect, compassion, responsibility, teamwork, and quality, consistent with the healing ministry of the Catholic Church.

*Baptist Health Care, Pensacola, Florida*
*Mission:* To provide superior service based on Christian values to improve the quality of life for people and communities served.
*Vision:* To be the best health system in the country.
*Values:* Integrity, vision, innovation, superior service, stewardship, and teamwork.

*Beloit Memorial Hospital, Inc., Beloit, Wisconsin*
*Mission:* To be a leader in assembling medical, employee, equipment, facility, and community resources in a manner which strives to deliver the highest quality medical services and improves the overall health status of the community. As a community hospital, these services will be delivered at an economic value and in a manner that creates the highest level of patient satisfaction.

*Cincinnati Children's Hospital Medical Center, Ohio*
*Mission:* To serve the health care needs of infants, children, and adolescents and to provide research and teaching programs that ensure delivery of the highest quality pediatric care to our community, the nation, and the world.
*Values:* To be the leader in the improvement of child health.
*Excellence:* We will strive to excel in every aspect of our services, recognizing that people are our greatest strength in all our accomplishments and achievements. We will respect and acknowledge the dignity and worth of each patient, family member, and employee.
*Integrity:* We will follow the highest standards of ethical conduct, truth, moral principles and ideals in providing patient care, teaching, research, and all related support services.
*Innovation:* We will encourage change, creativity, and the exploration of new ideas. We will reward the efforts of all who seek and share new knowledge and wisdom that contribute to the advancement of pediatric science and health care.

Although "mission" and "vision" are to an extent overlapping terms, the corporate vision articulates the organization's picture of the future. Hamel and Prahalad define this vision as the "quest for industry foresight" wherein the organization defines its future aspirations and figures out today the steps to be taken to make that future a reality. The real creative imagination of the management and the entire organization needs to be focused on articulating the vision and ways to achieve it. Hamel and Prahalad describe the difficulties involved in getting from here to there, from today to tomorrow:

> Although potentially useful, technology forecasting, market research, scenario planning, and competitor analysis won't necessarily yield industry foresight. None of these tools compels senior management to preconceive the corporation and the industries in which it competes. Only by changing the lens through which the corporation is viewed (looking at core competencies versus focusing on only strategic business units), only by changing the lens through which markets are viewed (functionalities versus products), only by broadening the angle of the lens (becoming more inquisitive), only by cleaning off the accumulated grime on the lens (seeing with a child's eyes), and only by occasionally disbelieving what one sees (challenging price-performance conventions, thinking like a contrarian) can the future be anticipated. The quest for industry foresight is the quest to visualize what doesn't yet exist.[4]

Sometimes an organization is created to fulfill a personal vision, as former Chili's CEO Norman Brinker said: "I have a vision, then I create an atmosphere that involves the people in that vision."[5] Similarly, Richard Scrushy, chairman and CEO of HealthSouth Corporation, began as a respiratory therapist who started out with a personal vision. He wanted to create an international company that would provide a full range of rehabilitation services in multiple locations. From modest beginnings, the company grew rapidly and has achieved Scrushy's vision of becoming the major rehabilitation corporation in the world, with a specialty in sports-related injuries.

### Mission

The organization's *mission statement* expresses the reason the organization was created and exists. It guides managers as they allocate resources, focuses organizational marketing efforts, and defines for all employees how they should deal with patients and other customers. The organization's statement of mission often includes its core values; as Wal-Mart founder Sam Walton said: "We put the customer ahead of everything else. . . . If you're not serving the customer, or supporting the folks who do, we don't need you."[6] Benchmark organizations recognize the importance of providing straightforward guidance to all employees on how the organization expects them to act in their jobs. Another benchmark of customer service, Southwest Airlines, started out in 1971 with this customer-focused mission: "Get your passengers to their destinations when they want to get there, on time, at the lowest possible fares, and make darn sure they have a good time doing it." Southwest's mission today "is dedicated to the highest quality of Customer Service delivered with a sense of warmth, friendliness, individual pride, and Company Spirit," and it is also "committed to providing Employees (with) a stable work environment with equal opportunity for learning and personal growth."

A 1999 study of hospital mission statements found that their most common components were a statement of purpose (76 percent), specific customers served (62 percent), one clear compelling goal (56 percent), statement of values and beliefs (56 percent), products and services offered (52 percent), concern with satisfying customers (50 percent), and concern for employees (41 percent).[7] In addition, the survey also found that top management satisfaction with financial performance was significantly and positively correlated with a mission statement that contains three types of information: customers served, concern with satisfying customers, and products/services offered. Moreover, top management satisfaction with financial performance was also higher if management was satisfied with how well each of the following mission statement components was written: specific customers served, concern with satisfying customers, and concern for employees. Although we cannot attribute cause and effect here, well-developed and well-written mission statements with a focus on internal and external customers appear to be associated with better financial outcomes.

## THE SERVICE STRATEGY

Once the external and internal factors have been examined in light of the corporate vision and mission, the healthcare organization is ready to define its *service strategy*. This strategy is critical to any healthcare organization's success because it guides decision making, from capital budgeting to handling patient concerns. Defining and creating the service strategy are as much art as science. The organization must now define its market, craft its service product to meet that market's needs, create the appropriate service environment, and design the service systems to reach the target market. If the organizational mission is to provide cosmetic surgery to an upscale, educated, retired socioeconomic group, then the service delivery system should be high-touch and the service environment should be elegant and congruent with what an upscale market wants. Discovering what any healthcare market wants takes us back to an important point: Ask the patient.

A healthcare organization must not only look inside to evaluate its core competencies but must also ask its patients to find out the key drivers of their satisfaction. Only patients can tell the organization what they really value, and these values should drive the decision process on resources allocations. The patients will tell the organization if its core competencies are important to providing value and satisfaction, and excellent healthcare organizations measure these key drivers carefully and frequently.

As a true believer in identifying key drivers, Disney surveys its guests constantly. On one such survey, Disney World guests were asked a variety of questions about their experiences and how those experiences related to both their intention to return and their overall satisfaction with the parks. Fast food in the parks and the park transportation system received relatively low ratings; however, analysis of the data revealed only a weak statistical relationship between these low ratings and both intention to return and overall satisfaction with Disney World. The quality of the fast food and the transportation system did not seem to matter all that much. On the other hand, ratings of hours of operation and fireworks were strongly related to both the return intention and the satisfaction measure.

Guided by the survey results, Disney decided to invest available funds in extending park hours and expanding the fireworks displays. Although the organization felt competent to improve fast food and the transportation system, it allocated scarce resources to improving areas of key importance to guests. The strategic planning process did not just involve managers introspectively looking at organizational core competencies, it also incorporated the wishes and expectations of guests into these decisions. Healthcare organizations should do the same as this guest-service exemplar.

Service expert Len Berry suggests that an excellent service strategy commits the organization to four key factors: quality, value, service, and achievement.[8]

### Quality and Value

First, the excellent strategy emphasizes quality. Without a commitment to quality, nothing else matters. Any healthcare organization can write a mission statement, but those truly committed to excellence start by committing the organization to providing the patient with an experience of high quality. Second, an excellent service strategy emphasizes value. It commits the healthcare organization to providing customers with more benefits from the experience than what the experience costs. Healthcare organizations must commit the necessary funds to measure the customer's perceived value of the services. No matter what the service costs, customers must believe that they are getting significant value for their money.

### Service and Achievement

The third characteristic of an excellent service strategy is that it focuses the entire organizational effort on service. This strategy commits the organization to hiring people who believe in service and possess clinical skills. The organization must ensure that employee-training programs emphasize the commitment to service quality, resources are allocated to serving the customer, performance and reward systems carefully include the entire workforce's commitment to service, and action plans support the service mission. The service strategy should ensure that everyone in the organization walks the service-quality walk by constantly emphasizing a total commitment to service excellence.

Finally, the service strategy should foster among employees a sense of genuine achievement. It should stretch and push each employee to grow and develop so that the employee group stretches and develops the entire organization to do things that no one thought were possible. Len Berry cites Taco Bell as an example of a company's ability to encourage employees to do the unexpected: 90 percent of the chain restaurants were at one time operating without full-time managers.[9]

Definition of the service strategy leads to the determination of the details and design of the service product, the service environment, and the service delivery system. If the organizational mission, for example, is to create and sustain outpatient surgical centers for the private-pay market in major metropolitan areas, then the product must be designed to meet that market's expectations, the environment must be designed to fit the product and match or exceed the patient's expectation of how this type of surgical experience should look and feel, and the delivery system must be designed to ensure that the service product is provided to the patient in a way that is congruent with how the patient expects to experience that service. The joint consideration of these three health-care experience components leads to the short-run action plans that can support and implement the components and thereby achieve the organization's mission.

## THE ACTION PLANS

The action plans represent the leadership's decisions on how to best implement the service strategy in specific terms that will motivate and guide the rest of the organization's members toward accomplishing the overall service strategy and the organizational mission. These plans lay out the specifics of how the organization will operate and what everyone needs to do in the next time period, usually a year.

The bottom of Figure 3.1 shows the five key areas in which action plans should be established: management performance, staffing, capacity utilization, finance, and marketing. Benchmark organizations not only develop plans in each of these areas but also make sure that each area has an appropriate means for measuring the degree to which those plans were achieved. Not only must employees understand the direction in which they are supposed to go, they must also know what getting there looks like. The performance measures ensure that the right things are done, the right goals are achieved, and that the employees themselves can see how well they are doing as they work toward achieving the service strategy goals.

All of the action plans need to be considered as a whole as well as individually. No marketing plan or capacity utilization plan, for example, should be set without also taking into account the financial/budgeting plan. Similarly no managerial performance plan can be set without carefully planning for the necessary resources that will allow health-care managers to reach their targeted goals. Putting a lot of resources into a marketing plan that will draw many customers without making careful capacity decisions is not sensible. Developing performance targets for managers without considering the physical, financial, marketing, and human resources needs to reach the targets also makes little sense.

Once the healthcare organization understands its patient satisfaction key drivers, it can then put in place a three-part accountability process for meeting customer expectations.[10] This accountability process, proposed by consultant Gail Scott, includes (1) defining the service expectation, (2) helping everyone understand the expectation, and (3) creating scripts and protocols. Table 3.2 provides an example of behaviors that you may require your staff to follow during service delivery. Table 3.3 lists scripts (what you say) and protocols (what you do) that can help the staff meet customer expectations.

## CONCLUSION

Healthcare service planning lays out the necessary path and identifies the mileposts that the organization must follow to fulfill its mission, to achieve its vision, and to serve its customers. Whether the organization is a large medical complex, an HMO, or a physician's office, it can lose its competitive stature if it foresees the wrong future, misdiagnoses its core competencies, poorly defines its mission, or chooses the wrong service strategy. Of course, unforeseen developments may disrupt or overturn even the best-laid plans. Good plans attempt to bring rationality and stability to the organization's operations and efforts, but organizations seldom operate in purely rational or stable situations. Indeed, the very plans that made an organization competitive under one set of circumstances may make it uncompetitive if managers get so wedded to the plans that they ignore or do not see changes in the marketplace.

The process of planning may be deftly tied to a yearly calendar and duly placed on everyone's time-management screen. But the plans laid out in August may be totally turned upside down in September by such external events as competitors' innovations or technological developments, an organizational disaster such as the illness or death of a CEO, a natural disaster, a terrorist attack, a prolonged worker strike, or an unfavorable judgment in a lawsuit. If such events occur, the organization cannot wait until next August to redo its plan. So plans must be designed to be flexible, not final. Effective healthcare organizations

**Table 3.2: Examples of Service Behavior Expectations**

1. *Make people feel welcomed.* Smile, make eye contact, introduce yourself, use customer last names, and offer help.

2. *Protect privacy and confidentiality.* Knock before entering patient rooms, cover patients, and watch what you say to whom.

3. *Show courtesy and respect.* Say "please" and "thank you," be sensitive to cultural differences, and find out what customers want and need.

4. *Explain what you are doing.* Let customers know what to expect, speak in ways customers can understand, check to see if the message is understood, and keep the staff informed.

5. *Handle with care.* Slow down and handle patients gently when moving or touching them, and listen and respond to what they are saying.

6. *Maintain a customer-friendly atmosphere.* Reduce noise and keep the environment clean and clutter-free.

7. *Follow-up and follow through.* Work to solve problems and complaints, let customers know what you can and cannot do, and find out who can help and then follow-up and "close the loop."

*Source:* Used with permission from *Journal of Healthcare Management* 46 (3): 153. (Chicago: Health Administration Press, 2001).

stay nimble in responding to the many uncertainties that can affect their operations and the services they provide. Many create contingency plans that offer alternative strategies to meet changed circumstances. But because no one can anticipate everything that may happen to an organization, contingency planning can go only so far.

Increasingly, healthcare organizations are including their employees in the planning processes as they have learned that good things come from widespread employee participation. First, the frontline employees know more about what makes patients happy or unhappy than anyone else does. They also have ideas about what products or services the organization could add, redesign, or delete to add value to the patient's experience or to reduce costs. Second, implementation of any strategic plan means that everyone has to understand it and accept its logic. What better way to gain understanding and obtain employee buy-in than to involve the employees in developing the plan? After all,

**Table 3.3: Key Drivers, Protocols, and Scripts**

| Key Drivers | Protocols (what you do) | Scripts (what you say) |
|---|---|---|
| 1. Respect for privacy and dignity | Knock on patient's door and say patient's name | "Mrs. ____? My name is ____. I am here to ____. Is this a good time?" |
| 2. Feel listened to | Ask if patient has any special needs or requests | "Is there anything else I can do for you?" |
| 3. Experience responsiveness to concerns and complaints | Ask if the previous concern (e.g., low room temperature) has been resolved | "Is the room temperature still uncomfortable? Can I get you another blanket?" |

*Source:* Adapted with permission from *Journal of Healthcare Management* 46 (3): 153. (Chicago: Health Administration Press, 2001).

if they understand the need to plan and how the plan will help the organization solve problems and reach the future, why would they not support it and try to implement it? Most managers have learned the hard way that the best plan in the world is worthless unless those who have to make it work want to make it work. When everyone is responsible for thinking strategically about how to fulfill the organization's service mission, the power of individual creativity can be unleashed in very positive ways.

## LESSONS LEARNED
1. Discover the key factors that drive the patient's determination of quality and value, then do the same for other customers.
2. Try to understand the future environment and what it might do to you and your future patients.
3. Use appropriate, powerful forecasting tools, but do not let them replace managerial judgment.
4. Know your core competencies and learn why they are your core.
5. Discover the core competencies you need to build for the future.

6. Use your vision to define your mission.
7. Prepare for the unexpected.
8. Involve employees in planning.
9. Understand how your customers define value and focus your competitive strategy on those values.
10. Develop action plans to implement customer service initiatives, including protocols and scripts.

## NOTES

1. For more extensive discussion on quantitative forecasting approaches, see J. A. Pearce and R. B. Robinson. 1997. *Formulation, Implementation, and Control of Competitive Strategy*, pp. 144–49. Chicago: Irwin.

2. Hamel, G., and C. K. Prahalad. 1994. *Competing for the Future*, pp. 221–22. Boston: Harvard Business School Press.

3. Nathan, S. 2000. "Hospital Mends Customer Service." *USA Today* (May 5): 7B.

4. Hamel, G., and C. K. Prahalad. 1994. *Competing for the Future*, pp. 114–15. Boston: Harvard Business School Press.

5. Brinker, N., and D. T. Phillips. 1996. *On the Brink: The Life and Leadership of Norman Brinker*, p. 191. Arlington, TX: The Summit Publishing Group.

6. Collins, J. C., and J. I. Porras. 1994. *Built to Last: Successful Habits of Visionary Companies*, p. 74. New York: Harper-Collins.

7. Barr, C. K. 1999. "Mission Statement Content and Hospital Performance in the Canadian Not-For-Profit Health Care Sector." *Health Care Management Review* 24 (3): 18–29.

8. Berry, L. L. 1999. *Discovering the Soul of Service*, pp. 65–68. New York: The Free Press.

9. *Ibid.*, p. 67.

10. Scott, G. 2001. "Accountability for Service Excellence." *Journal of Healthcare Management* 46 (3): 152–54.

*Chapter 4*

# Creating a Healing Environment

Healthcare Principle: *Provide the healthcare setting that customers expect*

The hospital, grey, quiet, old,
Where Life and Death like friendly chafferers meet.

—*William Ernest Henley*

THE HEALTHCARE EXPERIENCE takes place in all kinds of settings. It can be provided in a 500-bed university medical complex or in a small rural clinic. Although both the hospital and the clinic can create an environment that enhances and complements the total healthcare experience, differences between the two exist. Modern medical complexes communicate their ability to deliver high-quality medical care through their beautiful architecture, evidence of advanced technology, orderly layouts, and physical size. The small rural clinic, on the other hand, communicates a warm, caring environment that is focused on the individual patient; this environment is demonstrated by its small size, prominently placed registration desk, and attractive interior. Both benchmark hospitals and benchmark rural clinics know that the environment itself can be a positive influence on the patient's healing process.

Healthcare organizations are learning important strategies from the guest services industry. They are learning that a clean, safe, and easy-to-use environment can significantly improve the patient's mood, satisfaction, and perceived quality of the healthcare experience. Although some healthcare providers may believe that the setting is unimportant to patients who are focused on the medical procedure and clinical outcomes, research shows that the setting is a major determinant of

73

perceived quality and customer satisfaction and can lead to sustainable competitive advantage for the healthcare provider.[1] These studies reveal that specific aspects of the environment—such as comfort of resting areas, overall cleanliness, décor, layout, signage, and cheerfulness of facilities—are positively related to patient satisfaction and patient perceptions of service quality.

Successful service organizations structure their internal environments to promote a positive customer experience through a variety of strategies that include décor, displays, tangible customer amenities, and so forth. These organizations know that fulfilling the primary economic transaction sought by the customer is not enough. Customers also expect that the environment in which that transaction occurs will fulfill their other basic desires for comfort, convenience, safety, information, and even entertainment. Responding to customers' needs through managing environmental factors or *atmospherics* can affect the customer's propensity to consummate a purchase transaction, whether the transaction takes place in a Nordstrom's department store, Disney theme park, or the Mayo Clinic.[2] Positive customer responses to atmospherics have been shown to lead to customer satisfaction, continued patronage, positive word-of-mouth advertising, and an improved image for the organization.[3] The physical environment, in brief, is the least studied but could be one of the most important and controllable dimensions of healthcare customer satisfaction.

In this chapter, we discuss why and how the setting of the healthcare experience is an important determinant of patient satisfaction and other customer outcomes. We discuss the service setting, we list and enumerate the environmental dimensions and customer responses to them, and we address how a healing environment contributes to positive outcomes. We also give examples of organizations that have enhanced their clinical and patient experience/satisfaction outcomes by designing healthcare settings that appeal to all their customers.

## THE IMPORTANCE OF THE SERVICE SETTING

The service setting is important to healthcare managers for several reasons. First, it provides an excellent opportunity to meet or exceed patient expectations regarding the overall service experience. Second, it can create and enhance the moods of both patients and employees. Third, it can be seen as part of the service, if done in a memorable way or "themed." Fourth, it adds value to other functions. Taken as a whole, these aspects create a healing environment, which in turn can positively influence customer satisfaction, willingness to return, and intention to recommend to others.

## Meeting Patient Expectations

Until fairly recently, most healthcare organizations focused almost exclusively on the medical needs of patients. However, as patient satisfaction surveys became more widely used in the 1990s, organizations learned that patients and their families want and expect an environment consistent with their expectations. Hospital patients surveyed in focus groups mentioned physical features of the environment more frequently than any other determinant of their satisfaction and perception of service quality.[4] More specifically, they said they wanted privacy, cleanliness, quiet, closet space, and ability to control temperature.[5]

Other research indicates that the environment of most healthcare facilities often fails to meet patient expectations.[6] Patients in one major study rated their satisfaction with a hospital's physical appearance at the bottom of all factors listed, leading some patients to switch healthcare providers.[7] Surveys have also confirmed what common sense suggests: Because the customer derives a first impression of the healthcare organization's services and quality from its physical appearance, the first perception of the environment is a highly significant moment of truth. It influences the customer's expectations and quality judgments even before any clinical service is received. Healthcare executives have begun to use such survey findings to improve the design of healthcare environments.

## Creating and Enhancing the Patient Mood

Once the patient enters the facility, he or she should be greeted by an environment that fosters a positive mood. Although maintaining this positive-mood design can be a challenge in some areas, like trauma centers and emergency rooms, these may be the areas in which such a design is most needed to enhance the patient's and family's frame of mind. Family-friendly, patient-focused, and homelike designs can create a positive mood, support healing, and address the stress of patients and their families. Such an environment communicates to customers that the organization recognizes their psychological and social needs, as well as their medical needs, and wants to help fulfill them.[8]

Consider the psychological and social benefits found in a nursing home designed by healthcare architect Lloyd Landow. He lessened the usual depressing effect of long halls by placing small, angled alcoves at room entrances; Landow calls this technique "neighborhooding," as the design resembles a neighborhood street. The design produces an area that feels like a front porch, where the nursing home residents and visitors can sit and watch the goings on of the unit without feeling lined up along a corridor. This design allows residents to feel like they are a part of the life going on in their facility, instead of isolated in their rooms.[9]

Because fear of the hospital, doctor, or medical procedure stops many patients from seeking care or hampers treatment when they do, many older hospitals are introducing patient-centered touches to evoke a homey feeling.[10] Meanwhile, new hospitals are being designed to include architectural recognition of the mind-body-spirit connection. In healthcare organizations around the country, antiseptic white walls are being replaced by murals, such as of birds soaring toward tile ceilings; aquariums and soothing paintings are being employed to decorate hospital wings; and harsh fluorescent lights are being taken down in favor of softer lights that slant through fuchsia film. These trends represent a significant philosophical shift in the design of healthcare facilities.

According to Jain Malkin, a world leader in healthcare interior design and healing environments, such changes are not just an aesthetic issue; these interventions in the healing environment have their roots in reducing stress.[11] Most redesigned healthcare facilities include nonglaring lights, quiet halls, warm-toned paint colors, easy wayfinding, atriums, gardens, potted plants, and music.[12] To alleviate the patient's loss of contact with nature, many facilities are also providing more windows, balcony space, and solaria. To counteract feelings of isolation and powerlessness, hospitals are adding more bedside controls.[13] By one estimate, so far only about 20 percent of the 5,860 hospitals registered by the American Hospital Association have adopted designs reflecting this new philosophy.[14]

The philosophy, however, is gaining rapid acceptance in the healthcare industry as customers all around the country leave provider-driven healthcare organizations for those that are customer driven. One manifestation of this change has been the development of "healthplexes"— hospital-based complexes that attempt to move the industry's focus from acute care provision to wellness and health promotion and offer that focus within a single campus.[15] The driving force behind the success of healthplexes is the movement from a focus on patient-specific and episodic incidents of care to care for general populations, which maintains or improves the health status of the entire community. The goal of the healthplexes is to become a destination point, where wellness and community education can take place.

Here are some examples of healthplexes:

- Celebration Health in Celebration, Florida, offers a full-scale health club with a swimming pool and a basketball court.[16] It also has a cafeteria offering healthy meals, cooking demonstrations, and nutrition lectures. An octagonal, light-infused rotunda doubles as the main entrance and lobby for the hospital, the medical offices, and the health club.
- Health Central Hospital in Ocoee, Florida, welcomes visitors with an atrium and waterfalls. It also provides mood music, lighting, candles, and soft music in the Women's Center where mammograms are performed.
- Orlando Regional Healthcare System in Florida provides healing arts programs for children, which combine music, drama, and visiting animals.
- The Woodwinds Hospital in Woodbury, Minnesota, looks more like a resort than a hospital. In the main waiting room, rustic-looking rocking chairs are grouped around a limestone fireplace and two-story windows that overlook wetlands.

Major environmental designs or renovations can be costly. With cuts in government reimbursements and managed care constraints on reimbursement in the private sector, healthcare executives may find it difficult to justify the costs. But advocates like Florida Hospital believe the benefits justify the expenditures.[17] Moreover, empirical studies show that postsurgical patients who are assigned to rooms with views of nature (i.e., parks, trees, and flowers) give better nurse evaluations, take less medication, and have shorter hospital stays.[18] Studies have also shown that patients exposed to high noise levels and occupy windowless rooms require more powerful painkillers and suffer higher levels of depression.[19] Even painted nature scenes have a positive impact on patient outcomes.[20]

Adding humor to the environment is another way of enhancing customer moods. Integris Baptist Medical Center in Oklahoma City established the Medical Institute for Recovery Through Humor (M.I.R.T.H.) at a skilled nursing facility for elderly patients who are not yet ready to be discharged.[21] Humor rooms have been established as a therapeutic tool and are depositories of funny books, videos, games, props, and humor carts. The skilled nursing facility with the M.I.R.T.H. program is believed to be the only hospital ward in the United States that uses humor as its all-encompassing and defining treatment modality. The essential character of the ward is a lightness of being, an easing of the staid seriousness that pervades most hospitals.

## Creating and Enhancing the Employee Mood

Employees spend a lot more time in the healthcare setting than patients and other external customers do, and a well-designed environment can promote employee satisfaction, which is highly correlated with patient satisfaction. No one wants to work in a dangerous, dirty, and depressing environment. Employees want an environment that is clean, organized, pleasant smelling, and comfortable. A pleasant work setting allows employees to concentrate on the task at hand, shows them that management is interested in their well-being, and signals that the organization is committed to quality. In his book, *Customers for Life*, Carl Sewell relates a story of a service technician who complained about the employee restroom at Sewell's Cadillac dealership. The employee asked Sewell if he thought the employees lived that way at home and, if he did not, then why could he not show respect for his employees by providing a clean, nice restroom. Sewell says: "That was humbling. A week later we had a carpenter crew in there, and we tore it out and rebuilt it and did it right."[22]

Employees know that if their organization spends time and energy on the details of the facility, even those details that most patients will never notice, it must really care about the quality of the healthcare experience. The impact of this caring on the employees is immeasurable; in ways large and small, it shows employees the commitment that the organization expects from itself and from them. A healthcare organization that employs well-dressed, well-groomed people will have an atmosphere that is more conducive to healing than those facilities where everyone wears unclean, ragged attire. The dress and appearance code of most healthcare organizations is structured and specific; appropriate attire for employees indicates respect for customers.

Employee attitudes and behavior directly affect customer satisfaction and perception of service quality.[23] Because the healthcare environment affects employee attitudes (and therefore customer attitudes), employees should work in pleasant, safe, and comfortable environments. If they do, they are more likely to provide the level of service that will influence patients to return when they need healthcare.

As a contrasting example, employees in some public hospitals are often reported for rude behavior toward customers. In many of these facilities, the physical environment is old, dark, and depressing. Because limited public funding supports these facilities, very little is spent on improving the physical or ambient conditions. In fact, some hospitals are so old and dilapidated that they lack air conditioning, often forcing employees to work in an inefficiently laid out, noisy, and crowded atmosphere surrounded by tattered furnishings and old equipment. In addition, these facilities are often located in inner-city areas, which may once have been safe but are now perceived by customers and staff as having a high crime rate and a dangerous area. Even though the quality of care at such hospitals may actually equal or exceed the quality provided by suburban hospitals, the care can be perceived as being of lower quality simply because the physical environment is substandard. One large public teaching hospital in Atlanta, for example, had a poor public image in spite of the satisfactory healthcare it provided. Significant renovations and physical improvements led to a more positive public image.[24] The hospital's reputation and customer perception of healthcare quality increased substantially as a result of the renovations, even though healthcare quality actually remained about the same.

## Setting as a Part of Service

The environment may serve merely as a neutral backdrop for some healthcare experiences, but for others, the environment is so significant that it should almost be considered a part of the service. Patients are sufficiently familiar with hospitals to expect functionality, hygiene, and sterile conditions. But today's healthcare customers have also become accustomed to enriched environments in their homes, offices, entertainment sites, and automobiles. Organizing the healthcare experience around a theme while maintaining high-quality clinical services is called *theming*. Theming can add value to the healthcare experience. A theme can be reinforced by design elements, staged events, and activities. If used effectively, a theme can enhance the total experience, and the themed environment becomes a part of the service that the organization offers. Receiving high-quality clinical services within an effectively themed environment can add up to a memorable experience.[25]

Theming gives patients something to talk about when they get home; it reinforces their positive recollections and is additional confirmation of the experience's value.

Altura Clare Bridge of Tuskawilla in Winter Springs, Florida, provides a variety of services for residents who suffer from Alzheimer's disease and other memory impairments. Their unique housing theming helps residents distinguish their own private rooms. Rooms are arranged into intimate, easy-to-understand areas. Each house (consisting of several patient rooms) has color-coded walls and carpets that help residents distinguish theirs from others. Broad, circular walking paths are designed to lead residents past areas of activity and interest. Destination points, color cues, and contrasts of color and light help to orient residents as they walk. Security is a high priority for the facility, so the facility installed a discreet, unobtrusive security system and double-alarmed doors.

Some healthcare organizations have followed the hospitality industry's lead in viewing the services they offer as experiences that take place over time in a themed setting. A Long Island nursing home provides a 1930s-themed environment for residents to take them back to their youthful days (and perhaps to assure their relatives that the nursing home is not such a bad place to be). Pictures of Clark Gable and Lana Turner and murals of 1930's New York adorn the nursing home's walls, and they have built a replica of a stall at New York City's Fulton Fish Market complete with a tank containing live fish. Airports, hospitals, and banks have also themed their interiors to represent colorful locales.[26]

Theming does not need to be as specific as this 1930s New York nursing home. In a more general sense, a hospital can create a feeling of calm for its postoperative unit through the use of thick carpets, soft colors, and soft music. It can create a feeling of stimulation for its geriatric unit through the use of brighter colors, fast-paced music, and visual stimulation cues. A family-centered theme can be effective in children's and women's care centers. Homelike settings are less stressful, more comfortable, and more satisfying for expectant mothers and their families. For example, the women's health services wing at Brookwood Hospital in Birmingham, Alabama, has a homelike theme. Maternity patients stay in suites (instead of single rooms) that provide sofa beds for family members and other guests and have wallpaper, lamps with soft lights, comfortable chairs, and so forth. The wing also offers other amenities: Nurses pass out pink and/or blue bubble gum cigars to the family when a baby is born, the baby is kept in a crib and allowed to stay with the family in the suite, and visitors sign a "guest" book that becomes a keepsake for the family.

Similarly, Sutter Maternity and Surgery Center in Santa Cruz, California, has 12 birthing suites with window seats, French doors, and private terraces.[27] The suites host patients during labor, delivery, and postpartum recovery; custom-finished cabinetry hides the medical equipment used during childbirth. High-quality food service is available to patients 24 hours a day, and the cafeteria and pharmacy are accessible to families and visitors by a central public corridor.

The elements in the service setting should have a consistency. All aspects of the physical setting—layout of physical objects, lighting, colors, appointments, signs, employee uniforms, and materials—must complement and support each other and must give a feeling of integrated design. Theming is one approach toward achieving that integrated design. A themed environment may not always be appropriate, and theming can have its risks—it places limits on the service product, setting, and delivery system. A specialized theme is likely to narrow the healthcare provider's attractiveness to only those who like the particular theme. Thus, the competitive advantage that a theme represents for reaching one market segment may be a competitive disadvantage in other segments.

## Wealthcare

An important recognition of the healthcare setting is embodied in the development of what some have labeled "wealthcare."[28] For patients willing to pay, some major medical centers have built entire luxury floors or corridors with everything from chefs and concierges to high-end beauty products in the bathroom. These luxury suites have amenities such as mahogany furniture, personal safes, and kosher kitchens (as seen at Mount Sinai in New York); polished brass, hardwood floors, marble walls, patient services associates (Memorial Sloan-Kettering in New York); concierges and armed guards (Johns Hopkins in Baltimore); medical equipment behind picture frames (Duke in Durham, North Carolina); teatime pianists (Columbia-Presbyterian in New York); pet therapy (Cedars-Sinai in Los Angeles); private dining rooms (Methodist Hospital in Houston); and in-room kitchenettes (Washington Hospital Center in D.C.). Although some patient advocates complain that hospitals should be spending their money on improving service for everybody, supporters claim that the luxury amenities bring in extra revenue that helps defray overhead throughout the rest of the hospital.

## Adding Value to the Functions

The environment must be such that patients and their visitors and employees can enter, stay, and leave without getting lost, hurt, or disoriented. Patients and their families and friends worry increasingly about whether they will be safe from harm or injury when they go to healthcare facilities or leave home for any reason. Patients must perceive that service settings have a high level of safety and security. Light, open space, smiling employees making eye contact with everyone, cleanliness, well-lit parking lots and pathways, low-cut hedges that no one can hide behind, and the presence of uniformed employees are appropriate and reassuring. The Occupational Safety and Health Act, which requires that the workplace be safe for employees, also is an added reassurance to employees. Having a safe, easy-to-use, attractive, and clean healthcare environment adds value to the experience and satisfaction of all customers—patients, family, and employees alike.

## ENVIRONMENTAL DIMENSIONS

An attractive service setting is not just an amenity or a nice touch, it can be an important part of the healing experience. Because patients are often anxious about the healthcare experience they are about to face, the healthcare facility must show evidence of thoughtful concern for their needs and should be nurturing, responsive, and alive. It should be a place where healing is made visible and effective.[29] Figure 4.1 provides an overall model of how the environment can contribute to a variety of positive outcomes.[30] Figure 4.1 shows the four elements (Environmental Dimensions) that comprise the service environment as perceived by customers and employees: ambient conditions such as lighting and colors; spatial conditions such as the layout of services and equipment; signs, symbols, and artifacts such as signage; and other people. Consciously or unconsciously, each customer or employee selects the combination of environmental elements that comprises (for that person) the perceived service landscape or *servicescape*. People will respond differently to elements of that servicescape in terms of their cognitive, emotional, and physiological responses (Internal Responses). Their overall response to the setting will cause them to feel good or bad about the experience and to approach or avoid the organization (Behaviors). Such approach or avoidance, in turn, will positively or negatively affect a variety of outcomes valued by healthcare executives (Outcomes). Let us discuss the elements within the four boxes in greater detail.

**Figure 4.1: Customer and Employee Responses to Environmental Influences**

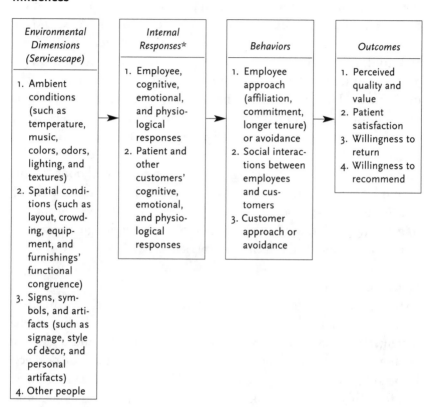

| Environmental Dimensions (Servicescape) | Internal Responses* | Behaviors | Outcomes |
|---|---|---|---|
| 1. Ambient conditions (such as temperature, music, colors, odors, lighting, and textures) 2. Spatial conditions (such as layout, crowding, equipment, and furnishings' functional congruence) 3. Signs, symbols, and artifacts (such as signage, style of dècor, and personal artifacts) 4. Other people | 1. Employee, cognitive, emotional, and physiological responses 2. Patient and other customers' cognitive, emotional, and physiological responses | 1. Employee approach (affiliation, commitment, longer tenure) or avoidance 2. Social interactions between employees and customers 3. Customer approach or avoidance | 1. Perceived quality and value 2. Patient satisfaction 3. Willingness to return 4. Willingness to recommend |

\* Moderated by the individual customer's mood, personality, expectations, and demographic.
*Source:* Reprinted with permission from *Journal of Marketing,* published by the American Marketing Association, M. J. Bitner, 1992, 56 (2): 60.

## Ambient Conditions

Ambient conditions—the "ergonomic" factors such as temperature, humidity, air quality, smells, sounds, physical comfort, and light—can have a major effect on the healthcare experience. The effect of a dark, dank, noisy room is different from the effect of a light, airy, quiet room. To many people, the first room will feel ominous and threatening, while the second will feel warm and comforting. Environmental sounds should be controlled and should serve a purpose. In general, the sounds provided (most often music) should complement the experience that the organization is trying to offer. In general, but with many exceptions, softer music in the service setting is soothing to patients; on the other hand, loud music and loud sounds are stressful. The sounds of music can also affect behavior—for example, people tend to eat faster and drink more if fast, loud music is playing; slow music encourages people to dine in a leisurely fashion. A study revealed that diners at the Fairfield University cafeteria chewed an average of 4.4 bites a minute to fast music and 3.83 bites a minute to slow music.[31] Some healthcare experiences are best delivered in bright lights, some in dim. Glare and lights at eye level are unpleasant in any setting. If you enter a service setting and do not notice the lighting, it is probably well done. Lights should be selected, turned on, and directed not just to avoid darkness but also to emphasize and to reveal. Like every other aspect of the setting, the lighting should be an element of a greater design whose purpose is to enhance the healthcare experience.

### Spatial Conditions

Spatial condition refers to the layout of the equipment and furnishings, the size and shape of those objects, their accessibility to the patients, and the distance between them. The nature and quality of the healthcare experience are affected by the organization's use of space. Depending on how the space is designed, waiting areas can feel open and friendly or they can make a patient feel closed-in and alone. How hallways or walkways are laid out to get from one part of a facility to another also influences the feeling of openness or closedness. Closed spaces evoke different feelings than areas with a lot of open space or green space. The basic decision about space is to lay it out as appropriately as possible to facilitate safe and easy use. Because physical elements within the environment may increase the risk that elderly persons or people with physical disabilities or injury may fall, healthcare facilities need to pay special attention to the spatial conditions to reduce the risk of falls and consequent injuries.[32]

Space must be used wisely. An assisted living facility has to balance the space allocated for patients' personal effects and items with the clinical requirements of the facility and the revenue-generation requirements of the total space. If in an attempt to achieve a homey feel the facility allows too many personal items, perhaps even personal furniture, to be placed in the space, then the personal items may interfere with the clinical requirements, and the cluttered space may depress rather than elevate the patient. The quandary is how to balance these conflicting goals. Similarly, an organization that attempts to increase its revenue-producing space at the expense of essential but non-revenue-producing space (for offices, kitchens, supplies, and utilities, for example) may have a memorable service environment, but its delivery system cannot reliably provide the service product required for a superior healthcare experience.

The space layout should also help people to know where they are. Healthcare managers must maintain the environmental feel of the setting while providing orientation devices to help patients, their families, and visitors locate restrooms, public phones, meeting rooms, and exits. Circus legend P. T. Barnum set up his exhibits and signage to guide customers from start to finish. Just beyond the last exhibit was a door labeled "This way to the egress." Circus patrons going through the door and hoping to view a rare animal or bird found themselves passing smoothly and effortlessly into the alley outside the building. Healthcare settings should be designed to ensure a safe, smooth flow for both patient and employee. Patients must feel that they can move smoothly and effortlessly through the service setting without feeling disoriented or lost. Employees must have enough space, clear traffic routes, and sufficiently short distances to travel to provide timely service to patients.

*Functional congruence* refers to how well something with a functional purpose fits into the environment in which it serves that purpose. The cabinetry in the birthing suites at Sutter Maternity and Surgery Center contains medical equipment—that is its function. The appearance of the cabinets is congruent with the homelike setting in which it appears. The equipment, layout of the physical landscape, and entire design of the service environment must fit together as well as serve a purpose. The functional congruence of environmental elements is given much consideration in a well-designed service environment so that whatever physical or other environmental element the patient requires is provided when needed and also fits with the other environmental elements. In designing new healthcare facilities, healthcare managers must realize that all areas need to have the ability to serve their customers' needs and easily adapt to changing healthcare delivery demands. Flexibility for future use is the key.[33]

## Signs and Symbols

Carl Sewell states that signs serve one or more of only three purposes: (1) to name the business (Walgreens Drugstore, Humana Hospital, Plaza Doctors Building); (2) to describe the product or service (X-Ray, Hematology, Restrooms); and (3) to give direction (Entrance, Do Not Enter, Pay Here, No Smoking, Employees Only, Wrong Way, You Are Here).[34] Signs are explicit physical representations of information that the healthcare organization thinks customers want, need, or expect to find. Signs must be easy to read, clear, and located in obvious places where they can direct and teach people how to use the service easily. In many clinics, signs at the entry point tell patients where to go to get the type of clinical service desired. In a facility serving a multilingual population, the signs need to be very clear in all appropriate languages.

Even such an apparently small and easy task as making a sign must take into account the customer's point of view, rather than the organization's. For example, large healthcare locations often use "You Are Here" signs and maps to help orient people. If these signs are not done carefully, and from the perspective of a total stranger to the facility, they can cause more confusion than having no sign at all. A customer confused by a sign is not only lost or disoriented but also feels stupid, and customers do not feel kindly toward healthcare organizations that make them feel stupid.

Some healthcare organizations do a good job of installing signs that get patients into the treatment areas but not so well at getting them out. A person who has had an uncomfortable treatment or perhaps nitrous oxide at the dentist's office needs large clear signs to be able to navigate himself or herself back through the maze of offices and hallways to the patient's room or the dentist's office exit.

Signs convey their messages through the use of symbols, often language itself. Some signs contain not words but other symbols, such as representational icons that can replace any specific language. These signs, of course, are especially important in very large healthcare settings to which patients from many different nations, cultures, and linguistic backgrounds may come. If the patient absolutely must remember the information on the sign, a symbol often works best.

Artifacts are physical objects that represent something beyond their functional use; as such, they are a type of symbol. Children's hospitals often use artifacts to create a friendlier setting. A little red wagon is a rolling toy, but it also represents freedom to move about for a child recovering in a hospital. It can also serve as a reminder of normalcy for children burdened with physical symptoms that tell them that they are not normal.

### Other People

Other people include employees, other patients, and visitors. Patients often want to see other patients so they do not feel as if they are the only ones with clinical needs; they want to see others in the same situation. Studies have shown that people tolerate pain better when they are in the company of other people suffering the same pain. "Misery loves company," but happiness and satisfaction are also contagious. Many healthcare settings would feel even more depressing and lonely without other people. In group therapy, other people are not just wallflowers or scenery; they are necessary to the experience and participate in coproducing that experience. Of course, even though the other patients may be an important or even a necessary part of a healthcare experience, and in fact can sometimes make it or break it, their presence is only rarely the reason why people seek out the experience. Other people, except for clinicians and other employees, are usually best thought of as part of the environment within which the service is delivered, rather than as part of the service itself, although the distinction is not always clear.

## THE SERVICESCAPE

The servicescape is the general overall perception or picture that the customer draws from the countless individual environmental dimensions—the temperature, lights, signs, green space, other people. It is what the individual environmental dimensions add up to for each patient.[35] Table 4.1 summarizes some of the major environmental conditions of the servicescape that are conducive to the creation of a healing environment.

Each customer or employee perceives different environmental elements; therefore, each has a different servicescape. The healthcare service provider must realize that each patient's reaction to the perceived servicescape is affected or "moderated" by the patient's mood, personality, expectations, and demographic characteristics. Even if they perceive the servicescape similarly, a 72-year-old female entering a vasectomy clinic by mistake is going to have a reaction different from that of a 24-year-old male.

**Table 4.1: Environmental Dimensions and Conditions Conducive to Creation of a Healing Environment**

| Environmental Dimensions | Environmental Conditions Conducive to Creation of a Healing Environment |
|---|---|
| 1. Ambient Conditions (i.e., temperature, music, colors, odors, lighting, and textures) | • No distressing noises, sights, or odors<br>• Adequate light; attractive colors; comfortable furniture; and suitable music, artwork, and reading materials<br>• Indoor nature (i.e., plants, gardens, aquariums)<br>• Cleanliness |
| 2. Spatial Conditions (i.e., layout, crowding, equipment, and furnishings; functional congruence) | • Adequate access to facility for parking and drop-off areas<br>• Attractive lobby, reception, and waiting areas<br>• Private rooms and bathrooms<br>• No barriers to mobility<br>• Handrails and grab bars<br>• Customer control of lights and temperatures<br>• Easily used call systems<br>• All technology user-friendly or staff available to provide assistance<br>• Patients close to nursing stations<br>• Adequate and comfortable seating for visitors<br>• "Homelike" designs |
| 3. Signs, Symbols, or Artifacts | • Adequate signage and wayfinding aids at all points<br>• Universal symbols used where possible<br>• Color-coded walls and carpets to assist customer wayfinding |
| 4. Other People | • Employees clean and appropriately dressed<br>• Other patients and families dressed and behaving appropriately |

## Moderators

*Moderators* are the individual, personal factors that cause customers to respond to the service setting in different ways. Customers bring a particular day's moods, purposes, cultural values, and personality traits to a particular day's healthcare experience. These factors affect or moderate each customer's response to the servicescape. Some people like to be alone and object to sitting in a crowded waiting room. Other people love to be around crowds and view the opportunity to share symptoms and gripes with other people as a plus. Some customers arrive in a happy mood, while others are angry or worried. Some older people have a hard time walking from one laboratory area to another, while young children do not mind.

Cultural values and beliefs also influence how customers respond to the servicescape. Some ethnic groups find red a happy color, and others find it threatening; some find handshakes a positive gesture, and others are offended. Each culture produces an infinity of cultural nuances, and healthcare managers can only do their best to recognize the individual variations that these differences create and then design an environment that will offer a healthcare experience of high quality and value to people from all types of ethnic and cultural backgrounds.

Moderators also include the individual moods that people bring to the servicescape. When people are upset or angry, they may not be able to perceive any environment as positive or pleasant. Patients coming to the emergency room with severe trauma will not perceive the environment positively, if they perceive it at all. People arriving either in a neutral mood or unfamiliar with the healthcare experience awaiting them will be most influenced by environmental cues. A person new to a particular hospital wants to smell the smells of cleanliness. Many healthcare facilities make sure to use cleaning products that will send the message, "This place is sanitary." The long-term patient is reassured by the smell or pays no attention to it, while the new patient (anxiously looking for cues about what the healthcare experience will be like) gets an impression of cleanliness from the aroma in the environment.

## Responses to the Servicescape

A healthcare customer or employee can respond to a service setting in one or more of three ways: physiologically, cognitively, and emotionally. The moderating factors discussed above will affect the nature of the response.

### Physiological

A physiological response results primarily from the servicescape's effects on the senses of patients, visitors, and employees. Figure 4.1 suggests that most physiological responses to the environment are responses to ambient conditions like temperature, humidity, air quality, smells, sounds, light, and the like. A second type of physiological response results from the information-processing activity of the brain. A well-known early study of how much unfamiliar information a human brain can process at any one time found that the capacity was seven (plus or minus two) random pieces of information, such as random numbers. The study was done for the phone company, which wanted to know how long a telephone number people could remember. The study results led to the use of combinations of words and numbers (like REpublic 7-5914) to help people overcome their physiological limitations. We can see variations of this method today in the word-based phone numbers used by organizations competing for our business with easy-to-remember 800 numbers, such as 1-800-I-FLY-SWA, 1-800-CALL-AVIS, 1-800-GET-WELL, and 1-800-HEALTHY.

The importance of this concept to those managing healthcare organizations is to recognize that a lot of random information coming in at the same time will quickly overtax the capacity of the human mind to comprehend the environment and feel comfortable with the healthcare experience. It does not take much unconnected information—several directional signs bunched together, for example, or a complex array of instructions—to confuse a customer, especially one who may have diminished capacity because of illness or old age, and many healthcare facilities are unfamiliar territory for their customers. Organizations must respect people's information-processing limitations; customers become frustrated when confused, lost, or overwhelmed with too much information or too many options.

Environments can be made rich or lean with information. They should be relatively lean when customers are expected to be unfamiliar with the setting or when they have to process a lot of information, and they can be rich when customers are familiar with the setting or have few choices or decisions to make. Thus, a waiting room should be rich in detail and content because patients only have to sit, observe, and wait for their names to be called. But if patients or visitors must make decisions about where they are or what to do next, as in a major medical complex, the setting should be kept relatively simple and familiar. This point ties in well with the cognitive aspects of the environmental experience.

### Cognitive

We enter every experience with a set of expectations based on what we have seen and done before, and we tend to look for similarities between what we have experienced and what we are about to experience. Our expectations then obviously influence what actually happens. If we enter a cafeteria similar to one we have visited before, then we expect to (and we do) perform the tasks scripted by the familiar cues in the environment—the arrow pointing to the beginning of the line, the stack of trays, the rack for the silverware, and the bars on which our tray should slide as we go by reviewing the food items available.

Physical aspects of the service setting can also evoke a cognitive response and can be viewed as a form of nonverbal communication. If healthcare customers or new employees see the nursing staff carrying portable computers, they link that information back to what they have learned previously about the relationship of computers to a provider's level of sophistication. If they see the nursing staff using manual typewriters, they wonder about the provider's overall level of technology. Sophisticated equipment suggests that the experience will produce an excellent clinical outcome and is worth the fees charged. Customers expecting cutting-edge technology will not accept a primitive facility.

Patients who enter healthcare facilities are typically under physical and psychological stress, which has important consequences on their interactions with the environment. Customers are easily frustrated by complex spatial configurations, which do not confuse long-time staffers.[36] Therefore, healthcare organizations should seek to introduce the environmental cues necessary to ensure that the present experience ties into some previously built and familiar script in the customer's and employee's minds. The more familiar the organization can make the experience for all its customers, the less confusion, frustration, and unhappiness.

### Emotional

Old grads get choked up when they return for reunions at their college campuses. Children and adults alike are emotionally touched by holiday decorations. Many patients are fearful of medical and dental offices and equipment or even of anyone wearing a lab coat. Emotional responses have two distinct elements of interest to the healthcare organization. The first is the degree of arousal—the extent to which the stimulus evokes any response. The second is the degree of pleasure/displeasure that the stimulus represents.

Many patients feel a heightened sense of displeasure in a healthcare setting. To counteract it and create a positive emotional response from its patients, the organization should try to provide environments and environmental features that have elements of arousal and pleasure. Clean restrooms, pleasant décor, and a smiling receptionist all contribute to arousal and pleasure. Pictures or murals on the ceilings of pre-op rooms can reduce the patients' heart rates and blood pressure levels. Similar results are created in hospitals that offer rooms with vaulted ceilings and varying ceiling textures, heights, and surfaces using fabrics, textured paints, and wood trim. People want to spend time and money in pleasurable environments; they avoid unpleasant environments if they can. The noise, confusion, and overstimulation of an emergency room on a Saturday night are high on arousal but probably low on pleasure for patients, their companions, and employees, and they would prefer to be elsewhere.

These three responses—physiological, cognitive, and emotional—lead the person to make one of two choices about the healthcare experience: approach or avoid (see Behaviors in Figure 4.1). Leaving the clinical service and its delivery out of the equation, the patient can decide that the effect of the service environment was, on balance, positive or negative. Servicescape perceptions can encourage internal and external customers or employees to feel comfortable and willing to come again or to go away and stay away. Healthcare organizations must work hard to create environments that encourage employee retention, repeat patient visits, and positive word of mouth—all of which normally lead to increased revenues. The model in Figure 4.1 should help healthcare managers choose and arrange environmental factors to provide servicescapes that enhance the service and its delivery and to which patients and employees, in their infinite variety, will generally respond in a positive way.

## THE HEALING ENVIRONMENT

Both theory and research indicate that a well-designed setting can influence customer satisfaction, employee performance, and clinical outcomes. Table 4.2 provides an action framework for creating a healing environment with the help of four environmental dimensions: ambient conditions; spatial conditions; signs, symbols, and artifacts; and other people. The objectives in each dimension represent the ideal end result for the customer, and each action step represents the tasks that must be performed to meet and exceed the objectives. How well these objectives and actions are understood and implemented can determine organizational success in creating a healing environment—a holistic entity composed of separate elements.

A positive first impression, wayfinding, feeling welcome, experiencing physical and psychological comfort, and feeling competent and secure are all attainable and mutually reinforcing objectives. Benchmark healthcare organizations think through their environmental dimensions from the perspective of their customers and then continually seek customer input on each dimension.

### Ask for Feedback

One way to ensure that environmental dimensions meet or exceed the expectations of customers is to ask customers for feedback. Dr. Milton Seifert and his physician partners in an Excelsior, Minnesota physician group practice meet regularly with a 60-member patient advisory council for guidance on everything from billing to aesthetics.[37] The advisers' recommendations have included installation of railings in the restroom and wheelchair ramps at the entrance and elimination of a blackboard that told patients in the waiting room who was next to be seen but also spelled out the health problems that motivated the visits. According to Dr. Seifert, "My patient advisory council is integral to nearly every decision we make. Their input is invaluable and our efforts are paid off by very positive patient satisfaction surveys."[38]

### Use Design

Healthcare organizations can also create a healing environment by using a variety of design tactics, including décor, displays, signage, and tangible amenities, that create an environment that feels comfortable, convenient, safe, informative and, if appropriate, entertaining. Here are some healthcare organizations that have employed the use of design elements that cater to the customer's sense of comfort, convenience, safety, information, and entertainment:

**Table 4.2:  An Action Framework for Creating a Healing Environment**

| Environmental Dimension | Action |
|---|---|
| **1. Ambient Conditions** | |
| A. *Objective:* Provide a feeling of physical comfort before, during, and after service delivery. | A. Provide a clean, organized, pleasant-smelling environment with appropriate comfortable temperature, humidity, and furnishings. |
| B. *Objective:* Provide a feeling of psychological comfort before, during, and after service delivery. | B. Provide a soothing décor in all rooms, with wall and floor colors, textures, and lighting that stimulate positive reactions from all the senses. |
| **2. Spatial Conditions** | |
| A. *Objective:* Create a positive first impression. | A. Create a clean, beautifully landscaped exterior campus with an entryway that has an abundance of greenery, artwork, and natural lighting. |
| B. *Objective:* Reinforce the initial positive impression. | B. Provide light, open space, well-lit parking facilities, and pathways with uniformed staff placed appropriately. |
| C. *Objective:* Create a comfortable well-laid-out patient room. | C. Provide adequate space that is well laid out, with obvious placement of all necessities. |
| **3. Signs, Symbols, and Artifacts** | |
| A. *Objective:* Create a facility that is easy to use and understand. | A. Provide signage that is easy to read, clear, and located in obvious places that direct and teach people how to use the service easily. |
| B. *Objective:* Create a layout that does not leave the customer feeling confused or lost. | B. Design the spatial layout so customers know where they are at all times. |
| **4. Other People** | |
| A. *Objective:* Require staff attire that meets customer expectations. | A. Survey customers regarding their preferences on staff attire, then implement these preferences. |

- Griffin Hospital (more specifically its inpatient facility and critical care nursing unit) in Derby, Connecticut, won the 1995 competitive design award sponsored by *Modern Healthcare* and the American Institute of Architects' Academy of Architecture for Health. Griffin created satellite nursing stations that each serve four patients, a U-shaped corridor around the critical care unit and separate staff and visitor corridors to avoid traffic problems, and rooms with two doors to allow easy access to the separate corridors.[39]
- The High Desert Medical Center in Lancaster, California, offers easy access to inpatient and outpatient services and health education for the expanding community.[40] The complex includes five buildings that have their own entrances and are connected by bridges or breezeways. Rows of eucalyptus act not only as shields from the wind, but they also divide areas and make them distinct. The use of courtyards, the arrangement of elements, and corridor placement make for easy patient and visitor wayfinding. This well-organized scheme integrates buildings, courtyards, and parking while maintaining the campus character.[41] Accent Health Network in Tampa, Florida, teamed up with CNN to broadcast health-related stories into the television sets in the waiting areas.[42] The service and hardware are paid for by advertisers. Helios Medical in Atlanta, Georgia, also offers advertiser-supported computer stations that provide interactive patient education in waiting areas. St. Luke's Episcopal in Illinois allows patients to tune to a 24-hour, closed-circuit television station offering nothing but soothing music and nature scenes.[43]
- Nursing facilities have also been active in environmental design. Arthur Schuster, Inc. (ASI) in Roseville, Minnesota, is now a leader in designing and furnishing nursing facilities with a home-like feel.[44] Among their innovations are carpets that are impervious to moisture and do not need a pad and chairs and couches with firm cushions.
- Sunrise Assisted Living in McLean, Virginia, has 163 facilities that look more like upscale family resorts than retirement homes.[45] All facilities have "signature touches," such as pets; fresh flowers; toy chests for visiting grandchildren; and a 24-hour snack bar stocked with cookies, fruit, juices, and coffee.

- Decades of research show that being exposed to landscape elements, such as water, fragrant plants, and labyrinths (winding walking paths), reduces stress, lowers blood pressure, reduces hospital stays, and inspires a more positive outlook.[46] Baptist Medical Center in Jacksonville, Florida, is one of a growing number of hospitals creating gardens specifically to improve their patients' recovery.[47] About the length of a football field, Baptist's garden has a smaller meditation garden, a labyrinth, and a contemplation garden. Children's Hospital and Health Center in San Diego, California, also provides a healing garden for their young patients and their family members.

### Patient-Focused Designs

The facility's physical configuration may also help to meet the customer's need for competence in navigating through the facility complex. Fallon/St. Vincent Medical Center in Fallon, Massachusetts, uses a decentralized, patient-focused design to respond more quickly to patient needs. The orthopedic section, for example, has its own rehabilitation and imaging components for the convenience of patients and staff. The Fallon/St.Vincent model calls for the integration of physicians' offices and ambulatory care facilities with the hospital to create a single consolidated healthcare campus.[48] This facility design allows continual monitoring of patients and quicker response times and has enhanced customer satisfaction.

Outpatient facilities should also be designed to reduce stress for patients, staff, and visitors. A sense of control, access to social support, and availability of positive distractions can all help reduce this stress. Careful environmental design is evident at the Medical Foundation in Palo Alto, California, where outpatient cancer patients may spend up to 18 hours undergoing chemotherapy. Because the treatment technology is located in the clinic's basement, daylight was brought into the space through the use of big windows and skylights to make the setting less depressing. Similarly, a day lounge for patients undergoing micrographic surgery for skin cancer, which may take up to eight hours, is located along an outside wall to give patients windows and a view.[49]

Julius Spears, the executive vice president and COO of Grady Health Systems in Atlanta, Georgia, is convinced that the creation of a healing environment has positive benefits. It increases patient outcomes, market share, and the viability of the delivery system.[50] Grady completed a major renovation and expansion project in the mid-1990s, and the aesthetic improvements significantly improved morale and satisfaction of both patients and staff and customer perceptions of healthcare quality. The renovation included improving the emergency room area, which was the main entrance for a large portion of the Grady patient population; moving ancillary services such as radiology and laboratory closer; providing amenities such as a new snack area adjacent to the waiting room; installing privacy walls at registration sites; and enhancing security measures. Mr. Spears believes that "the heightened self-esteem of our patients, the sense of pride exhibited by physicians and staff, and the overall positive aura surrounding this organization are directly related to our environmental improvements."

Table 4.3 provides a comprehensive, step-by-step approach that healthcare executives might take in creating a healing environment. First, the current environment needs to be evaluated to improve deficient areas. Second, action must be taken to provide a welcoming environment. Third, the healthscape must be designed to create the desired customer internal responses and behaviors. Fourth, the healing environment must then actually be established. These guidelines should help healthcare executives enhance their healthcare settings or environments as a means of improving their competitive advantage in an increasingly challenging market.

## CONCLUSION

Environmental investments can provide high returns in terms of patient satisfaction, reduced recovery time, perceptions of service quality, and intention to return. Healthcare executives must recognize the great impact of the environment on the patient and the patient's family. They must understand that how the environment is planned, designed, and structured can help create a healing environment that can add significant value and quality to the healthcare experience. Although considerably more study is needed to fully understand how the environment influences the health and well-being of patients and families, healthcare executives should recognize their responsibility to think through how their facilities are designed. Careful design can help patients and other customers feel comfortable, secure, and properly cared for. Thoughtful attention to colors, smells, light and darkness, uniforms, and themes can promote a sense of familiarity, comfort, and caring. Healthcare managers need to understand and use all the envi-

**Table 4.3: Steps in Creating a Healing Environment**

*1. Evaluate the current environment*
A. Analyze your service setting using the framework provided here.
B. Use interviews and focus groups to seek input from customers (i.e., patients, families, employees, and insurance companies) concerning ambient conditions, spatial use, signs and symbols, employees, and other customers.
C. Study the environmental dispositions of all customers (i.e., patients, families, employees, and third-party payers) before environmental changes are made.

*2. Take action to provide a welcoming environment*
A. Train frontline service personnel in customer relations, and encourage them to display a pleasing demeanor, clean uniforms, and proper grooming.
B. Provide a high level of customer safety and security: well-lit parking lots and pathways, low-cut hedges, and uniformed employees.
C. Make it easy for customers to go where they want to go and know where they are.
D. Continuously assess the current environment for deficiencies and fix them.

*3. Design the "healthscape"*
A. Develop a well-defined theme that is reinforced by all the design elements, including décor, displays, signage, customer amenities, and staged events.
B. Use warm colors and comfortable furniture to enhance "atmospherics."
C. Identify colors and styles that customers find both professionally reassuring and comforting (e.g., plush carpeting, well-appointed furniture, pastel colors, and color-coordinated fabrics).
D. Place new technologies in the environment, such as interactive games, computers with Internet access, multiplayer games, motion-based simulation, virtual reality, and other lifelike interactive experiences to engage customers in learning about their own health.

*4. Create a healing environment*
A. Create ambient conditions that promote comfort, convenience, safety, entertainment, and information.
B. Organize the spatial conditions to enhance customer satisfaction.
C. Create signs, symbols, and artifacts to enhance patient comfort.
D. Evaluate the environmental dispositions and preferences of all customers (i.e., patients, families, insurance companies, employees) before environmental changes are made.

ronmental tools at their disposal as part of their efforts to communicate to patients that they are in a clean, caring, and competent setting that will lead to a successful healthcare outcome.

## LESSONS LEARNED

1. Envision and create the environment from the patient's point of view, not your own.
2. Make it easy for patients and other customers to go where they want to go and to know where they are.
3. Supply rich environments when and where customers have time to appreciate and enjoy them; use lean environments when and where customers are trying to figure out what they should do or where they should go.
4. Do not overload the environment with information. Recognize that most people can process only small amounts of unfamiliar information at one time.
5. Know and manage the physiological, cognitive, and emotional impact of your environment on customers.
6. Manage the environment to maintain the customer's feeling of safety and security.
7. Create a healing environment by building in appropriate ambient conditions, spatial conditions, and signs, symbols, and artifacts.

## NOTES

1. Taylor, S. A. 1994. "Distinguishing Service Quality from Patient Satisfaction in Developing Health Marketing Strategies." *Hospital & Health Services Administration* 39 (2): 221–36; M. J. Bitner. 1992. "Servicescapes: The Impact of Physical Surroundings on Customers and Employees." *Journal of Marketing* 56: 57–71; J. Hall, J. Dornan, and M. Dornan. 1988. "What Patients Like About Their Medical Care." *Social Science and Medicine* 27: 935–39; Health Policy Advisory Unit. 1989. *The Patient Satisfaction Questionnaire.* Sheffield: HPUA, Sheffield University; Press Ganey Satisfaction Measurement. 1995. *The Satisfaction Report.* South Bend, IN: Press Ganey; M. Jun, R. T. Peterson, and G. A. Zsidisin. 1998. "The Identification and Measurement of Quality Dimensions in Health Care: Focus Group Interview Results." *Health Care Management Review* 23 (4): 81–96.

2. Kotler, P. 1973. "Atmospherics as a Marketing Tool." *Journal of Retailing* 49 (4): 48–64.

3. Bitner, M. J. 1990. "Evaluating Service Encounters: The Effects of Physical Surroundings and Employee Responses." *Journal of Marketing* 54:69–82; S.

Grossbart. 1990. "Environmental Dispositions and Customer Response to Store Atmospherics." *Journal of Business Research* 21 (3): 225–41.

4. Singh, J. 1990. "A Multifacet Typology of Patient Satisfaction with a Hospital Stay." *Journal of Health Care Marketing* 10: 8–21.

5. Malloch, K. 1999. "A Total Healing Environment: The Yauapal Regional Medical Center Story." *Journal of Healthcare Management* 44 (6): 495–512.

6. Lawson, B., and M. Phiri. 2000. "Hospital Design: Room for Improvement." *Health Services Journal* 110 (5688): 24–26; M. D. Fottler, R. C. Ford, V. Roberts, and E. W. Ford. 2000. "Creating a Healing Environment: The Importance of the Service Setting in the New Consumer-Oriented Healthcare System." *Journal of Healthcare Management* 45 (2): 91–106.

7. Bowers, M. R., J. E. Swan, and W. F. Koehler. 1994. "What Attributes Determine Quality and Satisfaction with Health Care Delivery?" *Health Care Management Review* 19 (4): 49–55.

8. Hair, L. P. 1998. "Satisfaction By Design." *Marketing Health Services* 6 (Fall): 5–8.

9. Montague, J. 1995. "Family Designs." *Hospitals and Health Networks* 69 (11): 94.

10. Owens, D. E. 2001. "A New Wave in Patient Care." *Orlando Sentinel* (February 20): D1, D4.

11. Malkin, J. (forthcoming). *Charting New Paths to Healing Environments: Designing Health Care Facilities in a Spiritual Context*. Cited in "A New Wave in Patient Care," by D. E. Owens. *Orlando Sentinel* (February 20): D1, D4.

12. Lowers, J. 1999. "Improving Quality Through the Built Environment." *Quality Letter for Healthcare Leaders* 11 (8): 2–9.

13. Rohnman, S. F. 1995. "Rethinking the Design of Patient Units." *Building Design and Construction* 36 (5): 52–55.

14. Owens, D. E. 2001. "A New Wave in Patient Care." *Orlando Sentinel* (February 20): D1, D4.

15. "Building Blocks: Is There a Difference Between a Hospital Designed to Care for the Sick and One Designed to Keep People Well?" 1996. *Hospitals and Health Networks*. 70 (5): 27–30.

16. *Ibid.*

17. Owens, D. E. 2001. "A New Wave in Patient Care." *Orlando Sentinel* (February 20): D1, D4.

18. Horburgh, R. C. 1995. "Healing by Design." *New England Journal of Medicine* 333 (11): 735–41.

19. Horn, M. 1991. "Hospitals Fit for Healing." *U. S. News and World Report* 11 (4): 48–51.

20. Wiley, J. P. 1999. "Help Is on the Way." *Smithsonian* 30 (4): 22.

21. Green, L. 2000. "He Who Laughs, Lasts." *Spirit* 16 (2): 74–78.

22. Sewell, C., and P. B. Brown. 1990. *Customers for Life*, p. 22. New York: Pocket Books.

23. Weisman, C. W., and W.G. Nathanson. 1985. "Professional Satisfaction and Client Outcomes." *Medical Care* 23 (10): 1175–92.

24. Fottler, M. D., R. C. Ford, V. Roberts, and E. W. Ford. 2000. "Creating a Healing Environment: The Importance of the Service Setting in the New Consumer-Oriented Healthcare System." *Journal of Healthcare Management* 45 (2): 91–106.

25. For additional insights into the importance of providing memorable experiences, see B. J. Pine and J. H. Gilmore. 1998. "Welcome to the Experience Economy." *Harvard Business Review* 76 (4): 97–105.

26. Kaufman, L. 1998. "Our New Theme Song." *Newsweek* (June 22): 46–47.

27. Hagland, M., K. Luchs, and C. Quayle. 1996. "Design & Construction: Building Blocks." *Hospitals and Health Networks* 70 (5): 27–29.

28. Rundle, R. R., and C. Brinkley. 1999. "America's Most Luxurious Hospitals." *Wall Street Journal* (August 27): W1, W14.

29. Weber, D. 1997. "The Empowered Consumer." *Healthcare Forum Journal* (September/October): 28.

30. Hutton, J. D., and L. D. Richardson. 1995. "Healthscapes: The Role of the Facility and Physical Environment on Consumer Attitudes, Satisfaction, Quality Assessments, and Behaviors." *Health Care Management Review* 20 (2): 48–61.

31. Peterson, A. 1997. "Restaurants Bring In Da Noise To Keep Out Da Nerds." *Wall Street Journal* (December 30): B-1.

32. Shroyer, J. L. 1994. "Recommendations for Environmental Design Research Correlating Falls and Physical Environment." *Experimental Aging Research* 20 (4): 303–08.

33. Knowles, E. W., and S. Latimer. 1992. "Integrated Care: A Look Inside Tomorrow's Hospital." *Hospitals* 66 (4): 47–51.

34. Sewell, C., and P. B. Brown. 1990. *Customers for Life*, p. 124. New York: Pocket Books.

35. Bitner, M. J. 1992. "Servicescapes: The Impact of Physical Surroundings on Customers and Employee." *Journal of Marketing* 56 (April): 57–71.

36. McKahan, D. 1993. "Healing by Design." *Interior Design* 64 (8): 108–11.

37. Childs, M. D. 1998. "Waiting Room Ambience Gives Competitive Edge." *Family Practice News* 28 (17): 64.

38. *Ibid.*

39. Pinto, C. 1996. "Going Natural By Design." *Modern Healthcare* 26 (45): 39–48.

40. Weber, D. 1997. "The Empowered Consumer." *Healthcare Forum Journal* (September/October): 39–49.

41. *Ibid.*

42. Childs, M. D. 1998. "Waiting Room Ambience Gives Competitive Edge." *Family Practice News* 28 (17): 64.

43. "Environments That Heal." 1995. *Healthcare Forum Journal* 38 (2): 39.

44. "Company Puts the Home Back in Nursing Homes, Other Facilities." 2000. *Orlando Sentinel* (December 29): B5.

45. Lau, G. 2001. "Home Operator Emphasizes Personal Touch." *Investors Business Daily* (January 20): A10.

46. Marcus, C C., and M. Barnes. 1995. *Gardens in Health Care Facilities: Uses, Therapeutic Benefits, and Design Recommendations*. Martinez, CA: The Center for Health Design, Inc.

47. Mattson, M. 2001. "Baptist Medical Plans a Place of Nature to Help Nurture Its Patients." *Florida Times-Union* (May 26): E1, E8.

48. Weber, D. 1997. "The Empowered Consumer." *Healthcare Forum Journal* (September/October): 28.

49. *Ibid.*

50. Spears, J. D. 2000. "Creating a Healing Environment: Practitioner Application." *Journal of Healthcare Management* 45 (2): 106–07.

*Chapter 5*

# Developing a Culture of Customer Service

Healthcare Principle: Define and build a culture committed to providing superb service for all parts of the healthcare experience

Work together with employees to develop a "can-do" culture of honesty, integrity, energy, and initiative.

—*Norman Brinker*

WHEN YOU WALK into Disney World, fly on Southwest Airlines, shop at Nordstrom's, stay at a Marriott hotel, or receive treatment at Baptist Hospital in Pensacola, Florida, you can sense something special about the organization and the people who work there. If customers of these organizations are asked about the experience, they invariably describe it as better than they expected. Even more amazing is that their employees will also tell you that their respective organizations are different. The Disney cast members talk about their commitment to the quality of the "show" they produce for park visitors, Baptist Hospital and Nordstrom employees talk about the commitment to customer service, and Southwest Airlines employees talk about their commitment to providing a unique and pleasurable flying experience. Not only do employees speak of these corporate values; they believe in them and show the customer their commitment in a thousand different ways every day. The healthcare manager seeking excellence can learn a great deal by examining how these organizations create and sustain their culture of service excellence.

An organization's culture is the shared philosophies, ideologies, values, assumptions, beliefs, attitudes, and norms that knit the organization's members together. All of these interrelated standards reveal the group's agreement, implicit or explicit, on how its members should approach decisions and problems. In other words, culture guides the way employees of the organization act and think as they go about doing their jobs. Any culture is dynamic and constantly changing. It influences its members and is influenced by its members. The interaction between members as they deal with changing circumstances changes the culture over time. In this chapter, we discuss the role of leaders in defining and teaching the culture, communicating the culture, and ways of changing culture.

## THE ROLE OF LEADERS IN DEFINING AND TEACHING A CUSTOMER-FOCUSED CULTURE

Getting everyone in the organization committed to high levels of customer service is a daunting challenge. Therefore, healthcare leaders must spend a great deal of time, personal time if necessary, (1) creating and sustaining the organizational culture that reinforces the values for which their organizations are famous and (2) convincing their employees and managers to believe in that culture as well. These leaders know that they are responsible for defining the culture. They have a strong commitment to excellent service and communicate it—through words and deeds—clearly and consistently to those inside and outside the organization. Can managers who are not the presidents or founders of organizations have the same kind of influence on the culture? They certainly can and they must, although managers and supervisors serve more often as translators than as definers of culture.

The most important influence on any organizational culture is the behavior of the organization's leaders. This influence can be traced from the bottom level of the organizational chart: Employees try to behave like their supervisors, supervisors are influenced by the behavior of their managers, managers look up to their own managers as role models, and so on, until top-level managers and the organization's chief executive officer become the role models for the whole organization and the ultimate definers of each organization's cultural values.

### To Keep and Translate the Culture

Supervisory personnel at all levels must realize how important they are as cultural keepers and teachers. If they do not perform this function well, then the service experience will suffer. Managers must not only walk the walk and talk the talk of excellent service, they must also consistently remind employees they supervise to do the same. If a hospital manager walking through a department sees an employee doing something inconsistent with the desired customer service culture and ignores it, the manager sends a message to all employees that such behavior is acceptable and that not everybody has to focus on customer service all the time. After a few instances of managers saying they value one thing but rewarding or overlooking another, everyone knows what the real level of service commitment is. Not only must all the public and private statements support the idea that everyone is responsible for providing excellent customer service, the organizational reward system, training programs, and measures of achievement must also support and reinforce this message. When managers publicly and loudly celebrate the service achievements of their employees, they send a very strong message to everyone else about what the organization believes in and what the culture values. They are cultural leaders.

Leaders are willing to do what others are not. They actually do what others only talk about, and their actions are consistent with their words. They are participative, highly structured, considerate, demanding, in touch with both staff and customers, and willing to do whatever it takes to develop and motivate staff to better serve customers. Although their expectations and insistence on results are high, so too are the rewards they provide for achievement. Their decisions are consistently based on the cultural values that the organization espouses. As a result, employees believe in the organization and what it stands for; they want to stay with the organization and serve its customers.

## To Reinforce the Cultural Reputation

A company's culture, like a person's character, drives its reputation. Healthcare organizations whose cultures honor patients, employees, and shareholders usually have excellent reputations. These organizations recognize the importance of a strong culture in the competitive marketplace and a strong culture that everyone believes in, understands, and supports. All organizations have a culture, whether or not anyone spends time worrying about it, shaping it, or teaching it. Managers of effective healthcare organizations understand the value of a strong culture and do whatever they can to reaffirm and support that culture. If the culture supports excellent service, then the employees learn from their managers that providing excellent service is what they are supposed to do. The more the members accept and believe in it, the more likely they will try to do whatever they can to create and sustain a service excellence culture.

Unfortunately, many healthcare managers do not understand their responsibilities in reinforcing the culture to get this level of employee commitment, and both their employees and customers can tell. Successful healthcare managers, however, spend enormous amounts of time and energy on teaching new employees the culture, reminding their existing employees of the cultural values, and rewarding and reinforcing these values at every opportunity. These managers, despite all they have to do, make the time to reinforce the culture. The successful use of the organization's cultural mechanisms—its stories, legends, heroes, language, rituals, and so forth—to convey the appropriate values is a good measure of leadership skills. When leaders concentrate on using these mechanisms in a holistic way, they can ensure that they convey to employees a consistent set of cultural beliefs, values, and norms. The more consistently used all these mechanisms are, the more powerfully reinforced the culture will be.

Disney is an outstanding example of an organization that has worked very hard to define and sustain its culture. Corporate culture is so important to Disney that it is included and defined in the employee handbook. But in addition to being words in a book, the Disney culture is real and important for cast members. After interviewing Disney employees, Author Jane Kuenz concluded about the people she met:

> These are frequently people who have migrated to Orlando specifically to work at Disney, often with exceedingly high, perhaps naive, expectations about the park. While these expectations are sometimes vague notions that Disney must be "the epitome of the fun place to work," at other times they reflect a high level of personal investment with the park and with its power to raise the innocuous or mundane lives of average people into the fantastical and magical existence of the Disney cast member.[1]

In other words, many people believe so strongly in Disney's ability to create a magical experience for its guests that they want to become a part of it. Whatever cultural training Disney provides after these people become employed is icing on the cake; they arrive already believing in the Disney standards of excellence. Similarly, most healthcare organizations have this same kind of a head start in getting employees to understand and participate enthusiastically in the organizational culture; most people enter the field because they are dedicated, devoted, and committed to helping others. Building, teaching, and sustaining the cultural belief that everyone is part of the team that enhances the health of patients, even saves their lives, is therefore fairly easy because the cultural belief and their personal belief are so similar.

In the past decade or so, a number of hospitals around the country have adopted a philosophy of "patient-centered" care. This approach has four principles[2]:

1. Treat everyone with dignity.
2. Share unbiased information with patients and their families.
3. Strengthen the patient's sense of control.
4. Collaborate with patients, families, and the broader community in deciding how the hospital looks and functions.

*Modern Maturity* sponsored interviews with organizations devoted to fostering patient-centered care as well as with other caregivers, health-care executives, and experts to determine which facilities are most respected by their peers.[3] Bergen Mercy Medical Center in Omaha, Nebraska, was one of the first to hire nurses based on attitude toward patient services rather than only for their technical skills. St. Charles Medical Center in Bend, Oregon, is renowned for compassionate end-of-life care, while Longmont United Hospital in Longmont, Colorado, has raised money from staff to send a nurse to China to learn Eastern healing techniques. Each organization, in its own way, developed a culture focused on the needs of their customers. As a result of their strong cultures, they have all created a service reputation that is attractive to present and potential customers. Their strong cultures have been instrumental in building a competitive advantage.

### To Walk the Talk

Healthcare executives often do not invest in what they claim to value. Although they say customer satisfaction and employee retention are the most important aspects of their business, they often fail to invest adequately in either.[4] Instead, their to-do lists focus on such areas as upgrading technology, building an integrated delivery system, diversifying their business lines, and reengineering their business and clerical services.[5] In contrast, their patients care most about responsiveness, information about their case, pain management, and positive attitudes of physicians and other staff.[6] The result is that top healthcare executives have been modeling behavior that does not give a high priority to the major concerns of their customers. Yet both employees and customers judge leaders not on what they say but what they do, and what they do is focus on organizational priorities and not those of customers.

Leaders must be careful about what they say to ensure that the messages they send are intentional and explicit. What gets the leader angry or excited tells everyone what is important. A leader who expresses outrage over a service failure caused by a careless employee sends a strong message to all the employees that good service matters. For example, Marriott Corporation founder Bill Marriott, Sr., reportedly fired an employee on the spot for insulting a guest. When this story got around the organization, there was no question in anyone's mind of the customer orientation that Marriott valued.

## THE IMPORTANCE OF THE CULTURE

Everyone has been in an organization that feels warm, friendly, and helpful, perhaps for reasons they cannot quite explain. Similarly, everyone has been in an organization that feels cold, aloof, uncaring, and impersonal. Although most people can readily give examples of organizations that fit the two types, few can really explain what makes the two types different. Making culture different in the right ways is the healthcare manager's responsibility. Service expert Len Berry says, "Sustained performance of quality service depends on organizational values that truly guide and inspire employees. And how does an organization get such values? It gets them from its leaders who view the infusion and cultivation of values within the organization as a primary responsibility."[7] Some leading writers even maintain that it is every manager's most important responsibility. In Chapter 3, we talked about defining a service strategy. That strategy is no more than a paper plan for achieving successful outcomes. Implementing it is impossible without a supporting culture. No matter how brilliant and well thought out the strategy is, it will fail if it does not fit with the organization's culture.

### Employee Commitment

The organization's competitive strategy provides the basis for such critical decisions as how the organization will be structured; what type of service will be delivered; what market niche will be filled; what production and service delivery system will be used; and who will be hired and how will they be trained, rewarded, promoted, and evaluated. But only employee commitment to implementing all those critical decisions can turn plans into actions. All the plans in the world are useless without employee understanding, commitment, and support.

Healthcare organizations require an especially high level of commitment and understanding. Because the healthcare experience is to an extent intangible and each moment during the experience is so critical to determining customer satisfaction with the experience, employees must have extensive knowledge of both clinical procedures and customer expectations and an ability to respond quickly to the many variations in those expectations. But knowledge is not enough. Employees must also have high levels of motivation to deliver the healthcare experience consistently, in the way it must be done to ensure the best clinical and customer outcomes. Consequently, a strong and focused organizational culture becomes an especially important managerial emphasis in healthcare organizations.

## Competitive Advantage

The organization's culture can be a significant competitive advantage if it has value to its members, is unique, and cannot be easily copied by others. If an organization has a thriving culture that others cannot readily duplicate, it can use that culture to attract both patients and employees. A good strategy for organizations is to identify other organizations in their industries with successful cultures and try to adapt the successful cultural elements to their own cultures, as appropriate. Southwest Airlines has a thriving culture that others can use as a benchmark for their own: The "Southwest Spirit is the twinkle in your eye, the skip in your step; it is letting that childlike spirit escape and be heard."[8] Working in a culture where the employees truly have the "spirit" is very different from working in a typical nine-to-five job. More importantly, being a customer who encounters this type of culture is unique and fun. The Southwest culture represents a competitive advantage over other airlines.

## Core Competency

The organization's strong culture becomes another core competency as well as a competitive advantage. As is true for other core competencies, the organization that seeks to do something incompatible with its culture is likely to fail. If, for example, the organization's culture is accustomed to providing a high-quality healthcare experience, any manager trying to implement a cost-saving move that somehow jeopardizes that experience will meet resistance. The basic principle is simple: If the organization is committed to a strategy of excellence in the total healthcare experience, then its culture must support such excellence. Otherwise, excellence is not going to happen.

### The Outside World

Culture helps an organization's members deal with two core issues that all organizations must resolve: (1) how to relate to the world outside of the organization and (2) how the organization's members should relate to one another. Author Ed Schein says that culture is a "pattern of basic assumptions—invented, discovered, or developed by a given group as it learns to cope with its problems of external adaptation and internal interaction—that has worked well enough to be considered valid and, therefore, to be taught to new members as the correct way to perceive, think, and feel in relation to those problems."9

Some managers define dealing with the outside world as taking a closed or negative view of the outside environment and encouraging an "us versus them" cultural mindset. Members of such a culture are unreceptive to new ideas from the outside; they tend to discard or downplay common industry practices or innovations and are generally secretive about what their organization is doing and protective of its proprietary knowledge. On the other hand, managers trying to create an organization with an open culture constantly encourage their employees to grow and develop by interacting with others in the industry, to benchmark against best practice organizations wherever they can be found, and to consider ideas and innovations developed outside the organizational boundaries. Not surprisingly, people in these learning organizations adapt more quickly to changes in patient expectations and respond better to patient needs.

### Customer Service Values

A strong culture with the "right" values can reinforce customer service. Healthcare executives are increasingly seeking ways to identify job candidates who share their organizations' cultural values. Irvine Medical Center in California uses testing and interviews to evaluate employee-hospital congruence on values such as service orientation, proactiveness, and teamwork.[10] The Center has found that selecting employees who share its core values has greatly reinforced its corporate culture. These hiring practices have achieved better results than the "chit-chat" interviews and reference checks that previously were the norm. Research indicates that nurses whose values are congruent with those of their employing hospitals have higher retention rates.[11]

Culture building should not end at hiring and initial employee orientation. The organization's cultural values also have to be reinforced. One method of doing this is at a staff retreat that focuses on reminding staff of the cultural values and the day-to-day practices that support these values. The retreat should have "building a customer service culture" as a clearly stated objective so that participants address such questions as: Who are our customers? What do they want? What values does the organization need to deliver what they want? What human resources practices will nurture those values?[12] Neutral outside facilitators can help participants differentiate between their individual and institutional values, and reconcile the two where necessary.

Because everyone brings to a new job the cultural assumptions of past experiences, managers of excellent healthcare organizations know they must start teaching new cultural values to employees from day one. Quint Studer, former CEO of Baptist Hospital in Pensacola, Florida, required all new employees to go through a day-long orientation program that not only covered the obvious topics of hospital policies and procedures, it also focused on teaching the cultural values of patient satisfaction and a customer service orientation. Studer made sure everyone knew that the hospital's mission rested on the values of service, quality, cost, people, and growth. These values were clearly defined, and organizational expectations of employees regarding these values were clearly stated. All employees were expected to remember the primary importance of customer service in their organizational decision making.

## The Gaps

The cultural teachings of leaders, managers, and other dedicated employees become beliefs about how things should be, values of what has worth, and norms of behavior. They provide guidance to the culture's members as they interact with each other and their patients. According to Schein, they guide the members in how they should perceive the world about them, feel about the events they face, and think about what they do and do not do within their jobs. Many bureaucratic organizations believe that the best way to make sure employees do the right thing in their jobs is to establish extensive rules and regulations to cover every possible contingency. Ideally, a rule can be written for every possibility. Excellent healthcare organizations, however, knowing that rules and procedures cannot cover everything, spend their time defining and teaching the culture so that their employees will know how they should act in treating their customers and one another. These organizations teach their employees as much as they can, then rely on culture to fill in the inevitable gaps between what can be predicted and taught and what actually happens when customers enter the service setting.

### Management by Culture

The stronger the culture, the less necessary it is to rely on the typical bureaucratic control mechanisms—policies, procedures, managerial directives—found in traditional industrial organizations. Because so much of patient care happens in the encounter between the patient and staff members, healthcare organizations must rely on staff to do the "right things" (i.e., exceed expectation) for their patients. Culture is critically important in ensuring these right things happen. A strong culture can help employees guide patients properly even when the supervisor is not nearby.

Unlike a manufacturing organization where the production process is fairly predictable, the process of providing a healthcare experience is subject to incredible variation—as many different things can happen as there are different types of people. Because defining all the possibilities is impossible, the healthcare organization must rely on its employees to understand what is expected and deliver it to the customer every time. The more uncertain the task, the more employees must depend on corporate values, instead of managerial instructions, formal policies, and established procedures, to guide their behavior.[13]

### The Nurse Culture

The culture of the registered nurse is particularly strong. The nurse is trained to provide the best clinical care possible for patients at all times. However, many nurses are frustrated because they find themselves in situations where doing their best is difficult because of understaffing and bureaucratic, time-consuming requirements and regulations.

Therefore, asking these clinically focused, time-stressed professionals to place a high priority on meeting nonclinical needs that are also important to achieving customer satisfaction is asking a lot. Nevertheless, clinically focused nurses must add the nonclinical dimensions of patient care to their value systems. Quint Studer required nurses at Baptist Hospital to end each service encounter with the phrase "Is there anything else I can do for you? I have time" to expand the cultural definition of the professional nursing responsibility. Other staff members (e.g., food servers, lab techs, etc.) were also required to ask the same question. Although asking this question significantly enhanced staff-patient communication and patient satisfaction scores, it did not significantly increase the time spent with each patient. In most cases, staff members found that either the patient did not need anything else or the patient's needs could be provided in a matter of seconds.

## BASIC ELEMENTS OF CULTURE

Culture-driven organizations seek to define their beliefs, values, and norms through what they do and say and what they reward, rather than through rules and regulations. The following section defines beliefs and values, norms, folkways and mores, and subcultures.[14] These are the basic elements of an organization's culture.

### Beliefs and Values

Beliefs form the ideological core of the culture. If culture is a set of assumptions about how things operate, then beliefs are formed to help the people inside the organization make sense of how those assumptions influence what they do inside the organization. Beliefs define the relationships between causes and effects for the organizational members.

Values are preferences for certain behaviors or certain outcomes over others. Values define for the members what is right and wrong, preferred and not preferred, desirable behavior and undesirable behavior. Obviously, values can be a strong influence on employee behavior within an organizational culture. If management sends a clear signal to all employees that providing good customer service is an important value to the organization, second only to achieving a positive clinical outcome, then the employees know that they should adopt this value. Employees are more likely, consequently, to behave so as to ensure that all of the patients' nonclinical, rather than just clinical, needs and expectations are met.

Top-performing healthcare organizations start with a values-driven culture. Although most have a mission statement that espouses their purposes, not all have articulated organizational values by which the organization will provide its services. Members of values-driven organizations are consistent in their behaviors and decision making. In organizations where customer service is a stated value, there is a bias for action to deliver and improve customer satisfaction, a bias for speed in solving customer problems, and a bias for clarity of decision making focused on the customer. Their values are integrated into every aspect of their management systems involving selection, performance appraisal, and rewards. Staff members are taught how to live the values. The entire value-centered system of management supports customer satisfaction.

Johnson and Johnson manufactures and sells a variety of products in the healthcare field worldwide, including medical equipment and devices; surgical instruments; joint replacements; and dental, diagnostic, and ophthalmic products. The glue that holds the company's separate divisions together is a document called "Our Credo," which affirms the company's commitment to its customers, employees, stockholders, and the communities in which it operates.[15] This credo is a statement of values that tells employees how they are going to operate the business with regard to each of these stakeholders. Every employee has a copy of the credo, and it is literally etched in stone at the corporate headquarters. "Our Credo" is a good example of how culture is embedded and conveyed in an organization.[16] It reflects the beliefs, expectations, and common values of management and provides a basic belief system that affects employee behaviors and attitudes. On a mandatory basis twice a year, every Johnson and Johnson division throughout the world surveys its employees to determine how well the company is measuring up to its credo. The collected data are used to help improve culture and the way things are done on a day-to-day basis. Based on the data, the divisions and departments come together to develop action plans.

### Norms

Norms are standards of behavior that define how people are expected to act while part of the organization. The typical organization has an intricate set of norms. Some are immediately obvious, but some require the advice and counsel of veteran employees who have learned the norms over time by watching what works and what does not work and what gets rewarded and what gets punished. Most outstanding service organizations have the norm of greeting a customer warmly—smiling and making eye contact to show interest. Some use "the fifteen-foot rule," which is a norm that requires employees to make positive contact with customers who are within 15 feet away; these customers include window washers, engineers, and grounds crew as well as customer-contact persons. Positive contact includes making eye contact, smiling, and briefly engaging the customer in conversation. Benchmark healthcare organizations have learned the value of these hospitality concepts in enhancing the healthcare experience and now teach these techniques to their patient-contact employees. All employees at Baptist Hospital have been instructed to say the script, "May I take you where you are going?" when they see customers who seem lost or confused.

Cultural norms are defined and shaped for the healthcare employee not only by fellow employees and supervisors but also by customers who make their expectations plain. Such customers are an advantage that healthcare organizations have over manufacturing organizations as customers become valuable assistants to the managers in monitoring, reinforcing, and shaping employee behavior. Patient expectations of how employees should behave help shape employee behavior. Orderlies learn quickly what is expected of them by the constant hints, looks, glares, and comments that patients make. Some healthcare organizations might consider doing what Disney, Ritz-Carlton, and other excellent customer service organizations do: They list their guest-service guidelines on cards for employees to carry with them. Figure 5.1 presents Baptist Hospital's behavioral guidelines for nurses. Scripts for staff in general and particular staff roles will be discussed later in this chapter.

Some healthcare organizations use advertising to market their services and to show the patient visually what the healthcare experience should look like. The advertising not only serves to inform and entice prospective patients about the organization, it also serves to teach employees the norms of caring and attentive behavior that patients expect. In addition to the norms of behavior, many healthcare organizations have adopted norms of appearance and standards of personal grooming—for example, employees must wear the organizational uniform, hair must not extend below a certain length, only women may wear earrings, and employees must wash their hands before treating or serving patients.

**Figure 5.1  Examples of Baptist Hospital's Behavioral Guidelines for Nurse Interactions with Patients**

- Greet all patients by name and introduce yourself during the initial meeting (all three shifts).
- Provide each patient with your pager number and phone number, and invite communication as needed.
- Discuss reasons for each procedure before it is done.
- Ask patients if they need anything else before leaving a patient room.
- Explain that doors and curtains must be closed to ensure privacy.
- Respond promptly to call lights.
- Ensure that proper levels of pain medication are available for each patient.
- Never talk negatively about patients or coworkers.

*Source:* Reprinted with permission from Baptist Health Care Leadership Institute. "Turning Customer Satisfaction into Bottom-Line Results," presentation by Q. Studer and G. Boylan, July 8–9, 2000, Pensacola, Florida.

Although such norms can lead to criticism about restrictions on personal freedom of expression, healthcare organizations must meet patient expectations in this as in all areas of service. If patients expect to see clean-cut, uniformed employees greeting them at check-in, then the organization had better hire clean-cut employees and put uniforms on them. Although organizations that do not serve external customers can ignore such personal appearance concerns, the healthcare organization cannot. It must carefully define and enforce its norms of appearance to ensure that employees have the "look" that patients and their families expect to see.

## Folkways and Mores

*Folkways* are the customary, habitual ways in which organizational members act or think. Shaking hands (or not shaking hands), addressing everyone by first or last name, and wearing or not wearing a tie are all examples of folkways. In a healthcare clinic, a folkway example is wearing white coats and uniforms. An organization's *mores* are folkways that are meant to preserve the organization's efficient operation and survival; examples include wearing gloves and washing hands. Mores require certain acts and forbid others. By indicating what is right and wrong, they form the basis of the organization's code of ethics and accepted behaviors.

## Subcultures

Cultures often split into subcultures. Usually, the more people involved in the culture and the harder it is for them to stay in communication with one another, the more likely it is that the organization will see some subcultures form. Subcultures can be good or bad, supportive or destructive, and consistent with or contrary to the larger organizational culture. Because culture relies on interaction to sustain itself, people who work together may well create a subculture of their own, especially if they do not interact much with other organizational units. Organizations that depend greatly on part-time employees are especially susceptible to subculture formation; the part-timers may not spend enough hours in the greater organization to absorb its culture. The organization will want to do what it can to ensure that the subcultures are consistent with the overall cultural values even if their behaviors, beliefs, and norms vary somewhat. Communication is the key to sustaining the overall culture.

The categorizing and subdividing of employees by place (laboratory personnel versus direct patient-contact personnel), type (Pediatrics versus Intensive Care Unit), shift (weekend versus weekday), and amount of work (full time versus agency) has the effect of forming many different and clearly identifiable subcultures. Employees tend to associate with others like themselves who are doing the same things in areas where they are likely to meet one another frequently. After all, a culture is a shared experience, and the more it is shared, the more definable it becomes for those sharing it. Surgical nurses tend to associate with other surgical nurses, anesthesiologists with other anesthesiologists, and so forth.

The subcultures forming within the overall culture can be a managerial challenge if they operate in ways that do not support the overall corporate culture. A common example in healthcare is the frequent conflict between the customer-focused culture of administrative staff, which seeks to treat the whole patient and family, and some old-line department heads who do not buy into that culture. The dominant culture must be strong enough to override the subcultures on issues important to the organization's survival. Although some cultural variation may be tolerated, the overall culture has to be defined and reinforced by management to ensure that the central values of the organization come through in the healthcare experience. Of course, a subculture (e.g., pediatric nurses) may sometimes be more customer focused than the dominant culture (e.g., those who perform administrative and clerical functions). In that case, the dominant culture has to be changed to emulate the customer-focused subcultures.

A study of the Northwest Regional Development Center of the VA Medical Center in Boise, Idaho, found two distinct subcultures within the organization: the provider culture and the executive culture.[17] These two cultures had different values that acted as barriers to understanding between them. The study found that nothing in the executive culture prevented it from continuing to add patients to the clinic beyond the clinic's capacity to provide high-quality service; similarly, nothing in the provider culture limited its willingness to spend money on diagnosing and treating patient illnesses even though the associated higher costs might make the clinic noncompetitive. Because such different subcultures exist in all healthcare organizations, their managers and executives need to find mutually acceptable ways to bridge gaps to provide the excellent service that both cultures seek to provide.

In cases like the Boise VA Medical Center, the information (feedback) that limits the behavior of each subculture comes from the other subculture. On a routine task, the information may be distorted, delayed, or not even available to each subculture. In that clinic, when the data regarding the two subcultures were presented to the executive team, it opened new areas for discussion and led to a tighter coupling between clinic capacity and new patient recruitment.[18] The result was better communication between the two subcultures and higher levels of patient satisfaction.

## COMMUNICATING THE CULTURE

### Laws and Language
The laws of an organization are its rules, policies, and regulations; these norms are so important that they need to be written down so everyone knows exactly what they are. They are quite similar to governmental laws and regulations. They tell the members what behaviors are expected within that culture and also detail the consequences of violating the norms. For example, safe disposal of hazardous medical waste is so important to both the healthcare system and the larger society

that such disposal is governed by very precise rules and regulations. Failure to follow prescribed procedures can result in serious legal and employment consequences.

In addition to the common language of the larger social culture, each organization develops a language of its own that is frequently incomprehensible to outsiders. The special language is an important vehicle for both communicating the common cultural elements to which the language refers and in reaffirming the identity with the culture that those who speak this language share. Terms an insider uses to talk with another insider communicate an important concept quickly and also distinguish that person from an outsider. For example, any nonclinically trained person listening to an emergency room conversation will have a difficult time understanding what is being said, who is asking what, and what directions are being given. A doctor saying "Palpate the axilla and check for idiopathic pediculosis" is giving very specific directions to the medical team that are incomprehensible to anyone else. A common customer criticism of healthcare workers is that they use the often incomprehensible lingo of the profession when talking to customers. A truly customer-focused healthcare service provider will use language that patients and their families can easily understand, not the specialized language of the field.

### Stories, Legends, and Heroes

Stories, legends, and heroes are another way of transmitting cultural beliefs, values, and norms. They communicate proper behaviors and the right and wrong way to do things. Many tales are told about Walt Disney and his attention to detail, service excellence, and the future direction of the parks. When he died in 1966, he reportedly left behind a series of films in which he conducted staff meetings to an empty conference room with the intention, and apparently the result, that they be shown monthly to his senior staff after his death. As one observer reported, he held filmed "conferences" into at least the 1970s in which he made statements like, "Bob, this is October, 1976. You remember we were going to do this or that. Are you sure it's underway now?"[19] Such attention to detail and commitment to service quality left an important legacy behind. For years after Walt's death, many decisions were reportedly made by trying to figure out "what Walt would have done" or "what Walt would have wanted." This thinking so permeated the culture that the organization continued for many years to work as if the brilliant leader were still somehow nearby and able to guide the new leadership's thinking.

All organizations need stories, heroes, myths, and legends to help teach the culture, to communicate the values and behaviors that the organization seeks from its employees, and to serve as role models for new situations. Most people love stories. It is so much easier to hear a story of what a hero did than to listen to someone lecturing about "responsiveness to patient needs" in a formal training class. Not only are the stories more memorable than some arbitrary points seen on a classroom overhead, but the tales can be embellished in the retelling and the culture thereby is made more alive. Every healthcare organization should capture and preserve the stories and tales of its employees who do amazing things and create magical moments when caring for patients. The effort will yield a wonderful array of inspiring stories for all employees and send a strong message about what the organization values and desires in its employees.

For example, here is a story used to inspire the staff of a nursing home and reinforce their cultural customer service value: An elderly resident in a nursing home seemed to be having a hard time sustaining interest in eating anything. When a nurse's aide found out that the patient had a passion for peanut butter milkshakes, she went out of her way, on her own time, to make such a concoction. The resident then was able to eat something. A top manager told the story of this "local hero" in an employee gathering and recognized the aide with a customer satisfaction award. The story and the recognition had an important impact on defining the culture of the facility: doing whatever it takes to create patient satisfaction.

### Symbols and Rituals

A *symbol* is a physical object that has significance beyond itself; it is a sign that communicates an unspoken message. Cultural symbols are everywhere in organizations. An office with a big window and a nice view, an office on the top floor, or a desk in a particular location communicates information about the status level and organizational power of the person that transcends the mere physical objects involved. In healthcare, white coats and uniforms are the symbols of a clean, germ-free environment.

*Rituals* are symbolic acts that people perform to gain and maintain membership or identity within an organization. At most healthcare organizations, all new employees go through a similar informational training program where they learn the organizational basics and the cultural heritage. Like military boot camp or initiation into a sorority, the employee training also has ritualistic significance because everyone goes through the experience upon entry into the company. Most healthcare organizations develop elaborate ritual celebrations of service excellence. These can range from a simple event like a departmental pizza party to honor all those receiving formal acknowledgments from patients to very elaborate Employee-of-the-Year awards ceremonies that resemble a major gala. What the organization celebrates ritualistically and how much effort it makes to celebrate tell the members a lot about what the culture believes in and holds valuable.

## TEACHING THE CULTURE

Managers of effective healthcare organizations constantly teach the culture to their employees, reinforcing the values, mores, and laws. Strong cultures are reinforced by a strong commitment by top management to the cultural values. Ed Schein suggests that the *only thing* of real importance that leaders do is to create and maintain the organization's culture.[20] Authors Davidow and Uttal make a similar point: "Leaders who take culture seriously are bears for internal marketing, selling their points of view to the organization much as they would sell a product or service to the public, with slogans, advertisements, promotions, and public relations campaigns. The largest single chunk of their time is spent communicating values."[21]

These leaders worship at the altar of excellent service every day, and they do it visibly. They are personally involved in showing their commitment to service excellence. They back up slogans with dramatic, often costly actions. To instill values, they stress two-way communications, opening their doors to all employees and using weekly workgroup meetings to inform, inspire, and solve service-related problems. They put values into action by treating employees exactly as they want employees to treat patients and their families.[22] They use rituals to recognize and reward the behaviors that the culture values, and they praise the healthcare "heroes" whose actions have reflected worthy cultural values. Other employees, as a result, are encouraged to use these hero stories as models for their own actions.

Schein offers further insights about how leaders can embed the culture, especially at the time the organization is being formed.[23] In the beginning, the leader defines and articulates a set of beliefs and assumptions about how the organization will operate. Because new members join the organization with mixed assumptions and beliefs, the leader must carefully and comprehensively define the new organization's culture. This process creates the definition of the corporate culture, embeds it in the organization's consciousness, and shows what behaviors are reinforced. Whatever the leader responds to emotionally or with great passion becomes a powerful signal to which subordinates also respond. Thus, at the time of an organization's creation, the leader has to spend some thoughtful time defining what is important, how the organization's members should interpret the world they face, and what principles should guide their actions.

Once the organization's culture is in place, the leader constantly adjusts and fine-tunes it as markets, operating environment, and personnel change. Schein suggests that leaders can use five primary mechanisms to define and strengthen the organization's culture: "(1) what leaders pay attention to, measure, and control; (2) leader reactions to critical incidents and organizational crises; (3) deliberate role modeling, teaching, and coaching by leaders; (4) criteria for allocation of rewards and status; (5) criteria for recruitment, selection, promotion, retirement, and excommunication."[24] One method by which leaders teach the culture is by "scripting" staff behavioral and verbal interactions with customers. Figure 5.2 provides some scripts that have been introduced at Baptist Hospital for staff interactions with patients and other customers. Figure 5.3 provides scripts for particular staff members.

Bill Marriott, Jr., is a constant teacher, preacher, and reinforcer of the Marriott cultural values of guest service. He believes in staying visible, so he flies more than 200,000 miles every year to visit his many operations and to carry the Marriott message to as many people as he can.[25] This intense commitment to personal contact with each and every Marriott employee and visible interest in the details of his operations have become so well known among the Marriott organization that his mere presence on any Marriott property serves as a reminder of the Marriott commitment to service quality. Marriott also demonstrates a fanatical and unceasing quest for perfection in all the details of providing his hotel guests with a consistent, high-quality experience.[26] His unceasing quest is embodied in his company's comprehensive manuals that detail how to perform each service function. For example, one guide lists the six steps for cleaning a hotel room in less

**Figure 5.2 Examples of Baptist Hospital's Housewide Scripts for Reinforcing the Culture of Customer Service\***

- "I'm sorry. Clearly we did not meet your expectations."
- "You will receive a survey from us in the next few days. Please complete and return, as your feedback is very important to us. If for any reason you cannot grade us "very good," please contact _____."
- "Is there anything else I can do for you? I have time."
- "May I take you where you are going?"
- "I am closing the door (or pulling this curtain) because I am concerned with your privacy."
- "I'm concerned about your comfort level. On every shift we will be asking you to measure your pain level."

\* Only three or four housewide scripts were introduced originally. Others were introduced incrementally over time as associates became comfortable with the concept.

*Source:* Reprinted with permission from Baptist Health Care Leadership Institute. "Turning Customer Satisfaction into Bottom-Line Results," presentation by Q. Studer and G. Boylan, July 8–9, 2000, Pensacola, Florida.

than 30 minutes. Marriott notes that if you want to achieve consistent results, you need to figure out how to do it, write it down, practice it, and keep improving at it until nothing else needs to be improved.

Southwest Airlines is also famous for this hands-on commitment to service. Former CEO Herb Kelleher walked through airports, planes, and service areas to show employees his concern for the quality of each customer's experience. Even today this tradition lives on as all Southwest managers are expected to spend time in customer-contact areas, both observing and working in customer service jobs. This same modeling behavior can be seen in the many hospital managers who visibly and consistently make eye contact, introduce themselves, and volunteer to assist patients and their families. Employees see and then emulate this care and attention to the customer.

Unlike the manufacturing industry, which can rely on statistical reports to tell managers how things are going on the production line, healthcare managers inform themselves about what is happening by staying as close as possible to the point where services are rendered. As Norman Brinker puts it, "There's no substitute for spending time with

**Figure 5.3 Examples of Baptist Hospital's Staff-Specific Scripts for Reinforcing a Culture of Customer Service**

Position:    Radiology technician
Script:       We have purchased a blanket warmer, and I am putting a warm blanket around you. We are concerned about your comfort.

Position:    Chaplain
Script:       We are also aware that you may have spiritual concerns. We do have chaplains here around the clock.

Position:    Parking attendant
Script:       We will be asking you throughout your stay how we can do things better. Let me remind you that we do have valet parking for the convenience of you or your visitors.

Position:    Department unit coordinator
Script:       How may your nurse help you?

Position:    Lab staff
Script:       In the lab, we have done a study and looked at the best techniques and needles to draw blood. I understand that this procedure may not be pleasant, but I am using the best techniques and sharpest needles available, so hopefully, this will not bother you too much.

Position:    Nursing staff
Script:       Your physician cares about you very much, and he has asked that we get a blood sample very early so the results can be posted on the chart by the time he makes rounds in the morning.
Script:       Hello, my name is _____. I will be your nurse until _____. Please let me know the moment we can do something better. My goal is to exceed your expectations and provide you with very good care. Any questions at any time, please let us know.

Position:    Nurse leader
Script:       Good morning, my name is _____. I am the nurse leader on this unit. I want to assure you that we will do everything possible to exceed your expectations. I need your help. . . . This is my pager number and my phone number. Please call me the moment you find something we can do better, or let me know of an opportunity where we can exceed your expectations. Our goal is to provide you with very good care.

*Source:* Reprinted with permission from Baptist Health Care Leadership Institute. "Turning Customer Satisfaction into Bottom-Line Results," presentation by Q. Studer and G. Boylan, July 8–9, 2000, Pensacola, Florida.

people in their own environment. You not only meet everybody personally, you are able to see and hear for yourself what's going on."[27]

Benchmark healthcare organizations accept the simple idea that the reason for the organization's existence and basis for its success is the patient. For these organizations, being available to patients, families, and employees, and interacting with them, is an important organizational value and not just a company slogan, and managers from the top down must set the example. As most of them know, the pressures of day-to-day administrative responsibilities can easily push aside this fundamental ingredient in service success, so they build customer-contact time into their schedules.

Schein notes that a leader can use many mechanisms to reinforce or define the organization's culture.[28] For example, a leader can define the value of a functional area by placing that area at the bottom or near the top of the organizational chart. Placing the quality-assurance function near the top of the chart and having its manager report to a high-level executive tells the organization members that the leader values quality. The important point is that who reports on what to whom is a major way in which cultural values are communicated.

The layout of physical space is another secondary mechanism that can send a cultural message. For example, office size and location are traditional symbols of status and prestige. If an HMO leader puts the chief of quality assurance in the nicest office, right next to her own, she tells the rest of the organization that high-quality clinical care is an important organizational value. Finally, the formal, published statements of mission, purpose, and vision teach employees the philosophy, creeds and beliefs by which the organization lives. Although some organizations don't say what they really mean in these public statements, the excellent healthcare organization will do so clearly, concisely, and consistently.

## CHANGING THE CULTURE

Because the world changes and the people inside the organization change, the culture must also change to help the members cope with the new realities. A culture that started out years ago with a strong and successful clinical orientation may have to change over time as patients demand organizations to pay attention to all aspects of the healthcare experience. No matter how good a job the founder did in defining the culture and getting everyone to buy into it, the next generation of managers must work, perhaps even harder, to sustain those cultural values that should endure while changing those that need changing. They have available, of course, the tools discussed above to do this. The communication tools of symbols, legends, language, stories, heroes, and rituals need constant attention to sustain the cultural values in the face of changing circumstances.

The most difficult task of all is changing an entire culture that is not service oriented. When Quint Studer took over the leadership of Baptist Hospital in 1995, he was confronted with low patient satisfaction (close to the bottom in national surveys), high employee turnover, low employee morale, negative community perception, and a fiscal deficit. He knew that survival depended on transforming Baptist Hospital into a patient-focused organization. He inaugurated a wide variety of initiatives that improved morale, enhanced patient satisfaction, increased occupancy, restored fiscal stability, and stabilized turnover. Studer succeeded in creating a culture built around customer service by setting ambitious service-related goals and objectives, measuring their attainment, holding individuals responsible for results, creating and developing leaders, aligning behavior with goals and values, enhancing employee satisfaction, communicating effectively at all levels, and recognizing and rewarding success.

Here is another example. When Duncan Moore became the new CEO of Tallahassee Memorial Medical Center (TMMC) in Florida, he had a vision of the "ideal" hospital.[29] Soon after he arrived at TMMC, he set about developing a new mission statement. At that time, each member of the executive team had some understanding of the hospital's mission, but each had different expectations and definitions of it. Duncan Moore followed the steps below in the change process:

1. Reach consensus on and ensure a clear recognition of a new mission focused on cost-effective customer service.
2. Develop a vision statement that can be easily transmitted to staff and with which staff can identify.
3. Ask key staff members in each unit to visualize what their unit or service would look like if it disappeared overnight and if they had abundant resources to rebuild and reorganize it.
4. Assess the current conditions within the unit or service, including such factors as physician satisfaction levels, staffing mix, adequacy of supplies, paperwork, and so forth.

5. Superimpose the assessment of actual conditions on the ideal vision to identify gaps or areas in which change must occur for the unit or service to become the ideal.
6. Prioritize the changes cited in each area based on their relative importance, potential impact on patient satisfaction, and potential cost savings.

TMMC followed two basic rules in implementing the change process. First, all teams that were assembled to find ways to fill the gaps had to include representatives of all the stakeholders directly affected by the planning function. Consequently, the core team was composed of a manager, the manager's immediate supervisor, the manager's direct reports, and representatives of affected stakeholders. Second, all plans needed to detail the means and resources by which the board might fulfill the plan. To maximize the impact of its interactive planning and management process and to promote an awareness of its mission and values among employees, TMMC provided support in the form of education, communications, and reward programs for employees. For example, intensive training in systems thinking, management styles, and systems model analysis were provided to team members.

In sum, TMMC created a profound cultural shift to a perspective that each employee "is doing the work for the patient" by revising the organization's mission and values and then implementing a planning process at the departmental level that focused on the departmental mission, customers, and needs. The process is continuous as TMMC attempts to move toward the "ideal hospital." According to CEO Moore, a positive culture is personally enriching for employees and not very expensive to achieve and maintain. The expectation is that the long-term improvements in cost-savings will offset the employees' time investment in the process. The assumption and expectation at TMMC are that a positive culture can give the organization a decisive edge on the competition.

## CONCLUSION

Here are some principles about organizational culture that seem to hold generally true.

- Leaders define the culture (or redefine it if necessary), teach it, and sustain it. Doing so may be their biggest responsibility in the organization. Culture is one of the most precious things a company has, so leaders must work harder at it than at anything else.[30]

- An organizational culture that emphasizes interpersonal relationships is uniformly more attractive to professionals than a culture that emphasizes work tasks.[31]

- Strong cultures are worth building or changing; they can provide employee guidance in uncertain situations where policies or procedures are unavailable or unwritten.

- Subcultures will form in larger organizations. A strong culture will increase the likelihood of keeping the subculture consistent with the overall culture's values in important areas.

- Sustaining the culture requires constant attention to the means of communicating culture so that they all consistently reinforce and teach the organization's beliefs, values, and norms of behavior to all employees.

- Excellent healthcare organizations hire and retain employees who fit their culture and get rid of those who do not. The fit between the individual and the culture is strongly related to turnover, commitment, and satisfaction.[32] Cultural change may be impossible without some change in personnel.

## LESSONS LEARNED

1. Leaders define the culture for everyone by what they say and do every day and by what they reward.
2. Culture fills in the gaps for employees between what they have been taught and what they must do to satisfy patients, families, and each other.
3. To create a culture of customer service, celebrate success publicly.
4. Leaders must think carefully about how everything they do support the cultural values of customer service.
5. Leaders must find heroes, tell stories, and publicize legends to reinforce important cultural values.
6. To be successful, a customer service strategy must become deeply embedded in the organizational culture at all levels.
7. Creating a culture of customer service requires consistent leadership at all levels, supported by values, clear mission and vision statements, objectives, strategies, measurement of results, selection of service-oriented staff, staff training, scripting, staff rewards, and persistence.

## NOTES

1. Kuenz, J. 1995. "Working at the Rat." In *Inside the Mouse: Work and Play at Disney World,* p. 139. Durham, NC: Duke University Press.

2. Guroff, M. 2001. "Hospitals with Hearts." *Modern Maturity* 44 (4): 67.

3. *Ibid.*

4. "Put Up or Shut Up: Study Finds Execs Not Investing in What They Claim to Value." 1998. *Modern Healthcare* 11: 42.

5. *AHA News.* March 9, 1998, p. 1.

6. Studer, Q., and G. Boylan. 2000. "Turning Customer Satisfaction into Bottom-Line Results." Presentation at the Baptist Health Care Leadership Institute, Pensacola, Florida, (July 8–9).

7. Berry, L. L. 1999. *Discovering the Soul of Service,* p. 38. New York: The Free Press.

8. Freiberg, K., and J. Freiberg. 1996. *Nuts! Southwest Airlines' Crazy Recipe for Business and Personal Success,* p. 154. Austin, TX: Bard Press.

9. Schein, E. 1985. *Organizational Culture and Leadership: A Dynamic View,* p. 9. San Francisco: Jossey-Bass.

10. Eubanks, P. 1991. "Hospitals Probe Applicants' Values for Organizational Fit." *Hospitals* 65 (20): 36–38.

11. Vandenberghe, C. 1991. "Organizational Culture, Person-Culture Fit, and Turnover: A Replication in the Health Care Industry." *Journal of Organizational Behavior* 20: 175–84.

12. "Retreats Advance Corporate Culture." *Hospitals* 65 (18): 58.

13. For more information on this point, see W. H. Davidow and B. Uttal. 1989. *Total Customer Service,* pp. 96–97. New York: Harper.

14. The following definitions are paraphrased from H. M. Trice and J. M. Beyer. 1993. *The Cultures of Work Organizations,* pp. 33–34. Englewood Cliffs, NJ: Prentice-Hall.

15. Atherton, E., and B.H. Kleiner. 1998. "Practices of the Best Companies in the Medical Industry." *International Journal of Health Care Quality Assurance* 11 (5): 173–76.

16. *Ibid.*

17. Smith, C. S., C. Francovich, and J. Geiselman. 2000. "Pilot Test of an Orga-nizational Culture Model in a Medical Setting." *Health Care Supervisor* 19 (2): 68–77.

18. *Ibid.*

19. Fjellman, S. M. 1992. *Vinyl Leaves: Walt Disney World and America*, p. 117. Boulder, CO: Westview Press.

20. Schein, E. 1985. *Organizational Culture and Leadership: A Dynamic View*, p. 2. San Francisco: Jossey-Bass.

21. Davidow, W. H., and B. Uttal. 1989. *Total Customer Service*, p. 48. New York: Harper.

22. *Ibid.*, p. 107.

23. Schein, E. 1985. *Organizational Culture and Leadership: A Dynamic View*, pp. 317–20. San Francisco: Jossey-Bass.

24. *Ibid.*, pp. 224–25.

25. Albrecht, K. 1988. *At America's Service: How Your Company Can Join the Customer Service Revolution*, p. 130. New York: Warner Books.

26. Grugal, R. 2002. "66 Steps to Cleanliness." *Investors Business Daily* (March 11): A4.

27. Brinker, N., and D. T. Phillips. 1996. *On the Brink: The Life and Leadership of Norman Brinker*, p. 191. Arlington, TX: The Summit Publishing Group.

28. The following discussion of secondary mechanisms is indebted to E. Schein. 1985. *Organizational Culture and Leadership: A Dynamic View*, pp. 237–42. San Francisco: Jossey-Bass.

29. Adapted from P. Eubanks. 1992. "Focusing the Culture on Customer Service." *Hospitals* 66 (16): 40–42.

30. Freiberg, K., and J. Freiberg. 1996. *Nuts! Southwest Airlines' Crazy Recipe for Business and Personal Success*, p. 145. Austin, TX: Bard Press.

31. Sheridan, J. E. 1992. "Organizational Culture and Employee Retention." *Academy of Management Journal* 35 (5): 1052.

32. O'Reilley, C. A., III, J. Chatman, and D. F. Caldwell. 1991. "People and Organizational Culture: A Profile Comparison Approach to Assessing Person-Organization Fit." *Academy of Management Journal* 34 (3): 487–516.

# PART TWO

## The Healthcare Service Staff

*Chapter 6*

# Staffing for Customer Service

Healthcare Principle: *Find and hire clinically competent people who love to serve*

There is a shortage of healthcare professionals across the country, as well as a shortage of registered nurses that is compromising patient care. This shortage will reach crisis proportions in the twenty-first century.

—*Kenneth Brownson and Raymond Harriman*

A YOUNG FATHER and his small children rushed to the hospital emergency room to see the children's mother. She had been critically injured in an automobile accident and the prognosis was negative. But hospital rules prohibited children under 12 from entering the emergency room. An emergency room nurse, who recognized the value of allowing this dying mother to see her children, broke the rules and allowed the children in to see their mother one last time. In the nurse's professional judgment, breaking the rules presented no adverse clinical effects on anyone and offered customer satisfaction. Skilled and thoughtful nurses like this one can make a tremendous difference to patients and their families. Rather than advocating that staff be told to "follow the rules," we believe they should be allowed and encouraged to use their intelligence, training, and creativity to find the best way to solve problems and be empowered to provide an outstanding service experience to each customer.

In this chapter, we discuss how and why employees are crucial to providing a high-quality customer experience in healthcare organizations, what challenges are posed by current staff shortages, and how to identify and hire those who truly love to serve others. The steps involved in the staffing process are detailed, beginning with job analysis and ending with employee selection.

## THE IMPORTANCE OF EMPLOYEES

Employees who are recruited, hired, and trained to provide a superior healthcare experience add value to the experience and the organization in important ways. First, they make the experience memorable and help keep the healthcare organization in the "top of the patient's mind" so that patients will speak favorably of the provider to others and even return when their healthcare needs call for such service. Second, they create a competitive advantage for the organization because no competitor can design into its service experience the same unique and personalized feeling that the well-selected, well-trained employee can. Third, they have high staff-retention rates as a result of their emphasis on providing a positive healthcare experience. An organization that encourages its employees to take every opportunity to be creative and individualistic with patients, show true caring, and use their professional skills fully tells employees that it appreciates their skills and trusts them to do the right thing with the patients. For healthcare employees who sought the job partly for the opportunity to demonstrate their creativity and originality in caring for patients and their families, this is the rewarding part of the job; these employees tend to stay in such organizations.

Part of the healthcare experience hinges on recruiting and selecting employees who are willing and able to create these memorable moments and to engage the patient in a unique way that enhances rather than detracts from the healthcare experience. Of course, not every employee is comfortable in this role, and not every employee needs to be. Many employees can be creative and original in more conventional ways, and every healthcare organization needs them too.

## WORKER SHORTAGE

The challenge of recruiting and selecting high-quality staff who will enhance customer service is made even more difficult by the current and projected future shortages in the health professions. The shortage of all types of healthcare workers has become a crisis.[1] In 1998, two different Memphis area healthcare organizations that employ approximately 8,000 employees each reported 400 to 500 job openings.[2] In the same year, New Hampshire reported a shortage of nurse aides, which some called a labor crisis.[3] The high average turnover rates of nurse aides (100 percent per year), which increased up to 400 percent in some regions, was one of the most important concerns facing nursing homes in 1997.[4]

Over the past five years, staff shortages have become more acute. Hospitals have been scrambling to find nurses as nursing school enrollments have declined.[5] The problem is especially acute among specialty nurses who work in operating rooms, intensive care units, and labor and delivery units. As a result, the New York State Association of Health Care Providers has formed a coalition with other industry groups to get more Medicare money for wages, to recruit retired police officers and firefighters into second careers, and to begin marketing efforts to attract young recruits to the healthcare industry. According to Daniel Sesta, president of the Healthcare Association of New York State:

> The work force shortage is one of the most crucial issues facing healthcare in New York State right now. I think it is affecting care. No health association wants to admit that, but I think that hospital CEOs are no longer in a position to guarantee the public that optimum quality of care is being delivered.[6]

Other hospital CEOs, as well as physicians, have expressed similar sentiments.[7] The continuing challenge for healthcare is recruiting and retaining staff members who are clinically competent and love to serve in an era of staff shortages.

## SERVICE LOVERS

Outstanding healthcare employees can easily be distinguished from the merely clinically competent. In his book *Positively Outrageous Service*, author Scott Gross calls such people "lovers" because they love to provide great service. In healthcare, these are the employees who connect with patients and build a relationship that make the patients "feel good" about their healthcare experience. Although the relationship may be brief, it makes the patient believe that something is special and memorable about his or her total healthcare experience.

Gross estimates that people who love to serve others represent only one in ten of the available workforce. As he states, "Ten percent can't get enough of their customers. Five percent want to be left alone. When it comes to customers, the vast majority can take 'em or leave 'em."[8] If Gross's percentages apply to the health professions, he raises two major challenges for healthcare managers. First, they need to work hard at developing a process that will systematically find, recruit, and select those ten percent of the clinically competent who are truly committed to providing excellent service. Second, they must work even harder to develop an effective process for showing the rest how to provide the same quality of service that the "lovers" do naturally. Because naturally talented people are so rare in the labor pool, the organization must identify what service skills are lacking in the people they do hire and train them in those skills.

Given the challenges of recruiting and hiring good employees in the healthcare industry, some organizations are tempted to place the "lovers" in the patient-contact jobs and hire the rest for support jobs that do not have direct contact with the patient. Because not all jobs in healthcare organizations require extensive patient contact, putting people not naturally good at service in these behind-the-scenes jobs might seem like a way out. The truly excellent organizations, however, recognize the fallacy of this reasoning. They know that all employees are somehow involved in serving customers—either patients or fellow workers. Knowing that service effectiveness depends on everyone throughout the organization taking their service responsibilities seriously, these outstanding organizations try not to hire anyone who cannot or will not provide outstanding service. Even the accountants must be sensitive to the needs and expectations of their customers—their colleagues. A hiding place does not exist anymore for those who may be outstanding technically or clinically but have no service skills.

After an extensive review of high-performance organizations, Jeffrey Pfeffer, a Stanford professor, reports seven human resources management practices used by these organizations.[9] One of the seven is selective hiring. For healthcare organizations that wish to be customer focused, this practice means they need to identify staff traits that are related to customer service and then recruit and select the best.

Although many healthcare organizations try to "select the best and train the rest," benchmark organizations have gained a competitive edge by developing recruitment, training, and placement programs that motivate all employees to provide outstanding service for both external and internal customers. If the organization is somehow able to attract and select the best potential employees, then it will gain a significant advantage over those organizations that do not systematically seek out and find these customer-service-focused people.

## SELECTION PROCESS

### Job Analysis

Selecting the best person for the job should begin by first looking not at the applicants but at the job itself, to see what employee abilities and characteristics the job requires. A careful, thorough job analysis allows the organization to identify the exact job specifications and required competencies for each job classification and type. A job analysis will tell you if you need physically strong people to assist patients in orthopedic rehabilitation, skilled nurses to monitor surgical patients, or multilingual people to speak to non-English-speaking patients.

### Knowledge, Skills, and Abilities

Evaluating the job enables the organization to deduce the knowledge, skills, and abilities (KSAs) necessary. Many organizations have spent considerable sums of money identifying the KSAs associated with each major job or job category and then have developed tests to measure the degree to which the applicants have these KSAs. If this measurement process is properly done, and if the tests have been shown to be both valid and reliable, then the organization has an effective and legally defensible means for putting the right candidates in the right jobs. Further, by doing the careful job analysis that allows this type of selection measure to be developed, the organization gets the added benefit of identifying training needs and building reward structures that are directly related to the critical KSAs that are closely linked with job performance.

Measuring the technical competencies necessary to serve patients is far easier than measuring friendliness, ability to stay calm under criticism by customers, professionalism, self-esteem, integrity, accountability, and willingness to help, which are all necessary to provide excellent customer service. Even so, healthcare organizations must try to assess the attitudes and values of potential employees as well as their job skills. Because skills can be taught and learned more easily and readily than attitudes and values can, new staffers must come in with a caring attitude. From the patient's perspective, the high importance of staff attitude is expressed in the healthcare saying "Patients don't care how much you know until they know how much you care."

## Staff Competence

In 1996, the Joint Commission on Accreditation of Healthcare Organizations (JCAHO) changed the human resources standards and interpretation statements about staff competence. Since then, hospitals have been required to assess, maintain, demonstrate, track, and improve the competence of staff.[10] Yet, as has been pointed out elsewhere, a wide gap exists between what JCAHO is requiring and what can and should actually be accomplished in the area of customer service with the competence model of performance.[11]

JCAHO surveyors are not currently defining competence beyond job skill and knowledge.[12] Competence is still narrowly defined and based mostly on job tasks rather than customer outcomes. This means that attitudinal and interpersonal skill issues, which drive customer satisfaction, are largely ignored. Competence is typically assessed by a supervisor (not a customer) through a pass-fail evaluation of each area of competence. Consequently, the demands of JCAHO to prove competence have been approached bureaucratically by both JCAHO and the hospitals. Culture is not aligned around customer service as should be done with a sound customer-service-focused model.

## A Competency-Focused Model

A sound model involves having the hospital or department management team define their customers, desired customer outcomes, and indicators of achievement for all outcomes. Generic core competencies are defined behaviorally for all employees, as are job-specific competencies in the area of customer service.[13] Obviously, competencies cannot be determined without first defining superior performance. In the current market-driven healthcare economy, the outcome desires of customers and the outcome desires of healthcare professionals should be the standards of superior performance.

Competencies are characteristics that are causally related to effective or superior performance on a job.[14] This means meeting or exceeding customer outcome expectations. There are five types of competencies:

1. *Motives:* things a person consistently thinks about or wants that cause action;
2. *Traits:* physical characteristics and consistent responses to situations or information;
3. *Self-concept:* a person's attitudes, values, or self-image;

4. *Knowledge:* information a person has in specific content areas; and
5. *Skills:* ability to perform a certain physical, mental task, or behaviroal task.

Some of these competencies are hidden (i.e., motives, traits, and self-concept), while others are visible (i.e., knowledge and skills).

Customer service problems and most management problems revolve around the hidden competencies. This is not surprising given the historical emphasis on hiring staff for their skills and knowledge and the fact that license and performance appraisal systems are based on task performance rather than customer outcomes. Competence cannot be determined without connecting customer-outcome expectations to worker characteristics such as motivation, interpersonal skills, and political skills.

Because motive, trait, and self-concept competencies related to customer service are more difficult and expensive to assess and develop than knowledge and skills competencies, selecting employees for these competencies is more cost effective than trying to develop them after hiring. Many possible clusters of competencies can be developed, but one author proposed the following: customer service/communication, professionalism, decision making/problem solving, resilience, cost control, political/system awareness, and support for the organization's values and goals.[15]

Among the customer service/communication skills and competencies, the following have been identified for benchmark healthcare organizations[16]:

- Speaks courteously to customers
- Offers and accepts constructive criticism
- Practices active listening
- Writes legibly
- Provides and asks for feedback to confirm understanding
- Maintains eye contact when speaking to someone
- Provides timely and clear information and follow-up to requests from patients and other customers
- Identifies self to all customers at all times
- Answers phone in four rings and identifies service and self
- Offers assistance without being prompted
- Helps maintain a quiet environment

- Is not involved in private conversations in front of patients or other customers
- Asks permission to put caller on hold and returns in one minute or less
- Does not complain to customers
- Listens to and educates customers
- Treats everyone as an individual
- Does not talk down to others
- Addresses issues directly with person involved in a calm tone of voice
- Greets people with a smile
- Focuses on customers' needs
- Shows dignity and respect for patients

Customer-focused organizations cannot afford to have staff members who respond to customers in any of the following ways: "It's not my job," "It's against policy," "I'll have to check with my supervisor, but she's out to lunch," and "You'll just have to wait until the doctor gets here."

Selection of new staff members should be done by the whole team, rather than a single individual, to allow for multiple imputs concerning the customer service competencies noted above. Once the candidate's clinical competence has been demonstrated, the selection interview should focus on the applicant's hidden competencies such as self-esteem, personal accountability, communication style, and customer service. Applicants should be asked how they have handled or will handle particular situations such as a difficult patient or family member. The goal should be to uncover the hidden competencies related to customer service usually possessed by 10 percent of the workforce.

### Competency-based Benchmarking

The intangibility of the healthcare experience and the uniqueness of what each patient expects from it have frequently led healthcare organizations to use a secondary strategy for selecting good candidates: study the organization's best performers and identify the personal traits, tendencies, talents, and personality characteristics that enable them to serve patients successfully. This approach attempts to define the necessary KSAs of successful people, instead of looking at the KSAs required in a particular job.

The logic of defining the KSAs in terms of the person is that the customer service aspects of the healthcare experience defy precise measurement or definition. Putting together a meaningful and useful list of job-driven KSAs for a hospital chaplain is difficult. If these job aspects defy definition and precise measurement, then the best alternative is to study or "measure" the people who have been successful in the organization and seek to determine the KSAs that allowed these people to become good at the roles they play. If these people have succeeded through a healthcare career across all types of jobs, then perhaps some universal KSAs, competencies, personality characteristics, or inborn talents can be identified and accurately (and scientifically) measured. The successful job performers in each job category can serve as templates for hiring new people for those jobs.

In essence this process is benchmarking against the very best practitioners of the job. If you hire only employees who have traits, skills, abilities, tendencies, talents, and personality characteristics that are similar to those found in the current strong job performers, then they should be more successful than new employees who do not have those same characteristics. Many organizations have followed this strategy based on work by the Gallup Corporation, S.R.I., J.D. Power, and other similar organizations. They look at an organization's strong performers and, based on their talents, develop talent profiles for each major job category. Then they use these benchmark profiles to screen new applicants. The use of this approach can even be extended to looking at the mix of talents in entire departments. If an analysis of a particular department shows that the current composition of people does not include some vital talent for departmental success, the selection process can ensure that the person next hired will have an ample supply of the missing ingredient.

Although competency-based approaches to selection have some obvious advantages, they also have some disadvantages. If they are designed for a single job or single job category, they can be quite expensive unless the organization has a lot of people doing that job. Because Beverly Enterprises, for example, employs so many nursing home administrators, developing a competency profile becomes worthwhile; however, a single independent nursing home may find that the considerable expense of having a professional survey organization come in to do this work cannot be recaptured in any selection efficiencies gained. Further, the competency models have a difficult time staying current with changing technology or changing job expectations. As the necessary competencies change, so too must the selection measures. Finally, many individual job-category competency measures are not interlinked with models in other parts of the organization. As Professor Richard Mansfield says, it may be "difficult to compare the competency requirements of one job to the requirements of another job or an individual's competency assessments in one job to the requirements in another job."[17]

Nonetheless, all competency measures are essentially anchored on the successful practitioners in the current organization. If the organization's success factors change over time, then the measures may become irrelevant. Finally, if the organization wants diversity in opinion, talents, and personalities to promote change and organizational growth, the use of existing executives to establish the norms for who should be hired in the future may impede the acquisition of diversity's benefits. Competency measures should be considered as only one tool in the selection process.

### General Abilities

In addition to looking for KSAs, competencies, licenses, and clinical training or experience of a prospective employee, healthcare organizations should also look for certain general abilities. Doing so does not downplay the vital role of clinical competence; it recognizes the equally vital role of caring about and effectively managing the total healthcare experience. General abilities include:

- *Enthusiasm.* Patients expect to be served by employees who are enthusiastic about the service, the organization, and the opportunity to provide service. Because enthusiasm is contagious, it positively influences patients' moods and satisfaction with the total healthcare experience.
- *Emotional commitment.* Healthcare jobs require a heavy emotional commitment from the service providers. Employees must stay upbeat, cheerful, enthusiastic, and genuinely interested in serving the patient even when they do not feel like it or are having a bad day or even when a patient is not reciprocally positive. Not everyone, no matter how service oriented, can make this heavy emotional commitment consistently, especially employees whose jobs require them to listen to complaining patients all day. For most

employees this type of constant negative experience eventually exacts its toll and results in burnout.

Some employees, however, experience burnout simply because they are tired of doing the same job in the same way every day. At some point most employees switch into an automatic- pilot mode, like the receptionist who tires of greeting everyone with the same smile and words many times everyday—because they cannot make the emotional commitment to treat patients with sincerity. Authors Schneider and Bowen term this emotional commitment a "passion for service," and they have developed a questionnaire for measuring it.[18] More importantly, their research reports that a passion for service is highly correlated with positive service outcomes.

• *Politeness, consideration, and willingness to make a genuine effort to help other people.*[19] Clinically competent staff members who exhibit emotional control, enthusiasm, and a caring attitude can help benchmark healthcare organizations provide an excellent total customer experience.

Recruiting, selecting, and retaining staff who possess all three general abilities will enhance the capability of healthcare organizations to satisfy their customers.

## Psychological Tests

Psychologists have developed a variety of tests to distinguish one person from another along different dimensions. Tests of mental ability measure logical reasoning, intelligence, conceptual foresight, semantic relationships, spatial organization, memory span, and a number of other cognitive factors. Tests of mechanical ability, physical ability, and personality are also available. Organizations have used these tests with mixed results. Physical and mechanical ability tests are more easily shown to be valid predictors of later job success than mental or cognitive tests. Personality and other mental measures are much harder to validate against successful job performance. "What makes a successful manager?" or "What personality type makes a more effective leader in a particular situation?" are difficult questions to answer and even more difficult to prove. The intelligence required to be successful is even harder to specify. Even so, Norman Brinker, former president of Chili's

Restaurants, says, "Look for people . . . who are smart. Remember, sinners can repent, but stupidity is forever."[20]

Research by Gomez-Mejia and colleagues[21] has indicated that personality can be reliably measured and summarized along five dimensions:

1. *Extroversion:* the degree to which someone is talkative, sociable, active, aggressive, and excitable.
2. *Agreeableness:* the degree to which someone is trusting, amiable, generous, tolerant, honest, cooperative, and flexible.
3. *Conscientiousness:* the degree to which someone is dependable and organized, conforms to the needs of the job, and perseveres on tasks.
4. *Emotional stability:* the degree to which someone is secure, calm, independent, and autonomous.
5. *Openness to experience:* the degree to which someone is intellectual, philosophical, insightful, creative, artistic, and curious.

Of these five dimensions, conscientiousness is generally considered to be the most valid predictor of job performance. In studies investigating the relationship between these five traits and service industry success, three dimensions showed some important correlation: agreeableness, emotional stability, and conscientiousness. Employees high in patient orientation are friendly, stable, and dependable.[22] Although these findings seem somewhat obvious, the implication of this research is that measures do exist that organizations can use to gain an indication of a potential employee's service orientation.

Although more complete studies need to be done before any claim can be made about reliability and validity for these measures, the fact that certain measurable and definable personality constructs are statistically associated with a tendency toward service orientation is useful information and confirms with data what the popular writers on service management have been saying: Certain personality characteristics, like those above, are commonly found in people who have a propensity to serve.[23]

Other types of psychological tests have been proposed as ways to assess characteristics of the job candidate. The key to their use is that they must be demonstrably related to job performance. Some healthcare organizations have succeeded to a degree in using psychological tests to identify the more motivated candidates in the available labor pool. Nonetheless, these types of tests can be difficult to link directly with job performance, and the key test of any measure used to screen potential employees is that it discriminates on the right characteristics and does not discriminate on the wrong. By law, selection strategies may not unfairly discriminate against those protected by antidiscrimination legislation.

## Job Crafting

Although job analysis provides the basis for development of job descriptions and job specifications (which specify the requisite KSAs of a given job), job boundaries are not fully determined in job descriptions and job specifications. Employees have latitude to define and enact the job, acting as "job crafters." *Job crafting* is the physical and cognitive change employees make in the task or relational boundaries of their work.[24] When employees know and buy into the strategic goals of an organization, they can use this knowledge to motivate and legitimate their own job-crafting behavior.

Job crafting is embodied in this example: A group of hospital cleaners who used the customer-oriented strategic goals of the hospital to frame their cleaning duties under the "care of customers"[25] rubric. In other words, they saw their jobs as an integrated whole related to customer care rather than a series of discrete tasks related to cleaning. This type of work framing helped the hospital cleaners to legitimize a different form of relating to patients and visitors and encouraged the addition of caring tasks to the work. Members of this work group liked their jobs, felt the work required high skill levels, and engaged in many tasks that helped patients and visitors and made the jobs of nurses and clerks go more smoothly. These cleaners not only added tasks, but they also timed their work to be maximally efficient to the workflow of their unit. Finally, they engaged in relational interactions that were intended to brighten someone's day (i.e., talking to patients, showing visitors around, and conversing with nurses).

Nurses have also engaged in job crafting by actively managing the task boundaries of their jobs to deliver the best possible patient care.[26] By paying attention to the patient's world and conveying seemingly unimportant information to others on the care team, these nurses recreated their jobs to be about patient advocacy rather than simply the delivery of high-quality technical care. They also extended the relational boundary of the job by expanding the relationship to include patients' family members, on whom the nurses relied for information and input.

Job crafting will occur whether or not it is encouraged by management. However, it will occur more frequently if management encourages it by selecting staff who are more likely to craft or fashion their jobs and then rewarding those who do. Customer-focused healthcare organizations need to identify and hire staff who will craft their jobs to meet customer needs in ways that may not be formally specified. How this might be done is covered in the remainder of this chapter and in subsequent chapters.

## RECRUITMENT PROCESS

### Internal Candidates
Jobs can be filled by recruiting either from inside or outside the organization. If suitable internal candidates are available, most organizations prefer inside recruitment.

### *The Known Quantity*
The internal candidate is a known quantity. That person's performance is available for observation and evaluation every day, and the person's strengths and weaknesses are known. Some people interview well and some poorly, so organizations can make wrong assumptions about any candidate's qualities. But the good and bad qualities of a person observed every day are evident, so organizations are fully aware. Perhaps even more important, the present employee has shown loyalty to the organization by staying on and seeking higher levels of responsibility and challenge.

Because customer relationships are so important in healthcare organizations, promoting current employees who have demonstrated job skills and have also proven that they understand and can interact successfully with the organization's customer base makes even more sense. If the job to be filled is at the managerial or supervisory level, another experience-related point in favor of hiring internally is that internal candidates have had the same experience, which is derived from the philosophy that one cannot manage someone doing something one has never done. The core technology of healthcare organizations is providing service, and unless managerial candidates have had experience in providing service, felt the pressure of patients in their faces, and found ways to resolve patient problems on the spot, they cannot really know what the job entails and hence cannot manage those who go through the experience.

Because the manager has to establish and sustain a customer-focused culture within the organization, the candidate needs to have real examples from his or her own real experience that help guide employees on how to provide excellent patient service. Although healthcare experience and real-life examples can be acquired in one organization and brought to another, the most relevant experience and examples are obviously those that are acquired within the organization one works for.

### Cultural Compatibility

The internal candidates already know the company's beliefs and values and have proven themselves comfortable in that culture. The cultural learning curve for new hires is substantially reduced when the organization promotes its own people as they already know the political structure, the corporate goals, and the way things get done. External hires still have to figure out what the organization really expects from them, while the internal candidates already know what management really believes in and rewards. As service expert Len Berry puts it, excellent companies "hire entry-level people who share the company's values and, based on performance and leadership potential, promote them into positions of greater responsibility."[27]

Church-based healthcare organizations promote people from within who share the same religious values for this reason. For example, Baptist Hospital in Birmingham, Alabama, gives preference to internal candidates who have demonstrated that they "live the mission." Candidates need not be members of any particular religious denomination, but they must demonstrate by their behavior that they "buy into" the organization's value of Christian service.

### Internal Search Strategies

A pool of internal candidates can be created in several ways. Many organizations use job-posting services, hotlines, newsletters, or other communication means to let eligible employees know about job opportunities throughout the organization. Some large hospital chains have created an electronic version of the traditional job-posting service by building a comprehensive database of jobs and employees looking for jobs. When a hospital in Boston has a vacancy for a cystoscopy technician, the manager can advertise for internal applicants through this online job vacancy service. All present employees looking for new opportunities within the system can list themselves and their qualifications on this online service. The Boston hospital manager can advertise for a licensed practical nurse (LPN) who is geographically nearby, has five years of experience, and is a graduate of a recognized LPN program. The database then produces a list of the top eligible and available candidates ranked according to the manager's criteria. The manager then contacts the leading candidates and explores the employment relationship further.

Such online, real-time, internal job hotlines are quickly growing even more sophisticated. Some in-house systems can now interface with college and university placement services, governmental employment services, and industry hotlines, permitting candidates to identify job opportunities with one stop on the Internet and organizations to post job openings for both internal and external candidates to consider.

### External Candidates

Not every job can be filled by an internal candidate nor do organizations always want to promote only from within. External candidates are desirable when the particular competency needed in a particular job is unavailable among the existing employees or when the organization thinks that an external viewpoint might help change a corporate culture that has become too inbred to consider new ideas. Healthcare organizations must recruit externally because nearly all clinical skills are taught in university programs and consist of academic training and clinical applications. Several major external search strategies are listed in Figure 6.1.

A major challenge for healthcare organizations is how to build a qualified labor pool when the competition for employees is strong. How can organizations provide outstanding service quality under such competitive conditions? Only by making creative use of all the available external recruitment strategies to build a large and talented pool of applicants. This means identifying the "best" recruitment sources for particular occupations, considering both the quantity and the quality of applicants generated.

The major problem that all healthcare managers are facing and will continue to face is the continuing staff shortages that have become the

**Figure 6.1. Strategies for External Recruitment**

**Advertising:** A message containing general information about the job and the organization is placed in various media (e.g., newspapers, radio, television). These media can have either a local, regional, or national audience and can serve the general public or a specific segment of population.

**Associations and Unions:** Many healthcare occupations have state, regional, or national associations that hold meetings, publish newsletters, and represent the interests of the occupation. Such associations frequently have job-placement units.

**Colleges and Secondary Schools:** Organization members are sent to schools to meet with individuals or groups of students to provide specific information about the organization or the job and to answer any questions. They may also perform the first review of applicants.

**Employee Referral Programs:** A word-of-mouth technique in which employees are provided with information about job openings and asked to refer individuals to the company. Often the employee is given a bonus if the individual who is referred is employed. Should the applicant be rejected, the employee is given a brief explanation.

**Employment Agencies:** Contact is made with agencies whose main purpose is to locate job seekers. The healthcare organization provides information to the agency about the job, which is then passed along by the agency to its clients. Clients can be either employed or unemployed. Agencies can be either public or private. Fees may be charged to either or both the client seeking a job and the organization seeking applicants.

**Walk-ins:** Although they may not literally walk in, unsolicited individuals frequently initiate contact with the healthcare organization. The number depends on such factors as the level of the positions open, the image of the organization, the frequency of job openings, and the physical proximity of the labor market.

**Employment Events, Job Fairs, Career Fairs:** A specially organized event to attract a large number of potential candidates to a specific location on a certain day to talk about and interview for jobs. These events can be held in conjunction with other organizations and may be in one's own labor market or in a distant location where unemployment is high. Job fairs are also increasingly being held in central business-district locations where any potential employee can talk to recruiters from sponsoring organizations.

*Source:* From *Human Resource Selection*, 5th edition, © 2001. Reprinted with permission of South-Western College Publishing, a division of Thomson Learning. Fax 800 730–2215.

healthcare crisis today. Shortages of technicians of all types are prevalent countrywide,[28] but perhaps the most dangerous and alarming kind of shortage is that of registered nurses. Florida reports that one of every ten positions for registered nurses went unfilled statewide, and turnover was 46 percent in some sections of Florida in 1998. The problem of nurse recruitment today (2002) is even worse. In specialty units, like intensive care, the emergency room, and pediatrics, the problem is life threatening.[29] A hospital president and CEO says that the nursing shortage is serious enough that it is having an effect on patient care in many hospitals.[30]

As a consequence of these shortages, healthcare organizations that aspire to provide outstanding customer service must make themselves the employer of choice and wage a multifront effort in their recruiting approach. The overall recruitment effort cannot offer only one "perk" (or perquisite) such as a sign-on bonus. Organizations need to combine perks with incentives that keep staff on the job after the bonus has been received. The organization should develop a total package that appeals to a wide variety of people. The package should include financial benefits, a flexible time-off schedule, flexible work schedules, and other incentives that current employees desire.

Some organizations form a cooperative program with college or graduate students to encourage the students to work for them after they graduate. New graduates are more likely to work for an organization where they are already employed, know their way around, and have made friends. Other organizations offer finder's fees to people (staff, patients, and others) who help recruit new staff members who stay for at least one year. Current employees have also been part of focus groups to determine the best selling features of a particular organization. These viewpoints might also be helpful in suggesting things organizations can do that will help to recruit and retain employees.

### Advertising

Besides the typical help-wanted ads in the newspaper and the less typical ads in magazines and weeklies, aggressive healthcare recruiters use more creative means. These creative means include programs such as an employee referral program, which provides a cash bonus to employees who refer candidates who are subsequently hired and retained. Another approach is to seek out and rehire employees who left on good terms; such individuals know the system already and do not need extensive orientation and retraining.

These creative approaches allow recruiters to reach people who may not read the want ads, may not be thinking about changing jobs, or may not even be thinking about working. Just as marketers segment their markets to find likely candidates for their products and services, healthcare employment managers increasingly segment their markets to reach and attract job candidates. As seen in Figure 6.1, there are many different ways to recruit, but some of them may be more useful than others in finding customer-oriented candidates in the employee segment that the organization hopes to reach.

### Professional Networks and Placement Services

Managers of healthcare organizations join professional organizations not only to advance their professional interests but also to find good employees and to find good ideas about how to find good employees. The amount of movement back and forth across healthcare organizations causes these networks and services to be strong, accurate, and informative. Thus, doctors join the American Medical Association, nurses join the American Nursing Association, and healthcare managers join the American College of Healthcare Executives or Medical Group Management Association to learn more about their professional interests and to network with others.

### Student Recruiting

An important strategy for finding the many young professionals that the healthcare industry needs is student recruiting. A number of different internship and residency programs develop pools of potential employees among young people who are either still in school or who have recently graduated. Healthcare organizations frequently get students to work for them as part of a required school experience, such as a cooperative (mentioned earlier), internship, or work-experience program. Most schools of health science, health administration, nursing, and medicine require their students to get some real-world work experience while they are taking academic coursework. Some clinical areas even require postacademic residencies or internships as part of their licensing requirements. The student not only makes some money to help cover college costs but benefits from seeing the practical application of classroom theory in the "real world." The healthcare organization also benefits from these programs as it gains access to an eager, young, trained labor pool that does not expect a permanent employment commitment. The smart organizations, however, keep a close eye on these student employees and make sure that impressive student workers know of their interest. They may offer them scholarships or put them in special work experiences that prepare them to be fully trained employees upon graduation.

For their clinical training, students seek out organizations that are known to have carefully designed work-experience programs that provide real learning opportunities and growth challenges. The point is that student recruitment programs can be designed and used to recruit good employees who learn, earn, and contribute to the organization. The best organizations know how to use these work-experience programs to identify the better students and keep them after they graduate. Because many of these same organizations also place a high premium on "dues paying," these programs give the students the opportunity to pay their dues in entry-level jobs while they are still in school, which put them in a better position for promotion to a higher-level and better-paying job by the time they graduate.

### Employee Referrals

The easiest way to get the kind of new employees you want is to ask your star employees to find them. Your good employees know what your organization is like, perform well in it, obviously like working for you, and can therefore be your best recruiters and spokespersons in the labor market. A bonus of this strategy is that existing employees who bring in their friends feel responsible for them and their performance. They exert positive peer pressure and encourage the new employees they sponsored to do well, which works to the organization's benefit. Some organizations pay a bounty to their existing employees if they bring in a job candidate who is hired and stays through a probationary period. The reward might be monetary or it can be something else that has value to employees such as a free weekend trip to a nice resort area, dinner at a special place, or some other inducement.

### Employers of Choice

An organization's reputation can also aid in recruitment. As authors Benjamin Schneider and David Bowen note, employers who have a positive image in the community and a satisfied and motivated workforce have a deep applicant pool from which they can pick the best.[31] These "employers of choice" are good neighbors to the community and have established their reputation for hiring and developing people for the long term. Their mentality, according to Len Berry, is to "recruit and hire well, offer a viable, expandable job, and expect most people to be productive, long-term employees. Invest in these people rather than save on those who leave."[32] In other words, hold out for the best employees, invest in those people so they grow and develop, keep them challenged and motivated in their current jobs, and offer them future opportunities with the organization.

Selling a healthcare employment opportunity is like selling the healthcare experience. If the company is known for offering its people high-quality job and career opportunities, it will attract high-quality applicants and build a pool of people who prefer to work for it rather than for the competition. Quint Studer of Baptist Hospital in Pensacola, Florida, took over a hospital with high turnover and low staff morale. Within three years, Studer's strategy of emphasizing customer service by focusing on employee selection, training, and rewards had reduced turnover by 67 percent and, according to employee satisfaction surveys, tripled the level of morale.[33] This facility became the "employer of choice" for northwest Florida.

In 2001, Griffin Hospital, a 160-bed acute care facility in Derby, Connecticut, was named one of the 100 best companies to work for by *Fortune* magazine. Its turnover and vacancy rates are half of the industry's average.[34] Griffin's CEO believes its success is due in large part to the hospital's commitment to patient-centered care. This approach to care aligns with the core philosophy of Planetree, a not-for-profit organization born of the consumer-movement philosophy of personalizing, harmonizing, and demystifying the healthcare experience for patients and their families. All staff members are required to attend a two-day retreat that is designed to immerse them in the patient experience.[35] At the retreat, employees engage in "helplessness" and "trustbuilding" exercises by feeding each other and providing other basic care. They stay in rooms that are semi-private, share bathrooms, and have no food choices. The purpose of the retreat is to show staff what the patient experience is like so that staff can be more sensitive to patient needs. The result is more satisfied patients and staff and lower staff-turnover rates.

### The Competition

Author Scott Gross adds another recruitment strategy: Go seek out excellent employees doing similar service jobs elsewhere.[36] Again, unlike the manufacturing sector where a potential employer is not going to be able to walk in and watch the best assembly-line workers work, many patient-contact employees can be observed relatively easily. Every time you visit someone receiving healthcare, if you are receiving care, at a different facility, you can evaluate the service provider as a potential employee in your own organization. Gross hands his business card to those that really impress him and tells them to come see him if they are interested in another job. Hiring people because you saw them working well elsewhere has the additional advantage of starting off the new relationship on excellent terms. New employees found in this way will be flattered that you sought them out and asked. Everyone likes to be recognized. By asking people to consider a job opportunity, you do a better job of recognizing than their boss has done, and the result may very well be the recruitment of some excellent candidates.

A variation on this strategy is to ask good people, whether they work for you or not, if they know about good people. A surprisingly large part of the existing workforce has a network of people who are like themselves or have similar jobs. Using the network to build a candidate pool can be a rewarding strategy.

### Callback
Candidates often enter the recruitment process but drop out before they can be interviewed or screened; some organizations call them back several months later to see if they are still interested. This callback is worthy because if people dropped out because they found another job, then after several months they may already be dissatisfied with their employer and/or may be ready for a change.

## SCREENING AND INTERVIEWING APPLICANTS

### The Application Form
Application forms are the first screen an employer should use in deciding whom to hire. A typical application form will include the applicant's past employment history, education level, possible conviction record, and similar demographic questions. The form should provide enough information to permit reasonable decisions about whom to keep in the pool and whom to drop. Obviously, a major tradeoff is involved here. The recruitment strategy should be designed to bring in as many legitimate candidates as possible. The advertising should

state the minimum required qualifications, work experience, or training. The application form serves as a preliminary check on whether or not the candidates do in fact have bona fide occupational qualifications, and they should really be bona fide to ensure that they do not lead unfairly to discriminatory hiring practices.

Sometimes the application form can be built into a job hotline, which applicants can call to find out about job openings and apply for those that interest them. The automated application and screening component of the hotline then collects basic information about the candidate. If the information given matches the organization's predetermined criteria, the automated interview ends with a request for a faxed or mailed resume. Sophisticated "optical character recognition" (OCR) systems can even scan the resumes, evaluate each candidate's suitability for the job, and have the summarized information ready for the employment manager the next time that person looks. These systems allow the employment function to operate 24 hours a day, 7 days a week; they guarantee that any applicant at any time will have an opportunity to be heard by the organization. Increasing numbers of people are working nontraditional hours. These "24/7" automated recruiting systems, which are just a phone call away from all potential applicants and particularly useful for people who may not be able to call during the usual work day, are a comparative advantage for those firms using them.

**The Interview**
If the applicant passes the initial screen, the organization will most often schedule an interview to see if the information on the application checks out, to see if the applicant seems to fit the organization, to tell the candidate what the job actually is, and to weed out applicants who do not really want to do the type of work the organization requires.[37] At Baptist Hospital in Pensacola, Florida, the first interview is structured to ask behavior-based questions and to tell candidates the standards to which they will be held as employees. Prospective employees are then asked to sign a document indicating that they will abide by the standards described. These standards of performance have been developed by employees and relate to such aspects as integrity, dependability, flexibility, and customer service. In the second interview, each applicant meets with at least two potential peer coworkers because the hospital believes that the peers should have a say in who their future coworkers will be.

Some believe that the right talents are the prerequisites for excellence in all roles. Talent is defined as any natural ability or repeated behavior that adds to a person's job performance.[38] It is a similar concept to the competencies discussed earlier in the chapter. The difference between an outstanding doctor and a good one (assuming equal clinical skills) may be the ability to communicate empathy, hope, and optimism to patients.

A separate interview focusing on applicant talent can serve as a supplement to the usual interview covering the job duties, work history, compensation, and the organization.[39] In the talent interview, the interview purpose should be made clear, the interview should be structured around the issue of relevant talents (i.e., customer orientation), and open-ended questions should be asked that mirror what the applicant will face on the job. Questions about hypothetical job situations should be broad enough to draw a range of responses. Ask candidates what kinds of roles they enjoy, find fulfilling, and have been able to learn quickly. Finally, ask for specific examples of past behavior reflecting the customer service values that the organization seeks to implement.

### The Background Check

Most healthcare organizations do police or background checks routinely to protect themselves and their patients. No organization that sends out its employees to provide an unsupervised service can afford to send out someone who has not been thoroughly checked out. But even if services are provided on the organization's premises, a background check is critical because employees are dealing directly with patients, with people. The healthcare industry is quite different from the manufacturing sector in this regard. A car does not care if a former car thief is part of the assembly team, but a hospital patient will care a great deal if the housekeeper is a former professional thief. Learning that you have hired a person who can do damage to your organization is not only embarrassing, it can cause legal troubles—a patient may sue you for not exercising due diligence in your hiring practices.

### Prior Work Performance

When hiring, Cadillac dealer and author Carl Sewell always finds out how well people have performed at their past and present jobs, figuring that if they have performed well in the past, they will probably perform well in the future.[40] His rule of thumb is to interview 25 people to find the one he wants to hire. In a competitive labor market like healthcare, a more realistic rule of thumb is to interview four people to find one good candidate; however, even this number may not be possible for all positions due to the tightness of the labor market. During interviews, Sewell measures candidates on five different dimensions: (1) history of success as a service-oriented person, (2) intelligence, (3) energy, (4) character, and (5) fit.[41] Because measuring energy and personality in an interview is hard, most interviews focus instead on clinical background, certification, and relevant experience. Although these clinical dimensions are vitally important for healthcare, Sewell's customer satisfaction dimensions are also vital to the modern healthcare organization.

### The Structured Interview

Structured interviews increase the likelihood that interviewers will assess all candidates according to the same criteria. When different interviewers interview many different candidates, consistency becomes both organizationally and legally important. A structured array of questions ensures that each interviewer collects the necessary personal and job-related data. Probing questions (e.g., "Tell me about yourself and why you're interested or qualified for this job") can sometimes add valuable information. They can also yield information that differs in quality and amount from candidate to candidate because of interviewer differences in ability to ask and interpret appropriate questions. A properly designed and administered structured interview ensures that the questions are job related, consistently scored, and asked of all candidates. Research shows that a well-done structured interview can be a valid predictor of job performance.[42]

A structured interview usually includes three types of questions. The first type is developed from *critical incidents*—positive or negative events that occur during a service encounter—that might be encountered on the job. A potential lab employee might have to respond to a hypothetical patient's question, "What are you going to do with that needle?" Scott Gross administers "Scott's No Fail 10-Percent Finder" test to prospective employees during an interview. He asks: "How many times in the past six months have you felt it necessary to get tough with a customer? Tell me about the worst incident."[43] He believes that the answers can tell him whether his potential employee is one of the 10 percent who loves to serve, one of the 85 percent who is average, or one of the 5 percent who does not have any interest in giving good service.

Here is a healthcare application of Gross's test. If the candidate says, "About twice a month, a patient tries to push me around. I tell the blankety-blank off," the interviewer will instantly cross that person off the list. If the candidate says, "I try to keep in mind that the patient is always right, but every now and then you get somebody who tries to take advantage and you have to throw this rule out the window," the candidate is probably a member of the great majority. If the candidate says, "I've learned never to get upset with a patient. The patient is always our guest, is probably under stress, and would probably rather be somewhere else. Even if the patient is wrong, I try to smooth the situation over," the interviewer has found a 10 percenter who truly believes in serving patients.[44]

The second type of question involves those related to clinical or other task competencies. For example, if the hospital is searching for someone to work at the admissions desk, questions will involve use of different admissions software packages and procedures for admitting patients, although admitting personnel basically do the same things across all hospitals. This part of the interview can be objectively scored, based on the candidate's correct and incorrect responses to job-related questions.

The third type of question focuses on the candidate's willingness to do the job as it is designed. The interviewer asks questions about the applicant's willingness to work overtime, long shifts, holidays, or weekends because many healthcare workers have to work when workers in other industries do not. If candidates say they cannot or will not be available when needed, then they are probably not a good fit.

## OTHER STAFFING CONSIDERATIONS

### Diversity

Benchmark healthcare organizations are interested in having diversified staffs, not just because of the legal and moral need to comply with antidiscrimination laws but because of three other reasons. First, thanks to advances in transportation and communication, a general state of economic prosperity, and the breaking down of many cultural and racial barriers, increasing numbers of patients are from diverse cultural and demographic populations. These diverse patients expect that service providers will be similar to themselves or will at least understand the expectations of people like themselves. They want service providers who speak their language, figuratively and perhaps literally. Many healthcare facilities in Orlando, Florida deliberately hire staff who are bilingual (i.e., English and Spanish) to facilitate communications with the large Hispanic population in the area. Staffing strategies should be designed to hire patient-contact employees who are sufficiently insightful to read cues indicating the expectations of patients from different cultures and backgrounds and flexible enough to meet those varied expectations.

Second, the healthcare organization's workforce may also reflect the diversity of its patient population. A typical healthcare employee no longer exists for whom the organization can design one-size-fits-all selection, training, and reward systems. Dual-career couples, same-sex relationships, single mothers with child care responsibilities, grown children with elder care responsibilities, and many other realities are apt to be represented in the healthcare organization's workforce. The manager of the modern healthcare organization must be sensitive to the needs of employees from these varied backgrounds and lifestyles.

Third, employing a diversified workforce by tapping all available segments of the general labor pool will result in the best workforce. In a competitive environment like the healthcare industry, all organizations must hire the best employees, regardless of background, cultural heritage, or other differences. Finding qualified, talented, motivated employees is not easy; recognizing the factors that make effective employees and ignoring those unrelated to employee performance is imperative. Some business organizations still do not fully appreciate the underutilized talent in many segments of the population. The best organizations gain a competitive advantage by seeking out and recruiting talent wherever it may be found.

Recognizing and appreciating diversity can be a stimulus to developing innovative ways to recruit. No matter how diverse the healthcare organization's workforce, however, the fact remains that patient-contact personnel will be different in most ways from the patients they serve. For example, most healthcare providers are younger than the patients. The organization must hire people who are adept at interacting with the variety of patients, who can take a reading of patient expectations during the first few moments of the initial service encounter, and who enjoy the challenge of providing personalized service to today's multicultural healthcare clientele.

### Retention

Although recruiting and selecting excellent customer-focused staff are highly desirable, little will be accomplished if the healthcare facility does not have a high retention rate. Experienced employees know how to get the job done, how to recognize and solve problems, and whom to go to if they have a problem they cannot handle alone.

Practices that create or maintain a highly loyal workforce with high retention also produce customer retention, according to a National Institute of Business Management study.[45] Their analysis suggests that an organization with employee turnover of 10 percent or less has as much as a 10 percent customer retention rate advantage over another organization with employee turnover of 15 percent or more. A factor that the study found to be critically important to employees' willingness to commit to an organization is the belief that the organization treats them fairly, considers their interests, and shares financial success with them.

Yet healthcare executives constantly struggle between controlling costs while providing patients with a consistent level of high-quality care. They frequently find it necessary to cut costs in ways that may increase staff workloads, which often leads to higher turnover. In 2001, the consulting firm Numeroff and Associates surveyed human resources administrators at America's best hospitals as listed by HCIA-Sachs, a healthcare information company, to learn how these hospitals retained their top employees.[46] Results indicated that providing advancement opportunities, fair pay and competitive salaries, and frequent and effective communication were the important retention factors. The bottom line is that satisfied employees provide higher quality service to their customers, which results in higher patient satisfaction and retention levels.

Authors Marcus Buckingham and Curt Coffman believe that "managers trump companies" when it comes to employee retention.[47] Their data indicate that each individual's immediate manager and what that manager does or does not do is more important in retention than the factors that cause any organization to be identified on any "best of" list. Simply, working for a great manager in a traditional organization is better than working for a terrible manager in an employee-focused organization. A great manager maximizes retention by informing subordinates of what is expected of them, providing necessary material and equipment, allowing employees to what they do best, recognizing and praising good work, caring about each employee, and encouraging the development of each employee.

## CONCLUSION

Although finding and hiring the right person is challenging for all organizations, it is especially difficult for those in the healthcare industry. Many jobs in other fields require definable skills that can be identified, measured, and tested; the healthcare industry has the extra challenge of ensuring that the patient-contact employees they hire are not only competent in the clinical and administrative skills but also have the interpersonal skills necessary to interact successfully with the patient and the creative skills to fix the inevitable patient problems. The difference between a good and great healthcare experience is so often the indefinable extra that patient-contact employees can bring to the experience. Finding, hiring, training, and rewarding the employee who happily and naturally gives that extra is one of the biggest challenges for healthcare organizations.

The best healthcare organizations view staff recruitment and retention as the responsibility of each staff member and as an organizational priority. As such, it is included in the agenda at every board meeting and it is included in the performance evaluation of each manager and supervisor.

## LESSONS LEARNED

1. Find the best people, train the rest.
2. Recruit creatively, use the major search strategies, and think of other means.
3. Build a large candidate pool; it will improve the odds of finding good people.
4. Do careful background checks on all applicants prior to hiring.
5. Identify and select the customer-focused competencies or talents.
6. Know and hire the knowledge, skills, and abilities necessary to provide outstanding healthcare experiences.
7. Look for clinical competence, strong interpersonal skills, and creative problem-solving ability.
8. Be the "employer of choice" in your local market.
9. Use peer coworkers in the selection interview.
10. Focus on retention of top performers by identifying and providing what they value most highly.
11. Make staff recruitment and retention one of the highest organizational priorities.

## NOTES

1. Brownson, K., and R.L. Harriman. 2000. "Recruiting and Retaining Staff in the Twenty-First Century." *Hospital Material Management Quarterly* 22 (2): 34–44.

2. Roman, L. 1998. "Lots of Help Wanted: Hospitals Scramble to Recruit." *Memphis Business Journal* 20 (29): 1–2.

3. Boyles, P. 1998. "Labor Crisis Looms With Shortage of Direct Health Care Providers." *New Hampshire Business Review* 20 (35): 31–32.

4. Kettlitz, G., I. Zbib, and J. Motwant. 1997. "Reducing Nurse Aide Turnover Through the Use of Weighted Application Blank Procedures." *Health Care Supervisor* 16 (2): 41–47.

5. Steinhauer, J. 2000. "Shortage of Health Care Workers Keeps Growing." *New York Times* (December 25): A1, A17.

6. *Ibid.*, PA1.

7. Curtis, R. 1999. "Nurse Shortage Now Critical." *Business Courier* 15 (41): 3–4; A. Goldstein. 1999. "Shady Grove Doctors Warn of Hospital Lapses." *The Washington Post* (October 17): C1.

8. Gross, T. S. 1991. *Positively Outrageous Service*, p. 159. New York: Warner Books.

9. Pfeffer, J. 1998. *The Human Equation: Building Profits by Putting People First.* Boston: Harvard Business School Press.

10. Decker, P. J. 1999. "The Hidden Competencies of Healthcare: Why Self-Esteem, Accountability, and Professionalism May Affect Hospital Customer Satisfaction Scores." *Hospital Topics* 77 (1): 14–26.

11. Decker, P. J., M. Strader, and B. Wise. 1997. "Beyond JCAHO: Using Competency Models to Improve Healthcare Organizations." *Hospital Topics* 75 (1): 23–28.

12. Decker, P. J. 1999. "The Hidden Competencies of Healthcare: Why Self-Esteem, Accountability, and Professionalism May Affect Hospital Customer Satisfaction Scores." *Hospital Topics* 77 (1): 14–26.

13. Decker, P. J., M. Strader, and B. Wise. 1997. "Beyond JCAHO: Using Competency Models to Improve Healthcare Organizations." *Hospital Topics* 75 (1): 23–28; P. J. Decker, M. Strader, and B. Wise. 1997. "Beyond JCAHO: Using Competency Models to Improve Healthcare Organizations: Part 2: Developing Competence Assessment Systems." *Hospital Topics* 75 (2): 10–17.

14. Spencer, L. M., and S. M. Spencer. 1993. *Competence at Work*. New York: John Wiley and Sons.

15. Decker, P. J. 1999. "The Hidden Competencies of Healthcare: Why Self-Esteem, Accountability, and Professionalism May Affect Hospital Customer Satisfaction Scores." *Hospital Topics* 77 (1): 14–26.

16. *Ibid.*

17. Mansfield, R. 1996. "Building Competency Models: Approaches for HR Professionals." *Human Resource Management* 35 (1): 10.

18. Schneider, B., and D. E. Bowen. 1995. *Winning the Service Game.* Boston: Harvard Business School Press.

19. Carraher, S. M. et al. 1995. "The Assessment of Service-Orientation with Biodata." In *Proceedings: Southern Management Association,* p. 172. Valdosta, GA: Southern Management Association.

20. Brinker, N., and D. T. Phillips. 1996. *On the Brink: The Life and Leadership of Norman Brinker,* p. 191. Arlington, TX: The Summit Publishing Group.

21. Gomez-Mejia, L. R. et al. 1996. *Managing Human Resources,* p. 210. Englewood Cliffs, NJ: Prentice-Hall.

22. Ones, D. S., and C. Viswesvaran. 1996. "What Do Pre-Employment Customer-Service Scales Measure? Explorations in Construct Validity and Implications for Personnel Selection." Paper presented at the 11th annual conference of the Society of Industrial and Organizational Psychology, San Diego.

23. For some measures that can help identify a service orientation in job candidates, see J. Hogan, R. Hogan, and C. M. Busch. 1984. "How to Measure Service Orientation." *Journal of Applied Psychology* 69 (1): 167–173; R. L. Frei and M. A. McDaniel. 1998. "Validity of Customer Service Measures in Personnel Selection: A Review of Criterion and Construct Evidence." *Organization Behavior and Human Performance* 23 (1): 1–27.

24. Wrzesniewski, A., and J. E. Dutton. 2001. "Crafting a Job: Revisioning Employees as Active Crafters of Their Work." *Academy of Management Review* 26 (2): 179–201.

25. Dutton, J. E., G. Debebe, and A. Wrzesniewski. 2000. "A Social Valuing Perspective on Relationship Sensemaking." Working Paper. University of Michigan, Ann Arbor.

26. Benner, P., C. A. Tanner, and C. A. Chelsea. 1996. *Expertise in Nursing Practice.* New York: Springer; R. Jacques. 1993. "Untheorized Dimensions of Caring Work: Caring as Structural Practice and Caring as a Way of Seeing." *Nursing Administration Quarterly* 17 (2): 1–10.

27. Berry, L. L. 1999. *Discovering the Soul of Service: The Nine Drivers of Sustainable Business Success,* p. 45. New York: The Free Press.

28. Brownson, K., and R.L. Harriman. 2000. "Recruiting and Retaining Staff in the Twenty-First Century." *Hospital Material Management Quarterly* 22 (2): 34–44.

29. Lundine, S. 1998. "Hospitals Reporting Statewide Nursing Shortage." *Orlando Business Journal* 15 (6): 1–2; General Accounting Office. 2001. "Nursing Workforce: Emerging Nurse Shortages Due to Multiple Factors." Washington, DC: General Accounting Office

30. Curtis, R. 1999. "Nurse Shortage Now Critical." *Business Courier* 15 (41): 3–4; A. Goldstein. 1999. "Shady Grove Doctors Warn of Hospital Lapses." *The Washington Post* (October 17): C1.

31. Schneider, B., and D. E. Bowen. 1995. *Winning the Service Game*, p. 115. Boston: Harvard Business School Press.

32. Berry, L. L. 1995. *On Great Service: A Framework for Action*, p. 171. New York: The Free Press.

33. Studer, Q., and G. Boylan. 2000. "Turning Customer Satisfaction into Bottom-Line Results." Presented by the Baptist Health Care Leadership Institute, Pensacola, Florida, June 2000.

34. Wolf, E. J. 2001. "Four Strategies for Successful Recruitment and Retention." *Healthcare Executive* 16 (4): 14–18.

35. *Ibid.*

36. Gross, T. S. 1991. *Positively Outrageous Service*, p. 159. New York: Warner Books.

37. Studer, Q., and G. Boylan. 2000. "Turn Customer Satisfaction Into Bottom-Line Results." Presented by the Baptist Health Care Leadership Institute, Pensacola, Florida, June 2000.

38. Buckingham, M., and C. Coffman. 1999. *First Break All the Rules: What the World's Greatest Managers Do Differently*. New York: Simon and Schuster.

39. *Ibid.*

40. Sewell, C., and P. B. Brown. 1990. *Customers for Life*, pp. 68–69. New York: Pocket Books.

41. *Ibid.*

42. Gomez-Mejia, L. R. et al. 1996. *Managing Human Resources*, p. 212. Englewood Cliffs, NJ: Prentice-Hall.

43. Gross, T. S. 1991. *Positively Outrageous Service*, pp. 164–65. New York: Warner Books.

44. *Ibid.*, pp. 165–66.

45. National Institute of Business Management. 2001. "Good HR Boosts Customer Retention." *Success in Recruiting and Retaining* 1 (1): 8.

46. Numeroff, R. E. 2001. "Retaining Employees: Lessons From the Best." *Healthcare Executive* 16 (2): 62–63.

47. Buckingham, M., and C. Coffman. 1999. *First Break All the Rules: What the World's Greatest Managers Do Differently.* New York: Simon and Schuster.

*Chapter 7*

# Training for Customer Service

Healthcare Principle: *Train your employees, then train them some more*

The dominant competitive weapon of the 21st century will be the education and skills of the workforce.

—*Lester Thurow, Dean, MIT Sloan School of Management*

SERVICE EXPERT LEN BERRY has identified five key factors that customers use to judge the overall quality of service.[1] Of these five, four are directly related to the ability of the service employee to deliver the service in the way the customer expects, and the fifth—*tangibles*— includes the appearance of the service employee. These four are *reliability* (the organization's and employee's ability to deliver the service consistently, reliably, and accurately); *responsiveness* (the employee's willingness to provide prompt service and help customers); *assurance* (the employee's knowledge, courtesy, and ability to convey trust); and *empathy* (the employee's willingness to provide caring and individualized attention to each customer).

The nonhuman, inanimate aspects of healthcare, such as the setting and the equipment, are clearly important in forming the patient's impression of the total experience. But the individual service providers, from the nurse's aide to the specialized surgeon, are the ones who can either make or break the organization's relationship with the patient in each and every encounter or moment of truth. Therefore, these encounters cannot be left to chance or the good intentions of employees.

For the medical staff to design an efficient clinical care system and the human resources department to select the right people are not enough. Healthcare organizations that consistently deliver high-quality healthcare experiences also extensively and continuously train their employees. Excellent healthcare organizations recognize the value of spending the necessary time and money on preventing service failures (and occasional disasters) and know that an excellent way to do so is to invest in management and staff training and development. In this chapter, we explore the elements of training, the factors to consider in developing a training program, and the concept of employee development.

## EMPLOYEE TRAINING

Although the average company that engages in training spends an amount equal to 1.5 percent of its payroll on training-related efforts, the best organizations spend a lot more. A commonly accepted rule of thumb is that each training dollar yields $30 in productivity gains over the next three years,[2] and the outstanding service providers are willing to make the investment to receive these productivity outcomes.

Benefits of customer service skills training may be a measured increase in patient satisfaction to healthcare professionals and substantial competitive market advantages to healthcare organizations implementing the training. One example substantiating these benefits is a study involving the emergency department at Inova Fairfax Hospital in Falls Church, Virginia. After providing eight hours of customer service training to all emergency department staff involved in patient contact (physicians, nurses, ED technicians, registration personnel, core secretaries, social workers, ED radiology, and ED respiratory therapy), researchers were able to show a link between this training and improved patient satisfaction and improved ratings of physician and nurse skill.[3]

Healthcare organizations have the special challenge of not only providing training on required job functions and clinical skills but also teaching service providers how to interact positively with patients and how to solve the inevitable problems creatively. Of course, patient-service employees must be trained in how to do the assigned clinical tasks, but they must also be trained to do it at the same consistently high level of quality for each patient in real time, with many different people looking over their shoulders, while maintaining a high level of customer service. This is a major training task; it goes far beyond the simple requirements of training someone in how to take an x-ray, draw blood, or register a new patient.

Equipping patient-service employees with scripts to be able to respond and show they care is not enough. These frontline employees must also be armed with knowledge and resources and must be empowered to address patient concerns directly and immediately so they can provide solutions, answers, and thus high-quality customer service.

Managers of clinically excellent healthcare organizations may wonder if it is really worth the time, effort, and money it costs to mount a serious and sustainable customer service training program effort. Baptist Hospital in Pensacola, Florida, confronted these concerns and came up with responses to each of six possible objections to customer service training. These are summarized in Table 7.1. Baptist Hospital's process for creating a customer-focused culture involves defining the desired culture, identifying the key competencies needed by members of the leadership team, providing a training program for leadership development, and then measuring and feeding back the tangible results regarding patient satisfaction to all organizational levels. The key leadership competencies to be developed were how to hire, fire, reward, and recognize staff associates. The training program focused on helping the leadership team do a better job in these areas.

## ELEMENTS OF TRAINING

Healthcare service providers should be taught the organization's values, practices, strategies, products, and policies to help them figure out what to do when the patient is unhappy and come up with solutions to service problems. Unless they understand the corporate values and beliefs, employees will not understand what the company expects them to do. Because the patient defines the quality and value of the healthcare experience, service providers should also learn about their patients' expectations, competitors' services and strategies, industry trends and developments, and the general business environment.[4] Even an x-ray technician needs to know something besides how to operate the machine to meet the service expectations of the patient on the x-ray table.

Healthcare consultant Patricia Spath has helped corporations improve their training programs for 25 years.[5] Her specialty is healthcare training. Based on her experience, she offers five guidelines for successful training programs:

1. *Set clear objectives.* If clear and specific objectives are not set, people will not know what to work toward. An example of a clear objective is

**Table 7.1  Barriers to and Benefits of Supporting Employee Customer Service Training Programs at Baptist Hospital**

| Barriers | Benefits |
|---|---|
| 1. "We don't need to." | • Sets sustainable results<br>• Lives values |
| 2. "We don't have enough time." | • It's the right thing to do<br>• Helps improve employee and patient satisfaction |
| 3. "We cannot be gone from the department." | • Shares responsibility and creates ownership<br>• Allows coordination and consistency within the leadership team |
| 4. "What more do I need to learn?" | • Speeds the skill set<br>• Tailor-made for the organization |
| 5. "It's too costly." | • Not as costly as having poor leaders create lawsuits.<br>• Creates a team that can adjust to environmental changes |
| 6. "We already do it." | • Raises the bar<br>• Networking builds relationships, trust, and support<br>• Creates a "built-to-last" culture |

*Source:* Reprinted with permission from Baptist Health Care Leadership Institute. "Turning Customer Satisfaction into Bottom-Line Results," presentation by Q. Studer and G. Boylan, July 8–9, 2000, Pensacola, Florida.

to cut the errors that occur during the delivery of drugs to patients. This objective is important because the National Academy of Sciences reports that more than 98,000 deaths a year result from medical errors.

2. *Show that training adds value to staff members.* Staff members need to see that the training will help them personally. Providing staff members with a chance to grow will increase the retention rate.

3. *Have role-playing sessions.* Realistic role playing can help teach a staff member and allow assessment of that individual's under-

standing of the material. Different staff members can play different roles to better understand the perspective of each customer.

4. *Set safeguards.* Without safeguards, things can go wrong. Knowledge is a critical safeguard in healthcare. Physicians and nurses, for example, can spot errors or potential problems in medications or treatment plans if they are trained and expected to do so. Each person in the patient care process should be trained to spot and correct errors.

5. *Hold employees accountable.* Set measurements to see how well employees are performing and how much more training they need.

Len Berry suggests five other guidelines, which complement Spath's, that he believes all service organizations should implement to develop an effective training strategy[6]:

1. Focus on critical skills and knowledge
2. Start strong and teach the big picture
3. Formalize learning as a process
4. Use multiple learning approaches
5. Seek continuous improvement

## Critical Skills

Critical skills are those skills that service employees are required to have. A healthcare organization can identify these critical skills through a systematic analysis of its service, delivery systems, and staff and also by asking its patients, employees, and external experts. Patients can tell you what employee skills are critical to their own satisfaction, and employees can be trained to ask patients what those skills are. Employees should become involved in the design of training, as they often have a pretty good idea of what skills are needed for their positions. Ask the best performers in the organization and study what they do and know, both clinically and nonclinically, internally and externally, to achieve at such a high level.

Disney has long been known for providing theme-park guests with a high-quality customer service experience. Less well known is the fact that Disney also offers a program specifically designed to teach healthcare organizations how to provide outstanding service to all of their customers.[7] Disney's "guestology" concept (see Chapter 2) translates well to healthcare, given that both the healthcare and hospitality industries strive to provide excellent experiences to their customers. The section below is an example of how Disney's principles of guest services were implemented in one healthcare facility.

Since 1991, East Jefferson General Hospital in Metairie, Louisiana, has been studying and adapting the Disney precepts of hospitality and service. According to Peter Betts, the hospital's president and chief executive officer: "From our perspective, guest relations is a definition of quality. We cannot expect our patients to be able to appraise the quality of radiology, laboratory, and operating rooms. A large part of the patients' perception of quality is how they're treated. Is the room clean? Are meals served on time? Does a nurse come when I press the button?"

East Jefferson has adopted Disney's four cardinal principles of guest relations: safety, courtesy, show, and efficiency. East Jefferson has altered them to suit its facility's needs. Beyond attending to the obvious safety concerns, the organization has also applied the safety precept to facilitate wayfinding, installing new signs to accommodate the weaker eyesight of their elderly customers. To execute the courtesy principle, the hospital has developed a "knock before entering" policy at patient rooms, allowing patients to give staff permission to come in. The show principle refers to everything the guest sees. To this end, East Jefferson has required that grounds remain manicured, everybody picks up trash in the halls, team members keep their work areas uncluttered, and murals are painted on the ceiling. Efficiency is enhanced by training staff to pick up litter, answer the phone by the third ring, and knock before entering.

As a result of East Jefferson's improvement efforts, it became the first healthcare institution to be awarded the first "Mouscar" (a takeoff on Oscar)—a trophy that honors companies that fully exemplify the guest-relations philosophy of the Walt Disney Company.[8]

## The Big Picture

The big picture includes the organization's overall values, purposes, culture, and the employee's role in the organization's overall success. New employees in any organization are usually eager to learn how their jobs fit into the big picture. This is why training must reinforce the big picture, letting employees know where they fit within the organization, what is expected of them in fulfilling the corporate mission, and how they can help contribute to achieving the company's goals. Employees perform more effectively when reminded of the value they bring to the organization, including the impact they have on customers.

In many organizations this big picture reinforcement occurs only periodically during infrequent training sessions or at the annual company gathering. Understandably, with the hectic pace of business, it is easy to lose sight of the big picture. But through ongoing communications (e.g., through staff meetings, customer and/or employee events, training programs, publications, or the intranet), companies can proactively reinforce the important contribution of the employees. For example, Baptist Hospital discovered that patient satisfaction improved significantly if patients received a personalized phone call after discharge. Key staff members were trained in when to call, what to say, and how to record the responses. Leaders also showed these staff members the link between the hospital's patient satisfaction goals and the telephone follow-ups. Once staff realized how important such a small task was to the big picture, they made time to make those calls in their busy schedules and phone follow-up increased dramatically.

When an employee is confronted after training with a problem or situation that does not exist in a handbook or a training manual, the core values and service culture learned and accepted during training should lead that employee to do the right thing for the patient. Because so many situations in healthcare are unplanned and unforeseeable, teaching the big picture and the core cultural values is especially critical. People who are taught the organization's values and beliefs from the first day are far more likely to make the right decision for the patient and the organization when a situation calls for decisive action.

If poor training becomes a regular occurrence in the organization, a domino effect can result: the organization's performance drops, which causes high turnover, which leads to low company morale and job dissatisfaction, which negatively affects the customer.[9] To improve the training process, training should be interactive, and participants should have a chance to offer suggestions for improvement. Training should also be an ongoing process beginning with a discussion of the corporate culture and continuing with a tie-in to the employee's regular job responsibilities. Training an employee once is not enough. Managers should continually reinforce what the organization is attempting to do in the area of customer service and the impact of the employee's responsibilities on the larger picture.

### Formalized Learning

Formalizing learning means building learning into the job, making learning mandatory for everyone, and institutionalizing that expectation. For example, employees should be sent regularly to learning opportunities on company time. By putting their money where their values are, organizations can send a strong message to their employees that learning is vital to the organization and that everyone is expected to participate. Motorola, an organization that has made a commitment to lifelong learning programs for its employees, has linked training programs to the company's strategic objectives. It set an objective of reducing product-development time and offered a course to teach its key employees how to achieve the objective.[10]

### Multiple Learning Approaches

Using a variety of learning approaches is important because people process information differently. No training opportunity should be left unexplored. In addition to traditional methods, organizations should sponsor book clubs, send employees out to observe exceptional organizations in the service industry, and constantly practice the necessary skills through a variety of means such as simulations, role playing, company skits, and case studies.

### Continuous Improvement

The initial training provides the knowledge, skills, and abilities that enable the employee to begin doing the job. But training should not stop there. Good service organizations and good employees both want continuing employee improvement, through on-the-job training and supervision, special training sessions, video demonstrations, and the full range of training methods available to modern organizations. Employees should also be cross-trained to enable them to perform another employee's responsibility when necessary. This additional training not only benefits the organization (as absence of a staff member will not slow down or stop service or productivity), it also benefits the employee (as he or she can learn another portable set of knowledge, skills, and abilities that give him or her an advantage in the present job or future job).

## DEVELOPMENT OF A TRAINING PROGRAM

### Needs Assessment

Training should always be preceded by a *needs assessment* to determine if perceived organizational problems or weaknesses are training related or the result of something else. Needs assessment answers the question "Will training give us what we need?" For example, a service problem might initially be identified as a training issue that can be solved by offering service providers a short training session. Upon closer examination, however, the issue might really turn out to be a fault in the nonhuman production part of the service delivery system. Constant patient complaints about slow and cold meal service might seem at first to point toward a training deficiency among the food service staff. But the real culprit may be that the elevators do not have enough capacity to transport all the meals in a timely way. All the service-provider training in the world cannot correct a flaw in some other part of the service delivery system.

Needs assessment takes place at three levels: organizational, task, and individual. Organizational analysis seeks to identify the skills and competencies that the organization as a whole needs and whether or not the organization already has them. For example, if the organizational analysis reveals a need for several more nursing supervisors on a unit and people to fill that need are not available, then the organization can initiate a training program to prepare either new or present employees to be nursing supervisors. Task analysis asks, "What tasks need to be performed?" "Are they being done well, or is training needed?" Most training in the healthcare industry is at the clinical task level, either to prepare new or newly promoted employees in how to perform the necessary clinical tasks or to retrain existing employees when clinical requirements change. Nonclinical functions related to customer service are less-frequently addressed. Individual analysis reviews the performance of people doing tasks to determine if they are performing up to job standards. Once the organization's needs at these three levels (i.e., organizational, task, and individual) have been assessed, training programs can be set up to meet them.

### Objectives

Needs assessment leads to identifying the objectives of training. If the needs analysis reveals a lack of an important employee skill, then the training objective should be to ensure that each employee needing that specific skill obtains it. For example, if patient comment cards show general dissatisfaction with the effectiveness of the personnel who register patients, then the training objective should be to improve the registration personnel's mastery of the registration procedures (assuming that the registration process itself is satisfactory and does not need to be redesigned). The point is that training should always be tied to solving a problem that can be identified, measured, and remedied through training.

### Feedback

Feedback about service problems or errors from patients or from medical staff, who are trained to check up on each other because the consequences of error can be so great, should serve as an important trigger for training. If patients or medical staff perceive a problem with how tasks are performed, then you do have a problem with your employee training, regardless of what you may think you have already done; you have a training need, whether your needs assessment has revealed it or not. Effective healthcare organizations constantly measure and monitor the performance of their people, systems, and services to identify training needs. Most problems that occur during delivery of the healthcare experience are caused by the delivery system staff. If managers learn about these problems quickly, either from patients, medical staff, or their own observations, they can quickly institute corrective training to get things right before other patients have the same problems.

Presenting current data on and future goals for patient satisfaction and a clear statement of customer service values can set the stage for a customer service training session. However, the impersonal nature of statistics sometimes permits managers and staff to explain poor patient satisfaction scores. The raw data may need to be personalized in some way. For example, at one facility, when tapes of focus groups held with former patients and community members were played, staff could then hear customers in a candid discussion about their experiences at the facility.[11] The human element made more of an impact than the numbers had done. Customer stories about staff, services, and departmental processes made a clear and lasting impression on those in attendance.

### External Versus Internal Training

Training can be provided by persons inside or outside the organization. Many healthcare organizations are not large enough to be able to afford their own training departments. Unless the operators of these smaller organizations are willing to do the training themselves, they generally turn to training consultants or to independent training organizations. These external training companies range from small, highly specialized organizations that have developed an expertise and a reputation in training within a specialized healthcare area to large organizations that offer training programs on just about any skill, area, or topic imaginable.

Universities and colleges are also important sources of healthcare training because their faculty members frequently have clinical and/or industry expertise as well as teaching experience and ability to convey what they know. Although many companies contract with training organizations that develop and deliver customized, onsite training, others send their employees to more generic, often less-expensive external programs. If the required training is in a highly specialized area or if only a few people need it, a company-specific program will probably not be worth the expenditure, so employees needing training are sent outside to get it. Advanced techniques of healthcare financial management, information systems design and use, and new marketing strategies are examples of specialized programs frequently offered through universities and professional associations. These programs can make up for their lack of specific application to particular healthcare organizations by being relatively inexpensive.

Many standardized customer service training programs exist that healthcare organizations can use to get the service message to employees. Organizations like the American College of Healthcare Executives, the Medical Group Management Association, and the American Medical Association offer educational seminars and training sessions focused on customer service.[12] In-house training departments are widely found in larger healthcare organizations, which usually have an internal unit that provides programs to employees. Adventist System of Florida, HealthSouth Corporation, and others have even set up their own "universities." Management consultants can also come into an organization to establish a customer service training program.

Although some organizations keep all training in-house to preserve organizational security and culture, the usual determinant of whether to use in-house or out-of-house training is cost. The number and location of employees who need training and the level of expertise that they need to acquire determine the cost of training. If only a few employees need highly technical training, the training will be expensive for the organization to deliver itself; if the employees are scattered at multiple locations, the training will cost even more. But if those employees need only some basic skills training, the organization will probably offer it internally. If many employees at a single location need training, the organization will probably find a way to do its own training.

### Employee Turnover

The high employee turnover prevalent in many healthcare organizations can influence the training decision. For instance, an organization of 1,000 employees that has an annual employee turnover rate of 200 percent has the same basic training requirements for new employees as an organization of 20,000 employees with a 10 percent turnover. Similarly, the level of expertise that the training must develop in these new employees will have an important impact on the cost of training. If considerable employee expertise will be required, training costs per employee will be high. Offering 100 training hours to 100 new employees who will be responsible for operating a sophisticated MRI system will cost about as much as offering 10 training hours to 1,000 employees hired to work as orderlies.

When the training costs associated with turnover are analyzed, as new employees have to be trained in skills that departing employees had already acquired, the importance of developing a managerial strategy that minimizes turnover and maximizes retention becomes apparent. For example, in the mid-1990s, Baptist Hospital had a large and expensive turnover problem. Quint Studer, the hospital's former CEO, investigated the problem and found that although the hospital's salary structure was competitive, the low levels of employee morale and high levels of patient dissatisfaction caused staff to seek job opportunities elsewhere. By introducing a customer satisfaction focus and by evaluating managers on morale levels and turnover rates among the employees they managed, Studer turned the situation around. Although part of the solution resulted from changing the managerial evaluation criteria (by adding employee morale levels and turnover rates to the evaluation system for individual managers), most of the success was a result of introducing training for all employees in how to increase patient and coworker satisfaction. Such training leads to lower levels of turnover, because employees are more likely to stay if they are serving satisfied customers. Unfortunately, many healthcare organizations are unwilling to invest sufficiently in this nonclinical training.

Employee turnover results in disappointed patients. Patients, especially those in long-term care facilities, frequently build relationships with service providers, and being served again and again by the same person is part of the value patients receive from the healthcare experience. If turnover is high, these relationships are destroyed or do not get built at all, and a powerful means of maintaining the satisfaction of these patients—the familiar face—is lost. As the "Cheers" television sitcom theme song reminds us, "You want to go where everybody knows your name."

## TRAINING METHODS

The most common training methods are live classroom presentations; video (either taped or through live feed); one-on-one supervised experiences (such as residencies and internships); home study; and computerized presentations (either online, interactive, or programmed). Although many training programs use a combination of these methods, emphasis has increased on the computerized and multimedia methods as computers have become more widely available and people have become more comfortable with them.

### Classroom Training

Live classroom presentations can follow a variety of formats; the most common of which is *lecture presentation.* In this format, a knowledgeable expert talks about concepts to employees in the hope that they can learn the necessary skill or knowledge within the available lecture time. This approach is based on the assumption that an expert can train the uninformed by speaking to them. For example, if one of the top performers in the company stands up and tells you what she knows, she does not typically believe that she needs to develop elaborate visual aids, computerized instructional screens, or anything else that takes time and money to produce. Because she has been there, done that, and done it well, she is obviously worth listening to and will have great credibility with all the employees she talks to. That is the assumption, and sometimes it can be true. However, this assumption has been disproved by research on how people learn. Regardless of those findings, those who use the lecture format do not seem deterred from continuing to do so. The lecture method does have advantages: It is inexpensive, time efficient, and to the point. Often, this format is combined with on-the-job training and mentoring to ensure that all the important points presented in the lecture sink in.

Another basic live classroom format is the *interactive case study*. Here, the organization provides learners with some case material for discussion. The material might be specific to the skill employees need to learn or it may be broad, relating to the more general skills of decision making or problem solving. In recent years, with the increasing emphasis on teams and team leadership, team-based training has become popular. Here, the leaderless group may be given a problem to solve or an issue to address, and the group is supposed to form into a collaborative problem-solving team.

With interactive, team-based training, people learn how to work together and how to discover and share the tremendous amount of knowledge that often exists within a team. Even in highly specialized training areas, teams can often teach each other specific skills more efficiently than a single instructor can, partly because the sum total of knowledge available in the group can fill in the gaps regarding how the skill is supposed to be performed. Teams also learn to monitor each other's ongoing performance, which should continue after the training program itself ends.[13] Smart managers take advantage of team knowledge; most managers, on the other hand, do not bother to find out about it.

### Video Training

Videos are frequently used in conjunction with a live presentation as a way to bring in new material beyond the expertise of the classroom presenter, to add variety to the presentation, or to make training available at odd times. For many healthcare organizations, videos are a cost-effective strategy. In larger organizations a centralized training department can make or buy video presentations and then ship them to individual units. Smaller, independent healthcare organizations can obtain a wealth of video instruction through commercial retailers or their trade and professional associations. With the high turnover in the healthcare industry, an instantly available video is useful and practical. For example, new employees can watch a video by themselves and learn the basics of how patient interaction, as one example, is supposed to be done. One of video's many advantages is it standardizes the presentation of the material so that everyone learns the same information.

A well-designed and well-produced video can do an excellent job of holding the new healthcare employee's attention, portraying outstanding role models of expected service behavior, and stressing important points. With professional actors in a video showing the correct means of providing patient service, a new employee can see far more easily what the expected behavior is than if an instructor talked for several hours. Truly, a picture is worth a thousand words when it comes to service training. The making of videos can be used as a reward technique. The organization can call on its best employees in the video subject area and have them create and produce the video. Such "homemade" videos show participants that the organization appreciates the quality of their job performance, gives them ownership in the training role, and provides live role models for their fellow employees to follow. Making a video is an enjoyable and status-enhancing recognition and reward for service jobs well done.

Live video is available to organizations willing to pay for the broadcast time or satellite feed capability. Live video is frequently what people are referring to when they talk about distance learning. Live satellite feeds and telephone line hook-ups permit the classroom to be in one location while the students may be at several other locations. The more elaborate versions of this technique have hook-ups that allow both sending and receiving of video and audio so that the learners and the instructor can talk back and forth, no matter where they are. The cost of live productions is still quite steep, so these training presentations are usually limited to important, new, or confidential information that must be sent to many people simultaneously.

New technology, diagnostic procedures, and clinical techniques are all appropriate subjects for live video. The increasing availability of teleconference facilities, advances in Internet technology, and the escalating costs of sending people to central training locations may make taped and live video presentations an increasingly desirable training option, especially when employees and service units are geographically dispersed. Video comes quite close to providing the just-in-time education and training that many organizations need in industries like healthcare, where the organization, the patient, the technology, and the employees change rapidly.

### Supervised Training

One-on-one *supervised experiences* are a typical on-the-job training method in healthcare. The trainee may complete an academic degree program and then be sent to a residency or internship program as part of the required preparation for a healthcare career. In such training, a supervising manager or clinician demonstrates, observes, corrects, and reviews the employee performing the required tasks. This classic learning-by-doing approach is often essential in the healthcare industry; the skills required to render proper treatment are often so unique, complex, or dependent on the needs of particular patients that the only effective training method is to put new employees on the job and let them learn it by doing it, under close supervision.

The traditional medical degree is a good illustration of this approach. After a lengthy academic experience, future doctors work in real hospitals treating real patients under the watchful eye of a residency supervisor. As experienced doctors help and teach new ones, so do experienced lab technicians supervise new technicians as they perform tests. The one-on-one technique is used extensively in healthcare because the many tasks to be performed are so varied and unique. Even if some healthcare tasks can be taught in the classroom, the variation among patients is so great that putting together a classroom experience or a training video to teach what is essentially unique is impossible. Much of the clinical training in healthcare adds up to a great deal of real-life one-on-one training experiences. Nobody will want to undergo a surgical procedure by a surgeon who has only read about the procedure in a book.

Some medical schools are beginning to train student interns to empathize with patients by having them assume the patient's role. At the Mayo Clinic in Rochester, Minnesota, Dr. Daryl Chutka has his first year medical students play the "Aging Game" to familiarize future physicians with the circumstances of the patients they will be treating.[14] For this game, students wear goggles to simulate cataracts, ear plugs to simulate loss of hearing, gloves to simulate arthritis, neck braces to simulate the nearly universal muscular stiffness of old age, and diapers to simulate adult incontinence. The students are then asked to read the labels on prescription containers through their goggles or count daily pills with fingers made less dexterous by rubber gloves. Near the course's end, students are placed in a mock nursing home, where other students are trained to act like uncaring ward attendants by failing to bring their food, shoving spoonfuls of applesauce into their mouths already full of marshmallows, or ignoring them altogether after wheeling them into a corner facing the wall. All of these experiences help medical students and future doctors to see the care process from the perspective of older patients.

All training programs focused on customer service should have staff members view the patient care they are providing from the patient's perspective. Such experience ensures that employees fully understand the customer and will therefore try to create the optimal healthcare experience.[15] Training programs should also incorporate group activities and team building exercises to increase communication and camaraderie within the organization.

## Computer-based Training

This training method can turn out to be the most exciting and valuable of all. Computers can be used for training in two ways. The simplest way is to use a stand-alone machine to teach a specific skill or body of knowledge by means of a preprogrammed presentation. To teach the relationship between seeing something and responding appropriately and immediately, a simple video game that practices eye-hand coordination skills can be used, such as games where the sight of an invader on the screen prompts the player to press a trigger that can eliminate the invader. This type of game is only one of the "edutainment" software programs that have shown considerable promise in the American educational system and hold even greater promise for the future training and development needs of the healthcare industry.

Training that is both fun and educational will reshape the nature of many corporate training efforts, dramatically improve the ability of organizations to teach all types of employees, and accommodate the wide cultural and linguistic variety of our increasingly diverse workforce. Computers never get frustrated with a slow learner and will stay with the student until the educational goal is reached.[16] The challenge is identifying computer-based training products that will help staff members improve their level of customer service.

Some skills can be taught by using computer simulation of the real situations that the new employee is expected to face. For example, if a hospital wants to teach a new employee how to handle patient complaints, it can provide the employee with simulation software with an interactive feature. This software will then take the employee through a simulated situation featuring an irate patient. The interactive feature of the software then leads the employee through the resolution process, allowing him or her to take steps to resolve the complaint. Afterward, the software program can then show the trainee the outcomes of his or her decisions, explaining the viability of each.

Similarly, a clinic can simulate its reception desk so trainees can practice using the reception desk equipment and responding to questions and requests from patients. After the trainee chooses a response by touching the screen at the designated decision point, the video will show what happened after that choice was made. Computer simulation use shows the organization's commitment to patient service and shows its investment in the employees because simulations help employees develop their decision-making abilities, improve outcomes, and show the personal and organizational rewards gained from giving good service. For example, if a patient in the simulation asks the way to a treatment room and the employee gives a highly service-oriented response —for example, personally escorting the patient to the treatment room—then the employee can be rewarded. Each option chosen in the simulated encounter can be rewarded (or not rewarded) by both patient and organization in a different way.

Medical schools have developed sophisticated computer programs that allow their students to perform virtual surgical operations. They use computer-connected gloves to operate on computer-generated patients. The surgeon can learn to perform a surgical procedure without actually touching a live patient or destroying a cadaver. Learning to do something without putting the patient, the organization's reputation, or oneself at risk is of course the point of a simulated experience. The more advanced simulations allow the employee to practice repeatedly until the performance meets desired standards and can then be done under supervision in real life.

Even more exciting than virtual-reality simulations and the increasing power of stand-alone computers to deliver useful and focused training are the new interactive training opportunities available through networked computers, mainly via the Internet. A Cisco Systems television ad says, "One day, training for every job on earth will be available on the Internet." The increased commercialization of the Internet has brought new applications. Now, live pictures and voice can both be sent over the Internet, which allows interaction between instructor and learner across the world. Expertise can be delivered anytime, anyplace, to anyone who is online, and online access is becoming increasingly available to everyone through many commercial providers. As the sophistication and quality of this type of training develop, it will increasingly challenge the monopoly of libraries as repositories of knowledge. Once on the Internet, the user can tap into the inventory of any major library anywhere or, if that is not sufficient, can tap into just about any expertise anywhere.

The more sophisticated applications of Internet technology mean that colleges and universities no longer have a monopoly on education in their geographical areas. These developments are a boon to the healthcare industry, as many healthcare organizations are multiunit and geographically spread out. Getting their employees to an educational center or a centralized training program is difficult and often impossible. However, getting these same employees to log on to the Internet is comparatively easy, and the amount of information, knowledge, and even training they can obtain though this medium is enormous.

### Other Methods

Training can be very specific or somewhat general. The specific is customarily used for entry-level employees who must quickly learn to perform a job skill well to justify their salary. General training can cover a wide variety of topics ranging from literacy to operating complex electronic systems. Some healthcare providers even find it necessary to teach employees basic bathroom usage and hygiene, such as teaching food handlers how to wash their hands.

The following are other methods of training that can be either specific or general:

- *Retraining.* This method is often made available to employees who have burned out, have become unable to perform their current jobs because of technological developments, or whose jobs have been eliminated. The rapid pace of technological change in healthcare has made retraining an increasingly important issue. Retraining strategies range from sending employees back to school to on-the-job instruction in new procedures. Some organizations, like those selling laser eye surgery equipment, send medical doctors to the buyers to teach proper procedures.
- *Role playing.* This method helps staff associates learn how best to relate to customers. Different scenarios can be role played for addressing a given customer service problem or issue, and then participants can select the most effective approach and role play

it. One example might be a patient who wants to go home today but needs to stay one more day. A question to consider in this scenario is: What are the options for communicating the "doctor's orders" and their rationale to the patient? The different approaches can then be role played to determine the most effective one. Other examples might include what to do or say when the patient, a physician, or a family member is angry or when a patient's family makes a request that is contrary to policy. Role playing can be helpful in dealing with situations such as the following:

1. How to advise patients or physicians that their requests cannot be granted
2. How to deal with angry or difficult patients
3. How to praise patients and motivate them to continue desirable behavior
4. How to recognize unacceptable staff language and behaviors
5. Where and how to voice concerns and problems
6. What *not* to say in the presence of patients
7. How to address patients and other customers

- *Orientation.* This training is for new employees and can include a segment on customer service that covers the organization's mission and vision, the importance of customer satisfaction, measurement of customer satisfaction, the new employees' roles' link to customer service, customer service standards, and the link between customer service standards and performance reviews.
- *Cross-functional training.* This method enlarges the workforce's capabilities to become multiskilled healthcare practitioners. For example, a Lakeland, Florida, hospital has developed a patient-centered healthcare delivery system that relies extensively on multiskilled practitioners to perform a wide range of tasks to meet patient needs. As a result, patients receive just as much care but from fewer people, employee-patient bonding has therefore increased, and patient satisfaction has risen to record levels. Cross-functional training provides task variety and higher interest levels for employees, which has significant benefits in improved employee motivation and morale. Cross-functional training is clearly a win-win-win situation for patients, healthcare organizations, and employees.
- *Special competencies training.* This method focuses on working as a team, creative problem solving, communications, relationships,

and patient-service orientation. Organizations using it realize that having the clinical skills is only part of the service requirement for their employees. They know they must also show their employees how to handle the many types of relationships that their patients will expect of them and how to solve the many problems that inevitably occur when different patients bring their different expectations to the healthcare experience.

- *Diversity training* and *attitudinal training.* These types of training focus on changing how employees view and interact with other employees and customers. With the changing cultural make-up of many communities, a heightened awareness of the issues, challenges, and opportunities faced by minorities is essential for those who provide healthcare services. As author Everard Rutledge reminds us, training is needed to ensure that caregivers recognize that "the 'one size fits all' approach does not work because all healthcare customers have unique life experiences and histories that influence the nature and effectiveness of their participation in and interaction with healthcare delivery systems and providers."[17] In today's competitive marketplace, healthcare organizations must educate their employees regarding such issues to expand services and programs to accommodate new markets.

## OTHER CONSIDERATIONS

### Training Message
Sending employees to a training program that focuses attention on service, no matter how effective or ineffective the actual training is, sends a powerful message to all employees that management cares enough about them and the topic that it invested real time and money. Any training tends to make employees feel more positively about the area covered because they recognize the training as a visible show of organizational commitment to improving the area.

### Measuring Training Effectiveness
If you do not know what your training is or is not accomplishing, you cannot know where to improve it. Obviously what you hope to learn is whether or not the content of the training has somehow been transferred from the trainer to the trainee. Four basic measurement methods are available, ranging in expense and degree of accuracy.

1. *Participant Feedback.* This method is the cheapest and most commonly used for assessing training effectiveness. It involves asking the participants to fill out a questionnaire that asks them some general evaluation questions. Because responses to these questionnaires often tend to reflect the entertainment value of the training rather than its effectiveness, they have relatively little usefulness for accurate program evaluation. At least they tell you if the participants enjoyed the training.

2. *Content Mastery.* If the point of the training was to learn some specific skill, competency, or content area, then test the knowledge gained by the participants afterward. Testing the level of mastery can be as simple as administering a paper-and-pencil examination or as elaborate as on-the-job demonstrations.

3. *Behavioral Change.* Many people quickly forget what they learned in classroom settings, especially if they do not apply it; "use it or lose it," as the saying goes. College students often say that they learn a subject well enough to get through the final exam and then they flush all the information out of their brains. To be effective in any meaningful way, training must be followed by real and lasting behavioral changes when the employee returns to the job. If the training is well designed and anchored to mastering specific service-related competencies or skills, and the behaviors are reinforced by positive results or what happens on the job, then positive measurable behavioral change should result.

4. *Organizational Performance.* Even if the training is well received, if the employees remember most of it on completion, and if they continue to use it on the job, the training is useless unless it eventually contributes to overall organizational effectiveness in some tangible way. To maintain the organization's competitive position, the training objectives and the training program require constant monitoring to make sure that they continue to prepare employees to provide the level of service that everchanging patients expect.

### Problems and Pitfalls of Training

Some possible problems with training are failure to establish training objectives, to measure results, and to analyze training costs and benefits.

1. *Not knowing the training objectives.* Training programs can run into trouble if the precise nature and objective of the training are unknown or imperfectly defined, or if the outcome expected of the training is hard to define or measure. Such programs are hard to justify or defend when senior management reviews the training budgets. Typical examples of areas in which the effectiveness of training is difficult to measure are human relations, supervisory skills, and customer service. Because these terms are vague and situationally defined, knowing what and how much training to offer to improve effectiveness in these areas and how to measure results is difficult.

   Healthcare organizations quite naturally want their employees to have a service orientation, but the concept is hard to define as is determining whether the training has resulted in such an outcome. What exactly that training should be and whether it is effective are much more difficult to determine.

2. *Not performing before-and-after measurement.* Although questions about effectiveness are difficult to answer, organizations should try to answer them. One measure of change in, say, patient-service orientation might be the number of patient complaints before and after training. Another approach is to use paid mystery shoppers to sample the level of service, both before and after the training. The point of any technique is to measure the value added by training. Without a "before" measurement, the organization has little way to know if the measurement after the training represents any improvement. Here, larger organizations have an advantage as they can use different parts of the organization to test different types of training and statistically determine whether or not one training type is more effective than another in terms of reducing patient complaints or increasing positive comments.

   Another strategy might be for the organization to measure the attitudes of its own employees toward patients, both before and after the training. Because we know that the correlation between the attitudes of healthcare patients and employees is positive, employee attitude may in general suggest how patients perceive the service level.

3. *Not analyzing costs and benefits of training.* Training programs have obvious direct costs, but they involve indirect or opportunity

costs as well; the time that trainees spend away from their regular duties costs money too. Training is too expensive for the organization to train everybody in everything, so it must try to get the best value for its money by using those training programs that can be shown to give the greatest positive results in customer service and patient satisfaction for the training dollar expended. All too often, organizations are at the mercy of consultants selling programs of unproven usefulness and value. Organizations should make the effort to ascertain the value of each training program, whether internal or external, in terms of whether it results in greater patient satisfaction.

## EMPLOYEE DEVELOPMENT

Training typically focuses on teaching people how to do new jobs for which they have been hired or to overcome deficiencies they may have in performing their current jobs. Development, on the other hand, is typically focused on getting people ready for their future. Training looks backward to identify and correct employee deficiencies in performing the job today. Development, on the other hand, looks forward to identify the skills, competencies, and areas of knowledge that the employee will need to be successful tomorrow. The problem with employee development is that knowing what the future will bring is difficult. Therefore, employee development programs tend to be more general, so measuring them and evaluating their effectiveness is even more difficult than for training programs.

### Tuition Refunds

A good example is the traditional employee tuition-refund policy that many organizations use to encourage employee development. Is the organization doing the right thing for itself or its employees if it pays a tuition refund only for those courses that are directly related to the employee's existing job, or is it doing a better job if it pays for any legitimate course at any legitimate educational institution? In the first case, the policy looks quite practical as it underwrites courses that directly enhance the employee's ability to do a current job. On the other hand, paying for any course regardless of field expands the total pool of knowledge available to the organization.

Consider a group of people who are studying different topics in different majors and then bring them together in a quality circle or problem-solving group session to work on an organizational matter. This group's total knowledge will obviously be greater than if everyone had gone through the same educational program or had majored in the same subject. A variety of learning experiences expands the creative potential of both the employee and the organization and therefore increases the possibility of finding new and innovative ways to perform existing jobs and prepare for the future.

### General Education

Supporting any legitimate employee effort to improve, grow, and learn is in the employer's interest. Such support sends a message to employees that the organization values their potential as much as it values their current contributions; it is also a relatively inexpensive employee and organizational development strategy. Even more important is that it supports a learning environment. An organization that actively promotes learning of all kinds sends a powerful message to its employees that it believes the only way it will stay competitive is to continuously learn. These learning organizations promote the active seeking of new knowledge that not only benefits the individual but benefits the entire organization by building its total pool of knowledge.

No matter how irrelevant the material may seem, the creative employee will use it to make organizational connections. The organization will eventually benefit from whatever creativity the educational experience spurred and from the increased loyalty and feeling of support that any employee gets from working for an organization that supports employee education. Forward-looking organizations understand that most of their revenues in ten years will be from products or services that they do not even know about today. Educational reimbursement programs that restrict people to those courses that the organization thinks are important today may be as silly as trying to predict which health-care services will be important ten years from now.

### Career Development

A good employee-development program should also include career development. Very few people picture themselves doing the same thing in the future that they are doing today. An organization concerned about customer service should pay careful attention to its current employee-development efforts so that the people who are helping the organization meet customer needs today are prepared to help it do so in the future. Employees tend to believe that the longer a person is with an organization, the more that person is worth to it. Many organizations support that belief by celebrating anniversary dates with parties and pins to show that the organization recognizes and appreciates the employee's commitment.

Pins and parties, however, are not enough. The outstanding service organizations recognize that the individual's need for personal growth and development must also be satisfied by permitting the employee to travel along a well-designed career development path. The entry-level healthcare manager should be able to see a path to the CEO's office that can be successfully traveled with hard work and dedication. Too many organizations typecast their employees, and these people know that no one expects them to go very far. Some employees do not have the ability, training, or desire to go very far, and they do not mind that. On the other hand, the American dream lives on in the minds of many entry-level employees in the service sector; even if presently content, they know that they may need or want to do something different some day. The outstanding organizations provide career paths that give talented, ambitious people the opportunity to realize their dreams. The opportunity is symbolically important, even if not all employees choose to take advantage of it.

## CONCLUSION

CEOs of the best healthcare organizations provide many opportunities for employees to grow and develop. Employee growth can be facilitated by means of the many training and development techniques covered in this chapter. Organizations should make it possible for employees with ambition, ability, and a willingness to make the effort to grow personally and professionally. Career paths should be available and visible. A major criterion for movement along these career paths in customer-driven organizations should be the ability and desire to provide outstanding customer service. The desire to learn, the encouragement of learning, and the assumption that learning can lead to advancement should be an important part of the organization's culture.

Too many healthcare organizations offer clinical training only and do not offer development programs at all, and consequently, their employees feel permanently stuck where they are. Although such organizations may think they are "economizing," other organizations will seek out these stuck people and invite them to join so they can find an opportunity to grow and develop. Competitors will always seek to hire your best people and not your worst. Ignoring the needs of all employees to learn, grow, and develop may be an inexpensive short-run strategy, but it will be a long-run expense. Not giving the employees opportunities to grow means that the healthcare organization itself may not grow and develop as rapidly. The best employees that you need for your future can always find opportunities elsewhere to use their talents if you do not give them the chance. The key idea behind organization training and development is that everyone must continue to grow and progress. Skill and knowledge development is a continuous process. It must be ongoing to meet the ongoing changes in the patient's expectations. It is a neverending journey.

## LESSONS LEARNED

1. Teach employees not only job-related skills but also interpersonal skills and creative problem-solving techniques related to customer service.
2. Use scripts related to customer service to teach staff how to respond to customers in a given situation.
3. Do not just train to be training; know what outcomes you expect from your training dollars, and measure your training results to ensure you get them.
4. Before training people, check the service delivery system; the problem may lie there.
5. Develop your people for your organization's future.
6. Do not just believe in your people; champion their training and development.
7. Reward behaviors learned through training to keep them alive.
8. Relate training to employee job responsibilities, especially those related to customer service.
9. Make training and development in customer service an ongoing process.

## NOTES

1. Berry, L. L. 1995. *On Great Service: A Framework for Action*, pp. 78–79. New York: The Free Press.

2. *Business Week*, March 28, 1994, p. 163.

3. Mayer, T. A., R. J. Cates, M. J. Mastorovich, and D. L. Royalty. 1998. "Emergency Department Patient Satisfaction: Customer Service Training Improves Patient Satisfaction and Ratings of Physician and Nurse Skill." *Journal of Healthcare Management* 43 (5): 427–31.

4. Berry, L. L. 1995. *On Great Service: A Framework for Action*, p. 188. New York: The Free Press.

5. Lau, G. 2000. "A Training Program Must Zero in on What Your Staffers Must Know." *Investor's Business Daily* (June 18): A1.

6. Berry, L. L. 1995. *On Great Service: A Framework for Action*, p. 191. New York: The Free Press.

7. Moore, J. D. 1997. "A Mickey Mouse Operation: Louisiana Hospital Learning Customer Service Lessons From Disney." *Modern Healthcare* 27 (15): 64–65.

8. *Ibid.*

9. "Dissatisfied Employees? Your Training Programs Could Be the Culprit." 2001. *ACHe-news* (April 16): 2.

10. *Business Week*, March 28, 1994, p.159.

11. Baird, K. 2000. *Customer Service in Health Care*, p. 89. San Francisco: Jossey-Bass.

12. Zeff, P. 1995. "Naughty or Nice." *American Medical News* 38 (December):13–14.

13. Davis, S., and J. Botkin. 1994. *The Monster Under the Bed: How Business Is Mastering the Opportunity of Knowledge for Profit*, pp. 98–99. NewYork: Simon & Schuster.

14. Okrent, D. 2000. "Twilight of the Boomers." *Time* (June 12): 72.

15. Oxler, K. 1997. "Achieving Patient Satisfaction: Resolving Patient Complaints." *Holistic Nursing Practice* 11 (2): 27–35.

16. *Business Week*, February 28, 1994, p. 81.

17. Rutledge, E. 2001. "The Struggle for Equality in Healthcare Continues." *Journal of Healthcare Management* 46 (5): 313–24.

*Chapter 8*

# Motivation and Empowerment

Healthcare Principle: *Motivate, empower, and reward your employees for achieving customer service goals*

Leaders think about empowerment, not control.

—*Warren Bennis*

IN ALMOST ALL healthcare experiences, the patient-service employees make the difference between a satisfied patient and a dissatisfied patient. Therefore, employees who provide the healthcare experience must be not only well trained clinically but highly motivated and empowered to meet the patient's expectations and to do so consistently. The leadership and managerial skills of the healthcare manager can influence employee attitudes greatly and are vital to employee empowerment and motivation. In this chapter, we discuss the process of motivating staff to provide excellent customer service, developing and working with teams, and empowering employees to take the initiative in identifying and solving problems.

## MOTIVATING EMPLOYEES

The challenge for healthcare managers is to discover what makes employees not only do their jobs efficiently and competently but also want to go the extra mile. Consider the following scenarios:

A nursing home resident had for some time been eating less and complaining more than usual. Her exasperated family thought her complaints were just another tactic to get attention, but an obser-

195

vant employee suspected that the patient's reluctance to eat might have a physical cause, so she arranged for the resident to see a dentist. The dentist confirmed the employee's suspicion: the resident's dentures were causing her discomfort, pain, and inability to eat. The situation was then corrected, and the thankful resident began eating regularly again.

A female chemotherapy patient was happily anticipating a trip to a dear friend's wedding. The event had been scheduled to fit between chemo treatments, when the patient could comfortably travel the long distance required. Then an attending nurse informed the patient that her high white blood cell count would require a change in the chemo schedule. The patient realized instantly that she would not be able to go to the wedding. The attending nurse recognized the look of dismay on the patient's face and initiated a request of the doctor to rearrange the treatment schedule. The change was made and the patient attended the event and had a wonderful time.

In both examples, the nursing home employee and the chemotherapy nurse took a creative path to solving their patients' problem not because they had to but because they wanted to. Something or someone motivated these healthcare professionals to go above and beyond their clinical responsibilities and job descriptions to provide extra service to their patients. Benchmark healthcare organizations are learning the importance of using the whole employee, from the neck up as well as from the neck down.

Every healthcare experience is unique, and any manager who believes it possible to predefine policy and procedures for handling any and all healthcare experiences is mistaken. Employees should know that they are encouraged, expected, and trusted to handle all the varied situations that come up in the patient-service areas for which they are responsible. If they were properly selected and trained in the first place, management must make it possible for them to do their jobs with responsibility, skill, enthusiasm, and enjoyment. But how?

The answer is simple. It is based on the well-accepted psychological principle that behavior that is rewarded tends to be repeated, and behavior that is not rewarded tends not to be repeated. Implementing the answer, however, is the challenge facing every manager. The way to keep employees performing at high levels, then, is to reward behavior associated with or leading to excellent healthcare experiences and to refrain from rewarding behavior that is not. In an intensely personal field like healthcare, acknowledgement of employee contributions is extremely important.[1]

Finding the right reward is the hard part. Employees are as varied as customers. Just as customers differ in what they expect, employees differ in what they expect in terms of rewards from their organizational relationships. In a sense, employees are the manager's customers. They define the value and quality of the employment relationship just as the customer defines the value and quality of the healthcare experience. The managerial challenge is to discover and then provide rewards in types and amounts that each employee believes are equitable and appropriate. Some reward possibilities include service awards, recognition for suggestions and improvements, and other types of incentives that recognize employees for serving customers well. Finding the right reward becomes even harder for the manager because over time employees' expectations, moods, and valuations of the employment relationship change.

For the most part, healthcare employees look for three things in a job. It must be fun (in the sense of enjoyably fulfilling), fair, and interesting. As Norman Brinker says, "If you have fun at what you do, you'll never work a day in your life. Make work like play—and play like hell."[2] Of course, some healthcare situations are no fun for anybody. Performing a painful clinical procedure or telling a parent that a child is terminally ill can be stressful or agonizing for the healthcare employee. Nevertheless, performing the overall job and accomplishing its goals should be fulfilling and enjoyable if not exactly fun. From the organizational perspective, the key to managing and retaining employees is to create job situations and provide rewards that the employees perceive as fun, fair, and interesting. If the organization can successfully build these elements into the job situation, employees will be motivated to work hard and follow directions. The trick is that everyone's definition of these three job characteristics is different.

Benchmark healthcare organizations determine how their own employees define the organization by administering a well-designed employee survey. Yale-New Haven Hospital in Connecticut surveys employees every two or three years. Similarly, at Baptist Hospital in Pensacola, Florida, a systemwide employee taskforce conducts focus groups to gather information that can be useful in determining rewards.

Benchmark healthcare organizations also attempt to minimize the effect of paperwork, administrative duties, and government regulations so that the staff can focus on serving their patients.

## Satisfying Employees

Leaders motivate people, develop their talents, provide them with proper resources, and reward them when they succeed. If healthcare managers and supervisors offer appropriate incentives and fulfill employee needs, then employees will find their jobs to be fun, fair, and interesting; they will be satisfied in their work. Consider, for example, the case of a conscientious, hardworking nurse aide in a long-term care facility.[3] The nurse aide is a single mother with school-aged children. She frequently misses work because of childcare issues. Because of her absences, management has informed her that she is on notice for termination. The aide was already worried, but the reprimand made her feel even more insecure about her future and depressed. Her personal problem and the threat of termination will surely have a negative effect on the quality of customer service and perhaps even the clinical care she renders.

This example presents the employee's manager an opportunity to turn around the situation and satisfy both the employee and hence her patients. But what can the manager do to motivate this employee to perform once again up to her potential? The first step is to diagnose the problem. The manager can determine the exact nature of her problems through facilitative listening. During the listening session, the manager can use her own personality, physical presence, and availability to motivate rather than give advice, instruction, or solutions to the problem. The major motivational ingredient is active listening.

The second step is to clarify to the nurse aide the organization's mission, vision, and expectations of the department and this employee in terms of patient care and customer service. These goals need to be related to the nurse aide's specific job so she will understand how her role fits into the big picture. Specifically, the organization's expectations of her—attendance, punctuality, continuing education, customer service, and so forth—and the reasons for those expectations need to be clearly spelled out. She must be shown how these expectations are related to the organization's and department's mission, vision, and goals. The manager should also describe and provide rewards for effective performance as well as penalties for failure to improve, including discipline and dismissal. The latter may be necessary for some employees who are unable or unwilling to meet expectations in a customer-focused environment.

The third step is to empower the employee to solve her childcare problem and provide input and support. The goal is to agree on a mutually satisfactory solution. If improvement occurs, recognition might include personal congratulations, personal notes, public recognition (oral or written), and promotion.

If employees are satisfied, then they are much more likely to try to meet the needs of the customers they serve. Customer satisfaction obviously translates into a positive relationship with the healthcare organization, which translates into community support and revenue enhancement. These relationships—the importance of leaders to employee satisfaction and the importance of employee satisfaction to customer satisfaction—make intuitive sense and are supported by research.

The research of Valarie Zeithaml and Mary Jo Bitner supports the relationship between employee satisfaction and customer satisfaction. They say, "There is concrete evidence that satisfied employees make for satisfied customers (and satisfied customers can in turn reinforce employees' sense of satisfaction in their jobs). Some have even gone so far as to suggest that unless service employees are happy in their jobs, customer satisfaction will be difficult to achieve."[4] Customer satisfaction obviously translates into a positive relationship with the healthcare organization, which translates into community support and revenue enhancement.

How do you find out if customers are satisfied? How do you find out if employees are satisfied? Ask them. Baptist Hospital in Pensacola, Florida, surveys all its employees every two years and conducts mini-surveys every 90 days on job aspects that they know lead to job satisfaction or dissatisfaction, such as employee relationships with their bosses and employee feelings about their pay and their working conditions. The organization understands the direct relationship between employee satisfaction and morale, turnover, and quality of the healthcare experience. Managers whose employees have low satisfaction scores are reminded of the low scores in their performance evaluations and compensation. The satisfaction scores are also posted for all employees to see. Employee satisfaction has led to increased patient satisfaction and productivity at Baptist Hospital.

Similarly, Sears Roebuck studied employees in 800 stores and found that attitudes about such job aspects as workload and how their bosses treated them had, according to Sue Shellenbarger, "a measurable effect on customer satisfaction and revenue. Basically, a happy employee will stick with the company, give better service to the customer, and recommend company products to others."[5] According to the study, if Sears employee attitudes improved by 5 percent, customer satisfaction improved by 1.3 percent, and revenue improved by one-half percent. If Sears executives "knew nothing about a store except that employee attitudes had improved 5 percent, they could reliably predict a revenue rise of .5 percent over what it would otherwise have been."[6] The Sears study supports our point: A satisfied employee gives better service to the customer.

## Rewarding the Desired Behavior

Most managers focus on their problem employees and ignore those who perform at their normal, competent level. Their employees quickly learn that "the squeaky wheel gets the grease." Rewarding the wrong behavior is as big a mistake as not rewarding the right behavior. The organization's reward system needs constant and careful review to ensure that the behaviors being rewarded are the behaviors that the organization wants employees to exhibit. For example, many hospitals tell their employees that they should make every effort to satisfy the patient. But many of these same hospitals evaluate and reward employee performance only according to the budget numbers and clinical results. This practice has been called "rewarding A while hoping for B." Most employees will naturally focus on the numbers and not on the patient-satisfaction ratings. Similarly, if healthcare managers tell employees how important team performance is but reward employees only as individuals, employees will realize that team effort does not really matter that much.

Here is an example of this point. Hypothetical Hospital hired Roberta Hunter to serve as a receptionist at the hospital's information desk. The manager told Roberta explicitly that her primary responsibility was to greet and welcome the patients and their families and to provide them with any information they needed. However, as time went on, to keep Roberta busy when patients were not entering the hospital, the manager added responsibilities to the position: doing routine but important paperwork. Roberta quickly realized that the manager never complimented her for cheerfully greeting the patients or giving helpful information nor did he say anything to her when she did not speak promptly with a customer because she was too busy with her other duties. But if she failed to get the paperwork done, she was strongly reprimanded. Therefore, by his actions or lack of action, the manager had redefined Roberta's job description. The manager made his real priorities clear, and Roberta adjusted her actions accordingly.

### Identifying the Rewards

The first step in satisfying the employees who must satisfy the customers is to identify the rewards desired by employees. Most employees begin new jobs with energy and enthusiasm; they want to do well. But this fast start cannot last forever without encouragement, reinforcement, and help. Employees' expectations that they will receive desired rewards for good performance are what keep them energized, enthused, and working hard on behalf of their organizations. Managers must learn techniques that accurately identify the issues affecting their employees.

The American Nurses Association conducted a national survey that found that staffing issues and mandatory overtime were the chief concerns among nurses.[7] Well-designed organizationwide surveys like this one can make managers aware of motivational issues (i.e., what rewards are most likely to motivate a given category of employees). Effective employee performance is a result of ensuring that the right people are in the right jobs for their talents, are properly trained to do the job the way it should be done to provide the healthcare experience that patients expect, and are rewarded in ways that keep them energized to perform those jobs with efficiency and enthusiasm.

### Necessary Managerial Skills

Managers must have certain skills to support and motivate employees, including administrative and leadership skills. *Administrative skill* is the ability to take care of the routine tasks, including paperwork, administrative procedures, and policies that directly influence each employee's ability to perform the job. A manager who forgets to submit the proper payroll, to provide the necessary information for employee decision making, or who schedules too few people to work in the ER on a Saturday evening creates situations in which even the most enthused, energetic employee cannot succeed. Managers must effectively administer the basic job-related requirements of employees.

*Leadership skill* is the ability to identify and provide those rewards that the individual employee wants from membership in the organization.

Although fear and the threat of punishment may be powerful short-term motivators, the ability of the organization and its managers to fulfill employee needs is what yields energetic employee commitment to organizational goals in the long run. What managers offer in return for employee contributions are the inducements that make the job fun, establish the fairness of how the rewards are distributed, and make the job interesting. These inducements are rewards or *eager factors*.

### The Eager Factors

What made the employee eager to join the organization in the first place? People join organizations to fulfill their needs. Although individual needs are infinitely varied, they usually include the need for financial security, to belong to an organization that matches and enhances one's self-image, to associate with people who think and feel the same way, and to grow and develop as a person and as an employee. Although every organization will have its misfits, most people work hard at doing what they love to do because the job satisfies their needs.

Thomas C. Dolan, president and CEO of the American College of Healthcare Executives, affirms the importance of competitive salaries and benefits.[8] He also believes that organizations should include incentive or gainsharing plans for all employees. Financial compensation policy, however, should be carefully designed because pay is not always linked to performance. Financial incentives may also have a negative "snowball effect." Consider a group of employees who receive a bonus for successfully completing a project. The group will probably be highly motivated to perform on the next project, perhaps even doing a better job. If the next job is of higher quality and they receive a lower bonus or perhaps no bonus at all, their motivation may decrease for following projects.

Most people enjoy being a part of a compatible group or team. Well-designed work groups can be helpful in managing employee direction and behavior in the workplace. As studies at the Hawthorne Plant of the Western Electric Company showed many years ago, the sense of belonging or not belonging greatly influences what people will or will not do in the workplace. The managerial focus here should be to work in harmony with the group to support each employee's effort to achieve the group goal, which will help achieve the organizational goal. The first managerial challenge in meeting employee belonging needs, then, is to identify those groups to which employees belong (which is not always obvious); the next is to identify group goals. The hope, of course, is that the purpose and values of the group are consonant with those of the organization. Only then will employees have a sense of pride, commitment, and loyalty to their organization.[9]

If groups offer members the opportunity to achieve something greater than themselves by being a part of the group, then the value of the group becomes greater than merely satisfying belonging needs. Membership in organizations with strong corporate cultures and whose purposes are respected by society as a whole is valuable to both group and individual. Asking the group to help accomplish the valued, respected organizational purpose becomes a powerful motivational tool for the organization and a primary means for keeping the individual and the group positively involved in the organization.

## WORK TEAMS

Workers in healthcare believe that their work is important and that they often make the difference between life and death. Healthcare employees know that they are essential parts of organizations that profoundly influence people's lives. If a healthcare organization calls a group of these people together and asks them to serve as a quality team to identify service-quality problems or find opportunities for improved patient care, they will work hard on behalf of that team's goal because they are so committed to the purpose of the organization.

The point is simple: People join groups to satisfy needs, and the group members can satisfy some of each other's needs without any organizational help. But if the organization enables the group to satisfy additional higher-level needs, then the organization is going to get the support of the group and its members. Although this sounds easy to do, it is not. Most organizations make no attempt to understand the relationships among the goals of the individual, the group, and the overall organization. Most organizations do not know what they can do or stop doing to enhance the positive benefits of these relationships. Figure 8.1 sums up what characteristics are required if a collection of people is to function successfully as a work team. The healthcare manager can use these characteristics to help weak work teams to be successful and to improve the performance of other teams.

### Benefits

Building strong work teams is worth the effort. Organizations reap many benefits from supportive and productive teams. First, the organization gains access to the many good ideas that a team can generate

**Figure 8.1 Successful Work Team Characteristics**

*The Successful Work Team:*
1. Has a meaningful team purpose that inspires and focuses the members' efforts
2. Has goals and objectives that are measurable, specific, realistic, and easy to understand with defined areas of authority
3. Is small enough to act as a true team (5 to 15 members)
4. Has members with the necessary skills to operate as a team (functional/technical skills appropriate for the decision area, problem-solving/decision-making skills, and interpersonal/team skills)
5. Has clear, well-organized work procedures and rules of behavior that are enforced by the team
6. Has a cultural value of mutual accountability, where only the team can fail or be a hero and not any one team member
7. Is supported by the organization's leadership and led by a team-building coach who builds a performance culture
8. Has enough group time to allow members to interact and learn how to care about one another
9. Understands the extent of its authority
10. Is provided with the resources necessary to succeed

by discussing and resolving problems affecting the team and the organization. Very few healthcare managers know everything nor are they capable of identifying the best answers to every customer's problem. Using team problem-solving processes provides a wealth of new ideas and frequently a better perspective than the manager alone might have. After all, those who deal with the customer and the problems that serving the customer may create know the details of those problems better than the manager with multiple responsibilities does.

Second, teams can assist in the supervisory role of management by providing an ongoing monitoring of each team member's behavior and productivity. If the team has a common performance objective, then the team can better monitor and oversee each member's relative contribution than management itself can. The group and the group's approval will likely have a more important influence on the individual employee's behavior than will the supervisor.

Third, teams help everybody learn more about the organization and what it does. By involving teams in solving problems and making decisions, the organization learns more about what it wants to do and how to do it, and the individual learns more about the job, why the job is done the way it is, what other team members contribute to the job's accomplishment, and the relationship of the job to the overall organizational purposes. Involving groups in decision making also forces the manager to understand clearly what the problem or issue is. After all, if you do not know what you are trying to do or why a particular issue is important, you cannot explain it to anyone else very well. Using team decision making helps the organization and its leadership to understand their own purposes, procedures, and reasons for doing things while it teaches the employees how to be more involved and accountable for their own work.

Fourth, when the team makes decisions for itself, it owns them, understands them, and becomes responsible for making them work and monitoring their outcomes. If a study team at the hospital decides that too many dishes are breaking on the foodservice carts while running over the tiled floor, it puts itself in the position of identifying the best solution and then making it work. In this example, the problem was caused by stacking the trays for food on top of one another without spacers; the team came up with a solution: put rubber spacers between the trays. Because the team and not management came up with the solution, the team members who were also the people pushing the carts made sure that they used the rubber bumpers and proved to themselves that their solution worked. Such problems are too frequently "solved" by an industrial engineer who comes up with an elegant solution that nobody uses. In such cases, the problem continues, and frustrated managers wonder what to do with the uncooperative employees.

The use of teams sends all employees the message that they are trusted. Employee morale improves, absenteeism decreases, and organizational recruitment efforts are enhanced.

### A Case Study
The Hospital for Special Care (HSC) in New Britain, Connecticut, uses self-directed work teams at the supervisory level of healthcare.[10] HSC is a 200-bed facility for rehabilitation and chronic disease management of children and adults. The hospital reorganized its management structure to better position itself as the most cost-effective provider of health-

care services in its area. One element integrated into this restructuring was self-directed work teams. Such teams are highly trained groups of employees responsible for turning out a well-defined segment of finished work. The teams at HSC possessed cross-functional skills and were given decision-making authority and ready access to information. They generally participated in planning, setting priorities, coordinating activities with other workers and teams, measuring output, and taking corrective action when needed. Management employees of HSC had previously worked as individuals toward common business goals under the direction of a senior supervisor. The purpose of the new self-directed work teams was to increase autonomy and group problem-solving ability and to facilitate change.

After a year of existence, members of the teams believed that the model had benefits at many levels. Pooling resources enabled teams to accept more complex patients from acute care earlier in their illnesses. High-quality, cost-effective education was provided to staff and members. A key characteristic of the self-directed work team was the cross representation among disciplines as a result of extensive information sharing. Finally, it was widely held that the collaboration between clinical managers and clinical resource consultants enabled good communication and resulted in more timely resolution of staff issues. HSC benefited from maintaining a centralized pool of experts who were able to plan and provide education to all levels of staff and the community.

According to authors Dreachslin, Hunt, and Sprainer, nursing care teams (NCTs) have emerged as a common approach to organization design and acute care in U.S. hospitals.[11] The authors describe an NCT as composed of one registered nurse, who serves as the team leader, and one or two nonlicensed caregivers, who assist the nurse in delivering care. Like other team approaches, complementary skills and commitment to a common purpose characterize the NCTs. The difference between NCTs and traditional nursing teams is that the boundaries of the latter are rigid while the boundaries of NCTs are permeable. NCT members are described as able to perform duties as needed to serve the patient, unhampered (within legal boundaries) by rigid role definitions. This design allows team members to experience more empowerment in terms of decision making in patient care.

## Possible Problems

Potential problems with teams are that they do not always work as fast as individuals do; they require managers to take on new attitudes and leadership behaviors; they cost money and time; and they should be limited to certain problems, situations, and tasks that lend themselves to team effort. Team decision making is not always the solution, and it can have disadvantages. First, without question, team or group decision making takes more time than an experienced manager takes to decide on a solution. Most team members do not intuitively know either how to make decisions systematically or how to collaborate in a team setting. Teaching members how to do these things adds to the time required to solve the problem. It takes time to teach group members what the problems are, why they occur, and how to work as a team to solve them. The team meetings themselves take time.

Second, managers and supervisors have to learn new behaviors that require them to relinquish decision-making responsibilities. Most managers and supervisors were promoted because they were the best at doing whatever job they now supervise—the best nurse becomes the head nurse, the best x-ray technician becomes the department head, and so forth. If the organization tells a manager who was promoted to the position that she is now assigned to coach a group that will make decisions, that manager may become confused and may wonder why the organization promoted her if it did not want her to make the decision. The message here is mixed, and many managers have a difficult time shifting gears to be coaches instead of doers or decision makers.

The other aspect of this problem is based on fear. Managers wonder what their own futures will be when they see employees being empowered to make decisions. If the job of the manager is to oversee people's work and to make decisions about how that work should be done, what happens to the manager's job once the team is empowered to make its own decisions and to oversee its own members? Many empowerment programs have not worked because middle managers, as a simple issue of job survival, have found ways to make sure they do not work.

Third, teams are neither cheap nor always effective. Taking people out of their jobs to make decisions has a cost. Furthermore, there are entire categories of decisions that teams are incapable of making or making well. A team has a difficult time making decisions about issues beyond its concerns or knowledge. A group of pharmacists, for example, will have a hard time making a good corporate strategic policy decision or a decision that has an impact on another group or unit within the organization. Even if the pharmacists received some training in grasping the big picture, they probably will not know about or be able to see all the ramifications of the issues involved.

Similarly, decisions that require technical expertise beyond that typically available to the involved employees will not likely be successful. Benchmark healthcare organizations often reward teams for good ideas and/or successful implementation. A potential downside of this effort is that employees who are not on a team may feel left out and become resentful. Some team members may become freeloaders and not contribute their fair share on the job. Finally, not everyone can work successfully in a team format, nor is every problem appropriate for a team solution.

### When to Use Work Teams

An organization needs to determine the answers to four critical questions before it uses team-based decision making. First, "Is management comfortable letting work teams make decisions about their job responsibilities?" Although this sounds easy to answer, it is not. Many managers are uncomfortable letting go of their managerial prerogatives. Even so, they often have to in healthcare because so many healthcare activities, such as surgery, can only be accomplished by teams. No one person has the time or skills to perform every task and make every decision.

Second, "Is management ready to let teams be accountable for their efforts and decisions?" Because most managers are evaluated on the basis of their unit's performance, this is a hard question also. If the manager is accountable for the decision, how can the manager be comfortable with allowing the group to make a decision that might come back to haunt the manager if it turns out poorly? Most people believe that if they have to be accountable for the results, they might as well make the decisions themselves, and they have a hard time trusting someone or some group to make those for them.

Third, "Is management ready to share the benefits of the decisions?" This question leads to others: If the group makes good decisions and saves the organization money, will management share the rewards with the group? In a related way, will management share the glory and other benefits that result from high levels of performance in an organization? If the team makes the decision that wins the boss the big bonus and the trip to Hawaii, will they ever work that hard on behalf of the organization (or that manager) again unless they too benefit in a meaningful way?

Fourth, "Is management ready to let team decision makers grow and develop?" If the group and its members do not get the opportunity to grow and develop, but they see management getting these opportunities as a result of the group's efforts, they will lose their interest in and enthusiasm for the team decision process. Management that wishes to use team decision making successfully must be ready to let the team and its membership participate in growth and development opportunities and organizational rewards and must be willing to trust them with the authority and responsibility for decision making.

Although work teams offer an important benefit to the employee by providing a sense of belonging, effective work teams do more for their members. They provide a sense of self-worth, the opportunity to grow and develop, and a means to recognize and share achievements and failures and to reinforce each other's values and beliefs. In brief, they help satisfy each group member's need to grow and develop as a person and as an employee.

For the organization to garner the benefits of teams, success in achieving customer service goals needs to be celebrated in public. Not only do data need to be publicized, but team success needs to be recognized in public because it reinforces the culture of excellence. Public praise played a major part in the successful turnaround of Baptist Hospital.

## Role Conflicts and Role Playing

This constant, ongoing process of working with teams is full of potential and real conflicts. A person who is sent different role expectations by different people will feel conflict and confusion. If the customer expects one thing and the company policy requires another, the employee faces the difficult choice of determining which way to go and which role to play. Conflict can also occur when the supervisor sends out conflicting role expectations, when the role expectations conflict with the focal person's fundamental values or beliefs, and when the roles themselves come into conflict. For example, if Sally's husband tells her to come home early for their child's birthday party and Sally's boss then asks her to work an extra shift tonight, Sally will have a role conflict.

Many healthcare employees identify themselves as members of a professional group (e.g., nurses, x-ray technicians, surgeons, dermatologists, and so forth). As such, they adopt professional norms of behavior and present themselves to their patients in a professional role. The norms that the particular professional group has promulgated to its members become the guidelines for how these professionals should play their roles.

Thinking of the job as the playing of a role, and an important role at that, gives new and greater importance to every job throughout the organization. Now, instead of a nurse thinking "I must empty bedpans," which may demean the nurse's many years of clinical education and experience, the employee can look at the task as a part of the "professional nurse role." In a professional responsibility, nothing is demeaning or lowly about dumping a bedpan if it advances patient care; after all, the nurse is not a bedpan emptier but a professional doing an excellent job of performing a professional task. This attitude helps eliminate role conflicts because it distinguishes the real person and her capabilities in her personal life from her skillful performance of her professional role.

Role playing helps solve another major personal challenge that healthcare personnel have to face: how to stay "up" all the time. People who deal with people have to be good at performing *emotional labor*—the consuming task of being friendly, upbeat, and sympathetic all the time. But thinking of the job as a role in a theatrical performance can help decrease the personal wear and tear of this emotional labor. Instead of actually paying the emotional price that results from getting personally involved in every patient's needs, the employee might instead display the emotional response required of someone in an acting job. Thinking of the job as performing a professional role makes it possible for healthcare employees to perform effectively without becoming emotionally burned out.

The research on this topic suggests that role playing is actually better for the employee and the organization than genuine emotional involvement. According to authors Ashforth and Humphrey, "Given the repetitive and scripted nature of many service roles, one may develop habitual routines for . . . acting such that emotional labor becomes relatively effortless."[12] Individuals who strongly identify with their organizational roles are apt to feel more authentic when they are conforming to role expectations, even if they are only acting rather than actually feeling the emotional involvement required. Further, acting like a certain type of person tends to commit one to actually becoming that type of person, especially if one volunteers to play the role to a public audience.[13]

The emphasis on being a role player also encourages people to think of themselves as being on stage even when they are feeling low or distracted by other role expectations in their lives. If you come to work bothered by the fight you had with your significant other that morning, once you go "on stage" at the hospital or clinic, you can usually get into the caregiving role and leave your nonwork problems behind.

Finally, managers need to spend time and energy in minimizing role conflict and maximizing role clarity. When the organization and its leadership do not spend the time necessary to clarify their role expectations for the employee, the potential for conflict is great. Effective healthcare training programs clearly define roles for the employees and thereby minimize the conflicts the employees will have to face. When they have finished training and begin to serve patients, they should know their roles thoroughly.

## EMPOWERING EMPLOYEES

Teams need to grow and develop, but so do individuals. One great asset that a team provides to its members is the opportunity to grow within the group setting. But the organization must provide additional opportunities for its members to satisfy this important need. The most widely discussed strategy for doing so is empowerment. Becoming empowered may add to the fun and fulfillment of the job for employees. It may also add a sense of fairness because well-trained employees may feel that it is only fair that they are given some responsibility for making decisions related to their own work.

The main benefit of empowerment is that the job that offers opportunity for growth and development through empowerment is more interesting. The organization benefits from interested, empowered employees too. As Norman Brinker says, "You can achieve so much more by empowering people to achieve on their own. Don't be too hands-on."[14] The empowered healthcare provider can personalize the healthcare experience to meet or exceed each patient's expectations and can take whatever steps are necessary to prevent or recover from service failure. On those complementary ends of the service experience can hinge organizational success or failure.

*Empowerment* is the assignment of decision-making responsibility to the individual.[15] It requires sharing information and organizational knowledge that enables the empowered employees to understand and contribute to organizational performance, rewarding them based on the organization's performance and giving them the authority to make decisions that influence organizational outcomes. Empowerment is broader than the traditional concepts of delegation, decentralization, and participatory management. Empowerment can stretch decision responsibility beyond a specific decision area to include decision responsibility for the entire job and for knowing how the performance of that job fits within the organizational purpose and mission.

Some organizations talk the talk of employee decision input but do not give employees any real power and authority to implement decisions. The purpose of employee empowerment is not only to ensure that effective decisions are made by the right employees but to provide a mechanism by which responsibility for job-related decisions is vested either in individuals or in work teams.[16] Empowerment also means that management is willing to share relevant information about and control over factors that impinge on effective job performance.

Empowerment is not an absolute; it has degrees. Managers may find that more is not necessarily better. For example, a manager can choose to provide higher degrees of empowerment for some individuals and teams doing certain tasks than for others. Indeed, even within a given individual's job or a given group's task responsibilities, different decision areas can be empowered to different degrees. A clinic, for example, may empower its nurses with complete authority to regulate who may visit patients and when, within a certain range of variation, to meet the level of patient satisfaction offered by competing clinics. However, the clinic might not be willing to let the same nurses make even minor modifications in clinical protocols or hours of clinic operation.

### The Job Content/Context Grid

Healthcare managers may need help in seeing how to use the empowerment concept in their own organizations. They may also need help in managing the delicate balance between giving employees control over their own work processes while retaining some supervisory control over what employees do. What will happen, for example, if management empowered a work group by assigning both authority and responsibility over the job and the group decided to do nothing at all related to the organization's goals or even the goals of the work group next to it? Obviously, empowerment must occur within some limits, and where to place them becomes a major challenge in implementing any empowerment strategy.

An organization wanting to empower its employees must first analyze its jobs. All jobs have two dimensions: content and context. *Job content* represents the tasks and procedures necessary for doing a job.

*Job context* refers to why the organization needs a job done, how one job interacts with related jobs, and how a job fits into the overall organizational mission, goals, objectives, and job setting. Managers trying to use empowerment will find it helpful to view decision making not simply as an act of making a choice among alternatives but as a five-stage process of (1) identifying the problem, (2) discovering alternative solutions, (3) evaluating the pros and cons of those alternatives, (4) making the choice and (5) implementing and following up on the impact of that choice. Employees can be empowered to participate in one, some, or all of these stages.

Figure 8.2 shows a grid with the job context on the vertical axis and the job content on the horizontal. The horizontal axis shows the way in which the employee's or team's decision-making responsibility over job content progressively increases in relationship to the decision-making process. For example, at the far left of the Figure in the first step of the decision-making process, employees have little responsibility; but the level of responsibility and decision involvement increases as one moves to the right. Similarly, as one moves up the vertical axis, responsibility and involvement over decisions related to job context increase. A manager seeking to empower employees may wish to increase decision responsibility over job content, job context, or both. The five points (points A through E) identified on the grid allow a better understanding of varying strategies for empowerment available to managers.

Point A (No Discretion) represents the traditional assembly-line type of highly routine and repetitive job. This is the classic fast-food job, designed by someone other than the worker and monitored by someone else. No decision-making responsibility is associated with this job in terms of either job content or job context. The employee is utilized from the neck down. Author J. B. Schor notes that the most stressful workplaces are electronic sweatshops and assembly lines where a demanding pace is coupled with virtually no individual discretion.[17] A good healthcare illustration of the latter is the job of a phlebotomist. The job is highly routinized, repetitive, and boring. Phlebotomists have little discretion about how to draw the patient's blood or how much to draw. The contact with the patient is so brief and the need to concentrate on the task so great that these technicians do not have enough time to interact much with patients to break up the task performance.

Point B (Task Setting) represents the essence of many empowerment programs used today. Here, the worker is given a great deal of

**Figure 8.2 The Employee Empowerment Grid**

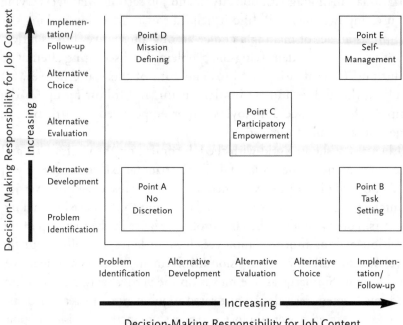

*Source:* Reprinted with permission from *Academy of Management Executive* 9 (3): 24, 1995. "Empowerment: A Matter of Degree," by R. C. Ford and M. D. Fottler.

decision responsibility for the job content and little for the context. The worker is empowered to make decisions about the best way to get the assigned task accomplished. In these cases, management defines the mission and goals, and the worker is empowered to find the best way to reach them. Management hopes that the empowered workers will apply their job knowledge and intellect to discover ways to improve what they do in their jobs.

Many healthcare jobs are in this category. The patient-service employee must do the job as defined by the clinical protocol but has flexibility to do it in a variety of ways to meet the needs and expectations of varied patients. The admissions person may be given the decision responsibility to prioritize patient treatments based on some triage protocol. Hospital nurses follow strict protocols but have a certain degree of flexibility in how they deliver care. For example, a nurse on the maternity ward may give an educated, married mother of four the postoperative instructions as clinically ordered but may choose to spend more time explaining instructions to an unmarried teenager having her first child. Nurses must make care decisions based on their judgments about the needs of each individual. A 90-year-old woman with a broken leg requires different care than an 18-year-old football player with the same condition.

Point B represents a significant departure from Point A because employees are totally involved in making decisions about job content. Jobs at Point B can be redesigned by employees or even teams of employees. They may redesign their tasks to add more content or develop a variety of new employee skills. Many Point B employees find such enriched jobs more motivating and satisfying, leading them to do higher-quality work. Even when management confines empowerment to job-content decisions, employee motivation may be enhanced for those who strongly value feelings of accomplishment and growth.[18] The success of the Point B strategy, however, will partly depend on factors beyond employee control, such as service delivery system design and organizational structure, patient expectations, clinical protocols, reward systems, and top-management support.

Point C (Participatory Empowerment) represents an area more typical of autonomous work groups that are given some decision-making involvement in both job content and job context. Such groups usually participate in problem identification, alternative search and analysis, and recommending the best alternative in job content; they participate similarly in job-context decisions. Although research is sparse, some evidence suggests higher job satisfaction and productivity in such groups. Benchmark healthcare organizations know that micromanaging is the surest way to minimize staff spirit and commitment. Consequently, they clarify the departmental goals and ground rules, then they empower departmental managers to take charge of their departments. These managers, in turn, then empower their staff to do whatever it takes (within ground rules) to improve customer service. Bureaucratic red tape is either minimal or nonexistent.

Point D (Mission Defining) represents an unusual situation and one seldom discussed in the literature of empowerment. Here, employees are empowered to decide on job context but not the content. In some small healthcare clinics, employees have fixed job functions but are very involved in defining the organization's mission, values, goals, objectives and strategies.

Point E (Self-Management) represents an area in which employees are given total decision-making authority for both job content and job context. Giving employees this much authority requires considerable faith in their ability to use their newfound empowerment in ways that will contribute to the organization's effectiveness. It requires extensive employee involvement in the development of the organization's mission and goals and confidence that employees are ready, willing, and able to make decisions about their work that will result in intelligent and appropriate contributions to the organization's objectives. Empowering a person to make both job content and context decisions that optimally respond to changing environmental conditions, technological innovations, and competitive challenges is the ultimate expression of trust. For obvious reasons, few healthcare organizations are comfortable permitting many people, other than those in the top-management suite, to operate at the self-management level.

## Point B and the Healthcare Industry

Point B empowerment perfectly suits many healthcare organizations and many healthcare employees. The clinical requirements define the job, and employees are expected to meet those requirements to achieve the desired clinical outcome. Some organizations expect employees to do the job strictly "by the numbers." But the benchmark organizations empower employees to provide service in a variety of ways. Even if a nurse in a burn ward has 25 different patients whose dressings must be changed every six hours in the same way, the manner in which that care is given and the interaction patterns that take place with each patient make each occasion somewhat different and potentially interesting for the nurse. It also presents an opportunity to perform a routine task with superb care and attention to each patient.

Benchmark healthcare organizations know that patient satisfaction increases when employees are empowered to spend more time with patients and go the extra mile to make them feel comfortable. Allowing staff to exceed patient expectations is particularly important when patients have complaints. Benchmark organizations empower all employees to provide token restitution (up to a certain dollar amount) when a patient believes that some type of service failure has occured. For example, at Baptist Hospital, each employee can go to the hospital gift shop and spend up to $250 to replace a patient's lost belonging or buy flowers to appease a complaining patient.

All in all, it can be said that a Point B empowerment level is the most suitable for many patient-contact jobs in the healthcare industry. It gives healthcare providers the flexibility to meet and exceed the patient's expectations and to prevent and recover from any service failures while maintaining the proper clinical protocols.

## Implementation

Successful implementation of an empowerment program requires knowledge of the available strategies and the determinants of their successful application and an awareness of the situations and people who can benefit from empowerment's potential. Implementation of empowerment should begin by focusing on decisions related to job content then moving gradually through the various decision-making stages from problem identification through implementation/follow-up. Later, after employees and managers become comfortable with empowerment in job content, increasing levels of empowerment in job context can similarly be added by raising the level of decision-making authority from problem identification up through implementation and follow-up.

At each step, management can determine what difficulties were created; how they should be addressed; and whether or not the individuals or teams were ready, able, and trained to move on to the next stage of decision involvement and responsibility. Alternatively, a company might empower employees to address problem identification and development of alternatives simultaneously for both job content and job context, much as was done at the General Motor's Saturn plant.

For either of these approaches or any other mid-range strategies, management needs to determine first where it would like to be on the grid in Figure 8.2 and then develop a plan to move its employees gradually toward that point. The grid simply illustrates the stages of employee empowerment, which allows managers to decide what level of empowerment their organization is ready for and what can be done to implement that desired degree of involvement in making job-related decisions.

The four key ingredients to any successful empowerment program are:

1. *Training* in knowledge areas, customer service, and decision making, and, if empowering a group (see work team discussion earlier), training in group interaction.
2. *Measurable goals or standards*, so empowered employees have a means to test whether or not the decisions they make are good or bad.
3. *Methods of measuring progress toward goals*, so empowered employees can tell if what they are doing is heading in the direction of the job goal or away from it.
4. *An incentive system* to reward the employees for making good decisions and to make it worth their while, both financially and in terms of other "eager" factors, to take on decision responsibility.

## Limitations and Potentials

Of course, employee empowerment has some organizational limitations. Employee empowerment may be less appropriate if (1) the basic business strategy emphasizes low-cost, high-volume operations; (2) the relationship to customers tends to be short term; (3) the technology is simple and routine; (4) the business environment is highly predictable; and (5) employees have low growth needs, low social needs, and weak interpersonal skills. Alternatively, employee empowerment can be highly successful and rewarding under the following circumstances (and note how many of them characterize the healthcare industry): (1) service is customized or personalized; (2) customer relationships are long term (sometimes but not always true in healthcare); (3) the technology is complex; (4) the environment is unpredictable; and (5) employees have high growth needs, social needs, and strong interpersonal skills.[19] Assuming (with respect to item 5) that employees are chosen with care, most patient-contact healthcare situations seem ideal for gaining the benefits of employee empowerment.

Within all organizations, including healthcare organizations, some departments, employees, or jobs may be better suited for employee empowerment than others. Managers hoping to gain empowerment's benefits can initially implement a limited form of empowerment in areas where the match appears potentially fruitful. From here, problems can be worked out and the empowerment process gradually expanded. Indeed, those healthcare organizations engaged in total quality management efforts, organizational reengineering, or attempts to reenergize their corporate culture's commitment to service through the introduction of more participatory management styles may all find the incremental strategy useful.

Because the workforce is so diverse, some employees will be better suited for empowerment than others. Part-time employees or contract (temporary) employees may not be interested enough in the goals of the organization or their long-term relationship with the organization to be good candidates for empowerment programs. The art of good management is to determine what degree of empowerment to extend to different employees. The grid is a useful first step in thinking about designing and implementing employee-empowerment processes, which will always be a matter of degree. Finally, empowerment can lead to problems if empowered employees make decisions that are disadvantageous to other employees. For example, if an empowered employee allows patients to check out two hours late, the housekeeping staff may have difficulty in preparing the room for the next patient, especially if another empowered employee allows the next patient to check in early. Empowering one employee must not be allowed to affect other employees negatively in the performance of their jobs.

The successful healthcare manager knows the vital importance of motivation and empowerment, if the organization is going to retain the employees it worked so hard to recruit and train. Doctors sometimes build strong relationships with patients. These relationships motivate patients to come back again and again; seeing familiar physicians adds value to their healthcare experience. A major problem with HMOs is that their managers seem unable to use appropriate motivation and empowerment techniques to keep physicians. This physician turnover is one reason for widespread customer dissatisfaction with HMOs.

## CONCLUSION

All employees seek certain types and amounts of inducements from their organizations; that is why they signed on. The manager able to provide those inducements can elicit effort, productivity, enthusiasm, and other contributions that the healthcare organization seeks from all employees. Determining the resources that are important to an individual or a group of individuals is a key responsibility of the manager seeking to retain the enthusiastic commitment of the people who work in that manager's area of responsibility. Providing the resources makes it possible for the employees to work in jobs that are fun, fair, and interesting.

## LESSONS LEARNED

1. Set clear, measurable standards that define expectations for job performance. Constantly reinforce these standards by setting examples; let employees know that the standards are important; reward employees when they meet them.
2. Walk the talk; set the example. Employees respond more to what you do than to what you say.
3. Make all tasks and goals measurable; people like to know how well they are doing.
4. Pay attention to communication; people cannot do what they do not know about or do not understand.
5. Be fair, ethical, and equitable. People need to feel that they are being treated fairly. If you do not show people why differentials are made between employees, they will assume the worst.
6. Reward behaviors you want, and do not reward behaviors you do not want. Among the most important rewards are public celebration of individual and team success in serving customers.
7. Praise, praise, praise. Give public reinforcement to people who are doing the right things. Reeducate and coach, in private, those doing the wrong things.
8. Show employees the relationships between their personal goals, group goals, and organizational goals. Find win-win-wins.
9. Do not just support your frontline employees; trust them as well.
10. Give people a chance to grow and get better, and then reward them for it.
11. Your frontline employees are heroes; make their jobs fun (to the extent possible), fair, and interesting.

## NOTES

1. Dolan, T. C. 2001. "Do You Still Walk the Halls at Night?" *Healthcare Executive* 16 (2): 4.

2. Brinker, N., and D. T. Phillips. 1996. *On the Brink: The Life and Leadership of Norman Brinker*, p. 195. Arlington, TX: The Summit Publishing Group.

3. Vance, A., and R. Davidhizar. 1998. "Motivating the Minimal Performer." *Hospital Topics* 76 (4): 8–13.

4. Zeithaml, V. A., and M. J. Bitner. 1996. *Services Marketing*, p. 76. New York: McGraw-Hill.

5. Shellenbarger, S. 1998. "Companies Are Finding It Really Pays to Be Nice to Employees." *Wall Street Journal* (July 27): B-1.

6. *Ibid.* A compelling discussion of the employee satisfaction-customer satisfaction link can be found in B. Schneider and D. E. Bowen. 1993. "The Service Organization: Human Resources Management Is Crucial." *Organizational Dynamics* 21: 39–52. See also B. Schneider and D. E. Bowen. 1995. *Winning the Service Game.* Boston: Harvard Business School Press.

7. *ACHe-news*, March 16, 2001, p. 1.

8. Dolan, T. C. 2001. "Do You Still Walk the Halls at Night?" *Healthcare Executive* 16 (2): 4.

9. Zairi, M. 1998. "Building Human Resources Capability in Health Care: A Global Analysis of Best Practice - Part III." *Health Manpower Management* 24 (5): 1–4.

10. Blejwas, L., and W. Marshall. 1999. "A Supervisory Level Self-Directed Work Team in Health Care." *The Health Care Supervisor* 17 (4): 14–21.

11. Dreachslin, J. L., P.L. Hunt, and E. Sprainer. 1999. "Key Indicators of Nursing Care Team Performance: Insights from the Front Line." *The Health Care Supervisor* 17 (4): 70–76.

12. Ashforth, B. E., and R. H. Humphrey. 1993. "Emotional Labor in Service Roles." *Academy of Management Review* 18 (1): 94.

13. *Ibid.,* p. 102.

14. Brinker, N., and D. T. Phillips. 1996. *On the Brink: The Life and Leadership of Norman Brinker,* p. 192. Arlington, TX: The Summit Publishing Group.

15. This discussion of empowerment is based on R. C. Ford and M. D. Fottler. 1995. "Empowerment: A Matter of Degree." *Academy of Management Executive* 9 (3): 21–28, and D. E. Bowen and E. E. Lawler. 1992. "The Empowerment of Service Workers: What, Why, How, and When." *Sloan Management Review* 33 (1): 31–39.

16. Plunkett, L. C., and R. Fournier. 1991. *Participative Management: Implementing Empowerment,* p. 5. New York: John Wiley & Sons.

17. Schor, J. B. 1991. *The Overworked American,* p. 11. New York: Bagle Books.

18. A classic book on this subject is J. R. Hackman and G. P. Oldham. 1980. *Work Design.* Reading, MA: Addison-Wesley.

19. Bowen, D. E., and E. E. Lawler. 1992. "The Empowerment of Service Workers: What, Why, How, and When." *Sloan Management Review* 33 (1): 31–39.

*Chapter 9*

# Involving the Patient and Family in Coproduction

Healthcare Principle: *Empower patients and their families to help meet their own healthcare needs*

God helps those that help themselves.

—*C. Simmons*

PATIENTS AND/OR their families can become involved in producing the healthcare experience. For example, patients walk after surgery to facilitate recovery, patients who have undergone lab tests bring their own results to a clinic, family members monitor their loved one's medication, and patients regulate their own pain killers. In this chapter, we discuss the reason healthcare organizations might want to increase the involvement of patients and their families in providing services, ways of facilitating this involvement, and the advantages and disadvantages of coproduction from all perspectives.

## CUSTOMERS AS QUASI-EMPLOYEES

Healthcare employees have to produce the healthcare experience consistently and flawlessly while coping with the many uncertainties that interacting constantly with anxious patients or their families can create. Healthcare organizations know they must help manage the confusion and uncertainty that customers can create for their employees while they are doing their jobs. One way to do so is by training the employees in both job skills and customer relations. Another effective strategy for managing this confusion is to think of patients and their families as quasi-employees and manage them accordingly.[1] This means

223

that organizations should design the service product, environment, and delivery systems to take advantage of the skills, talents, knowledge, and abilities that these extra "employees" bring to the organization.

If patient and family involvement in the healthcare experience is to the advantage of both patients and organization, then the organization must take on the responsibility of figuring out how best to enable these quasi-employees to do their jobs within the experience. Sometimes the patient will become a quasi-employee, sometimes friends and family, and sometimes all three. For the sake of simplification, we refer to coproduction roles that patients can play, although family, friends, clergy, and others can also play some of these roles when appropriate.

Here is a three-step strategy for managing these quasi-employees:

1. Define the roles you want patients or others to play, carefully and completely. In effect, do a job analysis: define the knowledge, skills, and abilities required to perform the jobs identified as desirable and appropriate for patients or their families and friends.
2. Make sure that patients and others know exactly what you expect them to do and that they are physically able, mentally prepared, and sufficiently skilled to do those tasks. Show them that performing the tasks is to their benefit. Give them a reason to do the tasks well.
3. Evaluate each of the nonemployees involved in patient care relative to their ability and willingness to perform well. In effect, conduct a performance appraisal on the patient to ensure that the experience being coproduced is meeting expectations. If it is not, identify what needs fixing. Does the patient need further training? Is something about the setting or delivery system impeding the patient's ability to successfully perform the assigned tasks?[2]

Of course, no outsider should be allowed to coproduce the experience if learning the necessary skills is too dangerous, time consuming, or difficult. By carefully assessing the entire healthcare experience, the healthcare provider can identify those parts that might discourage, encourage, or even require patient participation. A physician can allow a self-administered blood pressure test, or a hospital patient might walk to the cafeteria for dinner. In these instances, patients can choose to have an employee help them or they can perform their own test or obtain their own dinner. Some healthcare organizations do not give the patient any choice; they either make patient participation impossible or they structure the experience so that the patient has to participate to some extent to have it.

In the past, typical appendectomy patients were allowed to stay in bed until they felt like getting up and walking. Now, they are asked to get up and walk as soon as possible after surgery. Doctors know that resuming physical activity after surgical procedures promotes healing, so they do all they can to get patients up and walking. Today, the linkage between physical activity and postsurgical healing is so well accepted that patients are not usually given a choice; they have to participate to get better.

Organizations need to think through when to let patients coproduce their own experience and how much of it. Sometimes patient participation makes sense for the organization and the patient, sometimes it does not. The challenge is distinguishing between those situations.

## STRATEGIES FOR INVOLVING CUSTOMERS

The patient and others can be involved in several ways: as consultants or sources of expert information, as part of the environment for other patients, as coproducers of the experience, or as "managers" of the service providers and systems. Some of these involvements may sound unlikely, but they are all common.

### Consultants

One of the best ways for healthcare organizations to enhance their performance in customer service and customer satisfaction is to bring customers into the decision-making loop by allowing their input on devising new services and improving existing services. Fierce competition today has forced most organizations to become more flexible and creative in their dealings with customers to give them exactly what they want.[3] For example, Continental Airlines once had the worst on-time and customer service records in the industry. CEO Gordon Bethune changed that by putting customers first and involving them in service improvements through customer surveys and the airline industry's first 24-hour toll-free number, 800-WE-CARE-2, to deal with all types of passenger problems. Surveys included use of postage-paid comment cards, telephone interviews, and the company's web site. Customer service was renamed customer care, making passenger complaints and suggestions the top priority. Customer care's goal is to resolve customer complaints at the first point of contact—usually the initial phone call.[4]

When the healthcare organization asks its customers what they liked or disliked about their healthcare experience, they become unpaid consultants.[5] Because customers have gone through the healthcare experience, they are now experts at it. They are now the best sources of the information that management uses to review and adjust its service, environment, and delivery system. Using outsiders in this way is not unique to healthcare firms; many other types of organizations invite their suppliers, customers, and even communities to provide systematic feedback about how they are doing. Organizations also frequently invite customers to participate as members of focus groups.

All across American industry today, corporations are giving customers the tools to design and demand exactly what they want. Benchmark companies are inviting customers in as collaborators in product design and redesign.[6] Customers can help the organization design new services or redesign old ones. One way to do so is by using focus groups or having a team of administrators, physicians, and nurses interview individual patients after completion of a service encounter. A 24-hour-a-day hotline can be established to receive customer input. Comment cards, telephone interviews, and web sites are other methods of receiving customer input.

In many healthcare organizations, no real collaboration exists between patients and providers because a collaboration requires that people work together in mutual respect. Too often, when a person enters the role of patient, he or she no longer feels like an equal partner because he or she may experience feelings of helplessness, lack of technical competence, and emotional disturbance. No real balance of power exists between those giving and receiving health services in the traditional system of care. To change that system, healthcare providers have to see it from the patient's point of view and create a system based on the concerns of the customers.

One means of doing so is to establish a patient-family panel to build partnerships with patients. The organization can then combine professional knowledge with systematic input from experienced customers. Haukeland Hospital in Bergen, Norway, established a patient-relative panel in 1997 as part of their continuous quality improvement process.[7] The panel is composed of seven people, at least two of each gender and at least two in the patient and relative categories. Regular meetings are held about eight times per year, and the CEO of the hospital joins the meetings regularly. Two employees from the hospital's department of quality improvement provide the link between the panel and hospital management. What did the hospital learn from the panel? The hospital management and the panel learned each other's perspectives on how it feels to receive care, to meet different people every day, to adapt to a foreign situation where the staff are the ones "at home," and to live with sickness and pain.

These different perspectives were then used in the hospital's decision processes in areas such as involvement, continuity of care, safety, punctuality, accessibility, resources, information, and communication. For example, parents of sick children were previously given food tickets for meals in the cafeteria. Through the panel, the executive team learned the importance of parents eating together with their children and that many parents would rather skip meals than leave their children alone. The result was that parents were allowed to eat with children in their rooms.[8] Even though the panel cannot make any decisions, in acting as a consultative body for the CEO, it serves as an excellent model of how to create a successful partnership between customers and healthcare providers.

## Part of the Environment

Each patient is invariably part of another patient's healthcare environment and influences it—either positively or negatively. Research shows that patients sharing similar physical pain endure the pain better in a group than by themselves. Other studies show that patients in waiting rooms have more positive attitudes when in groups than when they are closed off by themselves. In such instances, patients have a positive effect on each other's experience.

On the other hand, the extremely intimate nature of some healthcare experiences requires that extraordinary precautions be taken to avoid patients being part of each other's experience. Customarily, though, for better or worse, other patients are part of the healthcare servicescape and therefore need to be managed like any other environmental element.

## Coproducers

Patients can actually become part of the production and delivery system of their own healthcare experience. A simple example is when patients pour their own water or feed themselves, minimizing the need for paid nurse aides. At a more complex level, many patients coproduce their own care by administering their own clinical tests, such as blood pressure, glucose level, or heart rate tests, eliminating the need to go to the doctor's office. The testing equipment can then be connected to a phone line and the results can be viewed on the Internet, allowing distant doctors to check them.

One way in which healthcare organizations have begun to enhance the ability of customers to coproduce their own health services is by giving them access to information they can use in making their own decisions on diagnosis, treatment options, and provider choices.[9] Anthem Blue Cross and Blue Shield of New Hampshire has partnered with the Foundation for Informed Medical Decision Making (started by Dr. John Wennberg at Dartmouth) to develop a program called Your Health.[10] This program gives patients educational tools such as videotapes, web sites, a self-care guidebook, and a 24-hour hotline they can use to evaluate and choose among competing treatment options. Results indicate that 70 percent of patients felt their quality of care improved after using these materials, while 90 percent were more confident in dealing with their medical conditions.[11]

## "Managers"

Patients can serve in a quasi-managerial role as unofficial supervisors and motivators of employees; they can even train other patients. Because patients have more contact with the healthcare service personnel, talk to them more often, and see more of their job behavior than their own supervisors do, patients can act as managers of their own experience and supervisors of the service providers. Patients have the opportunity and the motivation to act as supervisors and provide immediate feedback, whether satisfactory or not, on the service, the service provider, and the organization. The more familiar patients are with the organization, the more they know about what level of service should be provided and the more qualified they are to provide technical feedback.

When an unhappy patient tells the employee that he or she is not providing the service properly, that patient is in effect performing a supervisory function: providing feedback to the employee. Patients typically give great feedback to the caregiver by grimacing, smiling, screaming, or responding in other verbal and nonverbal ways to what the employee is doing. These responses are far more effective guides to the caregiver than any instructions that a supervisor can give. Although supervisors monitor the behavior of clinical staff as they perform their clinical duties, they also monitor the verbal and nonverbal behavior of the patients to gauge reaction to the staff service. Patients talk, smile, give directions, and complain, and those are cues to both staff members and their supervisors. All of these patient activities and functions are supervisory because the patients are observing, guiding, and motivating the behavior of employees, then "paying" them for good or poor service with a big smile and sincere appreciation.

Patients can be motivators. Having patients tell employees, in verbal and nonverbal ways, that they are doing a good job can be highly motivating. Most healthcare employees find great satisfaction in meeting and exceeding the expectations of patients. Healthcare employees usually enjoy the opportunity to be challenged by a patient who shares an interest or expertise in the subject of the experience. College professors often find the students who ask the most difficult questions to be the most fun to have in class. Most healthcare employees are constantly tested by the variety of patient expectations and variety of responsibilities in the service delivery process.

Patients can also train each other. For example, healthcare professionals can try to teach patients how to cope with a terminal illness, but it is an enormous challenge. Providers know that their patients are aware that the healthcare staff, whose lives are not at risk, cannot possibly understand the degree of emotional and physical pain that terminally ill patients are enduring. Support groups consisting of patients with similar diagnoses and treatment options can get together to talk about their experiences. The patients are credible with each other because they are all going through similar turmoils.

Most patients of healthcare organizations, like most employees, are anxious to fulfill their responsibilities and do whatever they need to do to help themselves get well and relieve their own suffering. They can frequently be seen watching or observing other people to learn how they can pattern their own behavior to be able to perform various tasks of the wellness production process. Pregnant women at birthing classes can, for example, teach each other proper breathing techniques to minimize pain and promote a safe and normal birth. Similarly, many amputees and breast cancer survivors gladly share their experiences with patients about to undergo or who have recently undergone the same experience. The organization can also use videos of experienced patients to show waiting patients what they are supposed to do. If the organization can use its patients or former patients to train other patients, the cost and time savings of such patient participation can be substantial. The situation can become win-win because the patients are often better able to help and train each other than the healthcare staff can.

## ADVANTAGES AND DISADVANTAGES OF COPRODUCTION

Coproduction of the healthcare experience has potential advantages and disadvantages for both the organization and the patients or other customers.

### Advantages for the Organization

First, coproduction can reduce employee costs. Every time patients serve themselves or produce their own products, they are replacing labor that the organization will otherwise have to pay to do the same thing while often improving the quality of their own experience. The more patients do for themselves, the fewer employees the organization needs to employ. Second, patient coproduction allows the organization to use the talents of its employees better. For example, at some hospitals families are allowed to conduct exercise routines for their patient-relative, so staff members are available for more complicated or life-threatening patient needs. If patients are allowed, encouraged, or forced to take care of some of their own basic requirements, employees are freed up to do more elaborate or complicated tasks that the patients do not enjoy doing or cannot do successfully or that are simply unsuitable for patients to perform.

### Advantages for the Patient

First, coproduction can decrease the opportunity for disappointment in the healthcare experience while increasing the perception, and perhaps the actuality, of service quality. Because the patients themselves define value and quality, having them produce part of their own experience means that they can produce exactly what they want. If patients adjust their own pain medication, for example, this opportunity creates the perception of real value because the patient receives neither too little nor too much. Second, the opportunity for self-service typically reduces the time required for service. A simple example is the customer at the bank who chooses to use the ATM instead of going inside the bank and standing in line for a teller. At-home testing procedures, with results forwarded electronically to healthcare providers, are a tremendous boon to patients who otherwise might have to drive great distances to receive routine check-ups. Third, self-service reduces the risk of unpleasant surprises for the patients. If patients at nursing homes are allowed to use the cafeteria instead of being required to eat whatever is on the tray, they are more likely to choose what they want and reduce the risk of being disappointed with unordered and unwanted food items.

## Disadvantages for the Organization

First, in this litigious society, participation exposes the organization to legal risk. Having a patient walk from his room to the x-ray room can lead to a lawsuit if the patient falls and is injured.

Second, the organization may have to spend extra money to train the service delivery employees so that they can not only do their usual clinical jobs but can also communicate effectively and easily with patients about what they are supposed to do. These employees are responsible for instructing the patients in how to provide the service for themselves as well as monitoring the experience to prevent the patients from creating any disasters. Because every patient is different; has different healthcare needs; comes to the healthcare experience with different skills, knowledge, and abilities; and also has different service expectations, service providers have to be alert, observant, and well trained in how to coach patients in all parts of the experience in which patients are participating. Hiring and training people to perform the necessary clinical skills at, say, a modern laboratory is one thing, but to allow or encourage self-service, the organization must go beyond basic job skills to hire and train people who can successfully teach patients to perform their own clinical tests properly.

Third, the organization may have to spend extra money to ensure that the service delivery system is user-friendly. If the organization wants the patient to follow a predetermined sequence of steps to create the desired experience, it must assign employees to guide patients and ensure that excellent directions are in place or the sequence is intuitively obvious to people from varied cultures and backgrounds. Only then can the organization be reasonably sure that all types of patients will do what they are supposed to do when and where they are supposed to do it.

If you are running a clinical laboratory, then the signs, directions, and instructions must indicate clearly where the entry point is, where the appropriate testing is done, how the patient is supposed to get there, and the payment procedure. Someone unfamiliar with a clinical laboratory might have no idea how to navigate this service delivery process. The clinical staff must be alert to confused-looking patients wandering around looking for signs, directions, and instructions on how to participate successfully in this laboratory experience.

Fourth, the organization may have to spend time and energy to ensure that the "back-of-the-house" areas, which patients do not normally see, meet the same appearance and quality expectations they have for the traditional "front-of-the-house" areas. Making the back of the house a part of the healthcare experience has an obvious impact on how the equipment is laid out; how shiny it is kept; and how the personnel dress, behave, and interact during service production. Instead of having laboratory technicians, who normally do not have to be particularly articulate, in an out-of-sight laboratory, active patient involvement in lab testing means that the organization must hire employees who can communicate easily with patients, look trim and neat, and ensure that the laboratory and other visible backstage areas are always clean to meet the patient's expectations. The cost of the uniforms, the extra interpersonal skills training for back-area employees, and the rearrangement of the back area all add up.

Fifth, organizations may have to deal with customers who cannot disengage from their role as coproducers. If patients enjoy coproduction and are reluctant to disengage, the organization that does not want to prod its patients along may have to add extra capacity. Clearly, when patients become coproducers, the traditional role of "service provider" in the healthcare experience changes and needs redefinition; the actual service providers then need additional training in the new roles they must now play—as coaches to the quasi-employees.

Sixth, unsatisfactory or unsuccessful coproduction can be disastrous to the organization if the cost of failure is great. If the organization lets the patient or family member transport the patient to the discharge area and the patient falls, trips, or has some other kind of accident, then the result for the organization will probably be negative. Good healthcare organizations make every effort to ensure that patients succeed as coproducers, but the risk of failure is always present. If the costs of failure are too high, then the organization must tactfully intervene to keep the patient from failing. The service provider must be sensitive and aware enough to recognize when a patient is about to fail, must take over before the failure occurs, and must be able to do so with sufficient grace that the patient is not embarrassed by failing when others all around are succeeding.

## Disadvantages for the Patient

First, paying patients may resent having to produce any part of the service for which they are paying. Some task-oriented patients do not particularly want much service provider interaction; they just want a health service. A production-line approach suits them just fine. Other patients, on the other hand, insist on and require close personal attention. If shifting part of the healthcare experience to patients themselves results in less "TLC," those patients will be dissatisfied.

Second, patients may fail to coproduce the service or any associated product properly. If you find that the physical therapy that you and your family have been conducting is boring and you quit, you will not have coproduced a satisfactory experience for yourself; worse, you cannot even blame the service provider for the unsatisfactory experience. Healthcare organizations try to protect patients against self-service failures, so they let patients try again or they offer to help. The risk is nonetheless present that the patient will fail to successfully perform in the coproduction and will create an unsatisfactory healthcare experience.

Patients can safely participate when they have the necessary knowledge, skills, and abilities, and they are motivated to participate if the service cannot happen without their participation or if they see some benefits. Some healthcare experiences can be completed only if coproduced. For example, if the physician asks you to say "Ah" and you do not do it, your throat examination will not be as effective. To take a more complex experience, patients must do their part during rehabilitation therapy, and mothers must push during childbirth. Many medical conditions are diagnosable only or primarily based on the patient's description of symptoms.

Many patients are motivated to participate because of their personalities, their familiarity with the experience being offered, boredom, or a desire/motivation to get well. By contrast, those who are not motivated to get well or even to survive will not want to participate in their own healthcare. Some patients just want to be a part of whatever it is they are involved in at the moment, no matter what, and constantly look for such opportunities. Some people always park their own cars, carry their own luggage, or walk up the stairs because they like to demonstrate for themselves (and anyone else who cares to watch) that they are physically fit enough to do these things. Others like to show how mentally fit or technically adept they are by doing things for themselves, whether taking their own temperature or doing medical research on the Web.

## DETERMINING WHEN PARTICIPATION MAKES SENSE

Sometimes both the organization and the patient benefit from patient participation and sometimes not. Distinguishing when, where, and how much the patient should or should not be involved in any part of the healthcare experience depends on a variety of factors. Generally speaking, participating in the service is in the interest of patients when they can gain value, improve quality, or reduce risk. Participation is in the organization's interest when it can increase patient satisfaction, save money, increase production efficiency, differentiate its services from those of competitors in some key way, or build patient commitment. Each opportunity for patient participation should be assessed on these criteria and designed into the healthcare experience when the factors are favorable and designed out when they are not.

### Value, Quality, and Risk

Although some healthcare situations require participation and some patients look for opportunities to participate no matter what, almost everyone is happy to coproduce if it adds value to their experience. By definition, value can be added by reducing patient costs (for the same quality), increasing healthcare quality (for the same costs), or both. Costs include not only the price but also the other costs incurred by being involved in the healthcare experience. For example, if a potential patient sees that the parking lot or waiting room of her usual walk-in clinic is full, the time cost to her of waiting for service may be so great that she goes to an unfamiliar clinic nearby. The patient may experience a decrease in quality but expects the greater decrease in overall cost to compensate for it.

Similarly, patients who want to be sure of service quality may want to participate in providing service. Those patients want to know that they are getting the service tailored to their specific needs and desires. Patients can "participate in providing service" without actually handling instruments and reading charts. Decisions about what clinical procedures and treatments might lead to the desired positive clinical outcome are a large part of any healthcare experience. The older notion was that patients followed "doctor's orders" without question; today, patients want to be involved. If the doctor says "Take two aspirin and go to bed," the patient may ask "Why?"

Many consumers, including healthcare consumers, have become activists regarding the goods and services they buy. Patients these days want to participate in the decision-making aspects of healthcare. They feel that they can improve the quality of the healthcare experience when they can choose from among available options offered or described by the healthcare professional. Computer-literate patients often derive their own second opinions from the Internet. They may go to informative web sites or to chat rooms and newsgroups to interact with people who have been in similar medical situations, then consider the gathered information and make a decision.

Another cost of coproduction for the patient is risk—the risk that the service may not meet expectations. Patients who provide or coproduce their own experiences minimize the risk that a healthcare employee will not provide exactly what is wanted. Many people now surf the Internet looking for medical information. Some of them believe that their doctor is more interested in processing a waiting room full of patients at the HMO-prescribed rate of eight or ten minutes per patient than in giving them the most advanced medical care, which may take longer.

### Customer and Organizational Reasons

Some research suggests that two factors of primary importance to patients are time and control. When patients can save time and/or gain control, they are more likely to want to participate. Each factor is of two kinds: real and perceived.[12]

With time, the feeling (perception) of how long something takes is as important to the patient as how long it actually (reality) took. The same is true for control. The amount of control over the quality, value, risk, or efficiency of the experience that patients think they acquire by participating is as important in determining the value of participation as the real control that patients actually have. As an example, patients are sometimes given real control over pain medication. They are allowed to administer more pain medicine when they decide the pain is too great; having this control adds to patient satisfaction.

From the organization's point of view, the most obvious reason to encourage or require coproduction is to achieve higher levels of patient satisfaction; another reason is to save money. As noted earlier, whenever the patient produces or coproduces the service, the patient is providing labor that the organization would otherwise have to pay for. A third reason is to increase production efficiency or increase capacity utilization. If patients are allowed or encouraged to do more things for themselves, then the nursing staff has more time for those patients who really need skilled nursing care. In this way, the organization can maintain a constant staffing level while still being able to accommodate the variability in patient demand for nursing care. Letting patients coproduce part of the healthcare experience increases the number of patients who can be served.

Organizations can also use patient or family participation as part of a product-differentiation strategy. For example, a hospital may distinguish itself from others by letting family members be present with video equipment during the birth experience or by the use of nurse midwives. Similar examples abound throughout our economy, from self-service gas stations to car rental agencies, cafeterias, and financial services. Many healthcare organizations have created web sites to provide information to patients. They distinguish themselves from nonelectronic sources of healthcare information by the ease and rapidity of access they provide to patients willing to help themselves.

A final reason is to build patient commitment and repeat business. If a patient feels that the organization trusts her enough to let her provide her own service, then the patient feels a bond and a commitment. Getting the patient involved in the healthcare experience is a positive way for the patient to feel ownership in that experience and a loyalty to the organization that provides this opportunity.[13] It also may be a way for that patient and the organization to express their tie to each other.

Many service organizations try hard to build such relationships because they recognize the lifetime value of a loyal repeat customer. Frequent flyer and "frequent patient" programs are both designed to build this attachment so that customers come back time after time to the organization that knows them. Benchmark healthcare organizations understand that their customers have many choices concerning where they will receive health services. Consequently, these organizations offer more incentives to keep the loyalty of their customers.

## Costs Versus Benefits

The key to deciding when to offer the patient the opportunity to participate is to do a simple cost-benefit analysis, by using material like that presented in Table 9.1. The organization needs to be sure, for both itself and the patient, that the benefits of participation outweigh the costs. The organization will want to ask itself the following questions: What are the knowledge, skills, and abilities (KSAs) necessary to perform successfully as a patient quasi-employee? Are we likely to find all, some, or none of them in our job candidates/patients?[14] What is the motivation for patients to participate, and how do we appeal to that motivation? What are the training requirements for successful performance in the patient/employee role, and do we have the time and personnel necessary to train the patients in the proper performance of that role? Will patients come back and use that skill again if we spend the time and money to train them? If so, the expenditure of time and money may be worthwhile. Is it cheaper, faster, or more efficient for the organization to provide the service or to allow the patient to do it? Are role models (especially other patients) available to help with the training, and how can we physically structure the service environment so that we can use these models? Will letting patients provide their own experience interfere with other patients or with other parts of the organization?

For patients to be effectively used in the healthcare experience, they must have the motivation and ability to participate and the training and KSAs to do what the organization wishes them to do; the role they must perform in the healthcare experience must also be clearly defined.[15] Organizations that see mutual benefits to coproduction and try to encourage it must always have a back-up plan to accommodate the fact that some patients will and some patients will not want to participate in the experience. Those organizations that find ways of utilizing patients and their families as much as possible will, however, decrease their costs and increase the value and quality of the service for those patients who do participate.

## Letting Patients Decide

The basic point is that many but not all situations lend themselves to using some self-service or patient participation. Two strategies are available for letting patients themselves decide on their participation level in such situations. First, healthcare organizations can let their market

**Table 9.1: Advantages and Disadvantages of Patients Coproducing the Service**

| For Patient | | For Organization | |
|---|---|---|---|
| *Advantages* | *Disadvantages* | *Advantages* | *Disadvantages* |
| Reduces service costs | May frustrate patient | Reduces labor costs | Increases liability risk |
| Increases interest | May diminish service level | Improves quality | Increases patient training costs |
| Saves service time | Patient KSAs inadequate | Reduces service failures | Increases employee costs |
| Improves quality | Learning curve too steep | Opens new market niche | Increases design costs |
| Reduces risk of disappointment | | Enriches employee jobs | Interferes with other units |
| Increases satisfaction | | Increases loyalty | Too much variability in patient KSAs and motivation |
| | | Increases satisfaction | |

segment know that everyone entering the service setting must provide some of the service themselves. For example, a mental health facility can communicate to all patients who are considering counseling therapy that they must agree to participate actively or the experience will not be worthwhile for them or the counselors and they should seek other healthcare options.

Second, segment the service process so that patients entering the service setting can choose to participate or not. Group therapy patients might be told that verbal participation, although it is to their advantage, is not required. Physical therapy patients might participate or not, depending on their energy levels and extent of their injury. If patients are unable, therapists can continue to exercise the muscles for them. Some patients seeking information about a hospital might be willing to do it themselves by navigating through the hospital's web site; but for those who want to receive information from a human being, the hospital should provide names and phone numbers.

## Firing the Patient

In a sense, all patients coproduce, or have the potential to coproduce, the healthcare experience for others simply by being in each other's company. If a well-mannered, well-dressed patient sits quietly and passively in a physician's waiting room, that patient may be no more than a minor enhancement, an adornment, to the experience of other patients. Unfortunately, some patients misbehave, and certain extreme behaviors are unacceptable in any healthcare setting. Patients and family members may become verbally and physically abusive, refuse to comply with reasonable organizational rules and policies, or make outrageous demands.

Not all employees work out, and not all patients work out. Sometimes the patient's "job performance" as a coproducing quasi-employee is so unsatisfactory that the organization must, as a last resort and employing clearly defined procedures, "fire" the patient. For example, if a clinic patient becomes unruly or abusive toward the staff or tries to damage or steal hospital equipment, the patient may be asked to leave. The organization should of course give patients the benefit of the doubt; but for those few patients who are demonstrably unable to participate appropriately in the service, the organization should not hesitate to show them the exit. However, the dismissal should be accomplished with minimal harm to the patient's physical or mental well-being and dignity. The patient who feels unfairly treated and who is really angry about being dismissed may become a source of long-term negative publicity, badmouthing, and even lawsuits.

Of course, firing the patient may be inconsistent with the organization's mission as this example supports. Doctors and nurses at Highland Hospital in Oakland, California, complain about the irresponsibility, rudeness, and bad smell of a patient who has serious heart and blood pressure problems. He begs lunch from hospital staff and bums cigarettes from strangers. He has been jailed for belligerence in the emergency room, and a restraining order has been placed against him, banning him from the hospital unless he is receiving medical care. He refuses to coproduce his healthcare experience and throws his prescriptions in the trash to ensure further trips to the ER. The patient seems ready for a pink slip. But Highland is a public county hospital with a mission to serve all who come in with a medical problem, whether they can pay or not. As a result the hospital (in 2001) was still serving the patient, who has gone to the hospital's emergency room more than 1,200 times since 1996 at a cost to taxpayers approaching $1 million.[16]

Most instances are not so extreme, and many patients are fired every day, perhaps for financial reasons or because a patient's changed condition exceeds the organization's ability to provide care. Assisted-living facilities fire their patients when they need nursing care services. Nursing homes fire their patients when their health benefits run out. Hospitals fire patients when their doctors think they are ready for discharge, whether the patients agree or not, or when their HMOs refuse to make further payments. HMOs fire their Medicare patients due to excessive regulation and inadequate reimbursement by the federal government.[17]

Although the firing of a patient may be a response to a patient failure of some kind, the organization must sometimes realize that it has also failed in some way. The rude, troublesome patient had expectations, whether reasonable and realistic or not, and the organization failed to meet them.

## CONCLUSION

Enhancing the opportunities for patients and others to coproduce the healthcare experience has many potential advantages for both the organization and the patient. However, the organization must provide training and support so that the individuals performing the procedure have the knowledge, skills, and abilities to do so. Moreover, the individuals coproducing the experience need to be motivated to do so. To achieve this kind of motivation, the organization needs to make clear how coproduction benefits the patient.

## LESSONS LEARNED

1. Hire and train your service personnel to coach, monitor, and supervise the coproduction of patients and others (i.e., family, friends, clergy, and so forth).
2. Train your patients to participate before you let them; be sure they have the knowledge, skills, and abilities to participate.
3. Motivate patients who derive value and quality from participation to coproduce.

4. Encourage patients to help monitor the service behavior of your employees.
5. Structure healthcare experiences in ways that encourage other patients to train your patients; provide pretreatment videos or prepare your patients to engage in the experience.
6. The more patients do for themselves, the less you have to do for them.
7. Patient involvement can improve efficiency and capacity utilization, especially at peak demand times.
8. If you have to fire a patient, try to preserve the patient's dignity.

## NOTES

1. For an excellent article on this subject, see D. E. Bowen. 1986. "Managing Customers as Human Resources in Service Organizations." *Human Resource Management* 25 (3): 371–83.

2. Adapted from B. Schneider and D. E. Bowen. 1995. *Winning the Service Game*, pp. 88–89. Boston: Harvard Business School Press.

3. Hiebeler, R., C. Ketteman, and T. B. Kelly. 2000. *Best Practices: Building Your Business with Customer-Focused Solutions*. New York: Touchstone Books.

4. *Ibid.*

5. Van Wersch, A., and M. Eccles. 2001. "Involvement of Consumers in the Development of Evidenced-Based Clinical Guidelines." *Quality Health Care* 10 (1): 10–16.

6. Coy, P. 2000. "The Creative Economy." *Business Week* 28: 77–82.

7. Enchaug, I. H. 2000. "Patient Participation Requires a Change of Attitude in Health Care." *International Journal of Health Care Quality Assurance* 13 (4): 1–6.

8. *Ibid.*

9. Friedewald, V. E. 2000. "The Internet's Influence on the Doctor-Patient Relationship." *Health Management Technology* 21 (11): 79–80.

10. Serota, S. P. 2000. "Focus on Customer Care." *Health Forum Journal* 43 (2): 38–41.

11. *Ibid.*

12. Bateson, J. E. G. 1985. "Self-Service Consumer: An Exploratory Study." *Journal of Retailing* 61 (3): 49–76.

13. For further discussion and examples of this point, see N. Bendapudi and L. L. Berry. 1997. "Customers' Motivations for Maintaining Relationships with Service Providers." *Journal of Retailing* 73 (1): 15–37.

14. For further information on how to determine if patients have the KSAS to become involved in their own healthcare, see G. Elwyn, A. Edwards, P. Kinnersley, and R. Grol. 2000. "Shared Decision Making and the Concept of Equipoise: The Competences of Involving Patients in Healthcare Choices." *British Journal of General Practice* 50 (460): 892–99.

15. Kelley, S. W., S. J. Skinner, and J. H. Donnelly, Jr. 1992. "Organizational Socialization of Service Customers." *Journal of Business Research* 25 (3): 197–214.

16. Foster, D. 2001. "California Man Finds Comfort, Solace in ER." *The Gainesville (FL) Sun*: 10A.

17. Carey, J. 2000. "Managed Health Care Isn't Healthy After All." *Business Week* (July 24): 40.

# PART THREE

## The Healthcare Service Systems

*Chapter 10*

# Communicating Information to Customers

Healthcare Principle: *Keep the patient, family, and employees informed*

Communicate everything you can to your associates. The more they know, the more they care.

—*Sam Walton*

WHEN PATIENTS AND other healthcare customers are confronted with uncertainty about any phase of the healthcare experience, most seek information to reduce uncertainty. Although they can sometimes obtain this information easily from a variety of sources, including the Internet, they often look to their healthcare providers to provide answers. Providers, in turn, have to be prepared to meet the information needs not only of their patients and their families but also of their employees, at the time they need it and in the format they can use.

This chapter discusses the advantages and disadvantages of healthcare information systems; their application in the three components of service product, setting, and delivery system; the importance of information flow; and the advanced systems that help in decision making. Our focus here is on how information systems can meet the needs of all the organization's customers rather than just the needs of the internal organization.

## THE VALUE OF INFORMATION SYSTEMS

In theory at least, the technology exists to assist in improving the practice of medicine in the twenty-first century as noted below:

Within a couple of years, patients all over the U.S. could have secure electronic medical records and go online to schedule appointments, shop for the best hospital, look up lab results, track the status of a claim, order a new drug or consult with a specialist. With existing technology, doctors can interview and examine patients hundreds of miles away or teach colleagues computer-aided surgery via the Web. There are pilot electronic monitoring systems to keep track of chronically ill people at home, and portable medical-alert devices that can monitor them on vacation. Computerized ordering systems in hospitals can help eliminate medication errors. Powerful data systems, if specially designed to link hospitals around the country, can analyze huge amounts of medical information and share it over a network to help identify and treat public health threats before they spread. Unfortunately, the chances that any of these innovations will actually show up at your local hospital anytime soon are remote. Unique among American industries, healthcare lags so far behind in adopting the latest in information and communications technology that some experts say it may never catch up.[1]

According to *Business Week*, inadequate information systems are the prime reason that administrative costs account for an estimated 15 percent to 20 percent of total healthcare spending.[2] Creating a system that manages information effectively is one of the most important and challenging issues facing any healthcare organization.

Information is data that inform, and an information system is a method to get the data to those who need to be informed. A well-designed information system gets the right information to the right person in the right format at the right time so that it adds value to that person's decisions. The "right" person in healthcare organizations can be the staff member, the patient, or both. Information that does not provide value to either customers or staff is useless. Informing a patient waiting in line to get treatment in the emergency room that the medical staff were standing around with nothing to do earlier in the day is not only useless, it is infuriating. Receiving x-ray results after the patient has left the hospital does not help the doctor to prescribe a course of treatment. Although healthcare traditionally focuses entirely on the information needs and requirements of the clinical staff, the patients and other customers also have needs and requirements that the healthcare organization should meet.

### Informing the Customer

Because service is by definition intangible, the information that the healthcare organization provides to help the customer make the intangible tangible is a critical concern of the information system. What information should the organization provide, in what format, and in what quantity to help create the experience that the customer expects? If the experience is a surgical procedure, then the operating team should organize all the information it provides to the patient to cue the perception that this is the proper surgical procedure and one that will be excellent at that.

The surgical theatre should be set up to look like a sterile, professional, well-organized place; the team members should be wearing clean surgical gowns; and all the other physical cues should be carefully structured to send the message to the patient, "Relax. You are in the hands of a skilled surgical team that will perform your surgery perfectly." One of the authors of this book remembers being wheeled in to surgery only to see the team standing around the room chatting and drinking Cokes. They did not seem to care that the message they were communicating by their casualness did not calm him in a situation that was extremely serious to him.

Because most patients do not know how to differentiate skilled surgical teams with good records from teams with bad records, the preoperative procedures and facilities must be carefully managed to ensure that every bit of information communicates clinical competence. Whatever the patient tastes, touches, hears, sees, and smells can be managed to encourage the patient to define the medical experience in the reassuring way in which the surgical team and hospital want it defined.

Regardless of the healthcare experience being offered, all informational cues in the service setting should be carefully thought out to communicate what the organization wants to communicate to the customer about the quality and value of the experience. The less tangible the service, the more important this communication will be. By recognizing that information can glue together the service product, the service environment, and the delivery system to make a total experience, the organization can use information to make the healthcare experience itself seamless. The organization can manage its information and use the available information technology to tie together all the elements of the healthcare experience to ensure that the customer's expectations are met or exceeded. Similarly, the healthcare organization that looks at each manager and employee, both clinical and nonclinical, as a customer for its information is better able to design its information system to meet their needs.

### Adding Quality and Value Through Information

Information can be used in many ways by organizations to add quality and value to the service experience. The availability of the Internet has greatly expanded the ability of healthcare organizations to communicate with their many different customers in new ways. Futurist Russell C. Coile, Jr., summarizes the Web-based strategies and activities in which healthcare providers and healthcare-related business can engage:

1. *Advertising:* Healthcare providers can reach consumers easily and relatively inexpensively via the Web.
2. *Providers:* Healthcare consumers can use the Web to find local providers, or they can search it to find the best medical organizations and physicians in the world.
3. *Customer information and referral:* Health insurers in particular are using the Web to provide information to their enrollees about benefits, available physicians, and healthcare consumer information and referral.
4. *Shopping:* Health-related products and services are quickly and economically available via the Web, such as prescription and over-the-counter drugs, medical supplies and equipment, vitamins, and home fitness equipment.
5. *Internet pharmacy:* Pharmaceutical refills are a high-volume possibility. Deep discounts plus the convenience of next-day home delivery will encourage many consumers to get their refills via the Web once online pharmacies meet state licensing requirements.
6. *Health insurance:* Health insurers and HMOs are looking to the Web for consumer registration, eligibility verification, and transaction processing. The biggest health plans and HMOs are already using this channel. But they may be vulnerable to Web-based "virtual insurers," including national Medicare HMOs whose low overhead enables them to offer low prices.
7. *Electronic medical records:* Numerous hospitals are expected to become virtually paperless in the near future. Providers and other authorized persons and groups will be able to access huge

amounts of medical information for diagnosis, treatment, and other purposes. Patients can have access to their own health histories, maintaining a record of their own health status.

8. *Health advice and telemedicine:* Health advice, both good and ill-advised, is readily available to Web users. Telemedicine promises to become a cost-effective method for remote diagnosis, case management, and medical consultation.

8. *Customer Service:* Health plans, hospitals, large medical groups, and others will increasingly provide customer service over the Web, including verification of health plan eligibility, explanation of benefits, search for plan-approved providers, after-hours questions, online enrollment, and patient self-scheduling; patients can look over physician office calendars and schedule an appointment.[3]

## The Transformational Power of the Internet

Information technology can transform an organization or even an industry. Online bookstores and travel agencies, custom book publishers, and e-mail are all transforming their respective industries in amazing ways. The growing impact of the Internet on healthcare is providing another dramatic illustration of such a transformation. The easier, cheaper, and faster way of providing information and services to customers (both external and internal) made possible by advancing information technology is rapidly changing the dynamics of the healthcare industry.

No one really knows how many health-related web sites are on the Internet; estimates range from 20,000 to 250,000. Both healthcare consumers and providers can quickly search the world for healthcare information. Almost half of the 72 million Americans with Internet access go online for health information at least once per month,[4] and in the last couple of years, 70 million people looked on the Internet for health information.[5] That number is expected to increase to 88 million by 2005.[6] Some estimate that half of all consumers who access the Internet are seeking health-related information.[7]

Medline, the National Library of Medicine's online search service gives Internet users access to 10 million articles in medical and other health-related journals. Web sites exist for general health topic information (e.g., healthfinder.gov, merck.com, mayohealth.com); drugs (pharminfo.com, ditonline.com); heart conditions (americanheart.org); cancer (oncolink.com); and health plans (www.ahcpr.gov/consumer).

Sites like WellMed.com and HealthMagic.com offer online personal health profiles that enable patients to record and track their own healthcare information, such as blood pressure and immunizations. ImpactHealth.com offers consumers a handheld, Web-based device for measuring and monitoring blood glucose and cholesterol.[8] These are just a few of the many web sites that have sprung up as resources for the healthcare consumer and clinical practitioner.

The Internet is breaking barriers to competition in healthcare; Web-based information is enabling patients to ask hard questions about the quality and cost of their healthcare. Now, because of knowledge available to healthcare consumers on the Internet, people no longer have the blind faith in their doctors that they once had. Physicians are being confronted by patients who know the cutting edge treatments, fully comprehend the implications of their health problems, and may not accept recommended treatments without question, as earlier generations of patients have done.

Many patients trust their Internet search engines more than they do their doctors; in some states, like Ohio and New Jersey, patients wondering if their doctors have been disciplined can find out (i.e., www.state.oh.us/med or www.state.nj.us). Similarly, those interested in the quality of specific nursing homes can now make that assessment by visiting www.medicare.gov. The use of the Internet for healthcare information and products continues to increase rapidly, as more people go online and health providers encourage patients to use the Internet for matters related to physician profiles, health insurance, drug prescriptions, and medical information. For example, www.ama-assn.org and www.bestdoctors.com provide information on physicians. Comparative information on health insurance is provided by www.ncqa.org and www.ehealthinsurance.com. Prescription information can be found on www.nabp.net and www.rxaminer.com, and medical information can be found on www.nlm.nih.gov or www.mlanet.org.

The Internet has a huge potential to improve our health and healthcare. It provides patients control, convenience, and access to services that may prevent illness, complications, and even death. By using it, physicians gain information and the ability to extend their services well beyond their offices and clinics. For example, patients with severe chronic wounds, such as those resulting from diabetes and circulatory diseases, can be provided with digital cameras with which to take pictures of their wounds. Pictures sent via the Internet enable physicians to check the wounds and recommend treatment, benefiting health plans as hospitalizations and other costly services are reduced. Even more dramatic is the Mayo Clinic's plan to develop a database that contains a patient's genetic make-up. Such a database will even personalize drug therapies, allowing doctors to check which drugs work best for individual patients.[9]

The Internet also has the potential to spread wrong information and to violate patient privacy rights because it can be easily tampered with, providing access to names and credit card numbers to those who should not have them. Medem, Inc., is a company that runs a network of physician web sites to facilitate physician-patient communication.[10] The company has recently established "e-risk" guidelines to help their clients—the doctors—manage their increasing use of e-mails to communicate with their patients. Among their recommendations is for doctors to adopt password-protected messaging systems.

Physicians can check on patients and give diagnoses through e-mail instead of office visits to manage time more efficiently. Oracle (software) and HealthSouth (rehabilitation hospitals and outpatient surgery centers) are partnering to build a "digital hospital" that will integrate information technology with patient care, automate systems, reduce paperwork and medical errors, improve quality, and reduce costs.[11] DiabetesWell.com has established a Web-based "e-clinic." Its doctors monitor 700 patients across the United States, collecting data from patients online then sending back evaluations and treatment instructions. Medical staff can use transmitted data and e-mail as the basis for digital "house calls."[12] Patients can use body media to keep track of their sleep, diet, and exercise patterns to promote healthier lifestyles; they can also wear a body sensor or "life vest" that plugs into their provider's data system to monitor heart rate, blood pressure, blood sugar levels, or other critical vital statistics.[13] Web-based respiratory devices help manage children with asthma, and Web-based pacemakers help evaluate patients with irregular heartbeats.[14]

WebMD's goal is to use the Internet to link virtually everyone in the healthcare industry: patients, doctors, pharmacists, hospitals, labs, suppliers, and insurers. It is already selling health and medical items online, taking orders for prescriptions, providing practice-management software to doctors, selling to clinics everything from bandages and sutures to scalpels and x-ray machines, and processing more than 2 billion medical claims transactions annually. The web site has nearly 10 million visitors a month.[15] All of these efforts at e-medicine are aimed at prevention, cures, and at keeping medical complications from occurring; such complications cost insurers billions of dollars.

Here is an example of how information technology might be used to help a heart attack victim who has just arrived in the ER. A "smart card" is an electronic repository of a person's health information and medical treatments. A person who is having a heart attack cannot fully explain his medical information, but his smart card can. When inserted into an optical reader, the card enables the attending physician to access the person's records and see the results of all previous cardiac tests. The doctor communicates any new findings and information to the person's records via wireless microphone, and the monitors attached to the person also electronically feed additional information to his record. Doctors can compare present results to earlier ones to arrive at a computerized diagnosis. All of this information is then transmitted to the person's physician. After consultation, medication is prescribed and the person is moved to the cardiac care unit.

In a 2001 survey, 212 healthcare providers were asked how the Internet and related electronic technologies might facilitate the work of physicians and hospitals. The respondents see the Internet as being more useful in improving the informational aspects of healthcare. Sixty-eight percent of respondents said the Internet facilitated the ordering of tests and obtaining of test results; physicians acknowledged their willingness to go online to order tests and get test results. Next in importance are data exchange among caregivers and access to medical information services online; these two uses have the double advantage of aiding in clinical decision making and reducing time and money spent on treatment. (For more detailed results, see Figure 10.1).

Among the less important features to respondents include improving message exchange between physicians and patients and maintaining personal patient records, which show that the provider perspective does not correctly give a high priority to the concerns of patients and their families. Yet nowhere is the need for convenient access stronger than in healthcare. Patients now want to be able to e-mail their doctors with questions and updates on their conditions. They want to be able to schedule appointments online and gain access to their test results and medical records electronically and securely.[16]

**Figure 10.1:  Ways in Which Web and Related Technologies Assist Hospitals and Physicians: Opinions of 212 Healthcare Provider Respondents**
(in percent)

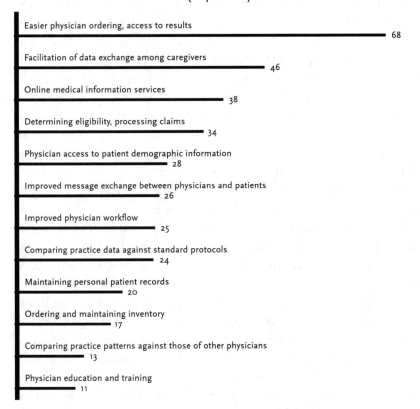

Easier physician ordering, access to results — 68

Facilitation of data exchange among caregivers — 46

Online medical information services — 38

Determining eligibility, processing claims — 34

Physician access to patient demographic information — 28

Improved message exchange between physicians and patients — 26

Improved physician workflow — 25

Comparing practice data against standard protocols — 24

Maintaining personal patient records — 20

Ordering and maintaining inventory — 17

Comparing practice patterns against those of other physicians — 13

Physician education and training — 11

*Source:* Reprinted with permission from *Modern Healthcare* (February 5): 68, 2001. "Wanting More from Information Technology," by John Morrisey.

## Personalized Service

Information can enable personalizing the service to make each customer, client, or patient feel special. For example, the use of direct linkages can allow a nurse who is monitoring many patients at many locations to contact a person whose vital signs are deviating from normal. Patients may be unaware that their vital signs are out of normal until a page or phone call greets them by name and gives them personalized attention to their problem.

Information and information technology can improve the service itself. While a bar code on a prescription drug provides the basis for recording the transaction, it also provides a wealth of other information that enhances the service experience for both organization and customer. Having a real-time record of the products being prescribed so the pharmacy can order more in a timely (or even automatic) way ensures that necessary drugs will be available when requested. Bar codes provide the opportunity to keep track of what types of drugs one physician is prescribing so that other physicians can be alerted to potential interaction problems and can even suggest alternatives. Even more interesting is the ability that such information gives to providers to identify needs before the patient is aware of them, based on monitored information. In a similar sense, if your doctor prescribes the blood-thinning drug Coumadin, then the information system can suggest that you purchase a blood-monitoring device.

The whole challenge of information systems is to figure out exactly how to gather the data that can inform, organize the data into information, and distribute that information to the people who need it when they need it. Healthcare organizations that are effective in getting information where it needs to go recognize that providing information is in itself a service, often as important as the organization's primary service, and is a necessity for the medical staff. They must therefore identify the information needs of both customers and healthcare employees in the service product, the service environment, and the service delivery system components. Let us talk about information as it relates to each of these components.

## INFORMATION AND THE SERVICE PRODUCT

Information about the healthcare experience is found within the tangible environment as well as the service itself. This information provides cues that lead customers to form favorable or unfavorable judgments about the quality and value of the healthcare experience (i.e., the service product). Sometimes, information itself may be a product. An illustration of this is the drug-management systems developed by Bergen Brunswig drug wholesalers. They put their terminals into any independent drug store that wishes to affiliate with their service. The terminals provide the stores with data on sales and inventory but also provide other services. The system will check on interaction effects of a prescribed drug with any other drug that the system knows has been prescribed for that patient and signal the pharmacist if it detects a potential problem.

In addition, Bergen compiles sales information for both drugs and sundries sold by the independent drug stores, and that information is used to help the drug stores manage their inventories. The information is used by Bergen to manage its own inventories and product availability, and may also be sold to drug suppliers for their marketing information. Bergen even has the capability of managing the drug inventory for any of its affiliated pharmacies and can provide just-in-time restocking based on its knowledge of consumer purchase patterns.

For the employee-customer, the service provided is often the delivery of the information that the staff needs for making decisions about how to serve fellow staff members. This information-product is provided to the employee-customer by another employee or employee unit acting as an internal information services organization. This concept is perhaps easier illustrated than explained in the abstract. Consider a rehabilitation therapy manager who must decide whether to revitalize or replace a room full of rehabilitation machines that have perhaps become dated, obsolete, or are no longer utilized at the expected rate. The manager will need such data as patient counts and utilization rates, wait times, patient surveys, and forecasts of future demand for rehabilitation. Each of these pieces of information is the end product of some other employee's or unit's information production and delivery system.

Providing information is the service activity for many internal employees-customers, and all healthcare organizations seek to provide it as effectively and efficiently as they can. Indeed, the entire movement toward patient-centered care that characterizes the benchmark healthcare organizations depends on employees having easy access to all patient-related information. Prompt, appropriate, and necessary patient care is impossible without some systematic way to acquire it. Managers and patient-contact employees alike must have accurate and complete information about patients to make good decisions and to measure the results of their decision-making activity.

## INFORMATION AND THE SERVICE SETTING

The service setting and its features and aspects can provide several kinds of useful information for patients. First, the service setting can be a source of information related to the service itself, and that information must be efficiently and effectively provided. If the tangible product in the healthcare experience is an x-ray at an outpatient clinic, then the patient needs to know how to find the x-ray department, the procedure for getting the x-ray, and what to do next after the x-ray is taken. Signs should therefore be placed in the service environment to facilitate easy access to the department. At the sign-in desk, directions should be posted in easy-to-see locations, and statements should be handed out to patients telling them what they are supposed to do after the x-ray procedure has been completed. Anyone who has tried to find a specific location in a large hospital knows that the healthcare industry has room for improvement in providing information on directions and locations.

Many hospitals have attractive graphics of the setting at their web sites, showing room interiors or even views from a hospital room window. These graphical renditions of the setting help to make the service tangible for potential patients so they can see for themselves the quality of the healthcare facility.

In a larger sense, the healthcare environment itself can be thought of as an information system of sorts by the way it is designed and laid out. The information provided in the environment can enhance or detract from the service experience. This information ranges from a simple orientation map posted at the entrance that tells patients and visitors where they are to more elaborate interactive computer systems that allow patients to obtain the information they need to acquire the healthcare services they seek.

## INFORMATION AND THE SERVICE DELIVERY SYSTEM

Information is required to make the service delivery system work. That system includes both people and the processes by which the service and any accompanying tangible product are delivered to the patient. Here again the nature of the service product and the delivery system unique to that product will determine what the ideal information system should be. If the end result of the service is effective healthcare treatment at a clinic, the information system needs to be set up in a way that communicates to the nurse and physician that the patient is ready for treatment, the vital signs have been measured and recorded, and the medical records are available. Many clinics use simple color-coded flags as an information system to indicate what stage the patient has reached and who needs to do what next in the treatment process.

## Service Quality

Perhaps one of the more important uses of healthcare information systems is in the systematic gathering of information on service quality. Acquiring this information, organizing it into a usable form, and disseminating it to managers and service providers is critical to ensure that service delivery and other problems are identified and resolved. Entering complaints into the information system about customers' annoyance with the constant paging of doctors over the intercom is a first step, but the step is worthless unless the manager and other employees responsible for customer satisfaction get the same information promptly. Finally, the information system must be designed to ensure that someone follows up on such service quality problems.

The information system can be used to ensure that all the people involved in delivering the service have the information they need to do their jobs in the best possible way. Here is where the most powerful applications of modern information technology have been developed. Providing the healthcare employee with the information necessary to satisfy and even impress the customer is an effective way to add value to the healthcare experience.

For example, when a patient appears at a doctor's office, the staff needs to know what insurance coverage the patient has. A customer can be cleared to pump gas at a self-serve pump in 18 seconds, but how long does it take for a patient to be cleared to receive medical service? Is the patient enrolled in a health plan and, if so, what services are covered? The patient has a coverage card, but is it current? The office staff must check a master list provided by the health plan. Unfortunately, the coverage card or the master list or both may be incorrect or out of date. Before the patient can even speak to the doctor, the records must be checked with the health insurer. Patients are naturally unhappy about the delay. Phycor, the nation's largest physician-practice management company, has devised a method enabling the doctor's receptionist to use the Internet to check the patient's insurance coverage quickly and reliably. Healtheon Corp. and IDX have implemented similar approaches.[17]

In many other situations, information systems, especially Internet-assisted systems, make it possible for the healthcare employee to provide service to customers quickly and efficiently. Indeed, this is the area in which the healthcare industry has worked the hardest to capture the benefits and economies of technology without losing the human contact that is so vital to the healthcare experience. It is a high-tech world, but because technology has taken over so many functions that used to be performed by people, patients value a "high-touch" experience even more than before. Len Berry says, "Most great service companies are high touch and high tech, not one or the other."[18] Healthcare organizations therefore try to use as much technology behind the scenes as they can, primarily to save on back-of-the-house labor costs, so that they can give patient-contact employees enough time to offer the personal contacts and touches that patients value so much.

### Electronic Expertise

In many ways, information technology now allows the healthcare organization to provide expert skills without paying experts to provide them. Rural hospitals often gain access to expertise they otherwise cannot afford by having online access to major teaching hospitals where that expertise is available around the clock. Acquiring this level of expertise takes time and experience that physicians in rural hospitals do not have, and the rural organization and its customers will have to pay more than they can afford to have that expertise on site all the time.

By having this expertise available through an online connection, a local general practitioner can call up from a bedside, get access to a specialist's knowledge and expertise, and enhance the quality of the local patient's care. If this knowledge can be provided online through an Internet connection in the patient's room or made available through a touch-screen device or even through an employee who can easily access a computerized database, the cost to the patient and the organization of providing that expertise is reduced while the quality of the information and the ease of access are increased. Clearly, this is a good illustration of using information and information technology to enhance the healthcare organization's ability to provide a valuable service for the patient.

### Customer-Contact and Healthcare Support Groups

Another major part of the healthcare service delivery information system ties together the customer-contact group (those people and functions serving healthcare customers) with the healthcare support group (those people and functions serving those who serve the customers). Coordination between these two geographically separate groups of the service delivery system is critical in providing a seamless experience for the patient. The patient does not care that the communications system between the pharmacist (who belongs to the healthcare support group) and the nurse (who belongs to the customer-contact group) is faulty. The patient cares only about the quality of the total healthcare experience, and the organization is responsible for providing the quality by ensuring that the right prescriptions get to the right patient at the right time.

For example, a patient may receive a physical exam in a primary care physician's office. If the physician does not have a laboratory to do medical tests on site, the patient might be asked to visit a medical laboratory, have certain tests done under certain conditions (e.g., no food for eight hours), and have the lab fax back the results to the physician's office. The probability of seamless service in such a situation is low unless directions for both the patient and the lab are extremely clear.

### Information Flow Across and Between Organizational Levels

The last major requirement of the information system in service delivery is to provide information flows between organizational levels. This level-to-level flow of information can take the shape of a simple employee newsletter or a document with a routing slip or can be embodied in a complicated online, real-time, data retrieval and decision system. Information can also be provided through a centralized database or intranet that is accessible to all employees, allowing them to retrieve specific information on corporate policy, dates and places of training opportunities, or availability of alternative jobs.

All of these methods of communication, whether on a piece of paper or on complicated electronic devices, are additional ways in which healthcare managers can reinforce cultural traditions, motivate employees, and educate them to enhance the healthcare experience. Of course, many other communication channels flow up and down between management and employees. Employee-of-the-month programs, for example, allow the organization to communicate to all employees the types of behavior desired and rewarded. Employee suggestion programs are another way for management to pick up new ideas and other types of information from their employees that enable quick identification of problem areas in the service delivery system.

Perhaps the most problematic example of information flow across levels is the chronic miscommunication problem between nurses and physicians. For example, a seemingly innocent problem with illegible physician handwriting can result in the misreading of orders by the nurse, which can then result in tragedy. Ninety-eight thousand patients die each year because of medication errors, many of which trace back to the nurses' inability to properly read the physician-handwritten prescription.

Technology can provide an avenue for improving such problems by providing a common database on the patient that records and tracks everything that physicians order for patient care and everything that all the clinical employees do in executing or implementing those orders. Indeed, in more sophisticated systems, orders can be automatically forwarded to other units and logged into schedule books so that the human error in information transmission is eliminated. Handheld devices and Palm computers can now link doctors' various databases to ensure that patients get the right medication. Such devices can also alert doctors if one of a patient's drugs conflicts with another.[19]

A consortium of large employers, known as the Leapfrog Group, wants hospitals to adopt computerized order-entry systems for doctors.[20] These systems require a doctor to input every order for a prescription, lab test, and procedure. The system checks for drug allergies or drug-interaction problems and even offers information on new therapies. The Leapfrog Group believes that developing such a system is an important contribution to reducing "preventable mistakes" or human error.

## ADVANCED INFORMATION SYSTEMS

Two types of systems that do more than simply provide information are decision systems and expert systems. They respond to information and choose between alternatives. Decision systems are particularly useful to organizations that want to establish lasting relationships with patients. Advanced forms of expert systems are sometimes called artificial intelligence.

### Decision Systems

Programmed into *decision systems* are rules that either help a decision maker decide or, in some cases, replace the decision maker altogether. An example of a decision system that aids a decision maker is an automatic warning that signals a monitor at the nurses' station when a critical care patient's blood pressure is too low or an icon that flashes on a computer screen to warn a nurse that a patient is having a medical emergency. A decision system can even replace a decision maker when real-life situations can be accurately modeled. In these cases, the information system provides a flow of information to a decision model that is programmed to respond when the monitored information indicates that a predetermined response is required.

Models can be built because research has revealed that certain relationships are always or nearly always true. If a blood sugar monitor registers a certain low level of sugar in the patient's bloodstream, then an IV drip can be automatically programmed to increase the glucose percentage in the drip. Because a drop in blood-sugar level can be dangerous, the information system can be programmed to check the level constantly. If the level drops, the system "decides" to increase glucose.

Other illustrations of automatic decision making can be seen in inventory reorders of low medical supply levels, recommended staffing levels and pre-preparation levels of surgical trays based on statistical projections, and a home monitor that automatically dials 911 when certain vital signs register in the danger zone. All this can occur without any human intervention and based solely on the data gathered and organized by the information system.

### Modeling Decisions

These decisions can all be modeled because the environment in which they occur is generally predictable. Because these decisions also recur frequently, it is worth the organization's time and trouble to develop a mathematical model describing the situation and to discover the appropriate decision rule. For example, an inventory system might have a built-in, preprogrammed reordering capability that ensures the continuous provision of necessary drugs without over-ordering. The challenge is to ensure that the system collects the data necessary to measure the depletion of inventory, so that the nurses using the drugs can define their usage rate fairly accurately. This way, they know how much of each drug they need to keep on hand and that the ordering system can predict accurately how long it takes to reorder and receive the necessary products. A system can be designed to collect and analyze this information to ensure that the proper quantity of each necessary drug is maintained in inventory.

As is true of any procedure designed to improve service to patients, the organization needs to assess the relationship between the value and the cost of the information before it establishes such a system. Because nurses are not accountants, they may not get around to gathering and organizing data on medical supplies often enough to justify the expense and sophistication of an online system. If the input of data is haphazard, the value of frequently out-of-date information is low and the expense of installing a sophisticated system is unwarranted.

### Relationship Marketing

The increased emphasis on relationship marketing or the "market-segment-of-one" concept has been made possible through the increasing power of computers to store, digest, and interpret large quantities of information. The idea is to find out so much about customers that the organization can treat each customer as a unique "market." When patients visit a physician, return patient satisfaction surveys, or seek out more information from a web site, they provide information about themselves that healthcare providers can use to gain a better understanding of their customers and their unique needs.

To improve patient care and save money, HealthSouth is constructing a $125 million, 219-bed, all-digital hospital near Birmingham, Alabama.[21] The hospital will be the first of its kind to digitize everything from prescriptions to surgical records and store it all on crash-proof, secure servers that will keep patients and doctors connected anytime and anywhere. Wireless monitors will send individual patient data to handheld devices carried by doctors. Every bed will have a video screen connected to the Internet, enabling videoconferencing with physicians and family members. Patient locations in the hospital will be traced using global positioning satellites. Medical observations will be entered on easy-to-carry computers rather than handwritten on medical charts.

The plan is to record and store the wide array of patient information in a totally integrated patient record system that will allow the clinical staff to have instant access to status, location, and treatment of every patient. The thousands of pages of medical records moved weekly to storage by most major hospitals will disappear into electronic storage, and the challenges of managing the paper trail that each patient creates will be met digitally. The hope is that greater efficiency will lead to fewer errors, practitioners spending more time caring for patients and less time entering information, and patients who will not be sick as long.[22]

Individual companies have information about you, based on what you did while interacting with them. In addition, organizations like

National Demographics and Lifestyles make a business of collecting and providing such data. Even the driver's license bureaus in some states make money by selling information on licensed drivers. The quantity and quality of information about consumers available in various databases is staggering. General Motors has information on its 12 million credit card holders, Blockbuster Video's database is built on 36 million households, and even Harley-Davidson has a database on its owners that it uses to encourage them to ride their motorcycles more often and buy Harley products specifically tailored for them. The more a company knows about its customer, the better it can target its marketing toward satisfying that customer's unique needs and the more it can increase the company's value to that customer.

Healthcare organizations that are able to build such personalized relationships make it tough for their competitors who cannot provide their patients with similar value through such personalized service. Information systems and the powerful advances in information technology make it happen, and many healthcare organizations now have access to the power of building personalized relationships with their present patients and offering such relationships to their future patients.

### Severing Relationships

Organizations try to establish close relationships with their best customers. At the other extreme, companies can use information technology to weed out customers with whom they do not want to continue a relationship. Instead of taking a come-one, come-all approach, many healthcare organizations are severing relationships with unprofitable customers or charging them higher rates. Technology has developed to the point that healthcare organizations can identify some profitable and unprofitable patients and patient groups.

If 20 percent of an organization's surgical patients generate most of the profit and 20 percent of ER patients actually detract from the bottom line because they cost more than the income they generate, the organization will probably take steps to intensify its relationship with the top group and diminish its relationship with the bottom. It might even reorganize itself into a purely surgical hospital and serve only that top 20 percent. After reorganization, if the hospital finds that elective cosmetic surgery is popular with patients and highly profitable to the hospital, it may decide to perform that surgery only.

For another example, healthcare insurers seek to avoid intensive consumers of healthcare services by developing screens. People with preexisting conditions or illnesses are screened out, or market campaigns are designed to not reach or appeal to undesirable parts of the market for insurance, or insurance policies are written to cover only a certain number of days in the hospital or to max out at a fixed dollar amount. One potential problem with severing relationship or "de-marketing" is that the organization may be cutting loose presently unprofitable patients who might generate large future profits or who might, if treated well, recommend the organization to friends. Furthermore, de-marketing may be inconsistent with the institution's mission or may create significant ethical or political problems. So healthcare organizations must move slowly in this area.

## Expert Systems

Systems can also be set up to make decisions that require choosing between alternatives when the correct decision is not clear cut; these are generally classified as *expert systems*. They seek to duplicate the decision process used by an expert who gathers information, organizes it in some way, applies a body of expertise to interpreting the information, and makes a decision that reflects the application of that expertise. An expert system, then, is built by finding out what information an expert uses, how that expert organizes it, and what decision rules that expert uses to make decisions based on the information.

Once these pieces of information are collected, usually through extensive interviewing of an expert or a group of experts, a series of decision rules can be written to duplicate the decision-making process of the expert. Healthcare journals frequently offer new illustrations of expert systems that assist clinicians in a wide variety of applications of these powerful systems. As clinicians face the same explosion of knowledge that all managers face, they will increasingly rely on these systems to help sort through the volume of information to find the best solutions to healthcare problems.

### *Decisions Requiring Judgment*

Expert systems can be developed to make decisions for use in a wide variety of recurring situations requiring judgment. They can schedule personnel for times and days to ensure proper staffing levels, keep track of hospital room inventory to ensure the maximum use for each day's inventory of available rooms, and can be used in similar areas where there is a straightforward algorithm or mathematical formula that can calculate the best or optimal answer. In these types of expert systems, the optimal answer can be determined once the data are gathered.

The key to using expert systems is to find experts, identify the criteria they use in making decisions, program their decision rules in a logical sequence, then apply the program to problems that lend themselves to computerized analysis. The net result is to create a category of decisions that can be made 24 hours a day for any person having access to the system. For example, a pharmacist wanting to find out about interactive effects of a newly prescribed medicine can call up the system from a remote terminal, at any time of day or night, and ask the system to investigate any interaction possibilities with any other drugs the patient is taking.

Clinical decision-support systems (CDSS) are computer-based information systems containing thousands of treatment options for different diseases. They are designed to help in the diagnosis and treatment of illnesses. Some CDSS simply collect, organize, and communicate data about patients to physicians, but others actually use medical databases to suggest diagnoses and treatment regimens. Some CDSS are expert systems that contain, first of all, a general knowledge base of medical information supplied by experts. Clinical information about particular patients is related to the information in the knowledge base. The computer then uses decision rules to draw conclusions and make recommendations to the attending physician.

Here are some examples of expert systems as employed in healthcare:

- A computerized system accurately monitors the fetal heart rate during the birth process. A rule-based expert system uses heart-rate data to classify the situation as normal, stressed, indeterminate, or ominous.
- A computerized voice response system provides medical advice for 100 common ailments. Callers receive advice based on their self-reported symptoms, consultation history, and the latest medical research. During follow-up calls, the system also tracks the improvement or deterioration of the patient's condition.
- An expert system spots irregularities in doctors' bills.
- An expert system detects and alerts staff about adverse drug events such as allergies, unpredicted drug interactions, and

dosage problems. The system is said to identify adverse drug events 60 times better than practitioners can.[23]

The existence of expert systems has far-reaching implications. As expert systems that are capable of providing up-to-date data and recommendations based on expert opinion become widely available, physicians may become obligated to use them. Not to do so might leave them open to legal liability for not using state-of-the-art methods for diagnosis and treatment.

### Advantages and Disadvantages of Advanced Systems

As Table 10.1 shows, several good reasons to use these systems exist, such as the fact that they give users instantaneous access to a "decision maker" that makes quick, consistent decisions, which may be critical for an ER doctor seeking a quick consultation on a tricky diagnosis. These systems also have disadvantages such as the user's inability to ask further questions if the problem or query is not quite what the model expects.

Customers have unique needs, and expert systems have to be designed from the customer's point of view if they are to be truly useful in problem solving within the organization. Obviously, because of the potential problems indicated in the Table, expert systems should not be used for trivial, unimportant, or infrequent decision situations because they are simply too expensive, nor should they replace human decision makers in life-and-death situations. They may, however, add greatly to healthcare quality by making medical expertise available any time and any place to assist an attending physician who needs help.

### Artificial Intelligence

More advanced applications of expert systems open the way to using *artificial intelligence* (AI). AI is used for situations where some decision rules are available but they are incomplete because part of the decision process is unknown or too unpredictable to model accurately. Artificial intelligence programs are designed to allow the computer to learn from successes and failures by ensuring that all decisions made by the AI program have a feedback loop. The feedback loop allows the result of implementing the decision to be fed back and tested against predetermined evaluative criteria to find out whether the decision was good or bad. If the outcome was good, the logic of

**Table 10.1 Decision and Expert Systems: Advantages and Problems**

| Advantages | Problems |
|---|---|
| • Makes consistent and impartial decisions | • May make bad decisions if problem is not routine |
| • Makes decisions quickly | • Eliminates human participation in decision |
| • Rapidly sorts through large amounts of information | • Assumes experts will reveal decision-making secrets and rules |
| • Frees up experts from making routine decisions | • Some decision processes are too obscure to duplicate in expert systems |
| • Allows instantaneous 24-hour access to a decision maker | • Legal issue of who owns decision rules |
| • Retains experts forever | • Circumstances may change too quickly for system to keep up |
| | • May frustrate users whose problems do not exactly fit system parameters |

the decision process used is affirmed. If not, the feedback allows the computer to learn not to make the same mistake the next time it faces the same situation.

The simplest and classic illustration is a chess-playing program. A computer can be programmed to behave like an expert chess player who knows all the rules and the traditional chess gambits. As it plays games against various opponents, however, the computer can also learn which moves lead to bad outcomes and which moves lead to good outcomes. Over time, this knowledge accumulates to improve the computer's decision-making capabilities just as accumulated knowledge improves the capability of a human expert.

Adding a learning capability moves an expert system's sophistication level up to that of an AI application. Obviously, the use of AI is still limited because of the cost and time required to develop this learning capability and the cost of errors while the learning takes place. Even so, it has a following: the Artificial Intelligence in Medicine Europe (AIME), which started in 1991, meets annually. This meeting offers a forum to dig deeply into the application of this powerful decision tool in healthcare settings.

From diagnosing congenital heart disease to scheduling patient tests to developing treatment protocols, AI can be a useful tool in absorbing the complex interdependencies of the human anatomic system and the volume of new science that advances the treatment of healthcare problems. This tool that never sleeps, learns continuously, and offers consistent expert advice may well be the only way for the human mind to adapt to and incorporate the increasingly complex world of clinical knowledge.

## PROBLEMS WITH INFORMATION SYSTEMS

Although no healthcare organization is going to give up its information system, these systems present potential and actual problems. One is information overload—the tendency of the system to produce and transmit too much data. Because these systems produce such apparently accurate numbers, managers tend to focus on the numbers instead of on less definite but often more important qualitative and human factors. Another problem is that an information system can produce bad information that looks good. Healthcare organizations have crucial and sometimes proprietary information within their systems, but they also have the challenging problem of keeping patient data private. For them, maintaining security is a very big issue. Finally, the costs of installing and learning the system must be matched against the benefits that the system can confer.

### Information Overload

Information systems are helpful and revolutionary but far from perfect. Too much information is as bad as not enough. Although sophisticated systems are designed to provide only the right information to the right person when that person needs it, many information systems provide a lot of raw data that users have to sort through until, they hope, they can find the needed information. Indeed, many systems are designed by having systems planners ask users what information they need. Most users will ask for as much information as they can get, instead of only as much as they really need. Most people believe that having too much is better than not having enough, and the proof is that they have seen people disciplined or even sued for having too little information but never for having too much.

A second aspect of this same issue is that when asked, most people indicate that they use many different informational data sources, instead of mentioning the one or two they actually use. Not wanting to admit ignorance or own up to how little information they use, they ask for a lot and then get lost in the pile. Benchmark healthcare organizations collect and feed back a lot of information on customer satisfaction.

## Focus on the Numbers

Because computers excel in transmitting, organizing, and analyzing numbers, much computer information is in numeric form. Although this form aids in accurate conversion of data into information, it does tend to focus attention on only those things that can be quantified or somehow expressed in numerical terms. Much of a manager's life in healthcare revolves around subjective, qualitative information rather than quantitative data. The availability of numerical information creates an overemphasis in decision making on such information and an underemphasis on qualitative information. Because many clinicians believe that medicine is an art, trying to determine what data should be processed to accurately represent the practice of the art is a difficult challenge.

## Bad Information

The old saying that garbage in leads to garbage out is quite true. A sophisticated information system can quickly get a lot of bad data to a lot of people; if that bad data get into the organization's decision-making structure, as they will with a sophisticated information system, then the data will be plugged in to multiple calculations used in many decision situations. What if the wrong financial information is submitted to Medicare, or the wrong lab result from a patient test gets into the system? The results can be worse than garbage; they can be catastrophic. Bad information widely circulated by means of a sophisticated information and decision system can lead to bad decisions and even disaster.

## Security and Confidentiality

How can the integrity of the database be maintained? Information systems have to be protected so that one organization cannot access confidential or proprietary data from another and so that only authorized persons can gain access to patient information. In many hospitals, anybody can walk into a hospital room and look at a patient's chart. In this era of telemedicine and doctors working at a distance, connected to the information system by modem or computer terminal, protecting the integrity of the database from unauthorized or inappropriate access is an important concern.

If hackers can get into the Defense Department and CIA computers, as they have, then competitors may well be able to get into healthcare databases. Protecting against such unauthorized entry is a big problem and big expense for organizations. The problem exists even internally, as database managers need to ensure that unauthorized persons cannot obtain confidential patient data. Outsiders and company insiders need to be prevented from snooping as well.

Acquisition of healthcare data by unauthorized users is one problem; misuse of information by authorized users is another. Healthcare organizations have not always preserved the privacy of patient records. When a patient in a Boston hospital learned that about a half-dozen hospital employees had looked at her records (concerning an unusual ectopic pregnancy) without her permission, she wrote to the hospital asking that her records be kept confidential and that an audit trail of her file be kept, so she would know who had seen it. Some seven years after she insisted on confidentiality, she asked to see the audit trail. Over 200 people, including medical insurers, had asked for and been granted access to her records without her permission.[24]

According to author Marcia Stepanek, "Even the best hospitals face increased pressure to profit off patient health data. In some cases, they may sell it to marketers, or position it as a key asset as they negotiate mergers or partnerships."[25] A study of 21 prominent health-related web sites revealed that 19 had privacy policies, but not one site actually preserved consumer privacy as promised.[26] The security and privacy of information in the system is of increasing concern to organizations and consumers as well.

### Value Versus Cost

Information is not free. Buying data terminals and computers, hiring programmers, running a data network, and building an information system are hugely expensive. On the other side of the expense are the largely intangible benefits of the information system. How does one measure the value of instantaneous access to a patient database so that the patient is identified by name, the information necessary for excellent patient care is immediately available, and the patient's unique requirements can be identified in advance and supplied? And how does one measure the cost of problems, including fatalities, that an adequate information system might have avoided?

In 1999, the Institute of Medicine shocked the healthcare industry by reporting that 98,000 people die each year from preventable medical errors. In a follow-up report issued in early 2001, the Institute said that the industry's problems only increased. No real progress had been made in applying advances in information technology to improve administrative and clinical processes.[27]

Deciding how much better a decision was, because the manager or the clinician had the right information available, is usually impossible. Yet, most organizations believe their systems are worth the cost. The problem is that when budget time comes and paybacks on investments are calculated, defending information system upgrades and improvements is difficult because evaluating the contribution of the system is difficult.

Although determining costs and benefits is difficult, companies can make estimates. About 85 percent of medical practice revenues come from insurance reimbursements, but the average time for processing claims is between 45 and 90 days. As the Internet becomes used more frequently for reimbursement, industry experts predict that within a few years, 30 percent of medical claims will be processed online.[28] The assumption is that the cost savings of more efficient claims processing will exceed the cost of the required investments.

### Cost of Learning the System

Top managers are the very people who need to learn how to use information technology, but often they are the very same people who are most uncomfortable and unfamiliar with it. Worse yet, given the problems in quantifying the value of the technology, these are the same people who make the decisions about buying the equipment and investing in the system. Obviously, a lot of learning has to take place before those who are uneasy talking about megahertz, bits, and bytes are totally comfortable in using the new information systems or accessing the Internet.

Even though the increasingly user-friendly software makes it easier for these managers to learn and use the powerful technology, the challenge for them is that as soon as they master one technology, a newer and more powerful one will come along that they will need to learn as well. Managers cannot learn about information systems once and then forget about them. The rapid changes in what computers can do in managing information require all participants in the healthcare system to change as fast.

## THE HEALTHCARE ORGANIZATION AS AN INFORMATION SYSTEM

Perhaps the easiest way to understand how information ties the healthcare organization together is by considering the organization itself as a big information network. Everyone is a transmission point on the organizational network, gathering, sending, and processing information into a decision-friendly format. Those responsible for designing the organization as an information system must consider how all these network participants are linked together and what each participant's information needs are.

If an admitting clerk is responsible for taking a phone call from a family member inquiring whether or not a relative has been admitted and, if so, what the medical status of that patient is, then the information system had better be designed to obtain and provide accurate information to the clerk when the phone rings. The system design will therefore require communication linkages, across all parts of the organization, that provide access to all information needed by the clerk so that person can respond helpfully and accurately. Reengineering the organization and its information system to focus on the needs of patients and their families is a necessity in the present-day competitive healthcare marketplace.

### The Primacy of Information

The logic of organizing around the flow of information changes the way jobs are organized, tasks are performed, the sequence of operations, and the organization of departmental units. The organization should be designed in a way that responds to information requirements. Jobs and departments dealing with uncertain, everchanging, ambiguous situations require a lot of information flow to ensure that the managers responsible for decisions on those units can get all the information they need to make them. Jobs or units that are relatively insulated from uncertainty, ambiguity, and changing circumstance may not require the same volume or quality of information; they can anticipate that whatever happened or was true yesterday will pretty much be the same today and tomorrow. Organizational units facing uncertainty need to add the information capacity that will allow the necessary information to be gathered, or they must find ways to reduce the need for that information. Both strategies involve integrating the organizational design into the information system and vice versa.

### Increasing Capacity

When the organization must increase its information-handling capacity, its system designers must look at all the ways information is transmitted across the organization. They will probably have to build an expert-level system with the capability to screen out unnecessary information while conveying necessary information. Furthermore, the system will have to create redundant sources of critical information. Information that a decision maker absolutely must not miss should be provided in more than one channel of communication to ensure that the end user has it when it is needed. That way, if one channel breaks down or fails to get the information to the person needing it, it can be provided through another means.

A simple example is sending someone an e-mail, followed by a fax, followed by a mailed hard copy, with the same information in all three communications. Building in this redundancy obviously creates additional demands on the information system, and organizations should carefully consider what information is so important that it really needs to be sent in more than one way.

### Reducing Need

The organization can seek ways to reduce the need to handle information. One major way to do this is to create self-contained decision-making units that are empowered and enabled to make decisions about their areas of responsibility. By increasing the number of decisions made at the point where the information is generated, the usage of the information channels is reduced. This is the classic strategy of decentralized decision making or, in the more current literature, the trend toward individual or group empowerment.

The idea here is that with proper training in asking for job-related data and turning them into information used for decision making, the individual employee or department can make many decisions that otherwise would have been routed up the administrative chain of command. The time and effort it takes to check with a supervisor or higher-level organizational unit can use up information channel capacity, but even worse for a healthcare organization, it also slows down the response to the problem. If a furious patient is complaining to an employee, that patient does not want to wait until someone upstairs gives approval for resolving a problem.

## Everybody Online

The most effective strategy for increasing the information flow is to put everyone online with immediate and easy access to the relevant parts of the organization's database. Increasingly, rather than sending masses of information through the communication channels, the trend is to put information online so that any employee with a computer terminal can ask for it.

Many organizations have internal e-mail or intranet capability that allows any employee to ask any manager any relevant question electronically. The flow of information back and forth across all levels of the organization is incredibly enhanced by this technique. The recent move by many healthcare organizations into external linkages with the amazing databases and informational resources available on the Internet means that even more information is available to anyone who needs it whenever they need it. Frontline employees now often have access to much of the same information that their bosses do and, with proper education about organizational goals and training in decision making, can make decisions in specified job-related areas of the same or better quality that their bosses could in previous eras.

## Integrated Systems

A few independent healthcare organizations in Dayton, Ohio, are grouping together to develop an integrated Community Health Information Network (CHIN). This network links 20 hospitals and approximately 2,400 independent physicians within a nine-county region covering a population of about 1.4 million. Initially the goal was to provide patient demographics, claim eligibility, a provider directory, and clinical results through the CHIN system. In 2000, the system was expanded to track patient visits, provide imaging services, record patient status by physician, and offer online links to pharmacies and long-term care facilities. Shands Hospital at the University of Florida has also developed an integrated patient care system. Clinical data, patient information, and financial records are integrated for all patients at all of the numerous Shands facilities.[29]

These sophisticated systems make so much information available online that management can operate "by exception," which means that it needs to spend its time and attention on only those departments, employees, and functions that are not performing up to a predetermined goal or standard. More sophisticated systems will take this informational resource even further by automatically registering the data in a corporate database that keeps track of daily revenues for the entire operation; reorders products and arranges for payment to and shipping from suppliers for those items that have reached predetermined reorder levels; and recalculates the statistics used for forecasting to maximize space utilization for each type of patient (or category of patient—e.g., acute care, ICU).

These more extensive, probably expert or AI level, decision systems use economic ordering quantity determinations, sophisticated statistical forecasting techniques, and automatic reorder points to ensure that the necessary quantity of products or rooms is available to support the predicted patient census. The same process can be used in managing outpatient visits, employee staffing levels, and on-hand perishable supplies.

## CONCLUSION

The impact that these communication systems have on empowering frontline employees to do their jobs better, quicker, and cheaper is astonishing now and will grow even more so in the future. The implications of these changes for middle managers, who historically were responsible for transmitting information from senior managers to frontline employees, is also important to consider in managing the healthcare organization. The impact that these technological trends have on organizational design, frontline employee responsibilities, and need for middle managers is profound. This electronic technology will change the way organizations are structured and managed; it will also change in a fundamental way the nature and role of healthcare employees who are concerned with delivering high-quality healthcare experiences.

The information systems of healthcare organizations ought to incorporate all the components of the healthcare experience. Such a total information system simultaneously provides the needed information to patients, management, patient-contact servers, and back-of-the-house staff, just when they need it in a way they can use it. Achieving this end requires the system designer to pay close attention to the needs of users, their capabilities, and their willingness to use information. It does no good to provide 30 pages of statistical output to a person who does not understand statistics or who does not have the time to sort through the data to find the necessary information. If you are out of anesthesia in the operating room for which you are responsible, you do not want to review statistical predictions of how much anesthesia you were supposed to use this week, or the usage forecast for next week, or the summary data for last week until somebody gets some more anesthesia to you. You need all that other information, but not right now.

## LESSONS LEARNED

1. Know the unique informational needs of each internal and external customer, and satisfy them.
2. Know the value of information to each internal and external customer.
3. Know the cost of providing that information.
4. Make information available in a format that each customer expects, can use, and will use.
5. Ensure access to information to people in the organization who need it, and exclude access to those who do not.
6. Put organizational information online, but protect confidential data.
7. Focus on generating and feeding back information relevant to customer service.

## NOTES

1. *Wall Street Journal*, June 25, 2001, p. R14.

2. *Business Week*, July 24, 2000, p. 24.

3. Coile, R. C., Jr. 2000. "E-Health: Reinventing Healthcare in the Information Age." *Journal of Healthcare Management* 45 (3): 206–10. This article is excerpted from *New Century Healthcare: Strategies for Providers, Purchasers, and Plans*, by R. C. Coile, Jr., Chicago: Health Administration Press.

4. *Orlando Sentinel*, May 30, 2000, p. D-1.

5. National Center for Policy Analysis. 2000. "Idea House." (September 28): 1.

6. *ACHe-news*, July 14, 2000.

7. *Business Week*, July 24, 2000, p. 24.

8. *Investor's Business Daily*, May 24, 2000, p. A10.

9. Hamilton, D. P. 2002. "Custom-Tailored Medicine." *Wall Street Journal* (March 25): B1.

10. Landro, L. 2002. "New Guidelines to Make Doctor-Patient E-mails Profitable, Less Risky." *Wall Street Journal* (January 25): A13.

11. *Wall Street Journal*, March 26, 2001, p. B13.

12. *Wall Street Journal*, January 17, 2000, p. B1.

13. *Wall Street Journal*, April 17, 2001, p. B1.

14. *Investor's Business Daily*, May 24, 2000, p. A10.

15. *Business Week*, July 24, 2000, p. EB64.

16. Seybold, P. B. 2001. *The Customer Revolution: How to Thrive When Customers Are in Control.* New York: Crown Business.

17. *Wall Street Journal*, October 19, 1998, p. R25.

18. Berry, L. L. 1999. *Discovering the Soul of Service: The Nine Drivers of Sustainable Business Success*, p. 189. New York: The Free Press.

19. Tsurvoka, D. 2001. "IBM Prescribes Technology for Doctors." *Investor's Business Daily* (July 2): A5.

20. Landro, L. 2002. "Deadly Hospital Errors Prompt Group to Push for Technological Help." *Wall Street Journal* (March 15): B1.

21. Cobbs, C. 2001. "A Digital Prescription." *Orlando Sentinel* (May 6): G1, G4.

22. For additional information on electronic medical records, see K. H. Dansky, L. D. Gamm, J. J. Vasey, and C. K. Barsukiewicz. 1999. "Electronic Medical Records: Are Physicians Ready?" *Journal of Healthcare Management* 44 (6): 440–55.

23. Cited in W. Raghupathi. 2000. "Information Technology in Healthcare: A Review of Key Applications." In *Healthcare Information Systems*, edited by P. L. Davidson, pp. 23–24. Boca Raton, FL: Auerbach.

24. *Business Week*, December 11, 2000, p. EB80.

25. *Ibid.*

26. *Ibid.*

27. *Wall Street Journal*, June 25, 2001, p. R14.

28. *Business Week*, July 24, 2000, p. 24.

29. Cited in W. Raghupathi. 2000. "Information Technology in Healthcare: A Review of Key Applications." In *Healthcare Information Systems*, edited by P. L. Davidson, p. 20. Boca Raton, FL: Auerbach.

*Chapter 11*

# Delivering the Service

Healthcare Principle: *Provide a seamless healthcare experience*

Being nice to people is just 20 percent of providing good customer service. The important part is designing systems that allow you to do the job right the first time.

—*Carl Sewell, Customers for Life*

ENSURING THAT ONLY well-trained, clinically competent, motivated, enthusiastic employees are serving patients is necessary, but it is not sufficient to produce an extraordinary patient experience. A healthcare organization must also ensure that the process by which the service is delivered is working as it should. Healthcare managers often assume that when a service problem arises in any part of the healthcare experience the employee has made an error. But reality frequently shows that the fault lies in a poorly designed system that makes it difficult, if not impossible, to deliver the service with the excellence that the organization, the staff, and the patient want.

If you talk with nurses, admissions officers, and laboratory technicians, they will tell you how frustrated they become when the service systems cannot help them do the jobs they are hired, trained, and paid to do and want to do well on. When the service delivery system fails, everyone loses. The patient is unhappy, the employee is frustrated, and the organization disappoints a patient and loses all the revenues that the patient's future business represents.

This chapter focuses on properly designing the service delivery system to make sure that all aspects of the healthcare experience are provided as planned. We also discuss planning, measuring, and improving the system and provide examples that are applicable in real-world situations.

## CHECK THE SYSTEM FIRST

According to authors Stephen Tax and Ian Stuart, "service design is among the least studied and understood topics in services marketing"[1]; yet, it is a crucial topic. Achieving patient satisfaction and avoiding problems in the healthcare experience can both be greatly affected by delivery system design. Every healthcare organization should invest time and energy on studying and planning the entire system to get it right. The total quality management (TQM) movement has taught organizational leaders several important lessons. First, everyone is responsible for delivering quality and monitoring the quality of the entire healthcare experience. Second, when a service failure occurs, the system must be checked for problems first before blame is passed down to people; after all, systems of even high-performing service organizations still fail from time to time.

Consider the following example of a system failure and the outcome that resulted from employee involvement.

After several doctors complained about their x-rays not being brought to the operating room in a timely manner and not having available x-ray technicians when needed, the chief operating officer (COO) of General Hospital decided to act using a nontraditional approach. The traditional managerial solution to the problem is to blame the staff. First, the section manager is loudly criticized for technical incompetence, poor supervisory skills, and other unsatisfactory outcomes brought about by the entire department. Then, the properly "disciplined" manager transfers the fault and criticizes or disciplines the technicians.

But the COO had a different problem-solving approach in mind. The COO organized a team of technicians and asked them to investigate the matter and to suggest ways to solve whatever problem they found. The team did exactly that. They found out that the cause of the problem was that not enough x-ray technicians were available in the hospital when the surgeons needed their expertise. This inadequate staffing level, the team discovered, resulted from a new manager's decision to change the hours of operation of the mobile x-ray unit. Some technicians served in both the in-hospital x-ray unit and the mobile unit. The mobile unit had previously been out in the field only when no surgeries were scheduled. A new supervisor had taken over the mobile unit, had been told to cut costs, and saw that costs could be cut by reducing the overtime hours worked by the driver of the mobile unit. That reduction forced the mobile unit to operate during some of the same hours that surgeries were regularly scheduled.

As a result, technicians who used to be available for in-house x-ray work were now sometimes out in the field when their services were needed back at the hospital. Because a new manager followed orders and tried to save some money in the mobile x-ray unit, the rest of the system was disrupted. This cost-saving move irritated the doctors, slowed down the surgical procedures for patients, and drove up the costs of surgery because the operating rooms and surgical teams were tied up for longer periods of time. Solving a problem in one part of the service delivery system, without thinking about its possible impact on the overall system, created problems for another part.

Three lessons can be drawn from this example. First, department managers often do not have enough time, information, or insight to figure out the best solutions by themselves. These managers tend to find the simplest, quickest solution and rely on the traditional theory of correcting the person to correct the problem. Second, employees may have a better chance of finding out the root causes of a problem than the manager does because they are more involved in the actual process of operating the system. Not using the talents, intelligence, and job-related knowledge of employees is a waste of these human resources. Third, every problem should be addressed first from the perspective of the entire service delivery system. Although one person may end up being the cause of a service failure, the fault is frequently in the system and not the person. Simply putting out one small fire ("we are spending too much money on overtime") without thinking about the system can cause big problems elsewhere.

### Self-Correcting Systems

TQM's goal is to use the people and the system designers to create a *self-correcting system*—an environment in which employees can override the system (or break the rules) to correct problems or failures.

Employees in a self-correcting system are responsible for telling management where the system has failed so that together they can fix it. Just as everyone is responsible for providing and maintaining quality, everyone is responsible for avoiding and fixing service failures. Here are two contrasting examples that present the importance of a self-correcting system.

A man was on vacation in France when he had a sudden attack of gout. Having neglected to pack his medication, he sought medical care from a local doctor. He received treatment, paid the bill, and kept the receipt for later reimbursement from his insurance carrier. He did not call the 800 number for HMO authorization (that number does not work in France anyway), and he knew that getting a referral form would be impossible. When he arrived home, he presented the bill to the HMO processing clerk for payment. The clerk told him that the bill could not be paid because the expenditure, although made for a covered ailment, had not been authorized. After several fruitless discussions and a brief phone talk with a manager, he still could not get reimbursement. "The rules" did not allow reimbursement for a reimbursable but unauthorized expenditure.

The HMO's clerk and its system both failed the patient. The HMO's procedures were not sufficiently flexible to handle the somewhat unusual request properly, the employee had been taught to follow the inadequate procedures to the letter, and the manager did not get sufficiently involved to find out what was really going on. If the HMO's employees had been sufficiently empowered and motivated, the failure might have been avoided. Contrast the HMO clerk's customer service with that of the motivated, empowered assistant administrator in the following example.

The assistant administrator was told by the hospital manager to handle a particularly difficult Medicare case. An elderly woman frequently came to the hospital claiming illnesses and diseases that required her to be admitted. The billing clerk had noticed that a large number of claims for treating the woman were being sent to Medicare; she then alerted the hospital's management to the possibility that the organization would be audited if they did not "stop admitting this malingering patient." When the woman appeared again, requesting admission, the assistant administrator was given the task of convincing her that she should go home. After some discussion, the woman agreed to leave if the assistant administrator would take her home. Because he knew that the organization's philosophy was to do whatever was necessary to satisfy the patient, or at least try to, he agreed and drove her to her apartment. The apartment was filthy and showed all signs that the old woman was unable to care for herself. The assistant administrator was deeply affected, so he arranged to fix the place up and clean it and volunteered to come back in a week to check on her.

The next Friday afternoon when he arrived, he found the place in worse condition than before. The power cords for the refrigerator, TV, and lights had been cut, and the phone line had been snapped at the box. Upon the assistant administrator's questioning, the woman revealed an attack (another in a long series) by a drug-driven nephew who periodically trashed her place in search of money. The assistant administrator called the hospital and, even though the woman was not "sick," arranged for an ambulance to transport her back to the hospital so she would be safe until the police caught the nephew.

The empowered assistant administrator solved a problem by going beyond the regulations. If he had not made two trips to the woman's apartment and had not brought her back to the hospital, the problem would not have been solved: the woman would have continued to return to the hospital for unnecessary and costly medical treatment and the abuse would have continued. Through the assistant administrator, the system "healed itself" to achieve the organization's primary goal: patient satisfaction. The system failed once when it concluded that the woman was simply a malingerer who needed to be sent home, but it redeemed itself by giving the frontline administrator the autonomy to solve the patient's problems.

The point is quite simple: Study your system in intimate detail, design accurate early-warning measures for each of the many possible failure points in both the clinical and nonclinical parts of the health-care experience, engage everyone in the organization in watching those measures, empower employees to ignore policies and rules that impede customer service, and follow-up on everything. If failures occur repeatedly at certain points, change the system design. If the organization has a patient service guarantee, be sure that the delivery system can meet and exceed patient expectations on that guarantee. Excellent healthcare managers know that they must keep a careful eye on all the places where the system might fail, and they do their best to keep these failures from happening. All healthcare organizations should design systems that ensure success and that avoid failure on the key drivers of an outstanding overall healthcare experience.

Because the patient is always the ultimate judge of the quality and value of the healthcare experience, designers of the service delivery system must ensure that they fully consider the patient's point of view, not just the clinical employee's perspective. Although the system should be user-friendly for clinical employees, the system must also cater to the patient's needs, expectations, and capabilities. The service delivery should be smooth, seamless, easy, and transparent from the patient's point of view.

## ANALYZE THE SYSTEM

Analyzing the service delivery system has three major components: planning, measuring or controlling, and improving. In the quality improvement literature, these components are known as *Juran's Trilogy* or the quality trilogy.

Any good delivery system must begin with *careful planning*. Years of experience in working with older people can give a new nursing home administrator a good head start in designing a comprehensive treatment, care, and recreation schedule. However, a careful analysis and detailing of every step in the entire service delivery process that provides comprehensive care and physical therapy for older people makes the difference between having it mostly right and reaching the level of excellence that the very best service organizations deliver.

The second component is *measuring for control*. We have said before that you cannot manage what you do not measure, and this is especially true of service delivery systems. The service industry in general and healthcare in particular have lagged behind in understanding how to apply measurements to the largely intangible patient services. The need for measuring not only the clinical status but also the patient care status in every step of the service delivery system is critical in understanding where any service delivery problems are and how one can tell when the solutions being tried are actually fixing the problem. Saying to a floor nurse, "I want you to do a better job of satisfying patients because patients on your floor seem unhappy," is easy but probably useless. Explaining to a nurse exactly what level of excellence was achieved last month, what level is being achieved now, and what the target level is can be extremely helpful.

In the best circumstances when the measures are clear, fair, and completely understood by the employees whose performance is being measured, employees are able to measure themselves. If you teach employees what is important to their individual job success and then train them to measure how they are performing on those critical factors, you have the beginning of a *self-managing workforce*. Ideally, the measures can permit employees to monitor their own delivery effectiveness while actually delivering the service. For example, if a nurse knows that the organizational standard for responding to a patient call is a maximum of three minutes, and a computerized device displays a running record of how many minutes it takes for the nurse to answer calls, she knows at all times where she stands in relation to the standard.

Much of the measurement these days is done by computer. For example, modern ERs, such as the ER at Overlook Hospital in Summit, New Jersey, use patient-tracking systems. Once Overlook decides to admit an ER patient to the hospital, its goal is to transfer that patient from the ER to a hospital bed in less than 90 minutes. The status of the eight critical steps in the admitting and treatment process is displayed on a screen, and reports are flashed every 15 minutes to let the ER know if it is meeting its time goals.[2]

After measurements have been developed, the third step in the analysis of the service delivery system is *improvement*. Information about what is actually occurring drives system improvement: If you can identify the failures, you can figure out where to fix the system. Once the plan is clearly laid out and the results of implementing that plan are adequately measured to yield insights into how well the system is operating, then both management and employees have the information needed to redesign the system or fix the problems to yield continuing improvement in the healthcare experience.

A major factor in improving the system is to train staff to put customer service ahead of policies and procedures whenever the two conflict. Frontline employees are often the first to notice or be informed of system faults or failures. If they have been properly selected and motivated, they will report the need for system improvement. For example, a nursing aide responsible for responding to patient call buttons, providing bed pans, and cleaning up was frustrated by the chronic understaffing that left her unable to respond promptly to patient needs. One day she noticed a predictable pattern: the call buttons began lighting up for bedpan requests at the same time food trays were delivered. She discovered that if she timed her visits to the rooms prior to food delivery, she could often be walking into the room to provide bed pans just as the patient was reaching for the call button. She is an example of a dedicated, motivated, observant employee who by observing the system improved it.

The cycle of planning, measurement for control, and improvement should never stop. The plan lays out what you think your service delivery system should be doing, the control measures tell you if what you planned is in fact happening, and the commitment to improvement focuses everyone's attention on analyzing and fixing the problems and moving toward a flawless healthcare experience. The point is that the design of any service delivery system should incorporate all three elements.

A good service delivery plan should include a way to measure how well the plan is being implemented at every step of the service delivery process as well as how the overall plan is succeeding. The measures should trigger an analysis of "exceptions" or variations from the plan and should quantify every critical part of the healthcare experience as well as the total experience. Most patients respond to the healthcare experience as a whole. Patients usually know why they are satisfied by the healthcare experience if the clinical outcomes were exceptional— the heart transplant was a success, the malaria was cured, or the therapy led to recapturing a physical capability.

However, in routine encounters such as an annual check-up, patients are often unable to identify how any one part of the experience influenced their determination of the experience's value and their sense of satisfaction. They can, however, give an overall impression of service quality that can trigger managerial investigation. If a patient is unhappy with the visit to the clinic, the clinic's managers will not know why until they carefully generate and analyze the data measuring patient perceptions of each step in the entire healthcare experience.

Management may not recognize that the dissatisfaction was caused by a long wait in x-ray, a rude doctor, or a dirty restroom. Knowing the system and having the measures can trigger the necessary corrective actions. A well-designed service system will include a way to measure every critical part of the patient experience as well as the experience as a whole.

## SYSTEM PLANNING TECHNIQUES

The first step in a customer-driven approach to service delivery system design is planning out the steps and processes in the entire system. At this stage, a detailed description of the steps involved is developed. Managers of benchmark service organizations start off their planning by surveying their potential patients to determine the key elements of the experience from the customer's perspective. Once those keys are determined, the delivery system can be designed to ensure that the patient's expectations regarding those key factors are met or exceeded.

If patient participation is included in the design, then the plan should account for the possibility that the patient cannot or will not participate in the treatment. For example, consider a professor who is used to having his healthcare needs met at the medical school and group practice affiliated with his university. He moves to another town, and his new primary care physician recommends that he visit a testing laboratory for certain tests. Accustomed to "one-stop shopping" for healthcare, the professor does not go to the laboratory and instead finds a new primary care physician who performs tests in the office. The first doctor's delivery system plan should have taken this possibility into account and included measurement of the customer's satisfaction with all parts of the delivery system.

Four basic techniques—blueprinting, fishbone analysis, PERT/CPM, and simulation—are commonly used to develop a detailed plan for delivering the healthcare experience. Managers can also use these techniques to focus on any part that patient feedback indicates is a problem area. These techniques are especially useful because they can readily incorporate the measurements necessary for control and analysis of problems that may appear in the system.

Each technique has its own advantages, but all are premised on the idea that a detailed written plan leads to a better system for managing the people, organization, information, and production processes that deliver the total healthcare experience. If effort and care are devoted to the plan, failures should be minimized. If situations regularly get to the point where problem-solving and problem-recovery techniques are necessary, some patients will inevitably become so dissatisfied that they will not choose the provider again if they can help it.

### Blueprinting

Detailing the delivery system through a blueprint or service process diagram has several immediate benefits to managers seeking to fail-safe the delivery of their service. First, managers can better understand and study a diagram (in a flow chart form, for example) that delineates all parts of the system. Second, managers can easily use the diagram to show the plan to others. Figure 11.1 is a simple flow chart of activities associated with a patient's visit to a physician office. All activities head toward and center on the patient's consultation with the doctor. Each activity related to the office visit must be successfully planned, designed, and managed if the healthcare experience is to succeed. Like most chains, the flow chart is only as strong as its weakest link. Although some activities are more important than others, each is a potential moment of truth that can affect the quality or value of the experience from the patient's perspective.

Employees must be trained and motivated to perform their responsibilities at each step on the flow chart. When the patient phones in for an appointment, staff must answer the phone promptly, be courteous and friendly, and find the earliest mutually convenient appointment time. If the patient arrives by car and parks, the organization must be sure that the parking area is clean and safe; if valet parking is provided, the patient must be given information about it ahead of time. As the first personal contact with the patient, the valet must be helpful and friendly. When the patient arrives at the front desk, staff must extend a friendly welcome and explain what is going to happen and when. At sign-in, staff must provide all necessary paperwork, assist in filling it out, and explain the organization's billing policies and procedures. During any waits, staff must stay in touch with the patient, explain any undue delays, and provide estimates of how long the wait may extend.

Although the patient may not be present at most other points of activity on the chart, which usually involve different organizational units serving each other as "internal customers," those points must also be similarly managed. For example, if the report of the patient's lab work (upper right on the chart) is not completed promptly to be inserted into the folder sent to the nurse, the doctor will not have that needed information at the consultation. Another consultation may have to be scheduled, and the patient will be inconvenienced.

*Blueprinting* is a more sophisticated form of flow charting. In effect, a good blueprint defines every component and activity not just of the delivery system but of the entire healthcare experience, from the

**Figure 11.1 Flow Chart of a Typical Patient Office Visit**

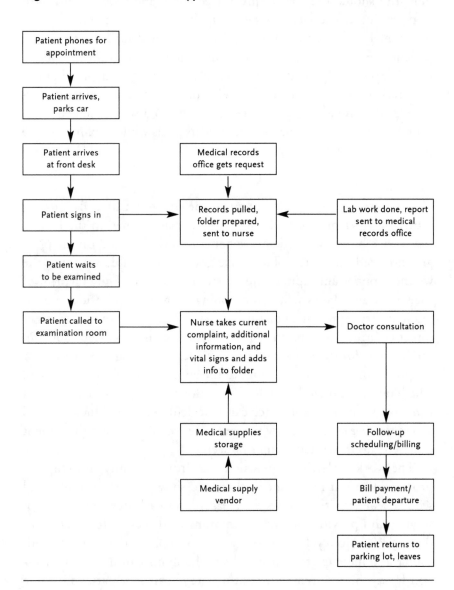

moment the patient sees the front door to the time the patient departs. Every event that is scheduled to happen in between is laid out on a blueprint, as is every contingency that can be reasonably projected. Those points at which service problems are most likely to occur can be identified, and early-warning mechanisms can be included. The blueprint should present not just the activities and processes involved in providing the service but should include times each activity takes to complete. If an excellent clinical visit is provided in 20 minutes, a patient may feel quite pleased; if in an hour, satisfied; if in two hours, the disappointed patient may never return. Finally, blueprinting not only satisfies the patient; it also helps the organization meet its revenue goals. Providing the service according to a well-designed blueprint will help the organization achieve its goals while maximizing the patient-experience quality and value.

### Example

Figure 11.2 shows a simple blueprint for treatment of a playground injury by an elementary school nurse. As diagrammed in the Figure, the service begins with the nurse being told that a child on the playground needs attention. The nurse goes to the child, examines the wound, applies antiseptics, and dresses the wound. The blueprint of the service also shows an arrow dropping from the application-of-antiseptic step to represent a potential area of failure where the nurse might forget to bring the antiseptic. If this happens, the next step shown in the figure is for the nurse to fix the problem by going to the office or supply room and then returning to the application-of-antiseptic step. The blueprint provides time estimates for each step so that the total time of the service experience can be calculated. The blueprint also shows the *line of visibility*, which separates the events that the patient can see from those that cannot be seen.

The work cycle times are calculated from carefully studying the process. The entire finished schematic shows clearly the planned sequence of activities, shows the measures for each step in the cycle of service, and provides an easily communicated picture for analysis of the entire service cycle. Obviously, this example in the Figure is both simple and incomplete. The excellent school nurse or healthcare manager for a school system will want to extend this schematic to include certain events that happen before the nurse is summoned to treat a student. The manager should start at the point where the overall strategy for student health was established in the first place. Doing so allows the manager to see all the other influences that have an impact on the student's total healthcare experience, including its many other intangible and tangible aspects.

## Figure 11.2 Blueprint for Nurse Treating Playground Injury

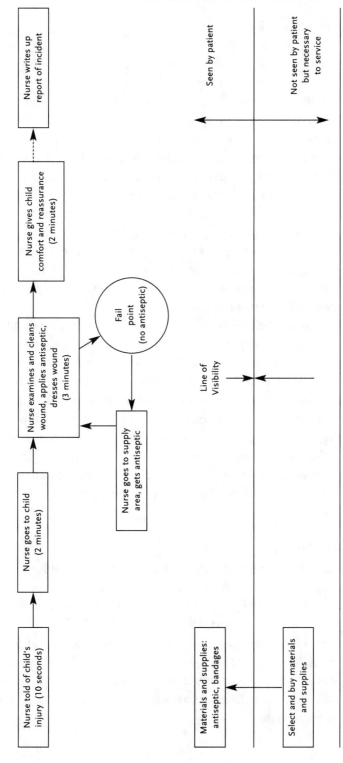

*Source:* Reprinted with permission from *The AMA Handbook of Marketing for the Service Industry,* published by the American Marketing Association, edited by C. A. Congram and M. L. Friedman, 1991.

### Adding More Detail

The simple example in the Figure can be extended and completed by incorporating all the fine points of elementary school nursing care; the blueprint can go into even greater detail by breaking down each step into a detailed subroutine and by adding complementary services such as administering shots, hearing and eyesight testing, and wellness counseling. In his book, *Service America*, service quality expert Karl Albrecht relates an example of a blueprint for a frontline bank employee that covered 36 11" by 18" pages.[3] The level of detail in Albrecht's bank-employee blueprint is similar to that used to study a manufacturing process. If the healthcare organization or unit is offering a mass service, the type and number of people being served may mandate extensive use of manufacturing production techniques and a "Taylorizing" (derived from the early work of scientific management founder Frederick Taylor) of the service delivery system, whether the healthcare organization wants to or not.

The need to treat hundreds of people a day in a large ER, serve dozens of people a day in a surgical center, or respond to countless phone calls on a health insurance information line may necessitate that the service delivery steps be broken down into highly specialized and routinized jobs to make the process as efficient as possible or to make the process work at all. The challenging question about those jobs is how to retain the human interaction component in the healthcare experience. The numbers of patients are so large and the service contact takes place so rapidly that the most personable professional will find it difficult to achieve a caring interaction with patients under the circumstances.

### Fishbone Analysis

If a widespread, often systemwide, service delivery problem is discovered, as opposed to a more localized service failure, one way to attack it is to use cause-and-effect analysis in the form of a *fishbone analysis*—a concept developed by Kaorn Ishikawa of Tokyo University in 1953. It provides a way to concentrate on the problem area and generally includes the participation of the area's employees. Although it analyzes the causes of faulty service outcomes, it can be considered as a planning strategy because its results are often used to make major changes in the delivery system.[4]

### Example

Figure 11.3 shows an application of this technique to a problem in the hypothetical General Hospital chain: too many blood donors show up at the blood bank for their set appointment times and subsequently experience unreasonable delays.[5] The problem (delayed blood donation) becomes the spine of the fish in the Figure 11.3 diagram. The general resource areas within which problems might arise that can delay blood donation are attached as bones to the spine. For example, "equipment" (which is a bone) is required to take blood promptly, so this resource area becomes a potential source of delay if, for example, equipment is already in use or otherwise unavailable. All of the possible contributors to the equipment failure are also shown as bones attached to the main equipment bone. The potential contributors to resource failure are typically identified through group discussion with the employees involved; they should know the reasons for treatment delays. General Hospital's employees readily identified the possible trouble spots.

The resources required for receiving blood donations can be categorized as equipment, personnel, material, procedures, and other. They are attached to the spine (problem). Within any one of them, a problem can arise that will cause the undesirable effect of unreasonable delays in serving blood donors. The potential problems associated with each resource will then be identified, listed, and prioritized by the employee group working on this problem. This technique, known as *Pareto Analysis*, calls for arranging the potential causes of the problem in order of importance.

In Table 11.1, the data representing the percentages of delayed service to blood donors associated with each cause are listed next to the cause in order of importance. The Pareto Analysis revealed that about 90 percent of all service delays at General Hospital chains were caused by only four of the approximately 30 possible causes. The most frequent reason for delay at all hospitals combined was donors being late for their appointments at 53.3 percent, followed by too few clinicians, late record updating, and computer system breakdowns. General Hospital realized that it was giving immediate service to the donors who least deserved it: those who arrived late for their appointments to give blood.

The data can also be analyzed by individual hospitals in the General Hospital chain to see if the overall problems with blood donation are

**Figure 11.3 Fishbone Analysis: Delays at the General Hospital Blood Banks**

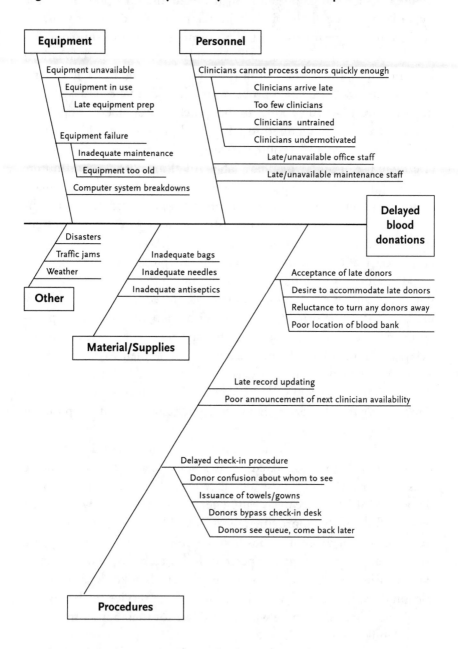

*Source:* Adapted with permission from *Cornell Hotel and Restaurant Administration Quarterly*, published by the American Marketing Association, D. Daryl Wyckoff, 1984, 25 (3): 158.

**Table 11.1 Pareto Analysis of Delays at the General Hospital Blood Banks**

| | All Hospitals | | Newark | | | Washington | | |
|---|---|---|---|---|---|---|---|---|
| Cause of Delay | Percentage of Incidence | Cumulative Percentage | Cause of Delay | Percentage of Incidence | Cumulative Percentage | Cause of Delay | Percentage of Incidence | Cumulative Percentage |
| Late donors | 53.3 | 53.3 | Late donors | 23.1 | 23.1 | Late donors | 33.3 | 33.3 |
| Too few clinicians | 15 | 68.3 | Late record updating | 23.1 | 46.2 | Too few clinicians | 33.3 | 66.6 |
| Late record updating | 11.3 | 79.6 | Too few clinicians | 23.1 | 69.3 | Computer breakdowns | 19 | 85.6 |
| Computer breakdowns | 8.7 | 86.3 | Old equipment failures | 15.4 | 84.7 | Late record updating | 9.5 | 95.1 |

*Source:* Adapted with permission from *Cornell Hotel and Restaurant Administration Quarterly*, published by the American Marketing Association, D. Daryl Wyckoff, 1984, 25 (3): 158.

the same as those found in each individual hospital. As the data show, both the percentages and the reasons for delay at the Newark hospital are somewhat different from those seen at the other hospitals. The fourth most frequent factor at Newark, failure of old equipment, does not appear as a problem for the Washington hospital, but computer breakdowns do. By arranging the information in this way, managers looking for causes of service delivery failures have an easily used analytical tool available. For each potential failure point, they merely collect and arrange the data that the fishbone categories tell them to gather. Recognizing the problem is the first step in improving the service delivery system; knowing the causes is the first step in solving the problems.

Once the impact of late-arriving donors was identified, General Hospital decided it would no longer wait for donors simply because they could not or would not arrive on time. Although this solution seemed to contradict the hospital's desire to attract blood donors, and staff naturally wanted to accommodate late-arriving donors, the hospitals in the chain had clearly been denying timely service to the many donors who made sure to get to the center on time. By setting up this fishbone and comparing the survey data against the key factors, the hospital group was able to identify the problem and discover a solution that worked: Do not wait on anybody. Of course, that solution initially caused a customer-relations problem with late arrivals, but General Hospital decided that it was less serious than the problems that the late arrivals caused. As a matter of fact, when word got out that General Hospital was not going to wait any more, fewer donors arrived late and the number of donors did not decline.

The individual parts of any delivery system can be broken down in the same way described above to discover the equipment, staff, procedures, material, and other factors that contribute to a service problem. Once managers measure each factor's contribution to the problem, finding a solution is relatively straightforward.

## PERT/CPM

Let us say you want to build a backyard barbecue. You design the barbecue and draw the figure, then you buy bricks and mortar. Then once you go out back to dig the foundation you find that you do not have a shovel and need to buy one. Finally, you start digging the foundation, and while you are doing so your neighbor tells you that you need permission from the neighborhood homeowners' association before you can build a structure of that size on your property.

The impediments to the process in the above scenario are merely a time waster and an annoyance to the barbecue builder, but these types of impediments can cause much bigger problems to a healthcare organization. Healthcare organizations cannot afford to start building a hospital or clinic and then find out in the middle of the process that it lacks material or permits to complete the project. When the planning and delivery of the service product involve different activities, and especially when those activities recur in a repeating cycle (like planning a heart transplant or rehabilitation therapy treatment), a helpful technique to use is PERT/CPM.

The PERT/CPM planning technique is frequently used in the construction industry and the military, but it has many applications in the healthcare industry as well. The PERT (Program Evaluation Review Technique) and CPM (Critical-Path Method) techniques are similar and have become merged into a single planning strategy. The combined PERT/CPM provides to the manager a detailed, well-organized plan combined with a control-measurement process for analyzing how well the plan is being executed. PERT/CPM is useful in planning major projects such as building a new hospital, setting up a new healthcare insurance plan, or opening a new clinic. It is also useful in smaller projects like planning a patient treatment or surgical procedure or installing a new MRI. Such activities have a beginning, an end, and a middle process. The steps in the process are (1) identifying the activities that must be done to complete the project, (2) determining the sequence of activities, (3) estimating how long each activity will take, (4) creating and diagramming the network of activities, and (5) finding the "critical path" running through the network. The successful use of the process may depend on the accuracy of the estimates made in step 3, and they are not always easy to make.

Using a PERT/CPM diagram like that seen in Figure 11.4 allows the healthcare manager to achieve several important objectives. First, the manager gains all the usual advantages of planning. Unforeseen events and activities can be identified, and how long something will take to do is readily estimated. Everyone involved in the project has an easily understood picture that shows all the pieces of the project, the sequence in which they are laid out and must be accomplished, and the time estimates for finishing each project step and the total time for completing the entire project. PERT/CPM can be used to plan any project

**Figure 11.4 PERT/CPM Diagram**

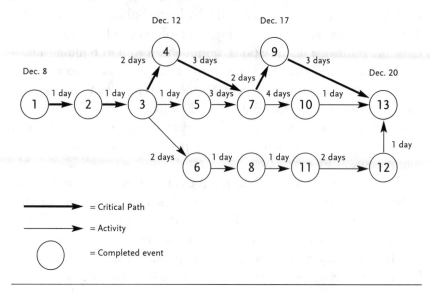

involving lots of activities that have to be accomplished on time to meet a deadline.

PERT/CPM diagrams are simple to create. They consist of circles or bubbles that represent completed events and arrows that represent the activities that must be done before an event can be considered completed. The arrows connect the circles, and the arrow points to the particular event for which the activity is necessary. In Figure 11.4, Event 1 must be completed before work can start on the activity that leads to the completion of Event 2, and the same is true of Events 2 and 3. Only after completed Event 3 occurs can work begin on the activities leading to Events 4, 5, and 6, which can be worked on independently of each other. Three arrows point at Event 13, which signifies that completion of Event 13 will first require completion of activities from Events 9, 10, and 12. As the diagram shows, Events 9, 10, and 12 cannot be completed before prior activities and events are first completed. The *critical path*—the sequence of events that must occur on time if the project is to be completed on time—in the diagram will be explained in more detail later in the chapter. It has no "slack" as the other two paths do.

Let us leave abstract events and consider the HMO plan for senior citizens that Universal HMO, Inc. wants to start in a new market. The final event in the sequence, the final circle on Universal's PERT/CPM diagram, will be "First Day of HMO Operation." One activity arrow leading up to that circle might be labeled "Hold three staff training sessions." But before those training sessions can be held, several other activities and events must take place. Universal HMO, Inc. must find a place to hold training, order training materials, hire and prepare a trainer, and hire the new HMO personnel. Some of those activities can be done simultaneously. Their completion might be indicated in the diagram by a circle labeled "Preparations for training sessions finished." Also included in the diagram are estimates of how long each activity will take. Summing the activity times will give Universal HMO, Inc. a pretty good estimate of how long it will take to have a trained HMO staff available.

Five steps are required to build a PERT/CPM network:

1. *Analyzing the Event.* The manager defines all events that must occur, and all activities leading up to those events, for the project to be completed at all. The real fruits of the planning process occur at this step. By taking the time and making the effort, the manager can detail every activity in the project and uncover every step that must be taken.

2. *Sequencing the Event.* The manager places defined activities and events in their proper sequence or the order in which they must be done. Developing the sequence may reveal previously undiscovered or unknown events that must be scheduled. If you are describing how to tie a shoelace, you may forget event number one—that you must first have a shoelace—unless you take the process step by step.

3. *Estimating Time.* The manager estimates how much time each activity will take so that an expected time for completing each event and the entire project can be calculated. Managers frequently use a simple formula to arrive at a weighted-average time estimate for each activity:

   Expected time = [optimistic time + 4 times most likely time + pessimistic time] / divided by 6.

4. *Diagramming the Project.* The manager puts all pieces together into the total project diagram. As seen in Figure 11.5, each activity and event is set out in the diagrammed network along with the expected times.

## Figure 11.5 PERT/CPM Diagram for Starting an HMO

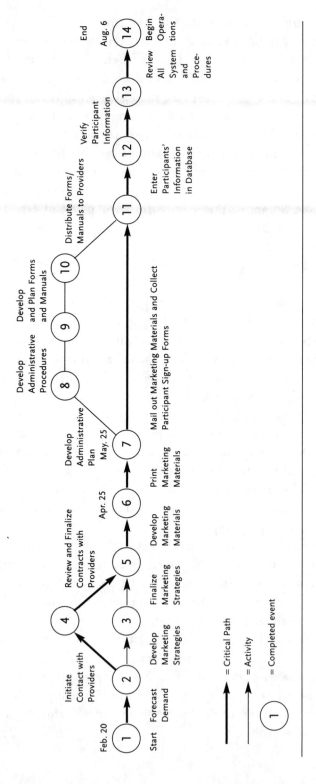

5. *Identifying the Critical Path.* The manager estimates the total time for completing the project and identifies the critical path—the sequence of activities that leaves no slack time—by summing up the activity times across the paths leading to the project completion. If these events do not happen on schedule, the project will not be finished on schedule. Other paths in the network may have a time difference between when the events must happen and when they are scheduled to happen based on the calculation of activity times. Event 6 must happen on April 28 or the entire project will get behind schedule, but Event 6 is scheduled for completion on April 25, so the project manager has some slack time. Even if Event 6 takes five days to complete instead of two, the delay will not affect the project completion date. Slack time also represents an opportunity to shift resources and attention away from events that finish earlier than they must and toward activities that need help.

The PERT/CPM network diagram also provides a terrific visual of what is involved in the project. Using the diagram, the project manager can show everyone what the whole project looks like, what each person's part in the project is, when each activity needs to be done, which are critical, and which events precede each person's job and which events follow. Even more helpful is that the manager now has a complete model that can be used to test what might happen under a differing array of assumptions. What will happen, for example, if some of the pessimistic time estimates come true (whatever could go wrong, did go wrong)?

Having the PERT/CPM diagram available gives the manager an easy and quick way to substitute new numbers and revise the time schedule for total project completion if necessary. Obviously, every major project involves a whole lot of uncertainties. With this technique, however, the manager can plug in the uncertainties and refigure their impact on the project if they occur.

Figure 11.5 represents the steps necessary to prepare for and begin offering a new HMO plan in a specific market. An HMO benefits manager followed the steps in building a PERT/CPM network to determine the activities, their sequence, and the time estimates. Then she set up the PERT/CPM network to show herself, the members of her organization, and the provider with whom her organization was contracting all the things that must happen to complete a successful introduction of the HMO plan to this market. This diagram serves as a daily planning guide to the benefits manager and members and providers of the organization; it can be hung on the wall to show everyone what activities they need to accomplish each day.

A well-constructed and complete PERT/CPM diagram may be used repeatedly because new product or service introductions generally have the same events and follow the same sequence of activities. The same is true for building a new hospital, planning a new clinic, or planning a particular operation in a surgical theatre. A caveat is in order, however. The PERT/CPM process assumes that the activities leading to a project's completion are independent and can be clearly defined, but that is not always the case. The process depends on the accuracy of the time estimates. Because these estimates are done by fallible human beings, they may be incorrect, and it does not take many incorrect time estimates to throw off an entire project.

Because the activities of healthcare organizations are often sequences or processes with a beginning and an end—from a brief clinical encounter to cleaning and preparing a room for the next day's patients—the possible applications of PERT/CPM to healthcare facilities and service situations are endless and surprisingly painless.

## Simulations

Making changes in the healthcare environment is often difficult because of the many issues that must be considered, such as cost and the effect on patient satisfaction. The organization must ensure that any proposed change does not have a negative effect. A properly run simulation enables the organization to "try out" changes before implementing them, without running the risks associated with actually making the changes.

A *simulation* is an imitation of the real thing. It is done either through illustration on paper or on a computer or reenactments and scenario performance. Some simulations are big, like a computerized simulation of activities in a university health center, and some are small, like a role-playing exercise at a training session. Some simulations involve professional actors enacting a specific healthcare experience to show the observing employees and managers where the problems in service delivery can occur. These simulations can reveal problems that the people who work there may not have thought about. They can also improvise patient-created problems to see if the system has safeguards to keep the patient from failing in the experience or, if a failure does occur, to keep the patient from irreparably harming the value and quality of the experience. Organizations can use all types of simulations when planning the service delivery system.

The computerized simulation techniques are the most sophisticated; they allow incredibly detailed simulation of the service delivery system and also provide ways to measure and manipulate the system to see what might happen under different assumptions. Computers can also simulate behaviors of patients, with their infinite needs and ranges of behavior, on the receiving end of the system.

The unique challenge in patient care is that each patient is different. Because predicting how any one patient is going to behave within the service experience is almost impossible, the opportunities for system failures are tremendous. Simulating patient behavior allows a better comprehension of how that variability in patients affects the system's ability to deliver the service at the level expected. Across the entire healthcare experience, simulation can identify problems created by both the organization and the patient.[6]

A good illustration of simulation is the recent trend in large urban hospitals to simulate their ERs on their computers. They gather data on arrival patterns and healthcare needs of patients at different times and days of the week and enter the data into the computer. The data may show that on a typical weekend evening, patients with trauma injuries will begin coming in early in the evening and that the frequency and severity of trauma will increase as the evening progresses. The data may also show that the "hangnail" type problems (e.g., minor cuts and bruises) increase during weekend days when physician offices are normally closed.

The ER can use the data generated by the computerized simulation to predict the type of medical care required by time of day and day of week as well as the number of staff required to serve the predicted patient population efficiently and effectively. Moreover, the hospital can estimate patient bed requirements, medical equipment demand, optimal stocking of supplies, and even the number of meals consumed in the cafeteria.

Not every healthcare organization has the patient volume to justify or pay for the creation of a full-scale computer model to study its service delivery system in detail. Nonetheless, with the increasing availability of computer technology in smaller, more user-friendly software packages, even individual physicians can now economically create computerized simulations of their systems.

Already available to small healthcare organizations is a software package called the General Purpose Simulation System for Personal Computer (GPSS/PC) on which organizations can simulate portions of their delivery systems or an entire delivery system. For example, an Atlanta clinic was expected to provide services despite some difficult circumstances: strict federal guidelines regarding delivery of services; clients who showed up late for appointments 40 to 50 percent of the time or did not show up at all; and frequent walk-ins who, according to federal guidelines, had to be accommodated.[7] The GPSS/PC was used to simulate client flow through the clinic. The simulation showed that simply reducing the wait time before filling a late appointment significantly decreased the average time spent in the clinic for all patients.

## CROSS-FUNCTIONAL ORGANIZATIONS

Thinking of the service delivery process as a system requiring the integrated, coordinated activity of people working in different departments leads to reflection on how the overall organization is designed. Is it designed so that individual departments can perform their individual functions smoothly, or is it designed so that the overall service delivery system functions smoothly? The two designs are not the same.

One method of organizing people and groups to enable them to work temporarily across the boundaries or functional units in which organizations are traditionally structured is the *cross-functional structure*. This term is also used to refer to an overlaying of a group or project team on the traditional functional organizational structure to work on a task for a limited time. Traditional organizational forms are characterized by a single line of authority running from top to bottom: A staff member reports to a supervisor, and the supervisor reports to a manager, and so forth.

A cross-functional organization is characterized by multiple lines of authority: A staff member may report to more than one person. In healthcare organizations, many situations arise that call for focusing everyone's clinical skills on solving a patient's problem or meeting a patient's expectation right now. Cross-functional structures are therefore especially useful in the healthcare industry, and in fact in any industry that is service driven.

In his book, Karl Albrecht tells a story about showing a group of hospital managers how the cycle of service appears from the patient's point of view. After an excited discussion in which they defined all the tasks necessary for delivering the hospital services needed by the patient, one manager suddenly said, "But no one is in charge." In other words, because of the way the typical hospital is organized, no one person was responsible for making sure that service was smooth, seamless, and focused on the patient. Every department and every function was someone's responsibility, but no one was responsible for being sure that all the subservices worked together for the patient's benefit. In elaborating on this point, the manager stated:

Our hospital is organized and managed by professional specialty—by functions like nursing, housekeeping, security, pharmacy, and so on. As a result, no single person or group is really accountable for the overall success and quality of the patient's experience. The orderlies are accountable for a part of the experience, the nurses for another, the lab technicians for another and so on. There are a lot of people accountable for a part of the service cycle but no one has personal accountability for an entire cycle of service.[8]

More and more hospitals believe that major change is needed to provide patients with a seamless service experience. Toward that end, many have reorganized their healthcare delivery systems to utilize cross-functional teams in delivering their services. A cross-functional team is a group staffed by a mix of specialists (i.e., physicians, nurses, nurse assistants, and so forth) formed to accomplish a specific objective. Team membership is usually assigned rather than voluntary. In healthcare, many such teams have involved the use of multiskilled health practitioners who are persons cross-trained to provide more than one function, often in more than one discipline. The combined functions can be found in a broad spectrum of health-related jobs ranging in complexity from the nonprofessional to the professional level, including both clinical and managerial functions. Research indicates that cross-functional teams have been successful in lowering costs, improving clinical quality, and enhancing patient satisfaction.[9]

At Lakeland Regional Medical Center in Lakeland, Florida, a cross-functional team concept has been successfully implemented. From

**Table 11.2 Advantages and Disadvantages of Cross-Functional Structures**

*Advantages*

1. Create lateral communication channels that increase frequency of communication across functional areas in the organization
2. Increase quality and quantity of information up and down the vertical hierarchy
3. Increase flexibility in utilization of clinical expertise and capital resources
4. Increase individual motivation, job satisfaction, commitment, and personal development
5. Enable achievement of clinical excellence more easily

*Disadvantages*

1. Violate traditional "single line of authority" and "authority must be equal to responsibility" principles of organization
2. Lead to ambiguity about control of resources, responsibility for technical issues, and human resources management issues
3. Create organizational conflict between clinical and team managers
4. Create interpersonal conflict among individuals who must work together but have different backgrounds; clinical training; and perspectives on work, time horizons, and goals
5. Create loss of status, causing unit managers to think that their autonomy has been eroded
6. More costly for organization in terms of increased overhead and staff, more meetings, delayed decisions, and more information processing
7. More costly for individuals in terms of role ambiguity, conflict, and stress

check-in to discharge, patients are looked after by a "care-pair," usually a registered nurse and a multiskilled health practitioner. The teams are cross-trained in functions ranging from EKG monitoring to recording patients' expenses. Patients' rooms have computer terminals and mini-pharmacies so that most of what is needed is close by. This approach minimizes idle time and cuts staff and paperwork. Time spent with patients has increased 60 percent, personnel costs have declined 40 percent, and patient satisfaction has increased.[10] The key factor in this success has been the team focus on the needs of the patient at all steps in the process.

Healthcare organizations use project teams, matrix structures, and other cross-functional forms. Because these forms generally involve people working under more than one line of authority, some traditional managers who believe that strict lines of authority are important have problems working with cross-functional forms. On the other hand, crossing functional areas and getting everyone focused on the patient can offer some important benefits. Table 11.2 presents the advantages and disadvantages of these organizational forms.

## CONCLUSION

Most service problems are caused by deficiencies in the service delivery system rather than individual staff members. Consequently, benchmark healthcare organizations analyze their delivery system from their customers' viewpoint, starting with their service expectations. Healthcare organizations need to use whatever organizational design best enables every unit and every person to focus on the patient's needs, wants, and expectations. Although the organization chart may show functional divisions with different people responsible for different things like maintenance, information systems, accounts receivables, nursing services, and so on, everyone in these excellent healthcare organizations knows that their real organizational function is ensuring that the healthcare experience meets or exceeds the patient's expectations.

## LESSONS LEARNED

1. Check for system failure before blaming people.
2. Detailed planning can avoid most service failures.
3. Plan for patient failures and how to recover from them.
4. Design the organization to ensure a seamless customer experience.
5. A bad system can defeat a good employee.
6. Use all available tools to break down the service experience into steps that can be studied.
7. You cannot fix a problem if you do not know what caused it.
8. Identify and eliminate current policies, procedures, and rules that may impede customer service.
9. Train staff not to use policies, procedures, and rules as excuses for not providing customer service.

10. Everyone is responsible for monitoring and maintaining the quality of the service delivery system; everyone is responsible for avoiding service failures.

11. Design the service system so that the overall service delivery system, rather than the individual departments, functions smoothly.

12. Designate a staff position that will be responsible for the entire cycle of service.

## NOTES

1. Tax, S. S., and I. Stuart. 1997. "Designing and Implementing New Services: The Challenges of Integrating Service Systems." *Journal of Retailing* 73 (1): 105–34.

2. *Wall Street Journal*, July 3, 2001, p. B1.

3. Albrecht, K. 1988. *At America's Service: How Your Company Can Join the Customer Service Revolution*, p. 89. New York: Warner Books.

4. For a particularly interesting use of fishbone analysis in healthcare, see R. Breiterman-White. 1999. "Continuous Quality Improvement in Anemia Management: Using the Fishbone Approach to Improve Outcomes." *ANNA Journal* 26 (2): 254–257.

5. Adapted from D. D. Wyckoff. 1984. "New Tools for Achieving Service Quality." *Cornell Hotel and Restaurant Administration Quarterly* 25 (3): 89.

6. For an excellent survey of the use of simulation to address healthcare problems, see J. B. Jun, S. H. Jacobson, and J. R. Swisher. 1999. "Application of Discrete-Event Simulation in Health Care Clinics: A Survey." *Journal of the Operational Research Society*: 50 (2): 109–23.

7. Brotman, B. A., M. Bumgarner, and P. Prime. 1998. "Client Flow Through the Women, Infants, and Children Public Health Program." *Journal of Health Care Finance* 25 (1): 72–77.

8. Albrecht, K. 1988. *At America's Service: How Your Company Can Join the Customer Service Revolution*, p. 38. New York: Warner Books.

9. Fottler, M. D. 1996. "The Role and Impact of Multiskilled Health Practitioners in the Health Services Industry." *Hospital & Health Services Administrators* 41 (1): 55–75.

10. Siler, J. F., and T. Peterson. 1990. "Hospital, Heal Thyself." *Business Week* (August): 66–68.

*Chapter 12*

# Waiting for Healthcare Service

Healthcare Principle: *Manage all parts of the customer's wait*

Hurry up and wait.

—*Old military saying*

HOW LONG WE wait and how long we are willing to wait are fascinating subjects. A British Airways TV commercial says that we spend 8 1/2 weeks waiting in lines during the first 30 years of our life. Parents put their children on the waiting lists of some exclusive preparatory schools before the children are even born. If you want to ride your own raft down the Colorado River in the Grand Canyon, rather than ride in a concession operator's raft, you will have to wait in line—at current use levels, that wait is about 20 years.

Waiting is a universal concern to all service organizations, but it can be critical in the healthcare industry. A poorly managed queue cannot only cause dissatisfaction with the healthcare experience but may cause a medical catastrophe as well. Effective management of waiting lines requires an understanding of both the mechanics and the psychology of creating well-designed queues. Building enough service capacity to handle the average patient demand is not the answer. The tremendous variation in patient care needs makes averages largely unrelated to the ebbs and flows of actual patient demand. Healthcare managers are especially challenged by the need to balance the healthcare organization's commitment to patient care and satisfaction with the huge costs of building and maintaining today's healthcare capacity.

In this chapter, we discuss the importance of the wait, present strategies for managing the reality and the perception of the customer's wait, and emphasize the importance of understanding capacity and psychology. Overall, we think that the secret to managing the customer's wait effectively is to use both quantitative and psychological techniques in the appropriate combination to make waits, even long ones, acceptable to customers.

## THE IMPORTANCE OF THE WAIT

Nobody likes to wait in line; yet, almost every healthcare organization relies on waiting lines to match its service capacity with the number of customers who want service. Managing the lines and how long customers have to wait in them is a major concern of any healthcare service organization that wishes to improve its customer satisfaction and capacity utilization levels. In some respects the wait is an inevitable part of the healthcare experience because no organization can perfectly prepare itself to meet the needs of all customers instantly. In another respect the wait is a service failure. Even if the wait at the physician's office is no surprise and therefore "meets the patient's expectations," the patient still does not like it.

Waiting time is the length of time customers wait to have their needs addressed efficiently. "Opportunity cost" is the time and other opportunities that customers must sacrifice to obtain needed or desired health services. Waiting occurs as a matter of routine in the admissions office, physician's waiting room, examination or testing rooms, and on telephone lines as customers attempt to schedule appointments, acquire test results, or resolve reimbursement issues. All patients wait to receive test results or prognoses, to be seen by a physician or nurse, to be told what to do or where to go. If they tire of waiting, and if not too ill to do so, they may just leave.

What makes patients wait? High expectations explain the large numbers of patients willing to wait for appointments with famous surgeons, respected dentists, or at well-known cancer clinics. The people waiting believe that the quality or the uniqueness of the medical treatment will outweigh the costs of waiting, despite the full patient schedule and the numbers on a waiting list. In effect, each person makes an "opportunity cost" judgment. If the expected benefits of that particular service or treatment outweigh the costs of idly sitting in a reception area, then the patient will wait.

Waiting time has unfortunately become an expected part of the service process in healthcare. As a result, to be served on time is a rarity. In spite of the pervasive use of appointments to balance healthcare capacity with patient demand, being served on time is a too infrequent event. Even more frustrating to patients is the fact that their time is respected in most other services. However, waits seem increasingly to be the rule and not the exception in healthcare. Staff may begin to feel that long waits are normal and to be expected and that customers should tolerate them.

Author Stephanie Sherman has identified four primary reasons why patients and physicians "defect" or leave a healthcare organization.[1] The most important of these reasons is that the waiting time is too long. Today's busy consumer demands and expects prompt service. When a customer defects, the healthcare organization may lose revenue that the customer represents for a lifetime. Even worse, further revenue may be lost from negative word of mouth, as each dissatisfied customer tells others to avoid using that provider.

Press Ganey Associates reviewed more than 1 million patient surveys in 545 hospitals in 44 states to determine the most important key drivers correlated with the patients' recommending a hospital to others.[2] The most important reason was "staff sensitivity to the inconvenience that health problems can cause." In other words, staff efforts to mitigate the negative impact of required health services on the customer's life (including waiting times) may enhance the probability that a patient will recommend a hospital or other health service provider.

Another study by Press Ganey Associates evaluated 25 physician practice qualities in terms of their relative need for improvement.[3] Seven of the top ten areas identified as needing improvement were related to customer waiting:

1. Availability of doctor on phone
2. How promptly phone call was returned
3. Lack of phone access to service
4. Speed of the registration process
5. Ease of obtaining a desired date and time for appointment
6. Length of wait in reception area
7. Waiting time to see the doctor

## CAPACITY AND PSYCHOLOGY

Managing the wait has two major components. First, ensure that the appropriate *capacity* has been built into the service facility to minimize the wait for the anticipated number of customers arriving at the anticipated rate. Second, ensure that the waiting customers' *psychological needs and expectations* are met while they wait.

The capacity decision results from careful study of the expected demand pattern. Whether one is trying to determine how many copier machines to buy to serve a medical records department, how many treatment rooms to build in the emergency department, how many phone lines to run into the hotline for an AIDS counseling center, or how many beds to put in a hospital, the need to make an accurate capacity estimate is the same. Management must predict and attempt to manage three factors: (1) how many people will arrive for the service, (2) at what rate they will arrive, and (3) how long the service will take. These three predictions drive the capacity decision.

The capacity decision would be easy to make if on each day that the provider is open for service the same number of people were to arrive for service, their arrivals were evenly spaced throughout the day, and serving each person took the same length of time. For example, a psychiatrist can schedule eight patients per day, schedule them to arrive on the hour, then serve each patient for 45 minutes and use the remaining 15 minutes to write up notes on that patient and prepare for the next. That psychiatrist has an easy capacity decision: one service facility (an office) containing one chair for the psychiatrist and one couch for the patient, plus other furnishings and equipment for one office.

If the service is an emergency room, the healthcare provider knows approximately how long each type of treatment will take, but the management will have to predict how many people will arrive for service at different times throughout the day and for what types of treatment. If the service has a less definite beginning and ending time, like some types of hospital stay, both the average time taken to deliver the service and the number of persons arriving for service will have to be estimated or predicted. We will discuss several methods for making these predictions later in this chapter.

Capacity designs can also affect perceptions of service quality. A doctor's waiting area with too many seats will appear empty to patients. The scarcity of other patients may lead those who did come in and sit down to conclude that the clinical quality or medical expertise is not up to par. This assumption predisposes patients to expect a less-than-superb medical experience. Further, they may feel foolish for choosing a doctor who is so obviously unpopular. The physician has two strikes against her, just because the office designers put in too many seats. From the physician's point of view, the excess capacity also has a serious disadvantage: it costs money! Fixed costs are tied up in unused chairs and other furniture, extra space, and so forth. Excess capacity may result in extra personnel costs as well.

In an ideal world, the organization has the exact clinical staff and physical capacity required to serve each patient immediately. Each patient needing care at Hypothetical Hospital's ER arrives just when medical staff and equipment are available to provide the desired treatment. Patients want that kind of service, and organizations want to provide it. Both are frequently disappointed, however.

## Organizational Options

Because people do not arrive at service facilities in neat, ordered patterns, they sometimes have to wait for service. When the organization sees that its waits for service are becoming unacceptably long, healthcare managers face several choices[4]:

### Refuse to Serve Additional Customers

This choice is highly undesirable; after all, healthcare organizations exist to provide service. But sometimes prospective customers must be told, "We do not have any appointments available until next fall," or "You will have to seek care at another facility."

### Add Capacity

Because this alternative is usually expensive, organizations do not choose it unless they believe that the high demand causing the waits will continue. Of course, certificate-of-need laws in various states also constrain if and when capacity needs to be added. The organization will be particularly hesitant to add capacity if the capacity of its design day—the theoretical day, and the number of customers on that day, for which the capacity was designed—is set at a high percent level; that is, the organization is already at or below capacity most of the time.

Stop-gap measures for adding capacity temporarily are sometimes available: Employees can be asked to work overtime; a SWAT-team approach can be used to reassign employees from their normal areas to help unclog a service bottleneck; temporary help can be hired; physical facilities, like trailers or portable buildings, can be rented; and so forth.

### Manage Demand

Simply informing customers of when the busy and slack times are may smooth out demand. Rather than being open to all patients at any time, healthcare providers typically use appointments to smooth out ebbs and flows of patient demand. Some providers offer inducements to encourage use of capacity at nonpeak demand times. "Early-bird specials" and discounts for off-peak use of wellness centers and health clubs are examples.

Reservations or appointments are useful and help balance capacity utilization when staff and equipment are too expensive to sit idle, such as at hospitals, dental offices, and MRI clinics. Most healthcare organizations have the market stature to insist that their patients make appointments, and the opportunity cost to the patient for not receiving the specific service at the specific time from the specific provider is usually so great that the patient is willing to make an appointment. When the cancer specialist is the only one in the city able to treat a certain rare form of the disease, or the heart surgeon is the only one you trust to do the bypass, or you love the physician who has treated your family for forty years, you will make an appointment and thereby help the provider organization efficiently manage its capacity.

Another way to manage demand is by *shifting demand*. A good example is shifting elective surgery from weekday mornings to weekends. An obstetrician will frequently estimate the due dates of those patients whose delivery is expected to be a normal birth and then schedule c-sections around those times. This shifting of demand for obstetrical services allows the doctor's capacity and the hospital's surgical capacity to be more efficiently utilized. Although these things cannot be perfectly planned, this type of demand shift allows far better utilization of obstetrical services than would otherwise be possible.

*Triage* is often used as one clinical solution to the problem of excess demand. Under triage, to ensure that the most serious medical problems are treated first, patients are divided into three groups: (1) those who must be helped now; (2) those who can be helped later; and (3) those who cannot be helped at all, which is rare.

Some ERs and clinics have taken this concept to the next level. They have established "fast-track" systems that put patients with routine or noncritical healthcare problems in a separate queue. Instead of using the more expensive doctors, this queue may use paraprofessionals, lower-skilled nurses, and low-tech treatment rooms. The fast-track queue reduces the cost of treatment and increases the speed at which both lower-level and more acute medical needs are met. One study by researchers Kirtland and colleagues found that using fast-track queuing, in combination with other efficiency measures, reduced average patient wait time by 38 minutes.[5] This strategy improves both clinical efficiency and patient satisfaction.

### Divert Patients While They Wait

At a minimum, waiting patients should be offered something else to do. The traditional diversion in a healthcare office is a stack of magazines or newspapers, though some organizations also provide television, instructional videos or videos that feature additional services available, aquariums, toys, crossword puzzle books, and computer games. Today, some emergency rooms hand out beepers, similar to those used in restaurants, to give their waiting patients freedom to move about without losing their turn in line.[6]

To give customers someplace to go and something to do while they wait, some hospitals have expanded their gift shops. The shop in Woodwinds Health Campus in Woodbury, Minnesota contains an alternative medicine salon that sells such items as exotic teas, healing oils, and plant-gel toothpaste and has a master herbalist on call. Many other healthcare gift shops are expanding their offerings of medical products; if a folding cane, pill-splitter, prosthesis, or heating pad is prescribed or recommended, why not sell it within the hospital? Other hospitals, following the lead of airports, are adding a variety of small shops. Because such establishments can serve as diversions for customers and are highly profitable for hospitals, these shops are truly win-win.[7]

### Improve Waiting Areas

Uncomfortable waiting areas can make a moderate wait seem excessively long. Many healthcare organizations give low priority to the quality of their waiting areas. Some still use plastic chairs with hard bucket seats, and the chairs are connected by a steel rod. Seating with sufficient personal space, attractive designs, and some padding can make the wait more tolerable. Similarly, attractive colors and noise-dampening rugs and drapes can help. A strict no-smoking rule should be enforced in all waiting areas. Although most healthcare organizations are officially smoke-free environments, sometimes the rule is not enforced. As a result, waiting areas can become intolerable for nonsmokers.

### Create and Implement Waiting Time Standards

An efficiently operating registration process should require only three to five minutes of patient time and can be conducted upon the arrival of each patient with no waiting. Office staff should return phone calls in 20 minutes or less, and physicians should return theirs in one hour. Physicians involved in surgery or emergency care may not always be able to meet this standard, but designated office staff can return the call for the physician to keep the communication channels open. Cell phones make these performance standards easier to achieve. Staff should not only inform customers that service will be delayed but also explain why the delay is occurring.

Stephanie Sherman says that no healthcare customer should wait more than 15 minutes for anything without receiving an explanation for the delay, including an apology and an estimate of how long the customer will have to wait to receive the service.[8] When delays exceed or are predicted to exceed one hour, the option to reschedule the appointment should be offered as should paid transportation, if needed. Table 12.1 indicates a possible format for collecting data on patient waiting time.

To correct unacceptable waiting times, the organization should look first at the service delivery system (discussed in Chapter 11). Did patients wait for staff, equipment, test results, or for some other reason? How long all customers waited and what they were waiting for should be recorded. Periodically, these reports should be summarized, disseminated to staff, and used as a basis for staff discussion focused on reducing waiting time through system adjustments.

### Calculate and Use the Design Day

Whether they realize it or not, or whether they do it consciously or not, all healthcare organizations use the design-day concept. The design-day capacity is a management decision that determines how much capacity will be provided to handle a predetermined amount of demand without compromising the healthcare experience. If demand is less than the design-day model, then customers are satisfied but the facility and staff are underutilized. If demand exceeds the design-day capacity, then some customers will probably be dissatisfied. Waiting lines may form on design days, but they will not exceed the length of time where customers perceive a decline in the quality or value of their healthcare experience.

**Table 12.1 Patient Record Data for Tracking Patient Waiting Times**

| | Patient Names | |
| --- | --- | --- |
| | *Jane Doe* | *Harry Smith* |
| Date | 2/23/03 | 2/23/03 |
| Time of appointment | 9:00 a.m. | 2:30 p.m. |
| Time of arrival | 8:55 a.m. | 2:35 p.m. |
| Time of sign-in | 9:00 a.m. | 2:35 p.m. |
| Registration completed | 9:05 a.m. | 2:39 p.m. |
| Times of communication regarding appointment | | |
| First | 9:10 a.m. | — |
| Second | 9:22 a.m. | — |
| Third | — | — |
| Time of first contact with clinician | 9:32 a.m. | 3:08 p.m. |
| Time of last contact with clinician | 9:47 a.m. | 3:17 p.m. |
| Time of departure | 9:54 a.m. | 3:32 p.m. |
| Total elapsed time | 59 minutes | 57 minutes |
| Service | 15 minutes | 9 minutes |
| Waiting | 44 minutes | 48 minutes |
| Did the patient receive timely communication about delays? Yes No | | |

Benchmark organizations know just how long waits can be and still remain within limits acceptable to patients. A physician practice might use a 15-minute maximum wait for any one part of the healthcare experience as its criterion. On the design day, the provider does not want anyone to wait longer than this maximum time because surveys have shown that customer perceptions of quality and value decline sharply with longer waits. Although 15 minutes is the maximum acceptable wait, seeing the physician, receiving lab results, or seeing a nurse may take longer on a busy day. However, based on the accumulated data, a 15-minute maximum targeted wait may be the best balance between having too much capacity and not enough.

A truly patient-focused healthcare provider may set its design day at a very high level, say 80 to 90 percent—that is, supply will be adequate for demand on 80 to 90 percent of the days of the year—because it appreciates the fact that most patients have only limited time in which to get the necessary treatment and have no choice but to wait. A patient with a broken hip cannot wait four weeks for treatment and expect a good medical outcome, so the design-day level for the hospital orthopedic facility must be set at a higher level than for, say, the pharmacy. The same may be true for the ER because ER patients must be treated quickly.

To provide a healthcare experience of high quality, the organization may set its design day high and build more capacity than might otherwise be practical. The cost of an unhappy customer to a major clinic that relies on return visits must be carefully balanced against the costs of building capacity. Similarly, not having adequate capacity to serve the needs of the medical staff (another type of customer) will lead to dissatisfied physicians looking elsewhere to send their patients.

### Calculate and Use the Capacity Day

Many organizations calculate and use a *capacity day*—the maximum number of customers allowed in the facility in a day or at one time. This number may be set by the fire marshal based on the number of square feet each customer must have available. Typically, however, the capacity day is set by the organization itself to represent a point beyond which overall patient or physician dissatisfaction with waits or delays in service is unacceptable.

### Do Nothing

The organization can accept the fact that waits will lead to unhappy customers and hope that they are not so unhappy that they vow never to return. In this increasingly competitive world with increasing numbers of healthcare options, this alternative is becoming less and less desirable.

An ER can use the above strategies in the following ways: turn patients away (if legally permitted); limit usage by diverting patients to other hospitals; build a new facility, expand present capacity, or have an "on call" staff group that can be summoned when needed; provide diversions for waiting patients with nonemergency needs; improve waiting areas, minimize waits, communicate regularly concerning the reasons for waits; or simply accept higher levels of customer dissatisfaction. Good customer satisfaction research can identify the best strategy. The goal is to find the strategy that ensures the greatest customer satisfaction with the lowest capital and staffing costs and allows both customers and the organization to satisfy their needs.

In 1996, the ER at Baptist Hospital in Pensacola, Florida, addressed the issue of patient waiting in a customer service program based on the following premise: "If we don't like to wait and be treated as unimportant, why should they? Every person is valuable and should be regarded as such! A human soul is a valuable thing."9 As a result of this initiative, lower wait-time standards were implemented, records were kept for all patients, staff were held accountable, and several other strategies similar to the list above were implemented. Patient satisfaction scores increased from the 29th percentile in third quarter 1996 to the 92nd percentile in third quarter 1998. Moreover, the percentage of patients waiting over two hours for service declined from 10 percent to 2.6 percent, and patients leaving without treatment declined from 4.0 percent to 2.2 percent.10

## THE *REALITY* OF THE WAIT

Few organizations in any industry have the luxury of adjusting capacity quickly or managing demand by getting customers to show up when the organization wants them to, instead of when customers want or need to come. Like organizations in other industries, most healthcare organizations must rely on predicting and managing the inevitable waits that are created when patients arrive seeking treatment. The dilemma for the organization is that although adding staff or capacity costs more, it reduces the wait, which improves the patient-experience quality, patient satisfaction, and patient loyalty. Reducing staff saves money but increases the wait, which decreases patient-experience quality, patient satisfaction, and patient loyalty.

How can a healthcare organization find the proper cost-benefit balance? The place to begin is using *queuing theory*, sometimes called *waiting-line theory*, and the mathematical solutions this technique offers.

### Queuing or Waiting-Line Theory

A typical queuing-theory problem might be: If an average of five patients per hour arrive at an ER or public health clinic with a single service provider, and if it takes the service provider an average of nine minutes to treat or attend to a patient, how long does the average patient spend waiting? During an average hour, how many minutes will the service provider be treating patients and how many minutes will the provider be idle?

Most applications of waiting-line theory in the healthcare industry are based on the idea that people who cannot otherwise be scheduled do not arrive in neat patterns. The typical approach is to sample the arrival and service requirement patterns of patients and use this information to simulate the distribution that best matches the reality for the particular organization's patients. A large clinic or ER might actually count all of its patients over a period of time, or sample them over a longer period using some appropriate sampling methodology, and let the actual patient patterns represent the distribution of both arrival rates and service requirements.

All waiting lines have three characteristics that any model must include:

1. *Arrival pattern*—the number of patients arriving and the manner in which they enter the waiting line. The arrivals can be random (like patients entering an emergency room), in bulk (like patients arriving after a natural disaster), or in some other distribution that is difficult to describe (like patients coming to a group practice facility in varying but not completely random intervals). Queue management is easiest when patient arrivals can be scheduled. Even if arrivals cannot be strictly scheduled, they can sometimes be controlled. For example, a dentist can set aside the first hour in the morning for all dental emergencies. If none show up, the dentist can focus on other practice-related tasks or paperwork.

2. *Queue discipline*—the manner in which arriving patients are served. Options are first-come, first-served; last-come, first-served; or some other set of service rules, such as severity of need. On the battlefield or the ER, for example, the triage principle is often used. As another example, patients waiting to have their teeth cleaned will not usually object if a patient entering the dentist's office with a painfully swollen jaw is attended to first. Patients understand service rules based on need; they do not understand an implicit rule like "Answer a phone call from someone

sitting at home before serving the client or patient standing right in front of you who may have traveled miles to visit the clinic."

3. *Time for service*—the amount of time it takes to serve patients. The time boundaries of some healthcare services can be carefully managed, like an MRI or the time spent in the recovery room after a routine appendectomy, but the time required for many services is unpredictable. Some ER patients suffer from severe wounds, while others have trivial problems. Some patients want to be treated and then sent home, while others want TLC with their flu shot. The amount of time it takes to serve the needs of different patients is as unpredictable as the patients themselves. If the waiting-line model is going to be an aid in managing the wait, it must take this variation into account. Although the previous examples involve people, waiting-line theory can be applied to anything that waits in line for something to be done to it. An insurance report waiting to be properly filed or a meal waiting to be served is as queued up and in need of managing as the arriving customer at the ER reception desk.

## Types of Queue or Waiting Line

In the following discussion, channel refers to a service provider, and phase refers to a step in the service experience once it is underway.

The first type is the *single-channel, single-phase* queue—one service provider, one step. This queue type is represented as the top illustration in Figure 12.1. For example, in a small clinic, a single physician practitioner provides single-phase service to patients, who come in, wait their turn, get treatment, and leave. In a larger, busier setting, patients might stand in any one of several single-channel, single-phase queues to get a flu shot. The patient looks the lines over, chooses one, stands in it waiting for service, and eventually reaches the clinician who gives the shot. Highway toll plazas and McDonald's counters are not the sites of multichannel queues, even though they may have multiple servers. They consist of a group of single-channel, single-phase queues, with one service provider per queue.

The second type is the *single-channel, multiphase* queue, like a cafeteria line or a medical clinic. Essentially, it is two or more single-channel, single-phase queues in sequence. The patient waits in one queue for service from a single service provider, then moves on to wait in another queue for another phase of service from another single service provider.

## Figure 12.1 Basic Queue Types

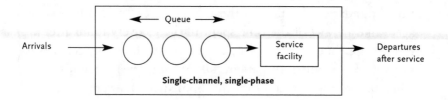

Single-channel, single-phase

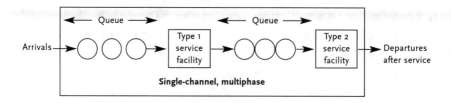

Single-channel, multiphase

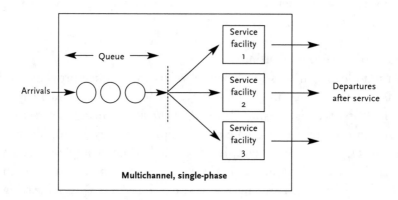

Multichannel, single-phase

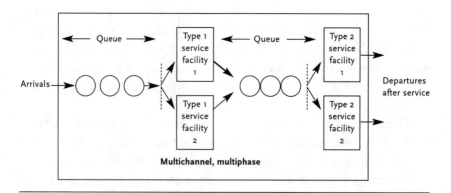

Multichannel, multiphase

At a typical clinic, patients queue up for the various phases. Each patient requiring treatment goes to x-ray, then to hematology for a blood sample, then to a waiting room for the physician.

The third type is the *multichannel, single-phase* queue. The patient begins in a single line that then feeds into multiple channels or stations for the service, each of which is staffed by a service provider. The patient waits to get to the front of the single line, then goes to the next available channel (service provider) for service.

An example is a multiphysician group practice where everyone waits in a single queue. The queue discipline is to tell the next person in line to come to the next available physician, who in turn renders a single service in a single phase. The Federal Personnel Office uses this method for incoming telephone calls. The automated system tells each caller how many callers are ahead, so the caller can decide whether to wait or call back later. The single phase of service is to have a phone call answered. The multiple channels for obtaining this service are the many operators handling calls. The queue is managed by having the next available operator handle the next caller waiting in line.

Many healthcare organizations find this method the most efficient way to manage their lines as it accounts well for the varying lengths of time that it takes to serve different patients. Everyone has had the experience of choosing to stand in one of several available single-channel lines (at the movie theater refreshment stand or the hotel front desk, for example), only to watch all the other lines move much more quickly. The use of a multichannel, single-phase system eliminates this feeling of inequity or bad luck; everyone starts out in the same line.

The last type is the *multichannel, multiphase* queue system, which is the most complicated to manage. Essentially, it is two or more single-channel, single-phase queues in sequence, which is similar to the post-September 11 check-in process at U.S. airports. The customer waits to get to the front of one line (check-in), then goes to the next available service provider. After receiving the first phase of service, the patient then gets in another line (security), waits to arrive at the front, then goes to the next available service provider/channel to receive the next phase of service. In healthcare, a patient may wait in line to see the first available doctor of several on duty. Then the doctor refers the patient to a lab where the patient waits in line to see the first available lab technician of several on duty.

A healthcare organization will often have numerous queues linked together in various combinations. For example, at a busy government clinic, patients may queue up outside the building before it opens in the morning, queue up at the cashier's office to pay a fee and "take a number" for consultation with a physician, queue up again in a waiting area for consultation, get in another queue for a specific diagnostic or treatment procedure, and then enter a final queue at the pharmacy if medication is needed. Managing the wait times associated with single and multiple channels and phases is difficult, but it is critical for ensuring a satisfactory healthcare experience and maximizing the provider's capacity utilization.

Common sense suggests that the best queue type for an organization to use is the one that enables customers to begin receiving service as rapidly as possible. In actuality, the best queue type is the one that patients prefer. For example, they may prefer to stand in a certain type of line because they think they will be served faster, even if they will not in actuality. For these reasons, organizations must know what queue types are most efficient and cost effective but also which queues their customers prefer.

### Simulation of Queue or Waiting Line

Although a statistical distribution can be used to describe the arrival and service patterns of many standard queues, some situations cannot be described by any statistical distribution. Here, only a simulation will yield the quality of data necessary to explain and predict the reality of a particular queue. Here is how a simulation might work.

The hotline of AIDS Aides is an extremely successful help and crisis telephone center for AIDS patients. The system has 20 phone lines that if fully staffed require one person at each line (for a total of 20 people). If on an average day only 50 patients call in, then full staffing of all the lines is an obvious waste of money because the probability of more than 20 people calling at the same time is small. But if AIDS Aides opens only one phone line, most callers will hear a busy signal or be put on hold; they may get no counseling or help but will experience considerable frustration. What staffing level best balances the cost of staffing the phone lines against the cost of frustrated or lost patients?

Over several weeks the floor manager can monitor the flow of calls and length of time callers are on a line plus how many times callers receive a busy signal and hang up or are put on hold. If sufficient observations are made, the manager can create distributions that accurately describe the number of callers, the arrival patterns of their calls, and their time spent either asking questions or seeking help. With this information the manager can then simulate the telephone experiences of AIDS Aides clients to determine how to staff the phone lines appropriately at different times and on different days of the week. Following is a simple illustration of how that might be done.

In his office, the manager can conduct a Monte Carlo simulation by setting up two roulette wheels that appear in Figure 12.2. Spaces are allocated on the first wheel to represent, in percentage form, the time between calls. From the observations already made, the manager knows that for 15 percent of the time, the time between calls was zero minutes—calls arrived simultaneously. For 20 percent, the time between calls was one minute; for 25 percent, the time was two minutes; for 10 percent the time was three minutes. For another 10 percent, the time was four minutes; for 12 percent, five minutes; and for 8 percent, six minutes. Spaces on the wheel are allocated to reflect these phone call percentages. To simulate the arrival patterns of the phone calls, the manager merely spins the wheel and writes on a chart the arrival time noted in the section of the wheel when it stopped.

The second wheel in Figure 12.2 is, in similar fashion, portioned off to represent the observations about how long each caller was on the phone. This total includes the time to answer the call, diagnose the situation, and either refer the caller to some specialized service or listen and counsel the caller. Because callers vary in their needs and desires, the time for service and the proportions on the wheel representing those times likewise vary. The observations might reveal that 5 percent of the time, the call took one minute; 15 percent took two minutes; 20 percent took three minutes, 25 percent took four minutes; 15 percent took five minutes; 10 percent took six minutes; 5 percent took seven minutes; and 5 percent took eight minutes.

Now the manager can simulate the phone demand by spinning the first wheel to randomly determine the time between customer phone-ins and spinning the second wheel to determine how long each customer took to be served once the phone was answered. By recording the numbers on a simple chart that notes the time between call arrivals, times for service, and time callers were waiting, the entire day's activities can be simulated to determine the maximum, minimum, and average length of time callers waited for service plus the total waiting time

**Figure 12.2  Wheels Representing Time Between Calls and Time for Calls**

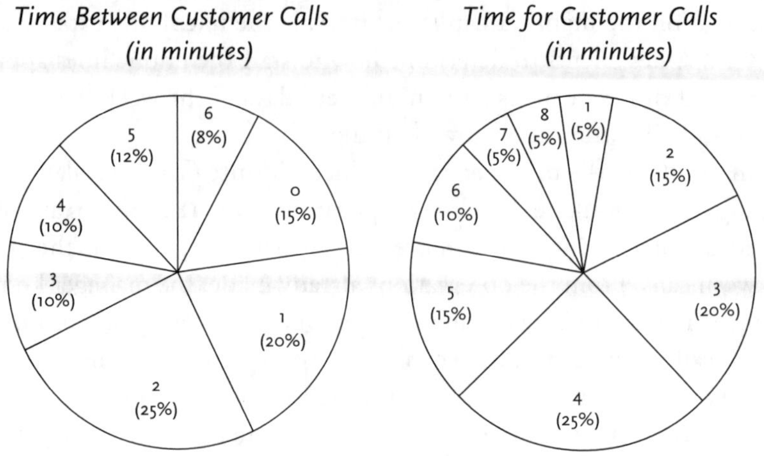

Time Between Customer Calls
(in minutes)

Time for Customer Calls
(in minutes)

for all callers. The chart simulates a day's activities by beginning when the phone lines open and recording the calls throughout the day until the phone center closes. Running this simulation many times (typically more than one hundred on a computerized model) allows the AIDS Aides's management to draw some statistical conclusions about the length of waiting time, counseling capacity utilization, and the impact on waiting (and customer perception of the quality and value of the experience) that opening up more phone lines presents.

Although this is a fairly simple illustration, it does show the usefulness of determining mathematically the relationship between the service provider's capacity and the average waiting time for the customer in a way that allows the healthcare organization to find the ideal balance between the two. This same technique can be used to determine the ideal number of monorails in a theme park, toll booths on a turnpike, beds on a hospital floor, servers and cooks in a restaurant, spaces in a parking lot, nurses in an emergency room, or any other application where an organization needs to balance the costs of providing capacity with the quality of the service experience.

Certain basic forces affect waiting lines, and they can be expressed mathematically. An explanation of the mathematics of waiting lines appears in Appendix A.

## Balancing Capacity and Demand

Determining the proper balance between supply and demand requires more calculations than just the basics. The AIDS hotline in the example has to gather more data about caller behaviors and expectations. If, for example, it finds that when clients are put on hold for more than one minute they will hang up, then a wait longer than one minute is unacceptable no matter what the remaining data might reveal. On the other hand, if the results show that callers are willing to wait because the help line is unique and they need assistance so badly, then the help center might be able to let the phone queues grow without much adjustment. The essential feature of the calculation is to determine that point beyond which the length of the wait damages the quality of the client experience beyond the level acceptable to the client and the organization.

Once the capacity-and-demand balance decision has been made, the organization now has to plan for accommodating the inevitable waiting lines that uneven demand patterns create. Here the challenge is to manage the wait in such a way that the customer is satisfied with it. Two major dimensions are involved. The first is the way the waiting feels to the customer. The second is how to minimize the negative effects of the wait by managing the value of the experience to the customer. The organization wants each customer to conclude that the experience made the wait worthwhile.

## THE *PERCEPTION* OF THE WAIT

Understanding what makes time fly or drag while waiting is a fundamental concern in improving the quality of the patient wait. Healthcare managers must remember that everyone is different, that individual differences will influence how people feel about waiting in line, and that how people feel about the wait is at least as important as how long the wait actually is. The following are factors that influence customers' perceptions of a wait:

1. *Occupied time feels shorter.* Most line waits can be made more enjoyable and made to feel less lengthy if people waiting can be distracted or diverted in some way. Many clinics and physician offices have gone beyond the traditional magazine rack by offering interactive video devices that help patients pass the time productively by learning something about their health. A cancer

specialist might offer an interactive video that answers typical questions asked by new patients; a dentist might feature a video describing a procedure to whiten teeth. A children's practice might offer toys in a play area, and an HMO waiting room might show CNN on TV. The Walt Disney Company is the master of managing time waits by providing diversion to its waiting guests. If the line for a particular Walt Disney World attraction has become extraordinarily long, Disney brings in a strolling band, acrobats, or some other distraction to entertain and occupy the guests. Although bands and acrobats might be inappropriate in a healthcare setting, pleasant diversions or distractions appropriate to the situation can be provided for customers.

2. *Time spent waiting to begin the service experience feels longer than time spent receiving the service.* In many offices, before patients are examined by the doctor, they are interviewed by a nurse who listens to the medical complaint, gathers vital signs, and generally obtains information. By the time patients are actually seen by the doctor, they have already had considerable contact with a medical person, so the wait to see the doctor does not feel so long.

   Another way to spend time is to teach patients in line what they are supposed to do once they reach the treatment area. The education provided during the wait time can improve or enhance the service experience and, in that way, actually becomes part of the experience. Videos in an orthodontist's office can teach kids how to insert and remove their braces before they actually get them. The orthodontist does not have to spend so much time teaching, and patients get engaged prior to actually having the braces installed. Some organizations use a similar technique while placing callers on hold. Callers listen to a range of options in the phone menu, which helps them make the right choice. They may also be presented with recorded instructional material so they may be better informed when they talk to a real person. Most medical offices require that patients fill out lengthy medical history forms. These forms provide useful information, but they also give patients something to do, which reduces how long the wait feels.

3. *Anxious waits feel longer.* Patients who are apprehensive about what will happen to them during an upcoming operation or about

results of a diagnostic procedure will feel their wait to be endless. Communication geared to reducing anxiety during such waits is highly desirable.

4. *Uncertain length of waits feel longer.* A patient is undergoing serious surgery; his family is naturally worried and anxious as they wait for the surgeon to come out and give a report. To the family, the wait seems endless because they do not know when the wait will be over. Healthcare organizations must alleviate this uncertainty by instructing their clinical providers to let patients and families know what to expect and when, if possible. A time estimate can help those waiting to set a mental clock to let time pass more quickly until the estimated time is reached.

   Patients want doctors to be on time for scheduled appointments. The wait before the appointed time is bearable because the patient knows its length. Once the appointment time is reached, in the patient's mind it is time to be served, and any time spent waiting after that will feel longer because it is uncertain.

5. *Unexplained waits feel longer.* When you do not know what is holding up the line or causing the delay, then the wait feels longer than if you know the reason. Effective managers keep people who are waiting informed, or they provide visual cues that explain the wait. For example, a longer-than-expected wait in a doctor's waiting room can be improved by explaining to those waiting that the doctor's schedule was interrupted by a serious emergency. On the other hand, effective managers of queues will ensure that unoccupied laboratory personnel or empty treatment rooms are kept out of sight of waiting patients so that managers do not have to explain why their personnel are not serving patients or why their treatment rooms have no one in them while the waiting room is full.

6. *Unfair waits feel longer.* If customers feel that the queue discipline is being consistently followed and fairly used, then the wait seems less than when they perceive that people are served out of sequence. Good organizations recognize this truth and manage their lines with this knowledge in mind. At times, very sick patients or some other special category of patient requires that the line discipline be broken. These patients can perhaps be smoothly integrated into the line flow by bringing them in through another entrance so that those waiting do not usually

notice that the discipline has been interrupted. For example, the ambulance entrance to the ER is usually some distance from the walk-in entrance. This separation allows serving emergency patients first as well as providing easy access for ambulances.

Organizations that for one reason or another need to break the queue discipline must find some way to communicate a reason for the apparent unfairness that patients will accept after hearing it, like "Heart attack case coming through!" or "Abdominal gunshot wound!" People generally defer their own needs to accommodate other people's more immediate needs as long as they know why. Passengers needing assistance go onto planes first, and nobody minds. Drivers pull over to let emergency vehicles move past the traffic queue. People seldom complain when a disabled person goes to the front of the line.

7. *Solo waits feel longer than group waits.* Waiting by yourself feels longer than waiting with family or friends or even with people you do not know. Organizations that recognize this perceptual issue try to organize their lines in such a way that people are grouped with other people. Under this logic, a double line feels shorter than a single line, and a line structure that encourages people to interact feels shorter than one in which people are allowed to stay inside their own personal and highly individual spaces. In waiting room areas, seating can be arranged to promote interaction and a sense of being part of a group.

8. *Uncomfortable waits feel longer.* Finding a way to keep people comfortable while they wait for treatment is a real managerial challenge. Besides the obvious methods such as providing comfortable seats and air conditioning or heating, healthcare providers must take special care of those with special medical needs. For example, a seriously injured person is given something immediately for the pain, and a comfortable bed is quickly found for the possible heart attack victim.

9. *Uninteresting waits feel longer.* Because most people like to talk about themselves, they will find interest in conversing with someone who asks questions about themselves. Having a nurse or a clinical assistant ask questions, take body measurements, and generally pay attention will make the wait time more interesting for those kinds of patients.

## Other Considerations

In all of these waiting situations, the customer's emotional state will have a significant impact on the wait for service. Different people react differently to anxiety, uncertainty, and pain as well as to the other perceptual influences on the waiting time. If the waiting line being managed is large and diverse, then the "typical" customer will drive the design of the line and the associated wait. Although healthcare managers must consider individual treatment needs as much as possible in designing and managing waits, the queue for a large customer volume must be designed to accommodate the waiting expectations of a typical, average customer.

If the people in line are a more select clientele with identifiable features, such as a queue on a premium hospital floor for big donors, then variability in treatment of the waiting patients may be possible and even necessary to ensure that the quality of the entire experience including the wait meets patient expectations for that upscale level of service. You want to make the wait enjoyable or at least bearable, and that is harder to do for a mass market patient base than for a select, known clientele.

In all of these waiting situations, the contrast effect will also influence the perception of the wait. If a customer's first wait is comfortable, totally explained, and predictable while the second wait is unpredictable, anxiety producing, and of uncertain length, the second wait will feel longer and less satisfying than the well-managed first wait. Similarly, if a customer has just had a long wait, a short one will feel even shorter in contrast. If the customer has just been in a wait where employees were friendly and all staff were busy assisting customers, that wait will in retrospect seem shorter than a following wait of identical length in which employees seem unfriendly and engaged in activities other than serving people who are waiting.

The key is to remember that the customer perceives the wait. If the objective data say that the wait at your facility is not too long or that the average wait at your organization is actually shorter than it is at a competitor's, those data do not matter to those customers who think they have waited too long for your service. Customers have mental clocks in their minds that tell them when the wait is too long or just right and extremely well managed. Managing the perception is as effective a technique as managing the actual waiting time, and if the organization is particularly good at managing perceptions, it can make even very long waits acceptable and tolerable to customers.

## Perceived Value of Service

The more value the customer receives or expects to receive from the service, the more the customer will wait without complaining. Because the customer defines the value of services rendered, the second major strategy for managing the perception of the wait is to manage the perceived value of the service for which the customer is waiting. This strategy can be implemented before, during, or even after the service is performed.

Before receiving the service, waiting customers can be provided with information (or even with some other service) that will enhance the value of the service that motivated them to enter the queue in the first place. A health spa or wellness center, for example, can enhance the perceived value of the healthcare experience by offering customers waiting in line healthy snacks, fruit, or chamber music in the background. Such thoughtful touches not only distract and occupy the customer, they also add value to the experiences that the spa and center are selling and for which the customer must wait.

During the performance of the service, its value (to the customer and as defined by the customer) can be enhanced over the customer's expectations by a number of strategies. The organization will want to employ these strategies in any event. But the idea here is that if the service meets or exceeds expectations when the customer gets it, the wait was probably worthwhile. Besides providing customers with a service that is beyond their expectations in the first place, some more subtle actions can enhance the value of the service experience. Some hospitals display their accreditation certificate, and doctors display diplomas from medical schools to indicate the quality of their training. These touches tend to encourage the patient to think that the medical treatment was worth the wait.

As a more direct response to the wait, the service provider can apologize for it and explain any unusual factors that may have caused the wait. This adds a personal touch that may increase the value of the experience for the customer. Many healthcare organizations are now instructing their medical staff to apologize for the inevitable waits.

After the service, the value of the experience can sometimes be enhanced to make the customers feel better about having taken the time to wait in the first place. Although advertising is generally used to attract the attention of potential customers, people who have already purchased services are even more attentive to ads than those who have not. The ads reinforce their wisdom in not only purchasing the service but also waiting in line to do so. Of course, ads seen ahead of time can also reduce the effects of the wait while it is in progress; the ads have convinced customers that the experience will be worth the wait, so they wait more patiently. Some organizations have found that a phone call to a customer that asks for reactions to the service can enhance the value of the experience and reduce the negative effects of the wait.

## CONCLUSION

Managing the customer's wait is a fundamental challenge for healthcare managers. The very expensive service cannot be stockpiled or inventoried, and the organization must find the right balance between having enough physical and personnel capacity to fill demand and having so much capacity that some healthcare services sit idle most of the time. In a perfect world, the flow of customers just exactly matches the supply. When one patient leaves the facility, another walks in the door seeking medical care. When the physician finishes with one patient, another arrives, and so on across the entire range of services offered by healthcare organizations. In our less than perfect world, effective queue management can get patients into the medical setting and meet their time expectations to their satisfaction.

## LESSONS LEARNED

1. Manage the wait; do not just let it happen.
2. Know how long your customers are willing to wait without becoming dissatisfied.
3. Know the psychology of managing waits.
4. Use queuing or waiting-line models to understand how your queues work.
5. Build in adequate capacity, and manage demand through calculation and implementation of design days and capacity days.
6. Minimize the negative effects of the wait before, during, and after the healthcare experience.
7. Create and implement new performance standards for waiting times.
8. To better balance capacity with demand, find out how much a dissatisfied customer costs you.

## APPENDIX A: THE MATHEMATICS OF WAITING LINES

The mathematics are quite simple for a single-channel, single-phase line. An understanding of a few calculations will reveal much about how to manage customer waits. In the following example, we will use a single-channel line for a laboratory facility with one lab technician. We will calculate the average amount of time that a patient waits for service and remains in the system (time waiting plus time being served). In addition, we will determine the idle time of the technician. These figures will be useful to a healthcare manager wishing to control the waiting time for patients and to reduce the idle time for the technician.[11]

These calculations for a single-channel, single-phase line can be done by hand. However, more complicated wait systems requiring more complex formulas should be (and can easily be) analyzed by computer. Standard spreadsheet products such as Lotus and Excel have the capacity to perform such wait analysis.

The Hypothetical Laboratory has a simple waiting room and one technician. Ben Blake, the manager, has been observing the wait at the laboratory for several weeks. Not wanting patients to wait too long, but hesitant to incur the cost of hiring another technician, he wishes to calculate the average wait for his patients over a one-hour period. He also wants to know how much idle time the single technician will have during that hour. If the technician has substantial idle time, Mr. Blake would like for her to perform some routine tasks such as fill out patient records, consult by phone with other technicians, and so forth. He has compiled the following information for this one-hour period. For this example, we ignore variability and use averages to describe both arrival and service rates for the lab's patients.

- The average time it takes to treat a patient is 4 minutes; the technician can treat about 15 patients per hour. This is the *service rate*—the units of service provider capacity per time period.
- 10 patients are expected to arrive during the hour. This is the *arrival rate*.
- The formulas use the following symbols:
  l = arrival rate per hour (10)
  m = service rate per hour (15)

  *1. Average time a patient waits:*
  $W_q = l / m(l-m)$  $W_q = 10 / 15(15-10)$  $W_q = .133$ hours or 8 minutes
  $W_q$ means waiting time before being served. This calculation tells

Mr. Blake that the *average* wait for a patient is 8 minutes. If that wait time is unacceptable to him, he may have to add another technician.

2. *Average time a patient spends in the system:*
$T_s = 1 / m–l$     $T_s = 1 / 15–10$     $T_s = .2$ hours or 12 minutes
This equation tells Mr. Blake that the average patient spends 12 minutes in the system, including both waiting time and service time.

3. *Average number of patients waiting:*
$L_q = l2 / m(m–l)$    $L_q = 102 / 15(15–10)$    $L_q = 1.33$ patients
$L_q$ means the average length of the queue, in number of patients. Knowing that only 1.33 patients are waiting at any one time, on average, reveals to Mr. Blake that the space available in the waiting area is sufficient.

4. *Percent of time the technician is busy:*
$b = l / m$     $b = 10 / 15$     $b = 67\%$
The laboratory has one or more patients in it, either waiting or being served, 67 percent of the time, or about 40 minutes out of every hour, on average.

5. *Probability that there are no patients in the laboratory at any given time:*
$p = 1 – (l/m)$     $p = 1 – (10/15)$     $p = 33\%$
This is obviously the inverse of the previous formula. If the wait-plus-treatment system has someone in it about 40 minutes out of each hour, it is empty for the other 20 minutes. Mr. Blake can use this information to assign other tasks to the laboratory technician.

## NOTES

1. Sherman, S. G. 1999. *Total Customer Satisfaction: A Comprehensive Approach for Health Care Providers*, pp. 26–27. San Francisco: Jossey-Bass.

2. Press Ganey Associates news release, January 10, 1997.

3. Press Ganey Associates, National Priority List—Medical Practices, March/April 1997.

4. Adapted from J. L. Heskett, W. E. Sasser, Jr., and C. W. L. Hart. 1990. *Service Breakthroughs: Changing the Rules of the Game*, pp. 138–41. New York: The Free Press.

5. Cited in J. B. Jun, S. H. Jacobson, and J. R. Swisher. 1999. "Application of

Discrete-Event Simulation in Health Care Clinics: A Survey." *Journal of the Operational Research Society* 50 (2): 112.

6. Groeler, G. 2002. "Beepers Help Reduce ER Tension." *Orlando Sentinel* (March 9): 81.

7. Mills, K. 2001. "Hospitals Offer More Medical Products." *Gainesville (FL) Sun* (August 26): 1G.

8. Sherman, S. G. 1999. *Total Customer Satisfaction: A Comprehensive Approach for Health Care Providers,* pp. 67, 122–123. San Francisco: Jossey-Bass.

9. Studer, Q., and G. Boylan. 2000. "Turning Customer Satisfaction into Bottom Line Results." Presentation at the Baptist Health Care Leadership Institute, Pensacola, Florida, June 8–9.

10. *Ibid.*

11. Although the following assumptions underlie these formulas, it is not necessary to understand them to follow the discussion:
- Queue discipline is first-in, first-out.
- No balking or reneging. Patients must accept service when it is offered, and no one quits or leaves the line.
- Arrivals are accurately represented by a Poisson statistical distribution.
- Service times must follow a negative exponential Poisson distribution.
- Arrivals are independent.
- Arrival rate does not change over time.

*Chapter 13*

# Fixing Healthcare Service Problems

Healthcare Principle: *Eliminate all sources of disappointments positively and quickly*

Those who enter to buy, support me. Those who come to flatter, please me. Those who complain, teach how I may please others so that more will come. Only those hurt me who are displeased but do not complain.

—*Marshall Field, department store magnate*

IF YOUR CUSTOMER is frustrated or angry about a problem in the healthcare experience, fixing the problem is at least as important as getting it right the first time. Everyone assumes that the service they are paying for will at least meet their expectations. When you make an appointment for a lab test, you expect that the appointment will be kept when you arrive and that you will have the test done correctly.

If your initial expectation is met, then you are satisfied. If your initial expectation is exceeded, then you are delighted and willing to return when the need arises. You will probably also tell everyone you know what a great healthcare provider that organization is. Exceeding expectations creates the apostles and *evangelists* that every organization hopes to have. These evangelists tell all their friends and relatives about how great the healthcare experience was, and this positive word of mouth reinforces the organization's favorable public image.

If your initial expectation is unmet, such as if the doctor unexpectedly cancels or if your name is mysteriously dropped off the schedule, then you are dissatisfied at best. If the problem is severe enough, it may turn you into the angry *avenger* that every organization fears. Although a typical dissatisfied patient may tell eight or ten people about the problem, an avenger may create a web site and tell millions.

337

Service problems, like clinical errors, are inevitable. Most health-care organizations plan well for clinical problems but fail to anticipate service problems with the same care. They incorrectly assume or simply hope that the service will always be as perfect as it was designed to be, the service delivery system will always be flawless, and the staff members will do their jobs exactly the way they were trained, every time. The well-managed healthcare organizations work hard to identify and plan for all types of problems and train their people to fix them. Service problems can vary considerably across the dimensions of frequency, timing, and severity. Not meeting patient expectations can occur anytime during the single healthcare experience or across multiple experiences with the same organization. Because first impressions are so important, a problem occurring early will weigh more heavily than one occurring late. Big errors count more than little ones.

This chapter shows the importance of fixing service problems, the reasons why such problems occur, and the strategies available to recover from and avoid them. Ultimately, if the organization fails by not providing the expected healthcare experience in the first place and does not resolve the problem quickly and fairly, then it has turned one problem into two problems.

## ELEMENTS OF A SERVICE PROBLEM

Despite the best-laid plans of the best service organizations, service failure is a reality in all organizations. The difference between the best service organizations and all the others is that the best group works hard not only to prevent service failure but also to remedy service failure when it occurs. Why do service failures occur? Two reasons are human error and system error. Another reason is external incidents as a result of terrorism, plane crashes, dam collapses, ship collisions, nuclear disasters, chemical plant explosions, and weather-related incidents such as hurricanes, floods, earthquakes, and fires. Although such incidents are relatively rare, healthcare facilities need to be prepared to cope with them.

The simple truth is that any system that is complex and interdependent (as healthcare systems are) will inevitably fail.[1] Most complex organization systems have everything tightly intertwined, and the tighter the intertwining, the more susceptible the system is to disaster if anything goes wrong in any part of the system.

Healthcare executives can either wait for these "normal accidents" to happen or take proactive measures that allow them to put off the day of reckoning as long as possible. Those that are effective in delaying the inevitable create what some call "high-reliability" organizations (HROS). HROS have beaten the service problem odds and have fewer accidents than expected.

According to authors Roberts and Bea, these organizations do three things to enhance their reliability[2]:

1. They aggressively seek to know what they do not know, hire well-trained professionals, empower them to act, and push patient care and treatment to the lowest level commensurate with appropriate medical knowledge.
2. They design their reward and incentive systems to balance the costs of potentially unsafe but short-term profitable strategies with the benefits of safe and long-run profitable strategies.
3. They constantly communicate the big picture of what the organization seeks to do and try to get everyone to communicate with each other about how they fit into the big picture and about any odd, unusual, or problematic situations.

HROS spend considerably more money than other organizations in training people to recognize and respond to anomalies. By contrast, organizations with higher frequencies of accidents tend to suffer from organizational hubris. They are not used to having problems and think that everything is under control. HROS have "disaster practice"— a simulation exercise that teaches staff members how to respond to catastrophes—to prepare them for the real thing when it eventually occurs. Such training reinforces the ideas people must not become complacent, that the hospital believes accidents might happen, and that the hospital worries about its ability to respond.[3] The training also gives staff an opportunity to see what responses work or fail and why. They can then locate areas where changes may be needed. HROS extensively use simulations to train so that when disaster strikes, service failure is minimized.

### Avenger and Evangelist

Customers want an active, interested, "concerned about my problems" attitude from any healthcare organization. They do not care about television, print ads, or billboards that market the organization as a good service provider if they have experienced the opposite. According to authors Sherman and Sherman, unhappy customers (who may turn into avengers) tell an average of 12 people about their unfortunate experience.[4] Each of those 12 then tells an average of five other people, so every unhappy customer then has an audience of 72 people on average. Further, if eight dissatisfied patients tell 12 others who in turn each tell five others, then 576 people are hearing the negative experience that only eight patients went through, which totals to over 70 negative messages per dissatisfied patient. Alternatively, customers who had a good experience (who may turn into evangelists) do not talk about it to as many other people.

If we assume that 92 out of 100 patients have a positive experience and they each tell (evangelize to) one other person on average, 92 people are spreading a positive message in the community. Retaining patients by providing excellent service and avoiding or fixing service problems is essential to organizational success. Authors Frederick F. Reichheld and W. Earl Sasser, Jr., showed that if a company can reduce its rate of customer defections (leaving the organization to go to a competitor) by only 5 percent, it can improve profits by 25 to 85 percent.[5]

When a patient has a service problem, one of three outcomes usually occurs. First, the problem is fixed and the formerly unhappy patient leaves the experience happy. Second, the problem is not fixed and the unhappy patient leaves unhappy. Third, the organization tries to fix the problem and only succeeds in neutralizing the unhappy patient. A happy patient may leave as an evangelist who spreads legends about a terrific experience. An unhappy patient may leave as an avenger who goes and tells many others about a terrible experience. A neutralized patient may leave and forget the whole experience and probably the organization as well.

In some cases, such as medical catastrophes, neutralizing the unhappy patient is the best that the organization can hope for. If the surgeon removes the wrong leg, the power system in the operating room quits working during the surgery, or the patient gets a serious staph infection while recovering from a successful operation, the best the organization can do is to neutralize the patient's level of dissatisfaction.

Indeed, some organizations have developed disaster plans to prepare their employees for such situations. For example, a hospital may have a quick-response team for certain emergencies. The team's primary responsibility is to attend to suddenly ill patients. A good quick-response team, however, will also provide aid and comfort to the patients and their families affected by the emergency, in part to restore their positive perception of the organization.

## DISSATISFIED CUSTOMER'S RESPONSE

The unhappy or dissatisfied patient is the focus of the service recovery. An unhappy patient can do any one or a combination of three things: never return, complain, and/or badmouth the organization. We shall discuss these possibilities in turn.

### Never to Return

The patient can leave vowing never to return. Because this angry patient is also likely to tell others about the negative experience, this is the worst outcome for the organization. In this situation, the organization not only loses the future business of the dissatisfied patient; it loses the future business of all those the patient can influence. The main reason for empowering staff to provide on-the-spot service recovery is to keep dissatisfied patients from leaving that way, if possible.

In a study that analyzed reasons that customers switch to other products or services, eight mutually exclusive reasons were identified, and they are divided into three categories[6]:

1. *Core service problems* (i.e., mistakes, billing errors, service catastrophes) was the biggest category; this category was mentioned by 44 percent of all respondents and noted by 11 percent of respondents as sole reason and 33 percent as one of two or more reasons.
2. *Negative employee attitudes or behaviors* was the second largest category, mentioned by 34 percent of respondents. If employees were perceived as uncaring; impolite or even rude; unresponsive or uncommunicative; and unknowledgeable (as in inexperienced, untrained, inept, out of date), they failed.
3. *Unsatisfactory employee response to service problems* is the third largest category, mentioned by 17 percent of respondents. When employees respond reluctantly, fail to respond with empathy or at all, or offer negative responses (for example, blaming the customer for service problems), customers understandably find those responses unsatisfactory.

Summing those percentages reveals that when customers switch from one product or service to another, they do so more than half the time because of the way they were treated or spoken to by employees. The people part of the delivery system failed.

## Complain

The second thing a patient can do is *complain* to someone in the organization. A popular book on this subject is entitled *A Complaint Is Your Friend,* by Janelle Brown and Claus Moller. Excellent healthcare managers know that benchmark organizations encourage patients to complain and thank them when they do. A complaint should be thought of as a positive opportunity for the organization because it gives the organization a chance to correct the errors and make the customer feel better. The service-management literature tells us that, unfortunately, only 5 percent to 10 percent of dissatisfied patients complain.[7]

Authors R.L. Day and E.L. Landon found that only 20 to 35 percent of people complained about the most dissatisfying consumer experience they ever had.[8] To complete the bad news, according to the research of Stephen S. Tax and Stephen W. Brown, most of the relatively few customers who do complain are dissatisfied with how companies resolve their complaints.[9] These dissatisfied customers are twice as likely to badmouth the organization as customers who are satisfied by the organization's response to service problems.[10]

The patients who tell the nurse about their unhappiness or write letters to the hospital manager describing their dissatisfaction may help identify problems while giving the organization the opportunity to fix problems or correct errors before those patients tell others about their dissatisfaction. Unfortunately, according to Tax and Brown, "most firms fail to document and categorize complaints adequately," which makes learning from mistakes more difficult.[11]

Healthcare organizations should encourage patients to complain, even teach them how to complain if necessary, then measure and follow up on complaint resolution. Customers who suffer service problems silently are more apt to leave without returning and to badmouth the organization than complaining customers are.[12] British Airways found that of customers experiencing service problems, only 50 percent stayed with the airline if they did not complain to personnel. But a full 87 percent of those who did complain stayed and did not defect to a competitor.[13]

Some companies claim even stronger results from successful complaint resolution. According to Sherman and Sherman, if you do make a mistake, most patients (about 70 percent) will do business with you again if you eventually resolve the problem. However, 95 percent will do business with you again if you resolve the issue on the spot.[14] The difference between 95 and 70 percent translates into large sums of money over the lifetime of patients and their families and friends.

This principle is why the benchmark healthcare organizations empower their frontline employees to handle many complaints personally and in whatever reasonable way they see fit, rather than seek the manager's authorization first. As Marriott vice president Roger Dow says, "The customer-contact employee is the only one close enough to the customer to recognize and evaluate a problem and make it right for the customer and keep that customer."[15] Authors Hart, Heskett, and Sasser agree: "The surest way to recover from service mishaps is for workers on the front line to identify and solve the customer's problem."[16]

Making sure that no customer leaves unhappy is obviously to any organization's advantage. The best way to do that is to seek out complaints from patients before they ever leave the hospital, clinic, or office. The results of a study conducted by the Technical Assistance Research Program for the U.S. Office of Consumer Affairs, which is also known as the TARP study, strongly suggest that customers who complain are more loyal than those who do not and that having complaints satisfactorily resolved increased the customers' brand loyalty.[17] These customers were happier with the organization after experiencing bad service than before because the dissatisfaction led to improvement.

### Badmouth

The third thing an unhappy patient can do is to *badmouth or spread negative word of mouth*.[18] If the negative experience was very costly for the patient or the family either financially or personally, the patient is even more likely to spread the bad word. The greater the costs to the patient, the greater the motivation to tell. The likelihood of people who listened to the negative message to spend their time and money at the same hospital, if they have a choice, is then substantially diminished. Obviously, the more important the experience is to the patient, the quicker the patient will become unhappy when the experience does not meet expectations. The more unhappy a patient is, the more likely that person will complain, leave, and tell people about the experience.

On the other hand, the value of a very satisfied patient who is an evangelist for the organization is considerable. This positive word of mouth not only influences others to utilize a healthcare provider but also blunts any negative word of mouth. If a potential patient hears strong testimonials about a healthcare experience from three trusted friends, disregarding a complainer will be easier.

Angry customers who used to be limited to writing letters to corporate headquarters or the Better Business Bureau, putting up signs in their yard, or painting "lemon" on the car now have a new tool: the Internet. For a few dollars a month, anyone with an Internet account can establish a web site to tell the world about any offending company. In this day of instant worldwide communication, an evangelist can praise or an avenger can complain over the Internet to millions of people.

### Credibility

Word of mouth is important for several reasons. People who tell other people tend to be more credible than nonpersonal testimonials.[19] When your friend tells you a physician is cold and uncaring, you no longer believe all the ads on television assuring you that the physician is the right person to go to for laser surgery. Not only is the personal information more credible but it tends to be more vivid. For either good or bad word of mouth, the richness of the detailed personal experience is more compelling than any commercial advertising.

### Dollar Values

When the lost revenue of unhappy patients who do not return is added to the lost revenue of patients who now will not come because of the negative word of mouth, the unhappy patient has created an expensive problem. Over the patient's lifetime, this potential revenue loss is tremendous. Carl Sewell of Sewell Cadillac in Dallas calculates that each of his customers is worth $332,000 in lifetime sales, service, and referrals.[20] Domino's Pizza estimates that over a ten-year period a regular customer spends about $5,000.[21] Club Med has calculated that one lost customer costs the company at least $2,400.[22] Although not everyone sells Cadillacs, pizzas, or resort vacations, every healthcare organization will benefit from calculating the value of its long-term satisfied customers. Because that lifetime value is so high, hardly any effort to fix a customer problem is too extreme.

Consider these numbers: A single patient might be admitted to a hospital three times over a lifetime. If the average hospital bill for one stay is $15,000, then the lifetime revenue loss for one patient who stays away is $45,000. If the patient is in a family of four, then the lifetime family revenue loss rises to $180,000. If the badmouthing damage is calculated (one unhappy person tells 12 others), then the lifetime loss might be $540,000 ($45,000 × 12).

Similar types of calculations can be made for an HMO that lost an employer representing 300 covered lives over the period of the contract, assuming annual premiums of $3,000 per enrollee over the five-year contract period (300 × $15,000 = $4.5 million) or a physician defection from a hospital, assuming two admissions per week for 45 weeks a year (90 × $15,000 = $1.35 million). The loss of a single customer (i.e., patient, employer, or physician) can be very significant.

To make these figures more meaningful to employees, the financial loss can be calculated at the department level. Such calculations can also lead to some surprisingly large numbers for even a small business. To show how a dentist might come up with numbers like these, assume that the dentist's satisfied patients come in for treatment twice a year and spend an average of $150 each time. The total value of each satisfied biannual patient's business for the next five years is $1,500. These numbers get even bigger when the number of other people that a positive word-of-mouth patient can bring to the dentist office is added in. Over the estimated lifetime visits of a typical satisfied patient, the total can be many thousands of dollars in potential revenues.

The point of these calculations is simple: the long-term impact of negative word of mouth is usually much more costly than the costs of correcting a service problem immediately.

## HANDLING OF THE RECOVERY

The organization trying to recover from a service problem can impress the patient positively or negatively.[23] Research shows that how the recovery is handled is more important to the customer than the original problem.[24] Following a problem, the healthcare organization can either end up much better off or much worse off, depending on the patient's reaction to the service recovery attempt. A small problem can become a big problem if the recovery effort is halfhearted or misguided. And a big problem can be turned into an example of great service when handled quickly and effectively.

In one study, the researchers discovered that the most important determinant of overall customer satisfaction was their satisfaction with those responsible for dealing with problems: the claims personnel.

Whether or not the organization could recover from problems also had the largest impact on intention to repatronize the organization and intention to recommend it to a friend.[25]

Authors K.D. Hoffman, Scott W. Kelley, and Holly M. Rotalsky asked a restaurant's customers to classify service problems from 1 (minor mistake) to 10 (major mistake). The two most serious problems identified were (1) product defects (cold, soggy, raw, burnt, or spoiled food; inanimate objects in food), which were rated 6.69, and (2) slow or unavailable service, which was rated 7.05. Doing nothing is the worst strategy (or absence of strategy), and recovery from problems by offering free food or a discount is the best. Although the organization should always apologize for its problems, an apology alone is seldom sufficient.[26]

The way an organization handles service problems, whether well or poorly, also communicates to the employees how committed the organization is to patient satisfaction. How the healthcare organization finds and fixes its service problems is a loud message to the employees about what the organization truly believes in.

Compare these two hypothetical organizations: Hospital A is defensive about patient complaints and keeps them secret (although employees will hear about them anyway), resolves complaints as cheaply and quietly as possible, and seeks people to blame for the complaints. Hospital B, on the other hand, aggressively seeks out and fixes service problems. It disseminates findings about complaints and problems to employees, makes quick and generous adjustments for problems, and seeks solutions rather than scapegoats. Which organization's employees do you think will give patients better service?

## SOURCES AND STRATEGIES

### Sources

Although some moments of truth are especially susceptible to problems, falling short of a patient's expectations can occur at any point in the healthcare experience. The service product may be inadequate, inappropriate, or fail in some other way to meet the patient's expectations. If the patient's teeth do not look as white as he expected when he walked into the dentist's office, a service problem is the result.

The nontangible part of a service delivery system can also fail. If getting a simple lab test done takes several hours, the system itself may have failed. The people part of the delivery system can certainly fail. If medical personnel are unfriendly, inept, poorly trained, or rude, then the experience will not likely meet the patient's expectations. The environment or setting can fail if the patient feels that the ambient temperature is too cold, the smell of antiseptic too strong, the examining rooms not clean, the parking lot unsafe, or the twisting pathways or unclear directional signs too confusing. These points of possible problems all have to be carefully managed to ensure that the healthcare experience meets and, hopefully, exceeds the patient's expectations.

Service problems come in degrees, ranging from catastrophic failures that make newspaper headlines, to insignificant slip-ups, to those problems that the patient does not even know about. Along this continuum is an infinite range of mistakes. Because the patient defines the quality of the service experience, the patient also defines the nature and severity of each service problem.

Different patients can be very unhappy or just mildly unhappy about the same problem just as different patients can be very happy or mildly happy about the same service. The healthcare organization and its service providers are not always at fault that the patient is unhappy; sometimes the patient is the source of the service problem. The doctor may have given the patient a perfect facelift, but the patient may still come out unhappy because she simply did not like the look. The patient may also be at fault for ignoring the warning sign at the exit door and setting off the emergency alarm, going to the wrong clinic, or filling out the forms incorrectly.

Even though these problems were not created by the organization, and are beyond the organization's ability to manage no matter how much they train their staff, perfect their systems, and refine their service, the organization must still plan for them and address how they will correct these patient-caused problems. The organization should also be ready to handle those problems that one patient causes for another—for example, the patient who sneezes on another patient's food, acts belligerently toward another patient, or cuts in front of others at the admissions desk. Although it should still do everything in its power to rectify such situations, the healthcare organization should not admit liability for unfortunate, unavoidable occurrences that are not its fault.

Attributing one's successes to oneself and one's problems to others is simply human nature. Healthcare organizations that want to keep patient-created service problems from destroying the healthcare experience and the patient's feelings about the organization build in strategies to help patients recover from their own problems so they can take a positive impression away from the service setting. Hospitals may offer different menus to particular patients so that they are not tempted to order items that will be detrimental to their recovery. Providing clear instructions to family members may also reduce patient-caused problems. Surgeons write with permanent ink to mark the correct side on which to operate. Benchmark organizations recognize the importance of helping patients solve the problems they create for themselves, without making them look or feel foolish or stupid. They help these patients to achieve a satisfying experience.

## Strategies

Three major strategies are available for dealing with service problems. First are strategies that seek to identify potential problems before they happen. These proactive or preventive strategies are built into the design of the service and its delivery system. Second are strategies that focus on monitoring the critical moments of the service delivery. Third are the outcome strategies that seek to find problems after the service experience has happened. Most of these strategies, such as SERVQUAL, will be covered in the following chapter.

### Preventive Strategies

Preventing problems is easier and less costly than recovering from them. Preventive strategies are designed to avoid a service problem. As Mary Jo Bitner and her colleagues put it, "The best way to ensure satisfaction . . . is not to have a failure in the first place."[27] These strategies seek to identify and fix any trouble spots before they become a problem for the patient.

#### Forecasting and Managing Demand

For example, if a statistical prediction of the patient demand for a hospital on a particular day indicates that the hospital will be full, then a preventive strategy will lead to the hospital's management calling in full staff, preparing extra supplies, and having available the full capacity of each department. Physician practices require appointments when the anticipated demand will be great. Having an appointment system means that patients will not be disappointed when they come to the physician's office for treatment. In addition, the medical personnel know the number of patients they can expect so that they can staff appropriately and have sufficient amounts of pre-prepared items to ensure that the healthcare experience is problem free. If the organization plans poorly, and patients have to wait too long, their perception of overall service-experience quality declines rapidly, and a service failure results. Keeping the wait down avoids that type of failure.

If the demand can be forecasted for a longer period of time, then other proactive strategies can be implemented. If demand for the next quarter or next year, for example, is expected to increase by 20 percent, then new capacity can be built, new employees hired and trained, and inventories can be increased to ensure that patients are not disappointed by long waits, unavailable supplies, or untrained and inadequate staff. Even if demand cannot be forecast accurately, employees can be trained to cope with major demand surges. Just as hospitals run disaster drills in conjunction with fire-and-rescue teams to prepare for unexpected, randomly occurring disasters, so can staff from other healthcare units be cross-trained through practice to handle the unexpected.

### Quality Teams, Training, and Simulation

The popular use of quality teams is another preventive strategy. Get the people who are directly involved in the service experience together and let them identify the problems they have seen or heard about and then try to identify strategies that will prevent these problems from occurring in the future. Adequate training of employees before they ever get the chance to serve a patient can prevent problems. Any organization that seeks to be highly reliable ensures that the people who deliver any of its services know exactly what the total experience should consist of and are motivated to ensure that the healthcare experience happens the way it is supposed to, every time, for every patient.

Another approach to problem avoidance is to use analytical models, like those discussed in chapters 11 and 12, to simulate all or part of the service delivery system or the service recovery process. Once a model is created to represent the patient-service provider interaction, the delivery process, or the entire healthcare experience, the manager and the servers can analyze a wide variety of different situations that might occur to see what impact each might have on the patient. On a simpler level, role plays and structured scenario simulations can help healthcare employees practice for all types of service problems and learn effective recovery strategies.

### Performance Standards

The organization can prevent problems by setting specific performance standards. Some are partly preventive, partly process, and partly outcome because the employees themselves can use them to monitor their own performance levels as they go through the delivery process. They can also use them as long-term measures to see how well they did over time. Some are purely preventive because they can be met before patients enter the door. For example, if a clinic has reliable predictions of how many patients come in on the different days of the week, those predictions can be used as a basis or standard for which medical supplies should be pre-prepared or ordered. If the prediction is correct and the standard is met, the service problem of "not enough medical supplies" should not occur.

Other examples of how performance standards can prevent problems might include hours of annual training required for staff, number of computer terminals to be purchased to accommodate anticipated patient demand, the number of examining tables to be set up or other facilities to be available when the organization can reasonably predict how many will be needed, and other inventory levels required to serve customers.

Performance standards can also be a useful indicator to patients of what service level they can expect. Examples of standards are "We will try to resolve problems of types A, B, and C within two hours; we will try to resolve problems of types D, E, and F within one week" or "If you leave a message on our help-desk voicemail, we will call you back within one hour." Many Ritz-Carlton hotel customers know that phone calls are supposed to be answered within three rings and that after a customer registers a complaint, a Ritz employee is supposed to make a follow-up call within 20 minutes to ensure that the complaint has been resolved. Hospital nurses in some facilities know that the patient call bell is supposed to be answered within 30 seconds.

### Poka-Yokes

To avoid wrong-side surgery, sometimes called bilateral confusion and symmetry failure, the National Academy of Orthopedic Surgeons has urged its physician members to sign their names on the spot to be cut. Surgical patients write in felt-tipped marker "I hurt here" with an arrow pointing to an elbow or "yes" on one knee and "no" on the other. These doctors and patients, probably without knowing the term, are using poka-yokes.

The *poka-yoke* is the final proactive or preventive strategy for avoiding problems in the service experience and keeping it operating as flawlessly as possible. Conceived by the late Shigeo Shingo, an industrial engineer at Toyota and a quality-improvement leader in Japan, the basic idea is to make service quality easy to achieve and service problems difficult to achieve by inspecting the system for possible problem points and then finding or developing simple means to prevent mistakes at those points or to make the mistakes obvious at a glance. A surgeon's tray and a mechanic's wrench-set box may have a unique indentation for each item, to ensure that no instrument is left in a patient or wrench in an engine. Hospitals have identification bands to ensure that the right patient gets the right treatment. Shingo gave these problem-preventing devices or procedures the name poka-yoke (POH-kah-YOH-kay), which means "mistake proofing" or "avoid mistakes" in Japanese.

Shingo distinguished three types of inspection: (1) *successive* inspection, where the next person checks the quality and accuracy of the previous person's work; (2) *self-inspection*, where people check their own work; and (3) *source* inspection, where potential mistakes are located at their source and fixed before they can become service errors. Poka-yokes are used mainly to prevent these mistakes.

An example of successive inspection is when the orderly checks the patient's chart to ensure that it corresponds with the directions given about where the patient is to be transported. An example of self-inspection is when the attending nurse personally compares the prepared drug against the patient's chart before administering the drug. An example of source inspection is when the surgical nurse monitors the pre-prepared medical supplies, such as surgical tools, bandages, or whatever else has to be assembled in advance of the surgery, to ensure that sufficient kinds and quantities of the items are available.

Poka-yokes are either "*warnings* that signal the existence of a problem or *controls* that stop production until the problem is resolved."[28] A warning poka-yoke may be a light that flashes when the patient's blood pressure is too low. It signals the nurse to adjust the drip before the patient goes into shock. A control poka-yoke may be a device that turns an x-ray machine off whenever the Roentgen level is too high. Warning and control poka-yokes can be of three types: contact, fixed values, and motion step. Contact poka-yokes monitor an item's physical characteristics to determine if it is right or meets a predefined specification. Some pharmacies prepare standard quantities of drugs to be sure the dosage is right before distributing to patients.

The second type of poka-yoke is based on fixed values. Surgical teams use prepackaged surgical supplies so they know exactly how many bandages, surgical tools, and so forth they have available for use. When the surgery is completed, the team can count every item to make sure nothing has been left in the patient. The third type of poka-yoke is the motion step. It is useful in processes where an error-prone step must be completed correctly before the next step can take place. A simple example is the start button on the x-ray machine. The button is outside the exposure area so technicians cannot take x-rays until they leave the room and are protected.

All poka-yokes should be simple, easy to use, and inexpensive. Something can go wrong at any point in most service delivery systems, so the poka-yoke is a useful concept in encouraging managers to think about what might go wrong and finding simple error-prevention strategies that are both inexpensive and foolproof.

### Process Strategies

Process strategies for finding service problems monitor the delivery while it is taking place. The idea is to design mechanisms into the delivery system that will catch and fix problems before they affect the quality of the healthcare experience. The blood pressure monitor and the heart monitor are examples of such mechanisms. The advantage of process controls is that they can catch errors as they happen, enabling immediate correction before they affect patients.

Process performance standards provide employees with objective measures so that they can monitor their own job performance while they are doing it. Specifying performance standards such as the maximum number of times the phone can ring before it is picked up is an example. Other illustrations include the maximum number of minutes a nurse may wait before responding to a patient call, the number of times per hour that a nurse must check on an intensive care patient, and the number of patients waiting for service before a cross-trained staff member stops doing regular duties and steps in to reduce the peak demand. These are all process-related measurements that allow the staff to minimize errors or catch them while the healthcare experience is underway.

Research shows clearly that the most important process strategy is to get unhappy patients to complain while they are still in the healthcare experience. This is a more difficult challenge than one might think because although some patients are all too happy to complain, most are not. Most patients are either unwilling to take the time, they believe that no one cares or will do anything even if they complain, or they are too angry to say anything and just leave. Research on complaint behavior has identified some important ways in which the organization can encourage its patients to complain:

- *All service personnel should be trained to solicit complaints.* Because many service problems involve service-provider errors, getting the providers to solicit complaints about their own performance is a challenge. The providers may see that mistakes are punished more heavily than catching errors is rewarded. Most people are less enthusiastic about admitting their mistakes than they are about sharing their successes, and the complaint strategy needs to accommodate this reality of human nature.

- *Service personnel can be trained to read body language for clues to an unhappy patient.* Taking this initiative can elicit complaints that might otherwise go unmentioned. Orderlies, nurses' aides, housekeepers, and other people who interact directly with patients should be trained to recognize the signs of unhappy people. Employees must also learn how to be receptive and sympathetic to the complaint once it is elicited. Patients must perceive them as interested and concerned. If patients do not think anyone cares, they generally will not say anything.

### Outcome Strategies

Outcome strategies identify service problems after they have occurred so that problems can be fixed and future problems can be prevented. The most basic outcome strategy is simply to ask the patient, "How did things go today?" Other more systematic illustrations include 800 phone numbers for former patients to use to report their dissatisfaction and brief questionnaires that patients can fill out when paying their bills.

Organizations should make unequivocally clear to patients that they want to hear about any problems. Studies show that whether customers seek redress of a problem or simply let it go is determined by their perception of whether or not the organization really wants to hear about it and will do something about it. Even patients who are reluctant to complain are more likely to do so if they perceive that something will be done about the problem.[29]

Obviously, the more dependent the organization is on repeat business and word-of-mouth reputation, the more critical it is that the complaints of its customers are acknowledged and acted on. Some healthcare organizations report their complaint investigations back to complaining patients in detail, including information on what people were affected and what systems were changed. In that way, the organization shows it is responsive to the patient's complaint and also gives that person a sense of participation in the organization, which may positively enhance loyalty and increase repeat visits. If the complaint identifies a flaw that the organization can correct, and if knowledge of the correction provides the patient with a sense of satisfaction for reporting a complaint that was important and acted on, a true win-win situation results.

Some numerical measures that organizations take as a matter of normal procedure can point up real and potential service problems. Total staffing or nurse staffing per patient day is an example. Although it is used primarily to keep track of costs, staffing varies by department, floor, or shift. If one shift is significantly below the norm, this may indicate possible service problems

## SERVICE RECOVERY

The organization failed. Now what? Healthcare organizations should train their employees to handle the problems when they find them. Their ability to creatively solve problems as they occur needs to be developed. Scenarios, game playing, video taping, and role playing are good ways to show them how to respond to an angry patient, a reaction to the wrong drug, or a surgical error. Just as umpires can be trained to recognize balls and strikes through watching videos, healthcare personnel can be trained to recognize service errors and to correct the problems that they find.

### Do Something Quickly

The basic service recovery principle is do something positive and do it quickly. Strive for on-the-spot service recovery. Its many benefits are one major reason why benchmark service organizations empower their frontline employees to exercise so much discretion in correcting errors. Employees of one service organization carry a card on which these three principles of service recovery are written:

- Any employee who receives a customer complaint "owns" the complaint.
- React quickly to correct the problem immediately. Follow up with a telephone call within twenty minutes to verify that the problem has been resolved to the customer's satisfaction. Do everything you possibly can to never lose a customer.
- Every employee is empowered to resolve the problem and to prevent a repeat occurrence.

Other suggestions for service recovery include asking the magic question (e.g., What can I do to make this right?), evaluating the complaint to identify significant dissatisfiers, getting specifics and writing them down, and handling the whole communication process in a pleasant manner.[30] The ultimate goal is to satisfy the customer.

Management must empower employees with the necessary authority, responsibility, and incentives to act quickly following a problem. The higher the cost of the problem to the patient in terms of money, personal reputation, or safety, the more vital it is for the organization to train the healthcare staff to recognize and deal with the service problem promptly, sympathetically, and effectively. Of course, empowering staff to recover from problems will not be sufficient if recovery mechanisms are not in place. If the rest of the system is in chaos, empowering the front line will not do much good.

A quick reaction to service problems has numerous benefits. Solving a problem immediately instead of over time reduces the overall expense of retaining patients. The sooner the patient is satisfied with the healthcare organization, the sooner the organization will benefit from the patient's positive word of mouth and repeat business. Fix their problems and most patients will be willing to come back. Fix their problems on the spot and they will almost certainly want to come back and recommend the organization to their friends. Rewarding and recognizing employees who have done an especially good job of successfully correcting a service problem offer strong incentives to other employees while providing role models of the organization's commitment to service quality.

## Address Root Problems

A necessary further step in any service recovery strategy is that employees should inform their managers about any system failures they encounter even if they initiate successful recovery procedures. If they do not, the problem may recur elsewhere.

The reactions of frontline workers to service failures caused by the system have significant implications for customer satisfaction. The common reaction is simply to remove the obstacle or solve the problem and to continue patient care. But an empowered staff should also be offered incentives for removing the root cause of the problem to prevent future recurrences. For example, a nurse may find that her newest patient was not served lunch. Assuming it was an oversight, she might call food service and order the lunch for the patient. This might solve the immediate problem, but if the underlying cause was that admissions failed to advise food service of the new patient's arrival, the same problem will occur in the future because the root cause was not addressed.

The best customer service organizations encourage staff members to address both the immediate service failure problem (the symptom) and the root cause. This is facilitated by including problem resolution as an explicit part of the staff's jobs, by allowing enough time to address the problem, by encouraging communication between staff, by dedicating proper attention to problems, and by giving incentives/rewards to those who engage in this type of "extra" work. Federal Express created the Golden Falcon Award to recognize employee initiative in service recovery. Recipients of the award not only get a pin to commemorate their success but also have an article published in the company newsletter about what they did, get a telephone call from the COO, and receive a few shares of the company's stock.[31]

All healthcare personnel should be trained to apologize, ask the patients about the problem, and listen in a way that gives patients the opportunity to blow off steam. Considerable research indicates that having the chance to tell someone in authority about the service problem and the resulting difficulties or inconveniences that it created is very important in retaining the patient's future patronage. This strategy is even more effective when the organization accompanies its thanks for the complaint with a tangible reward, even if it is small.[32] The tangible reward might be a voucher for a meal in the hospital cafeteria for family members or a letter of apology from the CEO thanking the customer for helping the organization recognize a service problem.

## Patients' Evaluation of the Recovery Efforts

Patients who have suffered a service problem and lodged a complaint want action. They use three criteria to evaluate the fairness of the organization's corrective actions: procedural, interactive, and distributive.[33] According to Tax and Brown, these three fairness dimensions explain 85 percent of the variation in customer satisfaction with how complaints are handled.[34]

*Procedural fairness* refers to whether or not the patient believes that organizational procedures for listening to the patient's side and handling service problems are fair or merely a procedural hassle full of red tape. Circuit City believes that not giving customers the best value possible is a kind of service problem, so it will pay customers a refund plus 10 percent off the lower price if they can show they were not given the lowest price in the market area on a purchased product. Customers feel that this is a fair policy. Customers also want an easy process for correcting problems. They feel that if the organization failed them, it is only fair that the organization makes it easy for them to receive a just settlement.

*Interactive fairness* refers to the patient's feeling of being treated with respect and courtesy and given the opportunity to express the complaint fully. If the patient has a complaint and is denied the opportunity to state it to someone because the offending service provider is rude, indifferent, or uncaring, and the manager cannot be found, the patient will feel unfairly treated. A study of traffic offenders in traffic court by Lind and Tyler revealed that many offenders whose cases were dismissed without a hearing were dissatisfied with the process and angry with the outcome, even though the dismissal was a favorable result for them.[35] Because they were denied their day in court, they were unhappy with the process. Common sense suggests and research studies show that a customer who is encouraged to complain and is then treated with respect, courtesy, and given a fair settlement is more likely to return when needing healthcare services than one who was given a fair settlement but only with reluctance and discourtesy.[36]

*Distributive fairness*, or outcome fairness, is the third test that patients apply to the organization's attempts to recover from problems. What did the organization actually give or distribute to the unhappy patient as compensation for the problem? If the patient complains about a rude housekeeper and gets only a sincere apology because that is all hospital policy calls for, some patients will feel unfairly treated; somehow "we're sorry" is not enough in the patient's judgment to compensate for the rude treatment.

Once again, it all comes down to meeting the patient's expectations. The issue is difficult because each patient is different. Finding the satisfactory compensation may involve methodical trial and error on the organization's part. Some research indicates that customers feel more fairly treated when organizations offer a variety of options as compensation for service problems.[37] For example, a physician can offer a patient the choice of an immediate appointment (if desired) or "free" prescription drugs.

## Characteristics of a Good Recovery Strategy

Hart, Heskett, and Sasser believe that service recovery strategies should satisfy several criteria.[38] First, they should ensure that the problem is addressed in some positive way. Even if the situation is a total disaster, the recovery strategy should ensure that the patient's problem is addressed and, to the extent possible, fixed. Second, recovery strategies must be communicated clearly to the employees charged with responding to patient dissatisfaction. Employees must know that the organization expects them to find and resolve patient problems as part of their jobs. Third, recovery strategies should be easy for the patient to find and use. They should be flexible enough to accommodate the different types of problems and the different expectations that patients have. The service recovery strategies developed should always recognize that because the patient defines the quality of the service experience, the patient also defines its problems and the adequacy of the recovery strategies.

A strategy that does not make some improvement in the situation for the complaining patient is worse than useless because the organization makes plain that it cannot or will not recover from a problem even when informed of it. The work of Hart and his colleagues suggests that most recovery strategies are in serious need of improvement. More than half of organizational efforts they identified that respond to consumer complaints actually reinforce negative reactions to the service.[39] In trying to make things better, organizations too often make them worse.

One reason that patients view many recovery strategies as inadequate is that they do not really take into account all of the costs to the patient. Doctor missed an appointment? Schedule another one. Busy signal on the telephone line for hospital information? Interject a recorded apology. The organization may think the relationship is back where it started. But for the patient, many costs are associated with problems, and the effective organization will try to identify them and include some recognition of them in selecting the appropriate service recovery. After all, the fact that the test results were not delivered by the promised date is not the patient's fault, so why should the patient have to suffer additional mental stress waiting for results? Why should the patient lose more work time as a result of a provider-cancelled appointment?

Patients clearly think that when a healthcare problem occurs, organizations need to do more than simply make it right by replacing it or doing it over again. The high numbers of malpractice suits substantiate that point. Of course organizations should do that, but they should do more. For example, if the excessively long wait beyond the appointed time causes the patient to miss half a day's salary, then the recovery strategy should not only include an apology but perhaps some compensation for the patient's loss of income as well. Outstanding healthcare organizations systematically consider how to compensate patients for economic and noneconomic losses and take extra effort to ensure that dissatisfied patients not only have their time and financial losses addressed in a recovery effort but also their ego and esteem needs addressed as well.

Even when the patients themselves make mistakes, good healthcare organizations help to correct them with sensitivity. They make sure patients leave feeling good about their overall experience and appreciating how the organization's staff helped them redeem themselves. Imagine how depressed you would feel if you came back to the hospital parking lot after a long day of visiting a terminally ill family member only to find that you have lost your car keys and are locked out of your car. You tell the parking attendant, and half an hour later a locksmith hands you a new set of keys, no charge!

Even though key problems are not its fault, the customer-oriented organization believes that the customer needs to be wrong with dignity. It knows that customers who are angry at themselves may transfer some of that anger to the organization. To overcome this very human tendency, customer-focused organizations find ways to fix problems so that angry, frustrated people leave feeling good because a bad experience has not been allowed to overshadow or cancel out all the good. By providing this high level of customer service, the healthcare organization earns the gratitude and future patronage of patients and enhances its reputation when patients and their families tell both external and internal customers stories of these service successes.

## Matching the Recovery Strategy to the Problem

The best recovery efforts are those that address the customer's problem. For example, suppose a patient tried to contact his physician by phone (as instructed) on a certain day and time, was put on hold, and ended up leaving a message asking the physician to return his call. If the return call was never made, a communications problem undoubtedly occurred, but the result for the patient is that the physician appears to be uncaring. An appropriate recovery effort might be to provide the patient with the physician's personal cell phone number.

Categorizing the severity and causes of service problems might be a useful way to show the type of recovery strategy that a healthcare organization should select. In Figure 13.1, the vertical axis represents the severity of the problem ranging from low to high; the horizontal axis divides service problems into those caused by the organization and those caused by the patient. When severity is high and it is the organization's fault (for example, when a service failure occurs that totally alienates the patient) the proper response is the red-carpet treatment. The organization needs to bend over backward to apologize, communicate empathy and caring, and address the patient's problem because it will take an outstanding recovery effort to overcome the patient's negative feeling. A less severe problem caused by the organization is illustrated by a physician who got far behind in his appointment schedule. The solution here is to apologize, offer an explanation for the lateness, and perhaps even offer compensation for any loss of income as a result of the excessive wait.

The two types of situations in the Figure where the patient caused the problem provide terrific opportunities for the organization to make patients feel positive about the experience even though the patients caused the problem. In a low-severity situation, a sincere apology is sufficient and will make the patient feel that the organization is taking some of the responsibility for a situation that was clearly not its fault. Indeed, some organizations will do even more, if the cost to make

**Figure 13.1  Matching the Recovery Strategy to the Failure**

|  | | Organization | Patient |
|---|---|---|---|
| **Severity of Failure** | Relatively severe | Red-carpet treatment and apology | Provide help to the extent possible and apologize |
| | Relatively mild | Apologize and fix/replace/ repeat | Apologize and extend sympathy |

Organization          Patient

**Cause of Failure**

a patient feel better is not substantial. Hospitals will often change meals if patients say they do not want them, even when the records show that the meals were just what the patients ordered. The wrong meal may not be the hospital's fault, but the patient feels good that the organization will not make patients pay for their own mistakes.

The upper-right box represents situations where the problem is relatively severe and the patient or some external force created the problem. These are opportunities for the organization to be a hero and provide an unforgettable experience for the patient. For example, if the patient is late for an appointment because she got delayed in traffic and arrived when the physician is busy with the next patient, the receiving nurse can come out and promise that the physician will see the late patient next.

## CONCLUSION

According to the TARP study, companies that invested in the formation and operation of units designed to handle complaints realized returns on the investment of anywhere from 30 percent to 150 percent.[40] These results, and the other research reported in this chapter, suggest strongly that putting money and effort into service recovery is good business.

Service recovery rules can and should be developed for staff. For example, if a customer is unhappy because of an unmet need and the staff member can meet that need for less than, say, $100, then the staff member should be allowed and encouraged to meet the need immediately.[41] If the cost of service recovery is more than $100, the customer should be informed that the staff member is working on a solution. The staff member can then contact the supervisor for permission to execute a solution of up to, say, $500. The important point is that staff should be empowered to do whatever it takes to fix any customer service problems immediately, at any reasonable cost, to avoid customer defection.

In addition to such empowerment, staff should also be trained in terms of what to do or say when service failure has occurred and a customer is angry.[42] Staff also need to know that they will not be criticized for "overserving" customers, that risk-taking in this area will be encouraged, that new approaches to customer service will be praised and encouraged, and that service failures and recovery will be monitored. The latter requires installing a system to gather information on customer dissatisfactions or defections and the reasons for them. Organizations must try to find ways to satisfy as many dissatisfied customers as possible. Gathering this information will also enable the organization to engage staff in identifying and correcting the causes of the service problems that are preventing the organization from achieving greater customer satisfaction.

## LESSONS LEARNED

1. If the patient *thinks* you created a problem, then you created a problem.
2. Service-failure prevention is superior to service-failure recovery.
3. Resolve their problems and most patients will come back; successfully resolve their problems on the spot and they will almost certainly come back.
4. All customer-oriented healthcare organizations should strive to be high-reliability organizations (HROS).
5. Encourage patients to tell you about problems; a complaint is a gift.
6. Train and empower your staff to find and fix problems.
7. Train your staff to listen to dissatisfied customers with empathy, and then record the service problem and its resolution.
8. Do not cause a service problem and then ignore it or fix it inadequately.
9. Find a solution that the customer believes to be fair.
10. Find ways to help patients fix problems *they* caused.
11. Unhappy patients will tell twice as many people about their unhappiness as happy patients will tell about being happy.
12. Even the best organizations let a patient down sometime. Be prepared for problems; have a recovery strategy in place.

13. Find out and share with employees how much a dissatisfied patient costs you; that will show your staff the importance of recovering from service problems.

14. Empowerment works only if the system works; even an empowered employee cannot recover from service problems without support from the system.

15. Encourage staff to address the root causes of service failure.

## NOTES

1. Perrow, C. 1999. *Normal Accidents: Living With High-Risk Technologies*. Princeton, NJ: Princeton University Press.

2. Roberts, K. H., and R. Bea. 2002. "Must Accidents Happen? Lessons From High Reliability Organizations." *Academy of Management Executive* (in press).

3. *Ibid.*

4. Sherman, S. G., and V. C. Sherman. 1999. *Total Customer Satisfaction: A Comprehensive Approach for Health Care Providers*, pp. 161–62. San Francisco: Jossey-Bass. Research reported by Hart, Heskett and Sasser is similar, showing that customers who have bad experiences tell approximately 11 people while customers who have good experiences tell approximately six people. See C. W. L. Hart, J. L. Heskett, and W. E. Sasser, Jr. 1990. "The Profitable Art of Service Recovery." *Harvard Business Review* 68 (4): 153.

5. Reichheld, F. F., and W. E. Sasser, Jr. 1990. "Zero Defections: Quality Comes to Services." *Harvard Business Review* 68 (5): 105–11.

6. Keaveney, S. M. 1995. "Patient Switching Behavior in Service Industries: An Exploratory Study." *Journal of Marketing* 59 (2): 71–82.

7. Dube, L., and M. Maute. 1996. "The Antecedents of Brand Switching, Brand Loyalty and Verbal Responses to Service Failures." In *Advances in Services Marketing and Management*, Volume 5, edited by T. Swartz, D. Bowen, and S. Brown, pp. 127–51. Greenwich, CT: JAI Press.

8. Day, R. L., and E. L. Landon. 1976. "Collecting Comprehensive Complaint Data by Survey Research." *Advances in Consumer Research*, Volume 3, edited by B. B. Anderson, pp. 263–68. Atlanta, GA: Association for Consumer Research.

9. Tax, S. S., and S. W. Brown. 1998. "Recovering and Learning from Service Failure." *Sloan Management Review* 39 (3): 76.

10. Blodgett, J. G., D. H. Granbois, and R. G. Walters. 1993. "The Effects of Perceived Justice on Complainants' Negative Word-of-Mouth Behavior and Repatronage Intentions." *Journal of Retailing* 69 (4): 408.

11. Tax, S. S., and S. W. Brown. 1998. "Recovering and Learning from Service Failure." *Sloan Management Review* 39 (3): 83.

12. Day, R. L., and E. L. Landon. 1976. "Collecting Comprehensive Complaint Data by Survey Research." *Advances in Consumer Research*, Volume 3, edited by B. B. Anderson, p. 407. Atlanta, GA: Association for Consumer Research.

13. Weiser, C. R. 1995. "Championing the Customer." *Harvard Business Review* 73 (6): 113.

14. Sherman, S. G., and V. C. Sherman. 1999. *Total Customer Satisfaction: A Comprehensive Approach for Health Care Providers*, p. 164. San Francisco: Jossey-Bass.

15. Quoted in S. S. Tax and S. W. Brown. 1998. "Recovering and Learning from Service Failure." *Sloan Management Review* 39 (3): 81. For more on the importance of the front line in preventing and recovering from problems, see L. A. Schlesinger and J. L. Heskett. 1991. "Breaking the Cycle of Failures in Services." *Sloan Management Review* 32 (3): 17–28.

16. Hart, C. W. L., J. L. Heskett, and W. E. Sasser, Jr. 1990. "The Profitable Art of Service Recovery." *Harvard Business Review* 68 (4): 150.

17. Technical Assistance Research Program (TARP). 1986. *Consumer Complaint Handling in America: An Update Study*. Washington, DC: Department of Consumer Affairs. Often referred to as the TARP Study.

18. For further information on negative word of mouth, see J. Singh. 1990. "Voice, Exit, and Negative Word-of-Mouth Behaviors: An Investigation Across Three Service Categories." *Journal of the Academy of Marketing Science* 18 (1): 1–15; M. L. Richins. 1983. "Negative Word-of-Mouth by Dissatisfied Consumers: A Pilot Study." *Journal of Marketing* 47 (4): 68–78; J. G. Blodgett, D. H. Granbois, and R. G. Walters. 1993. "The Effects of Perceived Justice on Complainants' Negative Word-of-Mouth Behavior and Repatronage Intentions." *Journal of Retailing* 69 (4): 399–428.

19. Day, R. L. 1980. "Research Perspectives on Consumer Complaining Behavior." In *Theoretical Developments in Marketing*, edited by C. W. Lamb and P. M. Dunn, pp. 211–15. Chicago: American Marketing Association.

20. Sewell, C., and P. B. Brown. 1990. *Guests for Life*. New York: Pocket Books.

21. Barlow, J., and C. Møller. 1996. *A Complaint Is a Gift*, p. 24. San Francisco: Berrett-Koehler.

22. Hart, C. W. L., J. L. Heskett, and W. E. Sasser, Jr. 1990. "The Profitable Art of Service Recovery." *Harvard Business Review* 68 (4): 151.

23. Hoffman, K. D., S. W. Kelley, and H. M. Rotalsky. 1995. "Tracking Service Failures and Employee Recovery Efforts." *Journal of Services Marketing* 9 (2): 49–61. See also S. W. Kelley and M. A. Davis. 1994. "Antecedents to Patient Expectations for Service Recovery." *Journal of the Academy of Marketing Sciences* 22 (1): 52–61; T. O. Jones and W. E. Sasser, Jr. 1995. "Why Satisfied Patients Defect." *Harvard Business Review* 73 (6): 88–99; R. A. Spreng, G. D. Harrell, and R. D. Mackoy. 1995. "Service Recovery: Impact on Satisfaction and Intentions." *Journal of Services Marketing* 9 (1): 15–23.

24. Berry, L., A. Parasuraman, and V. A. Zeithaml. 1994. "Improving Service Quality in America: Lessons Learned." *Academy of Management Executive* 8 (2): 32–52.

25. Spreng, R. A., G. D. Harrell, and R. D. Mackoy. 1995. "Service Recovery: Impact on Satisfaction and Intentions." *Journal of Services Marketing* 9 (1): 18–19.

26. Hoffman, K. D., S. W. Kelley, and H. M. Rotalsky. 1995. "Tracking Service Failures and Employee Recovery Efforts." *Journal of Services Marketing* 9 (2): 49–61.

27. Bitner, M. J., B. H. Booms, and L. A. Mohr. 1994. "Critical Service Encounters: The Employee's Viewpoint." *Journal of Marketing* 58 (4): 101.

28. Chase, R. B., and D. M. Stewart. 1994. "Make Your Service Fail-Safe." *Sloan Management Review* 35 (1): 36.

29. Blodgett, J. G., D. H. Granbois, and R. G. Walters. 1993. "The Effects of Perceived Justice on Complainants' Negative Word-of-Mouth Behavior and Repatronage Intentions." *Journal of Retailing* 69 (4): 421–23.

30. Grugal, R. 2002. "Draw Wine from Whine." *Investor's Business Daily* (May 21): A4.

31. Heskett, J. L., W. E. Sasser, Jr., and C. W. L. Hart. 1990. *Service Breakthroughs: Changing the Rules of the Game*, p. 155. New York: The Free Press.

32. Goodwin, C., and I. Ross. 1992. "Consumer Responses to Service Failures: Influence of Procedural and Interactional Fairness Perceptions." *Journal of Business Research* 25 (2): 160. See also S. S. Tax and S. W. Brown. 1998. "Recovering and Learning from Service Failure." *Sloan Management Review* 39 (3): 79–81.

33. Goodwin, C., and I. Ross. 1992. "Consumer Responses to Service Failures: Influence of Procedural and Interactional Fairness Perceptions." *Journal of Business Research* 25 (2): 149–63.

34. Tax, S. S., and S. W. Brown. 1998. "Recovering and Learning from Service Failure." *Sloan Management Review* 39 (3): 81.

35. Lind, E. A., and T. Tyler. 1987. *The Social Psychology of Procedural Justice.* New York: Plenum.

36. Blodgett, J. G., K. L. Wakefield, and J. H. Barnes. 1995. "The Effects of Patient Service on Consumer Complaining Behavior." *Journal of Services Marketing* 9 (4): 31–42.

37. Tax, S. S., and S. W. Brown. 1998. "Recovering and Learning from Service Failure." *Sloan Management Review* 39 (3): 80.

38. Hart, C. W. L., J. L. Heskett, and W. E. Sasser, Jr. 1990. "The Profitable Art of Service Recovery." *Harvard Business Review* 68 (4): 148–56.

39. *Ibid.*

40. Technical Assistance Research Program (TARP). 1986. *Consumer Complaint Handling in America: An Update Study.* Washington, DC: Department of Consumer Affairs. Often referred to as the TARP Study.

41. Sherman, S. G., and V. C. Sherman. 1999. *Total Customer Satisfaction: A Comprehensive Approach for Health Care Providers,* p. 195. San Francisco: Jossey-Bass.

42. *Ibid.*, p.197.

*Chapter 14*

# Measuring the Quality of the Healthcare Experience

Healthcare Principle: *Measure the important things, then pursue the superb healthcare experience relentlessly*

Standards—being able to specify what good, bad, and great service look like—are prerequisites to asking people to deliver.

—*Karl Albrecht and Ron Zemke*

ALL CUSTOMERS HOPE to be provided with an outstanding experience every time. Even though they know that perfection is elusive, they hope that whatever errors do happen will not happen to them. All healthcare organizations face rising patient expectations and an increasing unwillingness to settle for less than patients think they are entitled to have. This new customer activism has made service quality more important than ever as healthcare managers strive to meet both heightened patient expectations and increasing competition.

One way of creating a flawless experience for the patient in the future is for the organization to know what errors are being made or what problems are occurring now. Consequently, measuring the quality of the healthcare experience is an increasingly important part of the healthcare organization's responsibility. Satisfied patients are willing to come back, and dissatisfied patients go somewhere else if and when they have other healthcare options.

The best time to find out about possible service problems is before the patient leaves the service setting, while the information is still fresh in the patient's mind. Finding out on the spot also gives the organization the opportunity to recover from problems. Accurately measuring what patients think about their physical therapy, hospital stay, or laboratory testing is a difficult challenge for healthcare organizations striving to achieve service excellence. Nevertheless, it must be done.

This chapter focuses on finding out how the patient perceives the quality of the healthcare experience so that the healthcare manager can see problems from the patient's perspective. We present a range of measurement devices that show the organization where it needs to improve or change its service, service setting, its delivery system, or its personnel's skills to meet the patient's expectations.

## QUALITATIVE METHODS

The critical challenge for healthcare managers is identifying and implementing the methods that best measure the quality of the experience from the patient's point of view. As we have stated throughout, the patient determines quality and value. Consequently, an acceptable experience for one patient might be a superb experience for another and a serious problem to a third. The subjective nature of the quality and value of a healthcare experience makes identifying and implementing the appropriate measurement particularly difficult. No matter how well management or the medical staff planned the treatment, surgery, or therapy, the quality of the healthcare experience cannot be measured until the patient experiences it.

A variety of methods are available to measure the quality of the healthcare experience. These methods differ in cost, accuracy, and degree of patient inconvenience. Measuring healthcare quality can have many organizational benefits, but as usual the benefits must be balanced against the costs of obtaining them. In other words, the organization must balance the information needed and the extent and precision of the research expertise required to gather and interpret it, against the availability of funding. As a rule, the more accurate and precise the information, the more expensive it is to acquire.

Typically, healthcare organizations begin assessing customer service effectiveness through qualitative approaches and then move to quantitative methods later.[1] Table 14.1 outlines the major qualitative techniques and their advantages and disadvantages. The qualitative techniques are management observation, employee feedback programs, work teams and quality circles, and focus groups. Management observation, employee feedback programs, and focus groups are discussed below.

**Table 14.1  Advantages and Disadvantages of Various Qualitative Techniques for Measuring Patient Service Quality**

| Management Techniques | Advantages | Disadvantages |
|---|---|---|
| Management observation | • Management knows business, politics, and procedures<br>• No inconvenience to patient<br>• Opportunity to recover from service failure<br>• Opportunity to obtain detailed patient feedback<br>• Opportunity to identify service delivery problems<br>• Minimal incremental cost for data gathering | • Management presence may influence service providers<br>• Lacks statistical validity and reliability<br>• Objective observation requires specialized training<br>• Employees disinclined to report problems they created<br>• Management may be unfamiliar with processes and customers |
| Employee feedback programs | • Employees have knowledge of service delivery obstacles<br>• Patients volunteer service experience information to employees<br>• No inconvenience to patients<br>• Opportunity to recover from service failure<br>• Opportunity to collect detailed patient feedback<br>• Minimal incremental cost for data gathering and documentation | • Objective observation requires specialized training<br>• Employees not inclined to report problems they created |
| Work teams and quality circles | • Develops employee awareness of management's strong commitment to service quality<br>• Develops an understanding and appreciation of how each employee can directly influence service quality | • Employees may wish to avoid responsibilites of empowerment<br>• Team may not act cohesively and work together<br>• Necessary communication among team members takes large amount of time |

**Table 14.1** (*continued*)

| | | |
|---|---|---|
| Work teams and quality circles (*con't*) | • Through empowerment, improves employee morale, productivity, efficiency, effectiveness, and patient satisfaction<br>• Team working together conveys confidence and competence to patients | |
| Focus groups | • Opportunity to collect detailed patient feedback<br>• Opportunity to recover from service failure<br>• Qualitative analysis helps to focus managers on problem areas<br>• Other problems may surface during discussions<br>• Suggests that facility is interested in patients' opinions of service quality | • May only identify symptoms and not core service delivery problems<br>• Feedback limited to small group of customers<br>• Recollection of specific service encounter details may be lost<br>• One group member may dominate or bias discussion<br>• Inconvenience necessitates incentives for participation<br>• High cost of properly trained focus group leader<br>• Information may be withheld due to fear of disapproval by others<br>• May not be representative sample of the patient population |
| Service guarantees | • Provides feedback on service failures in significant areas<br>• Enhances both measurement and marketing | • Self-selected sample of patients not statistically representative<br>• Some patients may take advantage of organization |

*Source:* Adapted with permission from R. C. Ford, S. A. Bach, and M. D. Fottler, "Methods of Measuring Patient Satisfaction in Health Care Organizations," 22 (2), page 77, © 1999, Aspen Publishers, Inc.

## Management Observation

The simplest and least expensive technique for assessing quality is to encourage managers to keep their eyes open, especially to the interactions between staff and patients and other customers. This technique is sometimes called MBWA (Management by Walking Around). Some healthcare organizations call it "walking the front," which means observing what is happening first hand, looking for problems or inefficiencies, talking to patients to assess their reactions, and relaying to staff members any information that might enable them to improve the healthcare experience. Managers know their own healthcare operation, its goals, capabilities, and healthcare quality standards. They know, at least from the managerial perspective, when staff members are delivering a high-quality experience.

Managerial observations do not inconvenience patients, and they often permit immediate correction of patient-service problems. Further, managerial observation gives the supervisor the opportunity to recognize, reinforce, and reward the excellent employee and counsel an employee who might not be delivering the service as it should be delivered. It also provides a modeling opportunity where the supervisor observing a service problem can show the employee how to fix it.

When managers walk the front to serve as coaches and not as spies, their presence has a favorable influence on employee attitudes and performance and on patient satisfaction. However, some managers may not have enough experience or training to fully understand what they are observing, or they may have biases that influence their objectivity. More importantly, when employees know that managers are observing the service delivery process, they invariably perform it differently. Additionally, although management observation may ensure the quality of the experience for a particular patient, managers cannot watch every patient-employee interaction. The unobserved patient's reactions to unobserved experiences remain unknown to the manager.

Training healthcare managers in methods of observing patient-service provider interactions and measuring them against quality standards can eliminate both ignorance and personal bias. Unobtrusive observational techniques, random observations, and video cameras diminish employee awareness that the boss is watching. For example, many organizations tell both their telephone operators and callers that all phone conversations "may be monitored for training purposes" to eliminate the observation bias by making it uncertain when management is actually listening in. The operators know that someone may always be listening, so they do the job by the book. Some larger companies use managers from one location to observe employees at another location for the same reason. For obvious ethical reasons, employees and customers should be alerted that they may be monitored.

Besides observing the staff in action, managers of outstanding healthcare organizations also develop performance standards of measurements for every part of the healthcare experience so that they can monitor how well they are meeting their own definition of quality service. Some standards are more or less global in the healthcare industry—for example, three minutes to respond to a Code Blue, 20 minutes for breakfast trays to be served after arriving on the floor, and five minutes for a room call light to be answered.

Most standards are specific to the organizations that create them and are designed to meet or beat the competition as well as meet patient expectations. Emergency rooms define how many minutes it should take for a newly arrived patient to be triaged. If it has not happened in, say, five minutes, then the healthcare quality standard has not been met. Nurses may use number of rings for answering a patient call. If a nurse has not responded to the call within a certain number of rings, the quality standard has not been met.

These are quality standards that can be developed, measured, and used as ways to ensure that the healthcare experience is delivered as it should be. According to quality expert Phil Crosby in *Quality Is Free*, the price of not conforming to a quality standard can be calculated; that price is: How much it costs to fix errors and failures that result from not meeting quality standards in the first place? Although some may think that determining the cost of not answering the phone within three rings is impossible, quality experts like Crosby think it can and should be done.

Benchmark healthcare organizations measure quality in as many ways as they can. For example, the Central Florida Health Care Coalition conducts research for 12 large Central Florida employers to help these employers and other consumers of all types of health plans identify the plans that will best meet their needs.[2] Ten health plans are evaluated and data presented on 13 criteria including evaluations of the patient's personal doctor or nurse, specialist physicians, availability of help by phone, ease of getting appointments, wait times to see providers, helpfulness of staff, courtesy and respect, listening skills, physician explanations, time spent with physician, information provided by insurer, access to customer service of insurer, helpfulness of insurer customer service, and overall experience with insurer. Both the plan and the plan providers were evaluated in 1999 based on 3,659 employee responses from the 12 employers.

Results indicate that the weakest areas were related to customer satisfaction such as ease of getting advice by phone, ease of getting an appointment in a reasonable time, wait to see the physician, time and energy required to deal with insurer payments and approvals, wait to speak with insurer's customer service, and helpfulness of insurer's customer service.

In the above example, employees of the 12 companies received external evaluations from the coalition on *both* their health plans and their plans' providers. How the employees and their employers wished to respond to these data was their decision. However, the important point is that they supplemented their own observations and "hearsay" from other employees with more reliable and valid external data on how a representative sample of employees viewed the various health plans being offered.

To prevent customer service problems, the organization's own quality standards should exceed those of all but the most demanding patients. If they do, the organization's internal control measures may sometimes show that a standard has not been met, even if patients seem satisfied and no one complains. When that happens, some organizations in the service industry actually apologize! Patients will remember healthcare organizations that behave this way as much as they remember other service organizations that have learned the power of the apology. Healthcare executives may fear that offering apologies may lead to a lawsuit because it seems like an admission of liability. Benchmark healthcare organizations have learned how to gain the benefits of offering apologies without admitting liability.

## Employee Feedback

Employee feedback should supplement management observation. Employees can provide input on issues such as cumbersome organizational policies and control procedures, managerial reporting structures, or other processes that inhibit effective healthcare service delivery. They know firsthand about organizational impediments that prevent them from delivering high-quality service. *Employee work teams and quality service circles* are another source of feedback. Such techniques foster an understanding and appreciation of how each employee can directly influence service quality. Employee awareness of management's strong commitment to healthcare quality is affirmed through work teams. Using these teams requires employee training and management trust in employee judgment to correct problems.

### Focus Groups

Focus groups provide in-depth information on how patients and other customers view the service they receive. Typically a focus group of six to ten persons gathers with a facilitator for several hours to discuss perceived problems and to make suggestions. Marriott Corporation, for example, conducted focus groups of frequent-stay guests and incorporated their comments into the design of the Marriott Courtyard model. Many service organizations routinely invite customers to participate in focus groups. These invitations show customers that the company cares enough about their reactions to ask them to participate, and customers appreciate the dollars, complimentary dinner, or other expression of appreciation that compensates them for their time.

One reason healthcare organizations use focus groups is to supplement survey results, which often fail to produce information that is useful for program improvement because the information is not discriminating enough.[3] Customer expectations and the degree to which these are met are typically not considered. Surveys may also ask for satisfaction ratings about areas that are not of the greatest interest or importance to patients.[4] Finally, surveys may too narrowly frame the range of possible responses, which may result in overestimates of satisfaction.[5]

Patient focus groups can provide valuable feedback about what patients expect, and they are particularly effective in identifying factors patients find important.[6] Because focus group questions are open-ended and amplification is invited, participants' experiences, opinions, expectations, and suggestions are likely to be heard and understood.

The Mountain Area Health Education Center in Asheville, North Carolina, is a primary care healthcare facility that uses focus groups to assess patient suggestions for improving existing services or to suggest other services.[7] Thirty-two long-term patients (five or more years with the facility) participated in five focus groups that lasted about two hours. Among the findings were patient concern about the use of video cameras in examining rooms, wide variation in when and how test results were communicated, the heaviness of the clinic's front door, patient difficulty in changing infant's diapers, limited reading materials in the waiting rooms, inadequate signage, and inadequate telephone access to the clinic. Although some of these issues were immediately addressed, the more complex issues required additional research and were assigned to continuous quality improvement teams for further investigation. The resulting data proved exceptionally useful in making immediate, meaningful improvements in patient satisfaction and perception of service quality.

### Service Guarantees

This method is based on a given customer's subjective perception of whether an aspect of the service was or was not completely satisfactory. "Satisfaction guaranteed or your money back; no questions asked." "Satisfaction guaranteed or get 50 percent off your next purchase." Such guarantees have worked well across the service industry. For example, every Hampton Inn employee is empowered to approve a full refund if any customer is dissatisfied with any aspect of his or her experience. According to Steven Tax and Steven Brown, the Hampton Inn organization realized $11 million in additional revenue from implementation of its service guarantee and scored the highest customer retention rate in the industry.[8]

By contrast, such guarantees are quite rare in healthcare even though there is no indication that they will not work equally well. According to one study, the average business spends six times more money on marketing to potential new customers than it does working to keep the customers it has.[9] Healthcare facilities focus their marketing programs on recruiting new customers; yet, they typically offer no quality or satisfaction guarantees to their current or prospective customers to assure them of the excellence of their healthcare service.

One Texas hospital challenged its admissions office to process each patient admission in three minutes or less.[10] If the admissions process was not completed in three minutes or less, the hospital took $100 off the bill. Customers began to time the process. Although the employees were willing to put their hospital's money where its mouth was, they seldom had to pay money out on their guarantee. On those few occasions when they could not meet the standard and had to pay up, motivation was created to improve the system, not to change the guarantee. So why do healthcare organizations not offer some guarantees, similar to those offered by other service businesses? They should be able to guarantee that their customer service staff will answer the phone in a reasonable period of time, customer paperwork will be minimized, food will be up to standards, facilities will be clean, and staff members will be friendly and respectful.

As described by author Chris Hart, service guarantees provide a number of important advantages to organizations.[11] If a company has a strong and well-understood service guarantee that its customers can and do readily invoke, everyone in that organization can learn much about the service delivery system from its use. Hart notes several important benefits of a guarantee in measuring and improving the effectiveness of the service delivery system:

- *It forces everyone to think about the service from the customer's point of view* because the customer decides whether or not to invoke it.
- *It pinpoints where the service failed* because the customer must give the reason for invoking the guarantee, and that reason then becomes measurement data on the service delivery system. As we have discussed, a patient complaint is a good thing for a healthcare organization that hopes to be perfect. Guarantees are an incentive to get customers to complain if their expectations (and the guarantee's terms) have not been met. These complaints help the organization to fix whatever is wrong before other customers have problems.
- *It gets everyone to focus quickly on the problem at hand* because the costs of making good on guarantees can be quite large. Once a customer has to invoke the guarantee, the cost of the lost revenue forces management to direct its attention at correcting the problem.
- *It enhances the likelihood of recovery from a service problem* because the patient is encouraged to demand instant recovery, instead of writing a complaint letter and taking the business to a competitor.
- *It sends a strong message to employees and customers alike that the organization takes its healthcare quality seriously and will stand behind it.*

A good service guarantee, according to Hart, should meet several important criteria.[12] The guarantee must be:

1. *Unconditional.* The more asterisks or conditions attached to the bottom of the page and the more fine print, the less credible the

guarantee will seem to both employees and customers. Few or no conditions should be required to use the guarantee.

2. *Easy to understand and communicate* to both customers who invoke it and employees who honor it. Follow the old KISS rule: Keep It Simple, Stupid. The more complicated the guarantee is, the less likely anyone will believe or use it.

3. *Focused on the customer's needs.* The guarantee should solve the customer's problems, not fit the organization's needs.

4. *Clear on defining the standard for healthcare quality,* for everyone inside and outside the organization. If you are going to guarantee it, you better deliver it the way you are supposed to.

5. *Meaningful* to both the customer and the organization, in terms of what happens to both when the guarantee is invoked. The remedy should cover the patient's dissatisfaction completely. If invoking the guarantee only partially solves the customer's problem or is of little consequence to the organization, neither the customer nor the service people will value the guarantee.

6. *Easy to use.* Invoking the guarantee and receiving its benefits should be painless for the patient. The harder a guarantee is to use, the less credible it will be, and the less likely it will help identify serious service problems. Do not ask customers to fill out a bunch of forms and talk to several different departments to have their problem solved. It was not their fault that you messed up, so why should they have to do all the work to get it fixed?

7. *A declaration of trust* in both the customers you are trusting to use it only when they have a legitimate complaint and the employees you are trusting to correct the customer's problem quickly, fairly, and effectively without giving away the whole organization.

8. *Credible or believable* by the customer. If customers do not believe you will really make good, then they will not use the guarantee. The classic illustration is Pizza Hut's 30-minutes-or-free delivery guarantee, which was changed partly because people thought it was too good to be true.

## QUANTITATIVE METHODS

Although qualitative methods for assessing service quality have their benefits, good organizations are even more interested in measuring what patients themselves (and sometimes their families) think about their experiences in some quantitative format. Techniques to collect data directly from patients vary in cost, convenience, objectivity, and statistical validity. Table 14.2 provides an overview of quantitative methods and shows the advantages and disadvantages of each technique.

### Comment Cards

Comment cards are the cheapest and easiest to use of all data-collection methods. If properly designed, they are easy to tally and analyze. These advantages make them attractive for gathering patient satisfaction data, especially for smaller organizations that cannot afford a quality assessment staff or consultants. Comment cards rely on voluntary patient participation. Patients rate the quality of the healthcare experience by responding to a few simple questions on a conveniently available form, typically a postcard. Patients either deposit the form in a box placed near the healthcare facility exit, return it directly to the service provider, or mail it to the organization's office.

The following are six reasons to use comment cards, according to authors Leebov, Scott, and Olsen.[13]

1. To identify the particular needs and concerns of each major customer group
2. To be able to assess quickly and accurately the impact of service improvements from the customers' point of view
3. To speed up the feedback cycle, so you get customer input quickly
4. To have an easy method for getting candid feedback from customers
5. To supplement anecdotal feedback with quantitative data
6. To have a systematic way to find problems when you are implementing service improvements

Each healthcare organization identifies its customers for particular services, studies these customers, or asks them what is important to them in terms of service. Once these expectations have been determined, comment-card questions are developed. If studies reveal to a physician's office that its patients expect a friendly greeting, prompt attention, and detailed information about the treatment procedure, the office's comment card will ask patients about those elements of the healthcare experience. If an organization tries to differentiate itself from similar organizations in some particular way, that differentiating factor may also appear on the comment card, so that the organization can gauge the success of its differentiation strategy.

**Table 14.2 Advantages and Disadvantages of Various Quantitative Techniques for Measuring Patient Service Quality**

| Management Techniques | Advantages | Disadvantages |
|---|---|---|
| Comment cards | • Suggests that facility is interested in patients' opinions of service quality<br>• Opportunity to recover from service failure<br>• Minimal incremental cost for data gathering<br>• Moderate cost | • Self-selected sample of patients not statistically representative<br>• Comments generally reflect extreme patient dissatisfaction or extreme satisfaction |
| Mail surveys | • Ability to gather representative and valid samples of targeted patients<br>• Opportunity to recover from service failure<br>• Patients can reflect on their service experience<br>• Suggests that facility is interested in patients' opinions of service quality<br>• Allows comparisons of patient satifaction by department and patient demographics | • Recollection of specific service encounter details may be lost<br>• Other service experiences may bias responses because of time lag<br>• Inconvenience necessitates incentives for participants<br>• Cost to gather representative sample may be high<br>• Potential problems with the wording of questions |
| On-site personal interviews | • Opportunity to collect detailed patient feedback<br>• Opportunity to recover from service failure<br>• Ability to gather representative and valid sample of targeted patients<br>• Suggests that facility is interested in patients' opinions of service quality | • May not be representative sample of patients<br>• Other service experiences may bias responses<br>• Respondents tend to give socially desirable responses<br>• Inconvenience necessitates incentives for participants<br>• Cost moderate to high |

**Table 14.2** (*continued*)

| | | |
|---|---|---|
| Telephone interviews | • Opportunity to collect detailed patient feedback<br>• Ability to gather representative and valid sample of targeted patients<br>• Opportunity to recover from service failure<br>• Suggests that facility is interested in patients' opinions of service quality | • Individuals tend to find telephone calls intrusive<br>• Difficult to contact people at work; inconvenient at home<br>• Costs of skilled interviewers and valid instrument are high<br>• May not generate a representative cross-section of patients |
| Mystery shoppers | • Consistent and unbiased feedback<br>• Can focus on specific situations<br>• No inconvenience to patient<br>• Opportunity to collect detailed customer feedback<br>• Allows measurement of training program effectiveness | • Snapshot of isolated encounters may be statistically invalid<br>• Cost moderate to high<br>• Not applicable to all clinical areas (e.g., surgery)<br>• Ethical concerns |

*Source:* Adapted with permission from R. C. Ford, S. A. Bach, and M. D. Fottler, "Methods of Measuring Patient Satisfaction in Health Care Organizations," 22 (2), page 81, © 1999, Aspen Publishers, Inc.

For example, a cardiac surgery unit identified three key customer groups: patients, their families, and referring physicians.[13] Each customer group was asked what service was important to them. The four most important expectations for each customer group were then determined through interviews and focus groups. For patients, these expectations included efforts to relieve stress, clear explanations of the steps in the process, responsiveness of staff, and high levels of coordination among staff. Family members wanted staff to volunteer information about the patient's status and follow-up needs, staff to welcome questions, staff to be responsive to patients' needs, and respect from staff. Referring physicians wanted to be kept up-to-date about their patients, to receive timely communications, to be consulted, and to receive feedback from their patients. Once baseline comment card data were collected for each of the three customer groups, the data were compiled at frequent intervals to determine whether service to each group was improving, deteriorating, or remaining constant.

Comment cards give an indication of whether the organization is meeting the general expectations of the customers who take the time to fill them out. Written comments about long call-response waits, lines at the reception desk, or housekeeping problems reveal the strengths and weaknesses of the service delivery system, the personnel and their training, and the service itself. Positive comments provide management with the opportunity to recognize employee excellence. This recognition reinforces the behaviors that lead to good patient service and creates role models and stories about how to provide outstanding service that other employees can use in shaping their own behavior in their jobs. Negative comments can be used in training, without mentioning specific employees, to illustrate behaviors that caused negative healthcare experiences. Using comment cards in these ways allows managers to train employees in how to provide excellent patient service through the voices of the patients themselves.

Comments accumulated from cards may be plotted as numerical values on bar graphs and charts that visually display how patients perceived their experience. The plots will suggest whether service problems are occurring occasionally and randomly, or whether overall healthcare quality might be deteriorating. Although patient comments and their visual representations are interesting and helpful to management, the information is not statistically valid because, for one, the random-sample requirement of most statistical techniques is not met.

The greatest disadvantage of comment cards is that many customers ignore them and do not fill them out, so the cards received are not likely to be a true general picture of the customers' perceptions. Typically, only 5 percent of customers typically return comment cards, and they are usually either very satisfied or very dissatisfied. It is difficult to know what percentage of the delighted total or the dissatisfied total these responses represent. When the other 95 percent of customers say nothing, we cannot determine if they were happy, unhappy, or merely indifferent. Research shows that a large percentage of dissatisfied customers fill out no cards, leave quietly, and never return.

Another major disadvantage of comment cards, and in fact of many methods for acquiring feedback, is that the time lag between patient response and managerial review prevents on-the-spot correction of service gaps and problems. Once the moment of truth has passed and the angry or disappointed patient leaves after expressing negative responses on a comment card, the opportunity to recapture that patient's future business or loyalty is diminished. Even worse, negative word-of-mouth advertising generated by dissatisfied patients cannot be corrected.

### Surveys

Formal survey methods can obtain patient feedback about healthcare quality and value. Although surveying is more expensive than the methods already discussed, surveys can offer statistically valid, reliable, and useful measures of patient opinion that the others cannot. Surveys can range in sophistication, precision, validity, reliability, complexity, cost, and difficulty of administration.

#### Mail Surveys

Well-developed mail surveys, sent to an appropriate and willing sample, can provide valid information concerning patient satisfaction. Organizations can use mail surveys to their benefit, but many uncontrollable factors can influence patient responses to a mail survey. Inaccurate and incomplete mailing lists or simple lack of interest in commenting can produce a response rate too small to provide useful information. In addition, the time lag between the experience and survey response can blur a patient's memory of details

These surveys are usually used to generate reports that tend to be upwardly biased. The subtleties of the healthcare experience and patient perceptions cannot be fully expressed numerically. Also, averages may not be sufficiently informative. If some patients remember an experience as terrific and give it a high rating, while others rate it as terrible, the numerical average will suggest that patient expectations were met. The nature of medical treatment may also make interpretation of the ratings difficult. If the operation was a success but the patient died, it did not matter to the surveyed survivors that the rest of the patient's experience was above expectations. Finally, formal mail survey techniques are expensive because they require proper questionnaire development, validation, and data analysis.

### SERVQUAL

One well-accepted survey technique is SERVQUAL (short for "service quality"), developed by A. Parasuraman and his associates.[15] This survey has also been studied and adapted for healthcare organizations[16]; an adaptation of the SERVQUAL survey instrument, intended to evaluate service quality at Hallmark Hospital, is presented in Figure 14.1.

SERVQUAL has been extensively researched to validate its psychometric properties. It measures the way customers perceive the quality of service experiences in five categories:

1. *reliability*—the organization's ability to perform the desired service dependably, accurately, and consistently;
2. *responsiveness*—the organization's willingness to provide prompt service and help customers;
3. *assurance*—the employees' knowledge, courtesy, and ability to convey trust;
4. *empathy*—the employees' ability to provide care and individualized attention to customers; and
5. *tangibles*—the organization's physical facilities and equipment and appearance of personnel.

SERVQUAL also asks respondents to rate the relative importance of the five areas, so organizations can make sure that they understand what matters most to customers. In each area SERVQUAL asks customers what they expected and what they actually experienced to identify service gaps at which organizations should direct attention.

The SERVQUAL instrument reflects a point we have made throughout: the importance of the patient-contact staff to healthcare quality.

**Figure 14.1 SERVQUAL Application to Healthcare: Measuring Customer Perceptions of Healthcare Quality at Hallmark Hospital**

DIRECTIONS: Listed below are five features pertaining to Hallmark Hospital and the services they offer. We would like to know how important each of these features is to *you* when you evaluate a hospital's quality. Please allocate a total of 100 points among the five features *according to how important each feature is to you*—the more important a feature is to you, the more points you should allocate to it. Please ensure that the points you allocate to the five features add up to 100.

1.  The appearance of the hospital's physical facilities, equipment, and personnel
    _____ points
2.  The ability of the hospital to perform the promised service dependably and accurately
    _____ points
3.  The willingness of the hospital to help customers and provide prompt service
    _____ points
4.  The knowledge and courtesy of the hospital's employees and their ability to convey trust and confidence
    _____ points
5.  The caring, individualized attention the hospital provides to its customers
    _____ points

DIRECTIONS: Based on your experience with hospitals, please think about the kind of hospital at which you would prefer to receive healthcare. Please show the extent to which you think such a hospital would possess the feature described by each statement below. If you feel a feature is *not at all essential* for excellent hospitals such as the one you have in mind, circle "1" for Strongly Disagree. If you feel a feature is *absolutely essential* for excellent hospitals, circle "7" for *Strongly Agree*. If your feelings are less strong, circle one of the numbers in the middle. There are no right or wrong answers. All we are interested in is a number that truly reflects your feelings regarding hospitals that would deliver excellent service quality.

*[The 22 survey items for this section are the same as those in the next section, but without any reference to Hallmark Hospital.]*

**Figure 14.1** *(continued)*

DIRECTIONS: The following set of statements relates to your feelings about the service at Hallmark Hospital. For each statement, please show the extent to which you believe Hallmark Hospital has the feature described by each statement below. Once again, circling "1" means that you *Strongly Disagree* that Hallmark Hospital has that feature, and circling "7" means that you *Strongly Agree*. You may circle any of the numbers in the middle that show how strong your feelings are. There are no right or wrong answers. All we are interested in is a number that best shows your perceptions about the service at Hallmark Hospital.

*[On the instrument itself, the five category labels (Tangibles, etc.) will be omitted.]*

TANGIBLES
P1.   Hallmark Hospital has modern-looking equipment
P2.   Hallmark Hospital's physical facilities are visually appealing
P3.   Hallmark Hospital's employees are neat-appearing
P4.   Materials associated with the service are clean and sanitary at Hallmark Hospital

RELIABILITY
P5.   When Hallmark Hospital promises to do something by a certain time, it does so
P6.   When you have a problem, Hallmark Hospital shows sincere interest in solving it
P7.   Hallmark Hospital performs the service right the first time
P8.   Hallmark Hospital provides its services in the way it promises to do so
P9.   Hallmark Hospital insists on error-free service performance

RESPONSIVENESS
P10. Employees of Hallmark Hospital tell you exactly when healthcare services will be performed
P11. Employees of Hallmark Hospital give you prompt healthcare service
P12. Employees of Hallmark Hospital are always willing to help you
P13. Employees of Hallmark Hospital are never too busy to respond to your requests

**Figure 14.1** *(continued)*

ASSURANCE
P14. The behavior of Hallmark Hospital employees instills confidence in customers
P15. You feel safe in going to Hallmark Hospital and doing business with them
P16. Employees of Hallmark Hospital are consistently courteous to you
P17. Employees of Hallmark Hospital have the knowledge to answer your questions

EMPATHY
P18. Hallmark Hospital gives you individual attention
P19. Hallmark Hospital has visiting hours convenient to all its customers
P20. Hallmark Hospital has employees who give you personal attention
P21. Hallmark Hospital has your best interests at heart
P22. Employees of Hallmark Hospital try to learn your specific needs

*Source:* Adapted from "SERVQUAL: A Multiple-Item Scale for Measuring Consumer Perception of Service Quality," by A. Parasuraman, V.A. Zeithaml, and L.L. Berry. 1988. *Journal of Retailing* 64 (1): 38–40.

Although tangibles refer primarily to the setting and to the physical elements of the delivery system, and reliability reflects a combination of organizational delivery system design and service provider ability, the remaining three elements—responsiveness, assurance, and empathy—are almost exclusively the responsibility of the patient-contact employees.

## Assessing Internal Customers

Healthcare organizations too often overlook internal customers when they assess external customers. Many units within traditional full-service healthcare facilities provide service functions for other internal units either in addition to services for patients and external physicians or as standalone functions (i.e., human resources, training, and payroll). These internal service providers are often thought of as overhead activities rather than service providers with customers. As a result, many healthcare executives pay little attention to these activities.

One hospital developed and implemented an internal customer survey instrument.[17] This process included (1) an initial baseline survey of service managers concerning their satisfaction with internal nursing services, (2) feedback to service area managers regarding the survey results, (3) an interim survey to determine improvement, and (4) resurvey two years later to determine effectiveness of the implemented changes. In general, the scores in the initial survey were highly positive. Thirteen of the 15 areas received favorable composite scores and 11 received mean scores stronger than the "agree" category of 3.0.

After reviewing the results of the initial survey, senior nurse managers used the results as a baseline for service improvement. The service area nurse managers picked three specific problems identified in the survey and then developed and implemented plans to address those problems. Most of the nurse managers then solicited staff input on these action plans. After two years, the satisfaction levels of the customers (users of nursing services) showed that all 15 service areas were received favorably and 14 of the 15 areas had mean scores greater than 3.0.

Richard Lytle and his colleagues have designed a survey instrument (SERV*OR) to gauge employee perceptions of the organization's degree of internal service orientation.[18] The scale items are given below:

1. Customer treatment
2. Employee empowerment
3. Service technology
4. Service-failure prevention
5. Service-failure recovery
6. Service standards communication
7. Service vision
8. Servant leadership
9. Service rewards
10. Service training

### Personal Interviews

Face-to-face patient interviews provide rich information when trained interviewers, able to detect nuances in responses to open-ended questions, have the opportunity to probe patients for details about their experiences. Interviewing can uncover previously unknown problems or new twists to a known problem that cannot be uncovered in a preprinted questionnaire or reflected well in numerical data. However, personal interviews are costly: interviewers must be hired and trained, interview instruments must be custom designed, and inconvenienced patients must be compensated for participating. Without incentives, most patients see little personal benefit from participating in a patient interview unless they are either very satisfied or very dissatisfied. Finally, the most desirable time to interview patients and/or their families is at the conclusion of the healthcare experience. Getting their attention and cooperation when they probably prefer to leave is a challenge.

Another patient-interview approach is to employ consultants or employees (called "lobby lizards" in the hotel business) to ask randomly selected patients their opinions on several key service issues. In healthcare organizations, the individual conducting the customer interviews is typically a manager. Employees are often in an excellent position to gather patient perceptions of healthcare quality by means of structured interviews or surveys. For example, a billing clerk can question patients about their experience as they are leaving the clinic, office, or hospital. Because patients may not always be motivated to tell the whole truth, a systematic program should have questions that are professionally developed and validated to help ensure that the information gathered is useful, accurate, and sufficient.

An advantage of acquiring immediate feedback is that it may allow prompt recovery from service problems. Staff training should therefore include appropriate service-recovery techniques, given that research confirms that the organization benefits greatly from soliciting and fairly resolving patient complaints. Because service-quality information derived directly from the patient is highly believable to both staff and management, it motivates a serious consideration of the problems the patients identified.

### Critical Incidents

Another important survey tool is the critical incident technique. Through interviews or paper-and-pencil surveys, customers are asked to identify and evaluate numerous moments—classified as dissatisfiers, neutral, or satisfiers—in their interactions with the organization. The survey lets the organization know which moments are critical to customer satisfaction, and the critical dissatisfiers can be traced back to their root causes and rectified. In one study of convention hotels, for example, conventioneers identified guest arrival, coffee break, lunch, and the conference room itself as critical incidents and factors. Once the hotel knew which incidents convention patients viewed as critical, it concentrated on making them smooth and seamless.[19] In healthcare, the critical incidents tend to be related to customer expectations (discussed earlier) such as patients' concerns about personalized care, prompt attention, staff respect, physician and staff competence, a clean environment, privacy, and clear information. Critical incidents information related to these factors will generate useable information for service improvement.

### Telephone Surveys

Telephone interviews are another useful method for assessing customer perceptions of service. In the hospitality industry, some tour operators phone customers to obtain feedback about a recent vacation experience while paving the way for subsequent travel arrangements. Many healthcare facilities use telephone surveys within one week after the service was provided rather than a written survey filled out by the patient at the time the service was provided. More recently, surveys on the Internet have been used as a substitute for telephone surveys because web surveys are less intrusive.

Although telephone interviews or Web surveys eliminate the inconvenience to patients of gathering information while patients are still in the service location, they present other challenges. This technique relies on retrospective information that can be blurred by the passage of time. If the service received was too brief or insignificant for patients to recall accurately, or if patients have no special motivation to participate, the information they provide is likely to be unreliable or incomplete. In addition, in this age of intense telephone solicitation, customers often regard telephone surveys as intrusions on their time and violations of their privacy. Annoyed respondents feeling resentment toward the organization for calling them at home are likely to bias the data.

Red Lobster and Steak & Ale avoid some of these difficulties by building into their customer meal-checks system a code that prints an 800 number for every nth customer to call; the automated response system then asks customers to press touchtone buttons to answer questions about their experience at the restaurant. In return for participation, the restaurant offers coupons for free desserts or "two entrees for the price of one" on the customer's next visit.

Telephone interviews in which the patient responds directly to a trained interviewer who is administering a sophisticated questionnaire are expensive. When data analysis and expert interpretation are included, the total cost for a statistically valid survey can become quite high.

### Mystery Shoppers

Mystery shoppers provide management with an objective snapshot of the healthcare experience. While posing as patients, these trained observers methodically sample the service and its delivery, take note of the environment, and then compile a systematic and detailed report of their experience. They can sample an admissions process, a billing experience at an HMO, or an overnight hospital stay for a routine check-up. Shopper reports generally include numerical ratings of their observations so that reactions to the healthcare experience can be compared over time and with other organizations.

Although employees usually know that their organization uses a mystery-shopper program, they do not know who the shoppers are or when they will shop. Owners of smaller organizations, such as individual physicians or small clinics, can hire a commercial service, individual consultant, or ask a personal friend or university class to conduct a mystery-shopper program. Larger organizations and national chains may employ a commercial service or use their own staff as shoppers.[20]

Campbell Health System in Weatherford, Texas, decided the customer service data they developed from patient surveys was not effectively motivating their staff to improve the level of customer service.[21] After looking at several ways of giving customer feedback to staff, the board of directors, the medical staff, and the administrative team decided to use a mystery shopper. This individual, unknown in the facility, spent time as a patient to evaluate the facility's systems and customer service. He was admitted through the emergency room with chest pain and had an inpatient stay of two days. He went through the same channels a typical patient would travel and received the requisite tests and diagnostic services, including EKG and chest x-ray for his symptoms.

After discharge, the mystery shopper then carefully reviewed his experiences, developed a monologue, and produced a videotape presentation of his stay from admission to discharge.[22] He detailed the process by which each service or test was administered, identified employees who were positive role models, and listed experiences that were less than positive. At the end of the tape, he reviewed areas of exceptional customer service as well as areas for improvement. By being exposed to one person's intimate view of the session, staff gained meaningful insight into the importance of customer service and the factors that affect it.

Because visits by mystery shoppers are unannounced, employees cannot "dress up" their performance. In addition, shoppers can be scheduled at specific times to assess the quality of service during various shifts, under diverse conditions, with different employees, and through the eyes of different types of shoppers.[23] Mystery shoppers can also observe competing organizations in a particular market and systematically gather information on their service level, facilities, prices, and special services.

Some hotels employ mystery shoppers to test the ability of their properties to respond to anticipated service problems and service delivery failures. For example, shoppers can create a problem or intensify a situation by asking certain questions or requesting unique services to assess employee responses under pressure. Mystery shoppers can also gauge the effectiveness of a particular training program by shopping at a healthcare organization before and after the training.

The main disadvantage of a mystery shopper is the small size of the sample from which the shopper generates reports. Because anyone can have a bad day or a bad shift, a mystery shopper may base conclusions on unusual or atypical experiences. One or two observations is not a statistically valid sample of anything, but hiring enough mystery shoppers to yield a valid sample is impractical and expensive. Further, the unique preferences, biases, or expectations of individual shoppers can unduly influence a report. Well-trained shoppers with specific information about the organization's service standards, instructions on what to observe, and guidelines for evaluating the experience avoid this pitfall.

Finally, a healthcare mystery shopper can only sample so many aspect of the healthcare experience. Obviously, a mystery shopper cannot go through a surgical procedure.

## DETERMINING THE MEASURE THAT FITS

What gets measured gets managed, but determining which measure is most appropriate is another challenge. A major hospital in a for-profit chain, for example, may require more elaborate and expensive strategies to measure feedback because poor service can harm the reputation and bottom line of the hospital, the chain with which the hospital is affiliated, and the livelihood of countless employees up and down the line. The value to this hospital of finding and correcting service problems so that it can deliver the healthcare quality its patients expect is tremendous. Failing to meet patient expectations will quickly make it and everything affiliated with it uncompetitive in a dynamic marketplace. On the other hand, the office of a small independent physician who has a well-established reputation for providing superb clinical treatment in a caring manner will learn just as much from asking patients without incurring the expense of sophisticated quality assessment methods.

Costs and level of expertise used to gather data vary also. An important question to ask is who should collect data: employees, consultants, or a professional survey research organization. Using staff members is the least expensive alternative, but they also have the least expertise in customer service research and may lack the communication skills to interview effectively. Consultants and survey organizations cost more, but they are better able to gather and interpret more detailed, sophisticated statistical data using more sophisticated techniques. Employee surveyors are not able to measure eye-pupil dilation; professionals can.

Regardless of the evaluation technique selected to measure healthcare quality, one thing is certain: Patients evaluate service every time it is delivered, forming distinct opinions about its quality and value. All healthcare organizations that aspire to excellence must constantly assess the quality of their healthcare experience through their patients' eyes. Most patients and their families are happy to tell what they thought about their experience if they are asked in the right way at the right time. Telephone surveyors calling on Friday night at dinner time will get the turndown they deserve. Healthcare managers striving for excellence need to ask the right questions at the right time, of the right mix of patients, to obtain the information necessary to ensure service that meets and exceeds patient expectations.

Irrespective of whether qualitative or quantitative assessment methods are used or which particular methods are used alone or in combination, follow-up is crucial. If customers provide data to organizations that they perceive to be unresponsive to their input, then the quantity and quality of future input will be limited. Why provide new data if old data are ignored? It is better never to collect customer information in the first place than to collect and then ignore it. Follow-up might include communicating to staff clear and accurate economic measures of loss from the defection of one customer, setting service standards based on customer expectations, eliminating substandard performance and performers, communicating with customers and staff about service improvement, and anticipating a changing marketplace.[24]

Brazoport Memorial Hospital in Lake Jackson, Texas, found through patient surveys that the cancer center and rehabilitation unit were consistently satisfying their customers' needs.[25] However, some cancer patients who sought treatment in the emergency department were dissatisfied with long wait times. In response to the feedback, the hospital nearly doubled the size of the emergency department, added a fast-track clinic, increased physicians and nurse coverage, and dedicated an area exclusively to observation beds (thus removing nontrauma patients from the trauma area). The next step was reporting these reconfigured emergency services to the community both through testimonials from satisfied patients and communications with primary care physicians. The final step was to "close the loop" by using the same survey tool to determine if patient satisfaction with the emergency department improved as a result of the above initiatives.

## CONCLUSION

Numerous methods are available for measuring the degree to which service excellence is achieved. Each healthcare organization needs to make an assessment of which methods will work best for its own situation. Each organization also needs to determine whether to gather data using its own resources or contract the function to an outside group such as Press Ganey. The degree of sophistication required and the organization's internal resources will drive this decision.

Irrespective of whether the organization uses qualitative or quantitative measures (or both) or internal or external resources to generate the data, the purpose of the data collection on service quality should be identical: to enhance customer service. Once a baseline of information is in place, then the organization can focus on setting performance standards for a few behaviors at a time and spend several months achieving service excellence for these behaviors. Staff will not be overwhelmed, managers will be able to monitor a manageable number of behaviors, and staff will be able to learn together and support each other in the process. Once the original behaviors are improved based on customer service data, the organization can focus on additional behaviors to be improved (again, based on service quality data).

A major challenge is how to achieve and maintain continuous improvement. One major approach is to celebrate individual and group success in achieving service excellence. Staff need and want to be appreciated for their achievements and contributions. Among the more successful celebration methods are mentions in newsletters, posting letters on bulletin boards, sharing stories of excellent service at staff meetings, and sending thank you notes.[26] Every meeting should be viewed as an opportunity to teach, positively reinforce, and celebrate successes in achieving customer satisfaction. This process should be continuous.

## LESSONS LEARNED

1. The quality of clinical service and the quality of customer service are different. Benchmark healthcare organizations focus on both outcomes.
2. If you do not measure it, you cannot manage it; if you do not manage it, you cannot improve it.
3. Use the best combination of qualitative and quantitative methods to measure customer satisfaction.
4. Balance the value of service information obtained from patients with the cost of obtaining it.
5. Recognize the strengths and weaknesses of the available assessment techniques.
6. The more sophisticated the information needed from patients, the more expensive it is to acquire.
7. Consider offering service guarantees.
8. Assess the quality of service for both internal and external customers.
9. Follow-up on implementation of service improvement ideas generated from all quality assessment methods.
10. Get better or get beaten in the competitive healthcare marketplace.
11. Maintain momentum for customer service by continually using positive reinforcement and celebrating successes.

## NOTES

1. Ford, R. C., S. A. Bach, and M. D. Fottler. 1997. "Methods of Measuring Patient Satisfaction in Health Care Organizations." *Health Care Management Review* 22 (2): 74–89.

2. Central Florida Health Care Coalition. 1999. *1999 Consumer Assessment of Health Plans Study: Disabled Tabulations.* Princeton, NJ: Response Analysis Corporation.

3. Williams, J. C., and D. Healy. 1998. "The Meaning of Patient Satisfaction: An Explanation of High Reported Levels." *Social Science and Medicine* 47: 1351–59.

4. McComas, J., M. Rosseim, and D. McIntosh. 1995. "Client-Centered Approach to Develop a Scaling Clinic Satisfaction Questionnaire: A Qualitative Study." *American Journal of Occupational Therapy* 49: 980–85.

5. Batchelor, C., D. J. Owens, R. Read, and M. Bloor. 1994. "Patient Satisfaction Studies: Methodology, Management, and Consumer Evaluation." *International Journal of Health Care Quality Assurance* 7: 22–30.

6. Ford, R. C., S. A. Bach, and M. D. Fotter. 1997. "Methods of Measuring Patient Satisfaction in Health Care Organizations." *Health Care Management Review* 22 (2): 74–89.

7. Swarz, M., S. E. Landis, J. Rowe, C. J. Jones, and N. Pullman. 2000. "Using Focus Groups to Assess Primary Care Patients' Satisfaction." *Evaluation and the Health Professions* 23 (1): 58–71.

8. Tax, S. S., and S. W. Brown. 1998. "Recovering and Learning From Service Failure." *Sloan Management Review* 39 (3): 76.

9. Sherman, S. S., and V. C. Sherman. 1999. *Total Customer Satisfaction: A Comprehensive Approach for Health Care Providers*, p. 182. San Francisco: Jossey-Bass.

10. *Ibid.*

11. Hart, C. W. L. 1988. "The Power of Unconditional Service Guarantees." *Harvard Business Review* 66 (4): 54–62.

12. *Ibid.*

13. Leebov, W., G. Scott, and L. Olsen. 1998. *Achieving Impressive Customer Service: Seven Strategies for the Health Care Manager*, p. 90. Chicago: American Hospital Publishing.

14. *Ibid.*

15. Parasuraman, A., V. Zeithaml, and L. L. Berry. 1986. *SERVQUAL: A Multiple-Item Scale for Measuring Consumer Perception of Service Quality*. Cambridge, MA: Marketing Science Institute.

16. Shewchuk, R. M., S. J. O'Connor, and J. B. White. 1991. "In Search of Quality Measures." *Health Services Management Research* 4 (1): 65–75.

17. Weir, V. L. 1998. "Surveying Your Internal Customers." *Nursing Management* 29 (6): 31–34.

18. Lytle, R. S., P. M. Hom, and M. P. Mokwa. 1998. SERV*OR: A Managerial Measure of Organizational Service Orientation. *Journal of Retailing* 74 (4): 455–89.

19. Dansher, P. J., and J. Mattson. 1994. "Cumulative Encounter Satisfaction in the Hotel Conference Process." *International Journal of Service Industry Management* 5 (4): 69–80.

20. Cook, L. 1998. "Mystery Shoppers: Can They Help Head Off Major Quality Problems?" *Lodging* 23 (8): 78.

21. Millstead, J. B. 1999. "Mystery Shopping in Your Organization." *Healthcare Executive* 14 (3): 66–67.

22. *Ibid.*

23. Miles, L. 1993. "Rise of the Mystery Shopper." *Marketing* (March): 19.

24. Albrecht, K., and R. Zemke. 2002. *Service America in the New Economy.* New York: McGraw-Hill.

25. Oswald, W. W. 1998. "Progress Depends on Responsiveness." *Healthcare Executive* 13 (6): 42–43.

26. Scott, G. 2001. "Reviving Staff Spirit: A Key to Impressive Service." *Journal of Healthcare Management* 46 (5): 293–95.

*Chapter 15*

# Leading the Way to Healthcare Excellence

Service Principle: *Lead others to achieve a superb health-care experience*

A good leader is best when the people barely know he leads. A good leader talks little but when the work is done, the aim is fulfilled, all others will say, "We did this ourselves."

—*Lao-Tse, Chinese Philosopher*

PROVIDNG AN EXCELLENT healthcare experience is simple. Study your patients and other customers, know what they really want and expect, and then provide it and may be even a little bit more. Healthcare managers committed to providing a superb healthcare experience never stop studying their customers, using all the scientific tools available to know what they really want and value. Because all customers change, the study is never complete; the service product, the service environment, and the service delivery system must also change to make sure that each customer is satisfied. Leaders of outstanding patient-service organizations spend considerable time and effort studying the patient and using this information to shape their decisions on strategy, staffing, and systems.

This chapter brings together the book's important concepts to help the healthcare manager achieve service excellence. We also present our view of healthcare in the future and the leader's role. Again, we emphasize that service excellence is insufficient by itself in meeting customer needs. Excellent clinical service that addresses the patients' health concerns is an obvious prerequisite to service excellence.

397

## STRATEGY

In this era when an amazing amount of information about patients and what the competition offers in providing services to those patients is available, only organizations that truly understand what their patients and other customers want will survive and prosper. They first use this information to design a corporate strategy. They discover which of their competencies are considered core by the customers and concentrate on making these core competencies better. For example, they use the customer's wants, needs, and expectations to sharpen their marketing strategies; their budgeting decisions; their organizational and production systems design; and their human resources management strategy.

Southwest Airlines is an excellent example of a company that has used its understanding of the customer to discover and then provide what their passengers really want. Like most organizations, they originally used customer surveys to ask what customers wanted. They learned that customers wanted everything—cheap fares, on-time performance, great meals, comfortable seats, free movies, and more. Southwest realized that it could not give its customers everything, so it did additional research to dig deeper into customer preferences and learned that their customers really wanted low fares and reliable schedules with friendly service. The Southwest product is now exactly what its target market wants and, more importantly, wants enough to pay for and return to again and again.

The point of this example for healthcare managers is that they must dig deeper than the simple market survey of patient preferences to understand what preferences actually drive patient behavior. The organization can use the results from this deeper probing to match up the organization's core competencies and mission with what the customers want.

### Key Drivers

The outstanding patient-service organizations study their patients extensively to discover the key drivers of their healthcare experience. Some drivers are highly influential, and some seem relatively unimportant. Nonetheless, they all contribute to the impression that the patient takes away from the healthcare experience and are part of the determination of whether or not that patient will be satisfied. A trip to a hospital, or a visit to a physician's office or clinic, is a holistic experience to most people; excellent customer service organizations do the research necessary to identify all the separate components of this whole experience. Then they carefully manage them all.

In a sense, these drivers can be divided into two categories. The first category is composed of things that patients *expect* the organization to offer its patients to operate in the particular market segment. Customers expect the following basics from a hospital: nice clean rooms, acceptable food, appropriately trained and skilled medical and professional staff with a decent bedside manner, a caring attitude, efficient work systems, a clinical product of high quality, and no irritations in the environment. These are basic expectations that the organization must meet; otherwise customers will be dissatisfied. If the organization fails habitually to meet these basic expectations, it will fail altogether. The basic characteristics are the necessary but not sufficient patient-experience aspects that organizations must offer if they seek to maintain a reputation and attract the repeat business that leads to long-term success.

The second category of drivers is the characteristics and qualities that make the experience *memorable*. These are the features that differentiate the experiences provided by the excellent healthcare organizations from the experiences provided by others. These benchmark organizations find a way to go beyond meeting the basic expectations with which patients arrive when they come in the door to have a medical need addressed. The outstanding healthcare organizations know and provide the key factors that make a difference, make the experience memorable, impel patients to return again and again, and even motivate patients to tell all their friends about these exceptional organizations.

Holy Cross Hospital in Chicago; St. Mary's Hospital in Green Bay, Wisconsin; Parkland Hospital and Health System in Dallas; and Albert Einstein Health Network in New York all survey customers to determine how well they are providing the basics that customers expect. They also use a variety of techniques to identify the key drivers that determine how customers view the entire healthcare experience.

Albert Einstein Medical Center developed a satisfaction tool for its physician customers in the admitting service.[1] This tool was built around relieving physician anxiety for each step in their pathway through the service. These steps included admissions, preadmission testing, financial clearance, precertification, and bed assignment. For each of these steps, a series of questions is asked on a 1 (poor) to 5 (excellent) scale.

This tool monitors ongoing effectiveness of the admission department's service improvement efforts and pinpoints problem areas from the physician's perspective.

Baptist Hospital in Pensacola, Florida, continuously surveys its patients to learn everything about the healthcare experience. Baptist then uses that information to identify all its patients' basic expectations. In addition, Baptist identifies the factors that make its patients highly satisfied with the healthcare experience and strives to provide them.

The key drivers of patients and other customers will vary from one healthcare facility to another. For example, an HMO may find that its customers want easy access by phone, responsive and knowledgeable customer service representatives, and an unchanging panel of providers. For a primary care physician practice, the key drivers might be the possibility of quick scheduling of appointments, physician promptness in seeing the patient at the appointed time, and clear communication from the physician and nurse.

Generally speaking, the key drivers reflect expectations related to clinical outcomes, behaviors (i.e., being treated with respect and dignity), systems and processes (i.e., the way they are scheduled for tests), and the environment (i.e., cleanliness and ease of navigation). Each healthcare organization needs to identify its customers' key drivers in general and then do the same for customers in each department and/or service/product line. Customers for certain services or products may have different expectations from customers for other services or products. An ER patient, for example, has different expectations from a maternity-ward patient.

You do not know what factors in the service product, the environment, and the delivery system are the key drivers of patient satisfaction and intent to return until you carefully study all the possible drivers. Many times what management learns in such studies is a surprise because what management thought were keys when it designed the components do not turn out to be so from the patient's point of view. This difference between what the organization delivers and what the patient expects or really wants is the service gap that Len Berry has identified. No matter how much experience an organization has in surveying and studying patients, it will still be surprised occasionally by what patients say is really important to them.

Excellent patient-service organizations not only study their patients extensively but also accumulate the information that they have learned about patients, individually and collectively. Computerized databases and sophisticated techniques of database analysis allow the organization to know a great deal about its patients, either as a demographic or psychographic group or as individuals. The best organizations mine these databases to dig up as much information as they can about what is important to their patients so they can ensure that what is expected is provided.

## Extras

The outstanding patient-service organizations that attract repeat customers have an added advantage; they can accumulate information on their frequent patients and use this information to further customize the patient-service experience. In other words, they know that a key driver is to personalize the healthcare experience (everyone wants to be special and treated like an individual), and intelligent use of a customer database allows the best to get better at doing these things. The creation of such databases allows the organization to make each patient feel special through customizing the experience as much as possible. Customizing each patient's experience to match the patient's unique needs and expectations is becoming increasingly easy.

St. Francis Hospital and Medical Center in Hartford, Connecticut, has developed a system for making each patient feel special by letting each manager view the service experience for a particular diagnosis from the patient's perspective.[2] For example, a manager might follow an MRI patient and personally experience the procedure as part of the experience. Within 24 hours, that manager participates in a debriefing session with staff, during which they discuss the experience and brainstorm recommendations. Within ten days, the manager completes a documentation form that includes key observations, improvement opportunities, and recommendations. Not only does the organization improve its service product and its managers' commitment to customer service, but the patient being observed and monitored feels special.

Knowing what makes each patient feel special enables organizations to add the differentiating factors, the extras, that all excellent patient-service organizations want to provide to keep their patients so satisfied that they will want to return if and when they need treatment again. The "little bit more" than the patient expected can make the difference; it can turn the satisfactory experience into a memorable one and can keep the organization at the top of the customer's mind when thinking about where to go the next time that particular patient service is desired or when making recommendations to others.

These extras can be built into the service product, the environment, the service delivery system, or across all parts of the service experience. Based on knowledge about patient likes and dislikes, the designers of the experience can build in those things that will make a noticeable positive difference in the patient's mind. They should, however, always follow up to find out if they were successful and, if not, should try to find out where and why they failed.

The extras do not have to be expensive, complicated, or elaborate, although they may be. Bedside manner does not cost anything, for example, but certain environmental features may be quite expensive. When the State of Florida gives matching funds to construct a building, it also requires that a piece of artwork be placed in the building. At the Brain Institute building, which is part of the medical complex on the University of Florida campus, an artist constructed a $100,000 piece of abstract art that runs up the entire front facade of the building. Florida Hospital in Orlando, Florida, has created a staff position— "concierge"—for its orthopedics unit. This position involves being a contact person for each patient and making sure that this patient receives a seamless healthcare experience.

## Planning

Providing the patient with both the expected parts of the healthcare experience and the extra/differentiating factors is the result of extensive planning. And as we know, planning starts with the patient. Capacity and location decisions, staffing plans, the design of personnel policies, and the selection of medical equipment must all be based on the organization's best information on what kind of experience the patient wants, needs, and expects from the organization. If the organization's mission is to build a chain of freestanding "doc-in-the-boxes," then it must identify what staffing locations, medical equipment, exterior appearances, and clinic sizes it should have.

These decisions can be properly made if based on solid and extensive market research. Healthcare organizations that understand the key drivers of a healthcare experience use the best data they can find. Although many healthcare organizations still base these decisions on a variety of factors, benchmark organizations always start with the patient and make sure that every decision is based on a thorough knowledge and understanding of the patient.

### Feedback

Benchmark healthcare organizations also know that this discovery process is never ending, so they constantly seek feedback from their customers about what works and what does not. Patient needs, wants, and expectations change, and the best organizations change as well in response to evolving patient expectations. Those organizations that constantly seek to exceed patient expectations build in their own future challenges. Today's extras are tomorrow's standard patient expectations.

Outstanding organizations are constantly trying to outdo their present performance, and they survey customers constantly to determine how well they are satisfying their key drivers. For example, a medical group practice had a long history of complaints and frustrations associated with a paper scheduling system for patient appointments. As a result of survey data from three customer groups (i.e., physicians, staff, and patients), a new scheduling system was installed. Then success indicators were developed to evaluate the results of the new system. These results focused on key drivers suggested by each of the three customer groups. Significant improvement in satisfaction of all three customer groups resulted from this process.

### Culture

Managers of outstanding healthcare organizations need to remember the importance of the organizational culture in filling in the gaps between (1) what the organization can anticipate and train its people to deal with and (2) what actually happens in the daily encounters with a wide variety of patients. Anticipating the many different things patients will do, ask for, and expect from the service provider is impossible. The power of the culture to guide and direct employees to do the right thing for the patient becomes vital. Good managers know that the values, beliefs, and norms of behavior that the culture teaches its employees become critical in ensuring that the patient-care staff does what the organization wants done in unplanned and unanticipated situations, even if the organization has no specific policies relevant to that situation.

The culture must be planned and carefully thought through to ensure that the message sent to all employees is the one that the organization really wants to send. An important part of any strategy is to ensure that everything that the organization and its leadership says and does is consistent with the culture it wishes to define and support. The more intangible the healthcare product, the stronger the cultural values, beliefs, and norms must be to ensure that the provider delivers the quality and value of healthcare experience that the patient expects and that the organization wants to deliver.

## STAFFING

Staffing has become an increasingly important factor for all healthcare organizations as they realize that the most effective way to differentiate themselves from their competitors is through the quality of the service encounters that the patient-contact staff provides. Competitors can readily imitate the service product, the physical elements of the environment, and the technical aspects of the delivery system. For example, each hospital or clinic may have just about the same physical equipment as every other hospital/clinic. For one healthcare organization to duplicate the successful differentiating factor of another does not take very long. An MRI clinic is an innovation only as long as it takes the competition to offer the same service. People, not MRI machinery, make the difference. If one clinic has friendly employees and another clinic does not, customers will go to the friendly one, unless their HMO requires the second. When all other factors are equal or nearly so, the healthcare staff makes the difference.

The challenge for healthcare managers is to empower the service provider to engage each patient on a personal, individual basis while still maintaining production efficiency and consistent quality in the service delivery process. For example, a pharmacist is responsible for filling prescriptions exactly as prescribed in an efficient fashion that respects a patient's time constraints. He or she can handle the transaction in an impersonal manner (barely speaking to the patient). Alternatively, the patient can be engaged in a conversation about other prescriptions, any allergic reactions to drugs, the weather, or inquiries about family members (if known to the pharmacist). If the pharmacist just processed people, he or she may become bored. If he or she engaged them, the job becomes more interesting. The latter approach is much more likely to enhance the patients' relationship with the provider and provide a healthcare experience that exceeds expectations.

Some employees in these positions figure it out, engage their customers, and actually do have fun. They are usually the ones that were selected properly in the first place. Finding the right people for these jobs is an important responsibility of the selection process. Putting the right people in these routinized jobs eliminates many of the problems in delivering high-quality patient-service experiences. Some people are just plain good at quickly establishing personal contact with patients, and they can be identified through effective selection techniques. Finding these people and training them in the basic skills necessary for effective service delivery is a key responsibility for human resources managers in healthcare organizations.

Recall that patient-contact employees have three responsibilities in the service encounter: they deliver the service (or in some cases create it on the spot), they manage the quality of the encounters or interactions between the patient and the organization, and they identify and fix the inevitable problems. Too many organizations train only for the first of these responsibilities and neglect the other two. In many instances, receiving the service product is just one element in the patient's determination of the quality and value of the patient-service experience. Employees must also be trained to deal effectively with the variety of personalities and concerns that different patients will bring to the healthcare experience.

### Selection and Training

Selection of the right person for the job starts by clearly defining what the job requires. If you want a person to be a receptionist, who serves as a pleasant, reasonably informed first point of contact for new patients, then you hire a certain bundle of skills. If you want a person to be a triage decision maker, who not only serves as the first point of contact but also decides who needs immediate treatment and who does not, that takes an entirely different set of skills.

Any job has knowledge, skills, and ability requirements, and an "ideal employee" fits these requirements. Such employees can and should be identified so that the employment decision can be made properly. Selecting the right people and placing them in the right jobs is one real key to ensuring the quality of the healthcare experience.

The second part of the staffing issue is training. The right person in the right job must be trained to do it the right way. Some jobs in the healthcare industry are repetitive, simple, and boring; others are also repetitive, complex, and boring. They also require incredible attention to detail and concentration on task performance so that the employee provides the same healthcare experience in the same flawless way for each patient.

It is easy for an employee to "zone out," daydream, or otherwise lose interest in taking blood from the 30th person of the day. By that time his arms are tired, his attention span is short, and his interest in greeting one more patient with a friendly smile and positive eye contact is about zero. Part of that employee's training should include how to cope with the nature of the job.

When the encounters are short—as in a laboratory, billing office, or when delivering food trays to hospital patients—the training challenge is particularly difficult because the staff member does not have a chance to build a long-term relationship. The use of scripts helps the employee respond appropriately to the different expectations of different patients, even when the employee may be bored, tired, or stressed out.

### Patient Interaction

Similar jobs exist in the industrial sector, and job rotation, job enlargement, and job enrichment strategies have been tried with varying levels of success. The advantage that healthcare organizations offer to employees over most industrial settings is the positive feedback and stimulation that dealing with patients can bring, especially when employees know that what they do may make the difference between sickness and health or life and death. Once employees learn through experience or training how to derive some sense of satisfaction out of doing something that makes a patient smile or happy, they can enjoy their jobs and can feel a sense of accomplishment. Volunteers may be better able to engage patients and their families because they have more time to do so.

Many healthcare organizations have discovered that some of their best employees or volunteers are older, retired people who are often lonely, bored, and looking for something to do that will allow them to have positive contact with other people. Healthcare jobs are especially good in providing this particular opportunity. Some organizations that originally recruited older people because of labor shortages have found to their pleasant surprise that many older people bring an enthusiasm for service that makes them great employees.

If you just process people, you can get bored in many routine healthcare jobs. If you engage people, the job becomes interesting. Short-cycle jobs do not offer this aspect because in these jobs patient contact is so fleeting that the opportunity to engage patients is nearly nonexistent. By contrast, consider the attending staff members in a long-term care facility. With their longer time of contact, employees can utilize a variety of interpersonal skills to make the job personal and fun for themselves and their patients. They can interject their personalities to make the outcome a function of their own ability to provide a positive healthcare experience.

Taking blood from dozens of patients or serving dozens of dinners is a different matter and a far greater challenge for both employee and management. Patients receiving services at these points often are too tired, sick, or occupied to notice employees and their contributions to the quality of the healthcare experience. Knowing this, the level of employee engagement and subsequent satisfaction with making a difference is considerably less. The manager's challenge is to find ways to give each employee the opportunity to be unique, recognized, and noticed as an individual by the patient while not compromising the speed and efficiency of the production process used to deliver the service product.

Future employees will expect more job challenges and increased opportunities to be responsible for the patient encounter. Future managers will have increasingly efficient mechanized production and delivery systems available to them. Managers may have to choose between trusting these systems and trusting their employees to provide a high-quality and consistent service experience for their patients. The need to trust the employees will intensify as the competition for talented employees becomes greater. Good people want to take the responsibility, and successful organizations will be those that find ways to preserve the quality and value of the healthcare experience while empowering their employees to be responsible for patient satisfaction.

## Standards

Managers must define for the employees their job responsibilities, the standards of performance, and management's expectations. These must be clearly spelled out and reinforced and rewarded by managers every day. Once a manager lets an employee provide service of less than outstanding quality or overlooks poor employee performance, the message goes out to everyone that managers do not always really mean what they say about providing high-quality customer service. Just as a patient has many moments of truth during the course of a single healthcare experience, employees have many moments of truth with every manager every day. What happens during these moments of truth tells the employees a great deal about what management really believes in. This is where the organizational mission statement, corporate culture, and corporate policies about customer focus become real.

Just as one employee at one moment of truth can destroy the patient's perception of the entire healthcare organization and what it stands for, so too can one supervisor overlooking one violation of patient-care quality standards or job performance change the way an employee looks at an organization. Although most organizations have done a good job of developing selection techniques and providing the necessary job training, many fall short in the reinforcement area. When they let things slide, they miss the chance to reinforce the positive and coach away the negative aspects of employee performance.

The policy of many outstanding healthcare organizations requiring their managers to be in their job areas walking the walk and talking the talk is a vital part of how the message is sent to employees that everyone is responsible for customer service, including them. This policy also builds a sense of equality among the employees in that everyone is there to serve the customer. At Baptist Hospital, Quint Studer did not just "talk the talk"; he also "walked the walk." In other words, he modeled the behavior he was advocating for staff. If he came across a person wandering the hallways and looking confused or lost, he not only stopped to inquire if he could help, but he also personally escorted the person to the destination. After learning of an outstanding service provided by a particular staff member, he always called the person and/or praised the person in public.

### Celebration and Enjoyment

Because the frontline employee is such an important part of setting the mood for the patient, and because research shows the importance of employee attitude in determining the attitude of the patient, the patient-service organization needs to find ways of ensuring that its employees are experiencing genuine enjoyment while doing their jobs, rather than just going through the motions. Although this is partly a selection problem as discussed earlier, it is also a managerial challenge to find new and exciting ways to celebrate successes and introduce a sense of enjoyment and "playfulness" without letting the play get so far out of hand that it interferes with the quality of care or medical protocol of the healthcare experience.

Allowing playfulness is an important way to let staff release tension in stress-filled settings. Further, most people like to celebrate, and employees are no different. Celebrations of success can take the form of parties, balloons, banners, pictures of the honored managers and staff, and recognition dinners. No success should be allowed to pass unnoticed.

### Patient and Family

Just as organizations can benefit from thinking of their employees as customers, they can also benefit from thinking of their customers as employees. This gives the organization a different way of both looking at and thinking about their customers if they define them as quasi-employees.

Customers-employees can serve several important functions. They can be knowledgeable unpaid consultants, as they give helpful feedback to the organization regarding their level of satisfaction with the healthcare experience. They can help create the service experience for other patients, as they are typically part of the service environment. If being surrounded by other patients is a necessary part of each patient's experience, then how these customers-employees are employed in helping to create each other's experience becomes an important part of the management process.

Most importantly, they can become coproducers of their own service experience, with enouragement and training from the healthcare organization. This coproduction strategy can benefit both the patient and the healthcare organization. The organization saves on labor costs, and knowledgeable patients (perhaps with the help of their families and friends) are likely to receive a better healthcare experience because they helped produce it. Patients also do not have to wait for some services that they can do on their own.

### SYSTEMS

The best, most thoroughly trained people in the world cannot satisfy a patient if they deliver bad medicine or provide the wrong treatment perfectly. A huge, complex system (like a university teaching hospital) and a simple system (like a dental clinic) both have to be carefully managed so the right product is delivered to patients when they expect it to be. Patients do not care that the room is not ready yet because the laundry broke down, or that the organization misplaced a medical shipment so they cannot get the drugs they need, or that the staff specialists are unavailable because someone forgot to schedule them. The patient just wants a clean room, the right medicine, and the right specialist, and the patient wants those now. If these things do not happen, then the production system, the support system, the information system, or the organizational system has failed, and someone needs to fix it fast.

## Models

The most highly developed applications related to providing an excellent healthcare experience can be found in the clinical systems area. Models of patient behavior in many situations can be built and used to understand and predict ways in which the organization can best treat the patient's medical condition. Such clinical models can be extended into modeling all aspects of the healthcare experience. Simulations are an important technique for doing this, and with the decreasing costs of computers and increasingly user-friendly software packages, simulations will become more available and relevant to all types of healthcare organizations.

Once the planning process has gotten the design right and the measurement systems are in place to get patient feedback, the stage is set to use simulations of the entire healthcare experience to see if it all works as a system. Healthcare organizations need to ensure that the right capacity has been built into their service delivery system. The design-day selection and the parameters used (such as maximum wait times) drive the rest of the capacity decisions.

Because customers are not impressed by excuses such as "the computer system is down today," backup systems need to be in place so that customers are not inconvenienced. Having managers go through the service delivery process like a patient sensitizes them to potential problems.

In most healthcare organizations, the most visible part of the healthcare experience is the wait for care. This wait system, therefore, requires extra organizational time and attention to ensure that the inevitable waits are tolerable and within the limits patients will accept without becoming dissatisfied. Waiting periods are easily modeled and studied with simulation techniques and easy-to-use computer software. Everything from the number of beds in a hospital to the number of physicians on duty in an emergency room to the number of phone lines needed at an HMO call center can be simulated based on patient demand data. If you know how many patients are coming to your place of business and can estimate a predictable distribution to represent their arrival patterns and times for service, modeling how the waiting experience can be managed and balanced against capacity is relatively simple.

The management of the waiting time is important both from the capacity standpoint and the psychological standpoint. Because few organizations can build enough capacity to serve peak demand periods, and few healthcare organizations have the ability to stockpile their mostly perishable and intangible product, managing the patient's wait is critical for all healthcare organizations. The greater the perceived value of the healthcare experience, the longer the patient will wait. Again, this area is susceptible to empirical research; how long patients will wait for anything before they give up and leave can be studied, measured, and understood.

## HEALTHCARE AND THE FUTURE

The division between those healthcare organizations that figure out how to engage the entire employee and those who use employees only from the neck down will widen. Value added to the healthcare experience through the skills of employees engaging in service encounters will become a more important differentiating strategy as the decreasing costs and increasingly available technology make the healthcare product and service delivery system components (except for people) increasingly easy to duplicate and emulate by all competitors. If all eye exams are essentially alike, then the "feel-good" part of the eye exam becomes an increasingly important part of the total experience.

Advertising alone cannot provide this difference and in fact may be counterproductive if patients do not get what the glowing ads lead them to expect. Staff members make the difference in healthcare organizations. If your patients continue to think and speak well of you, you must be doing something right. If their continued high regard is vital to your organization's survival, you better find a way to keep it. If they do not speak well of you and hold your organization in high regard, then the principles outlined in this book, if implemented well, will move you toward healthcare excellence.

## Service or Price

Service organizations will tend even more than they do now to compete on service or compete on price. A successful group of organizations in every service sector will seek to add value to each customer service encounter (like the strategy of Pearle Vision) or seek to define value on price alone (like the strategy of discount opticals). By making sure that they focus on a particular niche of the market and advertising to that niche the services that will be provided and then providing them very well, these companies (like Southwest Airlines) will thrive. However, healthcare organizations typically market their services based on some combination of clinical effectiveness, service quality, and (possibly) price. In other words, they market based on value received rather than price alone.

The effective use of technology and efficient, well-designed service delivery system techniques will allow those healthcare organizations emphasizing price as their strategy for attracting their market niche to succeed in appealing to and satisfying the price-conscious market segment. The efficient users of high technology will find ways to offer low prices and still make money. The high end of the various service markets, like Sunrise Assisted Living facilities, will succeed for the same reasons. They too will use technology, but for them technology is only a means to the end of providing the maximum amount of service that their patients have come to expect at a price that is reasonable for the service level.

Both types of organizations will rely on technology to deliver the best value to their patients in the most efficient way. They will, consequently, make money through their efficiency where the less efficient competitor will fail. In addition, the high-cost providers can increasingly customize the product to each patient's expectations at the price point plus offer a little bit more as they can provide their employees with the necessary information to personalize the service in a prompt, friendly, and efficient way.

The healthcare businesses in the mass market between these two ends of the spectrum will have the most difficult challenge in the future as many are already having today. They will be challenged in offering patient services that are as personalized as those offered by the service-oriented firms in the marketplace and that patients now expect while providing the low prices that the price-oriented firms in a competitive marketplace have also led patients to expect. This middle group of organizations seeking to serve the mass market may do neither very well. They may find themselves in the position of overpromising and underdelivering, which is not the way to have satisfied, loyal, or repeat patients.

### Word of Mouth

The excellent patient-service organizations of the future will use every tool at their command to figure out what the patient wants and then provide it in a way that is consistent with the patient expectations of value and quality. If they promise a high-quality healthcare experience that includes friendly service, they better provide those features or patients with other options will not come back. Most healthcare organizations depend on the high regard of their patients, and disappointing them will cost dearly in a competitive marketplace.

Once you tell your customers what you will do for them, you have made a commitment and a promise. If the promise is broken or the commitment unrealized, patients will be unhappy and will tell everyone they know how unhappy they are. Few organizations can afford to break their promises, and the more a healthcare organization depends on a good reputation and positive word of mouth, the less chance it can take of violating that trust.

Information and opinions about service quality are freely available now and will become more so in the future. If a dissatisfied patient posts a negative comment on the Internet about your service, that comment may be readily accessible on a computer somewhere forever. Computers can be programmed never to forget, and the more they are involved in helping customers make selections among patient-service providers, the more critical it is to avoid failing the patient.

Some major healthcare organizations, like HealthSouth Corporation, now have an employee whose only job is to monitor relevant discussion groups on the Internet to detect and hopefully correct patient complaints and false rumors that show up on this increasingly powerful communication medium. A job classification that did not even exist ten years ago will become an increasingly important part of the organization's communication strategy as it seeks to avoid the negative word of mouth that can now travel almost instantly across cyberspace to the entire world.

### Consistent Improvement

The future will be information management, people management, increasing ability to understand what each patient really wants (a "market niche of one" that allows the organization to build a relationship with each patient), and focusing on the organizational core competencies that satisfy these patient expectations. The future will also bring forth more knowledgeable customers with ever rising expectations. The more that competitors in the marketplace try to outdo each other in providing superb healthcare experiences, the more familiar these experiences will become. Yesterday's exceptional experience becomes today's expected minimal level of service. Healthcare managers will need to engage the entire organization in constantly reviewing all aspects of the customer service product, the environment, and the service delivery system to find new and not easily duplicated features that make the experience memorable.

The easiest and most fruitful area in which to develop these features is in the interaction between staff and patients, where healthcare employees can make a memorable experience happen. The challenge here is to empower them without jeopardizing the quality and consistency of the clinical experience. Human error is inevitable, and the need to blend technology and people to provide a high-tech and high-touch experience of consistently high quality will be the biggest and most interesting challenge for the future healthcare manager seeking excellence in the healthcare experience provided.

## THE ROLE OF LEADERS

We end this chapter by stressing an idea that has been implied throughout this book: Managers must lead staff toward excellence. The leader is the symbol of what the organization stands for and believes. If the leader does not lead, all the efforts to discover the key drivers that cause the customer to seek out a particular healthcare experience, the expense of designing the service delivery system, and the effort to recruit and train the best people are wasted. Every day and in every way the leader must set the example and show all employees what their value is to the organization and to creating the healthcare experience.

Everyone wants to feel that what they do has value and meaning to a purpose larger than enriching a company's top executives and stockholders. Leaders not only inspire their staff to realize their individual worth to the organization; they also help staff see what contributions they make to the greater good by doing their jobs with excellence. Telling people how important it is that they do their jobs well is not enough; all employees must understand and believe that their contributions make a difference and that doing well whatever they do is vital.

Many healthcare organizations make efforts in this direction but only a few—the benchmark organizations—succeed. These organizations inspire their employees to believe that they are responsible for saving lives, relieving human suffering, and healing many who would not otherwise return to health. These organizations constantly remind all employees that what they are doing has a greater purpose than merely giving shots, cleaning rooms, or dumping bedpans.

Each job has value, and the person doing the job has value because of the contribution to the larger purpose. This is a vital part of inspiring people not only do a job but to do it with pride and commitment. Obviously, not every employee will be deeply affected, but this idea is planted in so many healthcare employees' minds that it creates the strong cultural reinforcement that focuses everyone's attention on producing an excellent experience for each patient. This is a powerful leadership technique and a valuable way to ensure that everyone stays focused on the patient.

The commitment and enthusiasm of great organizational leaders will lead to involvement and passion among organizational members. Leaders find ways to provide jobs that are fun, fair, and interesting. Leaders establish a culture of patient-service excellence and reinforce it by word, deed, and celebration. Leaders give value to employees by showing them they are valued for both their contributions to the organization and to the larger purpose toward which the organization aspires. Leaders have the joy and the responsibility of making it all happen: happy, motivated staff members; outstanding healthcare experiences; and highly satisfied patients whose loyalty, good will, and positive word of mouth in the community form the foundation of organizational business success.

Common sense and research suggest that a relationship exists among the behavior of organizational leaders, how employees feel about their jobs, and how that feeling is translated into the level of service they provide. If staff members feel positive, they provide a high level of service. Creative, high-quality service for patients links directly to patient opinions of the healthcare organization, and these opinions are a key part of any healthcare organization's success. This chain reaction all starts with the leaders. In the organizational units where employees rate their leaders as outstanding in such behaviors as listening, coaching, recognition, and empowerment, the patient satisfaction ratings are invariably the highest.

**Figure 15.1 Leadership Components**

Skills + Incentives + Resources + Delivery System + Measurement – *Vision* = Unfocused Employees = Unfocused Service = Confused Customers

Vision + Incentives + Resources + Delivery System + Measurement – *Skills* = Untrained Employees = Probable Failed Service = Disappointed Customers

Vision + Skills + Resources + Delivery System + Measurement – *Incentives* = Unmotivated Employees = Lackluster Service = Disillusioned Customers

Vision + Skills + Incentives + Delivery System + Measurement – *Resources* = Unsupported Employees = Inadequate Service = Complaining Customers

Vision + Skills + Incentives + Resources + Measurement – *Delivery System* = Unreliable Employees = Unreliable Service = Unsatisfied Customers

Vision + Skills + Incentives + Resources + Delivery System – *Measurement* = Uninformed Employees = Inconsistent Service = Unfulfilled Customers

Vision + Skills + Incentives + Resources + Delivery System + Measurement = Unsurpassed Employees = Superb Service = Highly Satisfied Customers

Finally, the leader blends together the strategy, staff, and systems so that everyone knows that they are supposed to concentrate on patients and other customers. The strategy, staffing, and the systems must be carefully managed if the combined effort is going to succeed in providing the outstanding healthcare experience that the healthcare organization was established to provide. If the leader sees that any element is not contributing to the employee's ability to provide outstanding experiences, the leader will fix it or have it fixed.

Just as the organization wants to fix any patient problem that detracts from the healthcare experience, the outstanding leader wants to fix any staff member's problem that detracts from that person's ability to provide the outstanding healthcare experience. Vision, skills, incentives, delivery system, and measurement are leadership components that leaders must manage if they are to meet this challenge effectively. As noted in Figure 15.1, all must be present to produce and maintain highly satisfied customers. More specifically, leaders must:

- Define an organizational vision of what patient segment is to be served and what service concept will best meet their expectations (vision)
- Establish a customer-focused culture to enhance clinical excellence (vision)
- Communicate the organization's mission and vision to all customers on a continual basis through a wide variety of methods (vision)
- Select employees with service-oriented attitudes and train them in the necessary clinical and customer service skills (skills)
- Train staff to exceed customer expectations on an ongoing basis using scripts, role playing, and other training methods (skills)
- Create standards of behavior and performance, and hold staff accountable for upholding these standards (incentives)
- Create and make available the incentives that will motivate empowered employees to provide unsurpassed customer service (incentives)
- Establish a service recovery system that empowers all staff to identify and rectify all customer service problems (incentives)
- Communicate and celebrate all individual and group successes (incentives)
- Ensure that employees have the proper resources to provide outstanding service (resources)
- Create a clean and attractive environment for all customers (delivery system)
- Design specific delivery systems that translate plans, employee skills, and resources into an experience that meets patient expectations and perhaps even wows the patient (delivery system)
- Focus on employee retention as well as patient retention (measurement)
- Provide the measurement tools that allow employees (and coproducing patients as well) to see how well they are doing in providing the targeted or desired healthcare experience (measurement)
- Continually identify and implement improvements in customer service because success is never final (measurement)

Measurement is critical for ensuring that all the other factors are correctly focused on achieving the best for the patient. Simply, if you do not know how you are doing, you do not know if you need to do better, so you do not know how to do better. If you try to improve patient service, you do not know if you have succeeded. Continual improvement is also necessary given that momentum can easily be lost.

CEO Mark Clement of Holy Cross Hospital in Chicago notes: "You are only as good as your last customer encounter, and things can change on a dime. Success is garnered one customer at a time."[3] Having built a performance record of consistently achieving national top-rated customer satisfaction, Holy Cross leadership and staff diverted time and attention away from customer focus. As they celebrated their success, customer satisfaction management was diluted. Consequently, their customer satisfaction ratings fell dramatically.[4]

Figure 15.1 shows how the customer and the customer's experience can be negatively affected when leaders fail to manage any one of these important leadership components. Negative effects will not always occur. Just as service problems happen in the best-managed organizations, so can patient-contact staff of poorly managed organizations sometimes provide successful healthcare experiences in spite of the organization and its faults. When one or more leadership components are missing, however, the chances of consistent service success are reduced. The exact effect on the healthcare experience may not be predictable in precise terms, but it will not be a happy one.

The Figure shows the effects that a missing leadership element can have on employees. Although managers will do as good a job as they can of managing the nonhuman elements, their ability to change them may be limited. If the clinic is already constructed and the laboratory set up, the clinic manager may not be able to do much managing of the patient-service environment and the mechanical parts of the delivery system. In a way this is good news because it enables managers to focus on the people part of the healthcare experience: the patients as part of the environment for each other, the patients as they participate in creating their own experiences, the clinical and support staffs as they try to provide outstanding customer experiences, and all support staffs as they provide the assistance that their internal customers require. These many and ever changing elements of the healthcare situation require and deserve each manager's attention.

If the organization's leaders lack an overall vision of a target market and its expectations, this lack will be communicated from the top throughout the culture and may lead to unfocused service. Staff members are not sure exactly what they are trying to achieve, and patients received mixed messages and inconsistent experiences. If managers put untrained people in patient-contact positions, service problems and disappointed patients are probable. If incentives are lacking or inappropriate, unmotivated staff will simply go through the motions of providing lackluster healthcare experiences.

Failure to provide resource support for all staff—clinical and non-clinical—will prohibit even a motivated and patient-focused staff from providing adequate service. Similarly, flaws in the delivery system will keep the best of personnel from providing reliably satisfactory healthcare experiences, much less superb ones; as the saying goes, "A bad system will defeat a good person every time."

Finally, if levels of service quality and patient satisfaction are not measured, employees will be frustrated by not knowing whether the healthcare experiences they are providing are achieving the healthcare mission or not; so in a hit-or-miss fashion they will continue to provide inconsistent service.

Only when these components are all in place can the leader be effective in enabling and empowering employees. Only then can empowered employees provide the outstanding healthcare experiences that fulfill the organizational vision of providing remarkable service that exceeds patient expectations. Every manager from the chief executive officer to the frontline supervisor must ultimately make sure that employees feel good about what they are doing, that they convey this feeling to patients, and that patients leave knowing the experience was worth every penny paid and maybe a little bit more. Leadership makes the difference between success and failure in today's healthcare organizations, and it will make the difference in the future.

## CONCLUSION

The healthcare experience, despite all its components—service product, service setting, and service delivery system—is not complete without the patients. Without the patient, the carefully designed service product; the detailed and inviting setting; the highly trained, motivated staff; and the finest facilities and equipment are just part of an experience waiting to happen. Throughout this book, we have made the point that everything starts with the patient. We conclude by saying that everything ends with the patient as well!

## LESSONS LEARNED

1. Train all staff members to think of the people in front of them as their guests.
2. Start with the customer—both external patients and internal staff members.
3. Build a strong culture and sustain it with stories, deeds, and actions.
4. Manage all three parts of healthcare—strategy, staffing, and systems.
5. Articulate a vision, transcending any single job, that gives all staff a sense of value and worth in what they do.
6. Organize, staff, train, and reward around the patient's needs.
7. If something is critical to organizational success, because it is a key driver, establish a standard of performance, measure it, and then manage it carefully.
8. Ensure that jobs are fun, fair, and interesting for employees to help them provide superb experiences for patients.
9. Keep in mind the strong relationship between highly satisfied employees and highly satisfied patients.
10. Prevent every service problem you can, find every problem you cannot prevent, and fix every problem you find every time and, if possible, on the spot.
11. Exceeding patient expectations today does not mean meeting those expectations tomorrow.
12. Never stop teaching; inspire everyone to keep learning.

## NOTES

1. Leebov, W., G. Scott, and L. Olsen. 1998. *Achieving Impressive Customer Service: Seven Strategies for the Health Care Manager*, p. 178. Chicago: American Hospital Publishing.

2. Leebov, W., G. Scott, and L. Olsen. 1998. *Achieving Impressive Customer Service: Seven Strategies for the Health Care Manager*, p. 122. Chicago: American Hospital Publishing.

3. Sherman, S. G., and V. C. Sherman. 1991. *Total Customer Satisfaction: A Comprehensive Approach for Health Care Providers*, p. 344. San Francisco: Jossey-Bass.

4. *Ibid.*

# About the Authors

**Myron D. Fottler, Ph.D.,** is director of Programs in Health Services Administration in the College of Health and Public Affairs at the University of Central Florida in Orlando where he teaches courses in healthcare human resources management, strategic management, and dissertation research. He was previously professor and director of the Ph.D. Program in Administration-Health Services with a joint appointment in both the School of Health Related Professions and the School of Business at the University of Alabama at Birmingham. He completed his MBA at Boston University and his Ph.D. in business at Columbia University. He has won awards from the American College of Healthcare Executives, American Association of Medical Administrators, and the Healthcare Management Division of the Academy of Management for his research.

Dr. Fottler is a member of the AUPHA/HAP editorial board and a founding coeditor of an annual research volume titled *Advances in Health Care Management*, sponsored by JAI/Elsevier Press. He is a member of the editorial boards for *Medical Care Research and Review, International Journal of Applied Quality Management, Journal of Health Administration Education,* and *Health Care Management Review.* He has been listed in numerous biographical publications, including *Who's Who in America, Dictionary of International Biography, Who's Who in The World, Outstanding Young Men in America, Who's Who in the East, Contemporary Authors, International Directory of Business and Management Scholars and Research, American Men and Women of Science, International Writers and Author's Who's Who,* and *Directory of American Scholars.* He is the author of 12 books and more than 100 journal articles.

**Robert C. Ford, Ph.D.,** is currently the associate dean for Graduate and External Programs and professor of management at the University of Central Florida's (UCF) College of Business Administration. He joined UCF in 1993 as chair of the Department of Hospitality Management after serving on the faculty of the University of North Florida and the University of Alabama at Birmingham. He has authored or coauthored over 100 articles, books, and presentations on organizational issues, human resources management, and services management especially as it relates to healthcare and hospitality applications. He won the 2001 Sodexho Marriott Health Care Division Faculty Publication of the Year for a coauthored article with Myron Fottler. His textbooks include *Principles of Management: A Decision Making Approach, Organization Theory: An Integrative Approach*, and *Managing the Guest Experience in Hospitality*.

Dr. Ford has also been an active professional serving the Academy of Management as the director of placement and the division chair for both the Management History and the Management Education and Management Development divisions. In addition, he has been the chair of the Accreditation Commission for Programs in Hospitality Administration and the president of the Southern Management Association. He currently is a Fellow of the Southern Management Association and the editor of the *Academy of Management Executive*.

**Cherrill P. Heaton, Ph.D.,** is a professor of organizational communications at the University of North Florida. In addition to teaching organizational and business communications in the MBA and M.Acc. programs, he has taught over 100 short courses for business and industry in these areas. He is the editor of *Management by Objectives in Higher Education*; coauthor of *Essentials of Modern Investments*; and coauthor of several articles and three books—*Principles of Management: A Decision Making Approach, Organization Theory: An Integrative Approach*, and *Managing the Guest Experience in Hospitality*. He is managing editor of the *Academy of Management Executive*.